# MASTERING
## THE
# TRADE

## Other Books in the McGraw-Hill Trader's Edge Series

*The Complete Guide to Spread Trading* by Keith Schap

*Pattern Recognition and Trading Decisions* by Chris Satchwell

*Mastering Futures Trading* by Bo Yoder

*One Shot, One Kill Trading* by John Netto

*Techniques of Tape Reading* by Vadym Graifer and Chris Schumacher

*Quantitative Trading Strategies* by Lars Kestner

*Understanding Hedged Scale Trading* by Thomas McCafferty

*Traders Systems That Work* by Thomas Stridsman

*Trading Systems and Money Management* by Thomas Stridsman

*The Encyclopedia of Trading Strategies* by Jeffrey Owen Katz and Donna L. McCormick

*Technical Analysis for the Trading Professional* by Constance Brown

*Agricultural Futures and Options* by Richard Duncan

*The Options Edge* by William Gallacher

*The Art of the Trade* by R.E. McMaster

# MASTERING THE TRADE

## TRADE

**PROVEN TECHNIQUES FOR PROFITING FROM INTRADAY AND SWING TRADING SETUPS**

## JOHN F. CARTER

**McGraw-Hill**

New York  Chicago  San Francisco  Lisbon  London  Madrid
Mexico City  Milan  New Delhi  San Juan  Seoul
Singapore  Sydney  Toronto

Copyright © 2006 by McGraw-Hill, Inc. All rights reserved. Printed in the United States of America. Except as permitted under the United States Copyright Act of 1976, no part of this publication may be reproduced or distributed in any form or by any means, or stored in a data base or retrieval system, without prior written permission of the publisher.

2 3 4 5 6 7 8 9 0    DOC/DOC    0 9 8 7 6

ISBN 0-07-145958-8

Trading the financial markets has large potential rewards, but also large potential risk. You must be aware of the risks and be willing to accept them in order to invest in the futures, currency and options markets. Don't trade with money you can't afford to lose. This material is neither a solicitation nor an offer to buy or sell futures, options, or currencies. No representation is being made that any account will or is likely to achieve profits or losses similar to those discussed in this book. The past performance of any trading system or methodology is not necessarily indicative of future results.

McGraw-Hill books are available at special discounts to use as premiums and sales promotions, or for use in corporate training programs. For more information, please write to the Director of Special Sales, Professional Publishing, McGraw-Hill, Two Penn Plaza, New York, NY 10121-2298. Or contact your local bookstore.

This book is printed on recycled, acid-free paper containing a minimum of 50% recycled de-inked paper.

**Library of Congress Cataloging-in-Publication Data**

Carter, John F.
    Mastering the trade : proven techniques for profiting from intraday and swing trading setups / by John F. Carter.
       p.  cm.
   Includes bibliographical references and index.
   ISBN 0-07-145958-8 (hardcover : alk. paper)
   1. Investment analysis. 2. Portfolio management. 3. Day trading (Securities)
4. Electronic trading of securities. I. Title.
HG4529.C374 2006
332.63'228—dc22

*To everyone out there who is courageously facing the task*
*of turning themselves into a professional trader*

# ACKNOWLEDGMENTS

**W**riting and trading have a lot in common in that they are essentially solitary professions that are made much more enjoyable by anyone who is willing to lend a helping hand. In regards to this project, I would like to first thank Hubert Senters and Priyanka Rajpal for holding down the fort while I was "working on the nightmare." Also thanks to your contributions to this project, which helped to keep me sane toward the end when things were getting crazy. Although the book deadline was firm, July Soybeans were moving and I couldn't just ignore them.

Thanks to Kira McCaffrey Brecht, Gail Osten, and everyone at *SFO Magazine* for helping me to realize that writing about trading could be a worthwhile thing to do. Larry Connors and Eddie Kwong at Trading Markets for advice along the way and for keeping me on track with this original project, making sure I didn't spend a lot of wasted time reinventing the wheel. Kelli Christiansen at McGraw-Hill for initially contacting me about this project and turning it from idea into reality, and to Executive Editor Stephen Isaacs at McGraw Hill for helping to keep this project on track.

I thought I could rest easy once I completed the first draft, but little did I know that the real work was about to begin. Thanks to Bill Shugg, Tim Sambrano, Pamela Snelling, and Don Allen for reading early drafts and providing feedback. Also thanks to the staff at McGraw-Hill, who performed the herculean task of bringing this book to life: Scott Kurtz, Editing Supervisor; Maureen Harper, Production Supervisor; Roberta Mantus, copy editor, and Eric Lowenkron, proofreader. Thanks also to Mark Douglas for insightful feedback in the later stages of the project.

For help with my trading and trading related projects along the way, I'd like to thank Marcia Wieder, goddess of Maui, for kicking things off in regard to my leaving corporate America and trading full time. Scott Sether, who was truly in this from the beginning, for helping to redefine the term "market research." Tracy Alderman, Rosa Hernandez, and Michael Duwe, for helping to get things kicked off. Page Rossiter, for keeping me on track during the transition. Skip Klohn, as an early mentor in the process. Eric Corkhill . . . where do I start? Thanks for acting as a consultant on a multitude of topics, and thanks for giving me enough red wine so that I only remembered the good stuff the next morning.

Thanks to Barbara Schmidt-Bailey and Jeff Campbell at the Chicago Board of Trade, and Marty Doyle at One Chicago for good ideas and great feedback along the way. John Conolly, for a multitude of solid insights into the business. To the gang at Mirus, for continued support. To the gang at Newport, for clarifying what not to do and how not to do it. Cooper Bates, for keeping me on track on the meaning of it all. Steve Patrow and Becky Herman, for keeping things entertaining while I was in the beginning stages of this journey.

Of course, it makes sense to thank family members where appropriate. Thanks to my mom, Francie Cobb, for supporting me while I "did my thing" along the way, even if it was sometimes scary to watch. Thanks to my step-father, Lance Cobb, for being a father and introducing me to the world of financial markets at an early age. To my brother, Jason Carter, for being a great sibling. It's nice to have another person in the world who understands. Maria Carter, my wife, for her unflinching support in the face of it all, and also for becoming passionate about the Home Decorating Channel while her husband played "catch up on the book" over the weekends. Next time I swear we'll just go to Hawaii. I'm pretty sure I can write and drink Mai Tais at the same time.

Thanks also to the memory of my father, Bill Carter, who was taken away too soon, but in so doing passed along valuable lessons to his kids. And to the memory of Joanne Wolfram, a good friend, who reminds us all to live life while you have the chance.

# CONTENTS

## Chapter 20

# When It's Not Working for You, No Matter What You Do   381

## Chapter 21

# Mastering the Trade   391

# FOREWORD

In early 2003, I was attending an online trading conference in an effort to educate active traders on a new class of products called Security Futures. I had joined OneChicago after having been in the managed money business for over 20 years because I believe these products will enhance equity trading in the cash, futures, and options markets. Having avoided these events for many years, I was surprised when I had the pleasure of listening to someone who was incredibly articulate and thoughtful. I said to myself, "He really gets it."

John Carter was not speaking about security futures, but rather he was presenting his intellectual framework and approach to trading. It is a method to which I relate strongly, so I introduced myself. We spoke at length on many subjects, including the idea that his methodology could be applied to security futures and that successful trading is one long journey, not a destination. John became an early supporter and trader on OneChicago, another indication of his innovativeness. We have continued to exchange ideas, and therefore I was honored when John asked me to review *Mastering the Trade*.

I judge a book on trading according to one simple criterion: Have I learned something new? *Mastering the Trade* not only introduces new concepts, but is insightful and easy to read. This is indeed a rare combination in the trading literature. In addition, John stresses that there is neither a single approach nor a single answer to successful trading. In fact, he emphasizes that before one can be a profitable trader, one must fully understand one's own personality. Every decision from the holding period of a trade to the amount of one's capital to risk per trade is a reflection of the inherent preference curves of the trader. In fact, *Mastering the Trade* begins by emphasizing the importance of the proper approach to trading prior to discussing methodology.

Once the book turns its attention to the process of trading, it sparkles once again. Regardless of how long one has been in the markets, there are new approaches or enhancements to existing ones that I find quite beneficial. For example, as an active participant in the stock index futures markets, John's unique application of extreme tick readings is very insightful. I can then decide whether to apply it toward my own trading, test it further or ignore it entirely. The beauty of trading is that there is not one size that fits all and John does not try to force fit his ideas on anyone. They are presented, discussed and then demonstrated. Amazingly enough, every trade is not always a winner. The set-up is a probability outcome that if followed over time should lead to trading success. That is the essential message that John drills repeatedly. Bad trades happen all the time; it is how one reacts to them that determines future success.

Another point that *Mastering the Trade* makes is that there is no a single answer to the question: Should one be short or long a market? There are always valid reasons to be both ways. The markets provide some clues, but ones trading style needs to provide the rest. That is why John shows how to use everything from monthly charts to one-minute pivots. A full-time trader should have different volatility and risk parameters than one who can only examine the market before and after the close.

Trading is an emotionally debilitating business. One can always explain yesterday perfectly. The weekly trader says "if I only followed the one-minute chart, I would not have gotten caught in that position." The one-minute, intraday trader says "if I had only leaned against that weekly pivot point, I wouldn't have gotten stopped out and had a huge winner." John doesn't play this game. He applies an intellectually honest process to trading, suggests risk-reward set-ups and then lets the markets do the rest. Remember the market is always right. It is the analysis or set-up that is wrong.

*Mastering the Trade* reinforces what successful traders intuitively do every time they place a position: Trade small, stay in the game and try and let time be your ally. Losing streaks are bound to occur and knowing that they will occur and living through them are two different things. Diversify across markets. Some set-ups will be working well in a market and then stop. The market hasn't changed nor the set-up failed; the more opportunities, the greater the chance of success. But if one is trading too large, then one may not be able to initiate the next trade after a series of losses. John is very helpful in outlining what unit sizes to trade.

I would suggest studying the list of markets recommended and being prepared to participate in many of them. We all have a tendency to pick and choose the set-ups in those markets where we have a pre-defined bias. The message of *Mastering the Trade* is that the set-ups are objective and can help eliminate the emotional battles that are constantly being fought. Today a single stock future will look great on a chart, but the set-up will indicate that it is time to sell. If one is looking for excuses not to follow the signal, then don't buy *Mastering the Trade*. However, if one is tired of saying "I knew this would happen," but does not have anything to show for that knowledge, then John Carter's new book is an outstanding place to start a realistic, grounded approach to mastering the trade!

*Peter Borish*
*Chairman, OneChicago*
*Former Head of Research for Paul Tudor Jones*

# INTRODUCTION

The best lesson I've ever learned about short-term trading happened while on a white water rafting trip. Eight of us were in the raft when it hit a rock and flipped, launching us into the air like a catapult, sending everyone headfirst into the icy water. Half of us remembered that, in the event of a spill, to stay calm and position ourselves on our back, feet facing downstream. We zipped around rocks and through cascades of water, eventually dragging ourselves safely ashore. An hour passed before we learned what had happened to the rest of the group. For them, a rescue operation went into effect, and the end result was a gashed leg, a concussion, and a near drowning. Later, when speaking to the abused, I learned that all of them had experienced a type of brain freeze. They could see the danger around them. They knew they were in trouble. They even knew they needed to act, to do something. But they literally could not make a decision about what action they should take. So, they took the one option left to them: They froze like the proverbial deer in the headlights and did nothing. In the absence of a decisive path of action, the river grabbed them by their lapels and, like an angry pimp with bills to pay, slapped them senseless.

I remember one member of the group saying, "That river was out to get me!" Extreme paranoia and self-centeredness aside, the river was not out to get anyone. It did what it was supposed to do; move quickly and rapidly through a canyon in order to get to the ocean. The riders who understood the nature of the river were prepared and took the roller coaster journey in stride. The riders who were unprepared got thrashed.

The similarities between this event and a typical trading day are nearly identical. The unprepared trader (newbie) is in the same situation as the unprepared white water rafter. In the event of extreme conditions, both will freeze, and both will be lucky to survive the experience. One bad trade can wipe out months or years of profits.

Professional traders make money not because they are right more often than not, but because they know how to take advantage of all the "fresh meat" that is sitting out there in the form of amateur, unprepared traders. "Fresh meat" refers to anyone who has been trading for less than 10 years. That said, many traders never make the leap, and remain in this victim-like state all of their trading lives. The minority who endure and join the ranks of consistent winning traders are the ones who have learned the following truths:

- The financial markets are naturally set up to take advantage of and prey upon human nature. As a result, markets initiate major intraday and swing moves with as few traders participating as possible. A trader who does not understand how this works is destined to lose money.
- Traders can know more about a market than anyone else in the world, but if they apply the wrong methodology to their trading setups, they will lose money.

- Traders can know more about an indicator or group of indicators than anyone else in the world, but if they apply the wrong methodology to those indicators, they will lose money.
- Traders can know exactly what they are doing, but if they are trading the wrong market for their personality, they will lose money.
- Trader can know exactly what they are doing, but if they apply the same strategies they used to make themselves successful in other areas of their life, they will lose money.

Without this knowledge, a trader is like a wounded antelope in the center of a lion pride, where it is not a question of "if" the antelope is going to get torn to shreds and swallowed, but rather of "when." For a trader without this knowledge, the possibility of ruin it not a question of "if." It's only a matter of "when."

Nevertheless, even with the odds stacked against them, each year tens of thousands of unprepared traders flock to the markets like lemmings to the sea, their heads filled with visions of easy cash, first class tickets, and of telling their boss to go pound sand. By the time most of them sense that spark of an idea that would have allowed them to understand how trading really works, they have already flung themselves over the cliff and are plunging towards the rocks below. All they have to show for their hard work is ample amounts of frustration and despair, perhaps a furious spouse, and a trading account that has been ravished and ripped off by a professional.

Trading is not about everyone holding hands, belting out the lyrics to John Lennon's *Imagine*, and making money together. The financial markets are truly the most democratic places on earth. It doesn't matter if a trader is male or female, white or black, American or Iraqi, Republican or Democrat. It's all based on skill.

The only way to become a professional trader is to obtain that blunt edge of a weapon that separates you from the rest of the migrating sheep. That edge is gained by utilizing specific chart setups and trading methodologies that take into account the five key points listed above, as well as the psychology of the trader taking the other side of the trade. Otherwise, as you enter the revolving door to the financial markets, filled with excitement and anticipation, the predators are merely licking their lips, because what they see is a slab of freshly cured meat, ripe for the eating. And feast they will.

## WHO SHOULD READ THIS BOOK?

This book discusses a unique approach to the markets that focuses on the underlying reasons that cause market prices to really move, and is applicable to trading stocks, options, futures, and forex. In reality, markets don't move because they want to, they move because the have to. Margin calls, stop runs, and psychological capitulation all force a series of rapid fire market orders in a very short period of time. These generate sharp intraday moves lasting a few minutes to a few hours, and, on a bigger scale, swing moves that last a few days to a few weeks. These moves inflict pain on a lot of traders who do not understand how this process works. Yet, there is always a group of traders who profit from these moves. This book discusses specific ways to get positioned "on the other side of the trade" in order to take advantage of these moves, relying on a unique interpretation of many classical technical analysis and chart patterns.

More specifically, the book discusses strategies with exact entry, exit, and stop loss levels for the intraday trading of stocks, options, ETFs, e-mini futures, 30-year bonds, and the forex currency markets. There are also swing trade setups discussed on stocks, options, single stock futures, and e-mini stock index futures.

It is my hope that traders at all levels of experience will welcome this book's broad market overview and specific trading strategies. Beginners will be treated to a no-hype reality check on how the markets really work, will be introduced to clear concepts and trade setups, and will come to understand why newer traders are destined to lose money until they grasp the basic market mechanics that are constantly happening behind the scenes. They will also understand how they are repeatedly taken advantage of.

It is my goal that intermediate traders will appreciate the knowledge included in this book, which is designed to take them to the next level of trading. In addition, I hope that professional traders and other market insiders will find this book is able to clarify some of the truths in which they have instinctively found to be true, in addition to providing fresh ideas to improve their bottom line. Stock traders who have never traded e-mini futures or forex will learn how these markets work and how to get enough information to decide whether the addition of these markets would be appropriate for their own trading. They will learn how the futures markets affect specific stocks and thus better position themselves to profit from their stock trading.

Day traders will learn why relying on indicators alone is a losing game, discover specific strategies to get into a trade early, and learn the differences between knowing when to bail and knowing when to hang on for the ride. Swing traders and pure stock pickers will learn how to read the ebbs and flows of the market, and know whether they should be focusing on the long or the short side. Investors that are overlooking their retirement accounts will discover specific ideas for timing their investments on a monthly and quarterly basis in order to improve their returns. While this book is aimed at full-time traders, there are special sections throughout the book that focus on individuals who are working full time and are only able to trade part time. This does have advantages if done correctly.

While I feel this work will be a welcome edition to anyone who is interested in the financial markets, it is important to realize this book assumes a working knowledge of the basics. There won't be a chapter discussing the nuances of support and resistance, or a chapter with 25 examples explaining the differences between an uptrend and a downtrend. While I'm going to spend a chapter on option plays, I'm not going to spend a chapter discussing how options work. In other words, if it has already been written about, or if it can be Googled, then it won't be rehashed here. This book focuses on new concepts that have not been written about before. That said, the work does provide an introductory chapter on futures and forex trading and the types of markets that are focused on in this book. If you're not sure what a bond tick is worth, or what 10 Euro pips mean to your P&L, then this section is for you. I will also discuss websites and other books that are great for getting up to speed.

In addition to specific trading setups, the book discusses practical aspects of trading such as the type of hardware and software to use, as well as money management allocation and developing a game plan that fits the trader's personality. Finally, there is a strong focus on specific information that can be used the next trading day.

Let's get started.

# MASTERING
# THE
# TRADE

# PART ONE

## Trader's Boot Camp

*I don't want the cheese;*
*I just want to get out of the trap.*

Spanish Proverb

C H A P T E R

# MARKETS DON'T MOVE BECAUSE THEY WANT TO— THEY MOVE BECAUSE THEY *HAVE* TO

## AVERAGE TRADER PROFILE: THE WRONG SKILLS IN THE WRONG PLACE AT THE WRONG TIME

Individual traders live in a state of constant flux, stuck between two worlds that combine both the best and the worst that trading has to offer. On the one hand, they can move in and out of markets with an ease and efficiency large funds can only dream of. Traders have the freedom to carve out specific niches for themselves that the manager of a pension plan could never achieve or duplicate, and in so doing have the opportunity to create an independent life, free from the hassles of the average Joe. These perks are extremely appealing and impossible to duplicate in any other profession.

Reasons for trading full or part time are many, and can range from wanting a career change, a wish to be more independent, the desire to escape the responsibilities of running a large corporate division or individual business, or choosing to be a stay-at-home parent. This is a "job" that provides the chance to make a very nice living, and it's a lot more interesting and fun than any other profession—except being a rock star, of course. But if sharing the stage alongside U2 seems slightly out of reach, then trading is a good alternative.

It can be done from anywhere that has reliable Internet access. There are no bosses spewing forth inane, ever-changing contradictory orders as they struggle within a system that has promoted them right up to—and through—their level of competence. Employees are not necessary. Those of us who have survived the corporate world can find nothing on this earth that equates to the freedom and beauty that come from no longer having to manage a large group of dispassionate human beings. Start-up costs are minimal thanks to leasing programs from companies like Dell. Trading in your robe or nothing at all is perfectly fine. Best of all, a trader can choose his or her own working hours. Some examples of schedules from successful traders I work with include: trading actively October through April and then taking the remaining five months off; trading only the first two hours of the market open and taking the rest of the day off; trading until they make 50 percent on their capital and then taking the rest of the year off. The list goes on and on. With so much to offer, it is no wonder that tens of thousands of people toss their hats into the ring, trying to make a go at this most appealing of professions. It truly represents the proverbial American dream.

However, with so much freedom comes a cruel price. Simply put, the markets cannot protect a trader from himself or herself. Individual traders, unlike fund managers, are unsupervised and have the freedom to act unchecked in any way that they choose. And for some traders this means acting like a 7-year-old child who has just been dropped off at a Toys-R-Us after chugging two cans of Mountain Dew. Unfortunately, this kind of freedom reinforces bad habits, and the net result is a market that moves and thrives in such a way as to prevent as many people as possible from consistently making money. Why is this? It has to do with traders being the best salespeople in the world.

Although used-car salespeople are saddled with reputations as being pushy and dishonest, they don't hold a candle when compared to the average trader. A trader, once in a position, can deceive himself or herself into believing anything that helps to reinforce the notion that he or she is right.

When faced with a loss, Joe Trader will look at a chart and tell whomever is within spitting distance, "The market is acting as if a reversal is about to happen." Net result: he does not exit the position, and his losses mount. When faced with a profit, Joanne Trader hesitates to pull the trigger, telling her cat, "The market is acting great. It would be premature to sell at these levels." Net result: She does not exit the trade, and it turns into a loser. The mistake these traders are making is a common, yet fatal affliction most traders suffer from. They are unaware of how the market naturally programs their reactions so that they will lose. And they are unaware of the key factors that really move the markets I discuss in the introduction. The net result is a trader who "eats like a sparrow and defecates like an elephant." This is a situation, of course, that no account can withstand. Worse, this cycle of emotional slavery will not end until it's met head on. Unfortunately, professional traders understand this all too well, and they set up their trade parameters to take advantage of these situations, specifically preying on the traders who haven't figured out why they lose. One trader's disaster is another trader's bread and butter.

## IT'S ALL ABOUT PAIN AND SUFFERING

The problem is simple and twofold. First, although traders certainly know that not all trades are going to work out—they do get a distinct feeling right after placing every trade that *this trade is going to work out*. A study done by a pair of Canadian psychologists documented this fascinating aspect of human behavior. Just after placing a bet at the racetrack, people are much more confident about their horse's chance of winning than they were immediately before laying down the bet. Obviously, there is nothing about the horse that changes, but in the minds of those bettors, its prospects improved significantly once they placed their bet and got their ticket. Without getting into a large psychological treatise on why humans behave like this, it has to do with a strong, underlying social influence to appear consistent with our choices. Once we make a choice, we respond to external and internal pressures in such a way as to justify our earlier decisions. If we made a good choice, then this process works out very well for us, and we will continue to build upon our good choice. However, if we made a bad choice, whether it is regarding a trade, a job, or a boyfriend, then this process will take this bad choice and make it emphatically worse. We will simply refuse to let go and move on, being more concerned about trying to act consistent regarding our earlier decision. People can waste an entire lifetime living within the justifications of a bad choice. What a waste.

Second, many traders feel they can rely on their judgment *while in a trade*. On paper, this makes a lot of sense. After all, before a trade is placed, traders are at their most objective. However, once the trade is on, the degree of objectivity diminishes immediately and in direct proportion to the number of shares or contracts being traded relative to the account size. Think of it this way: If one trader is long 10 Emini S&Ps in a $10,000 account, and another trader is long 1 Emini S&P in a $100,000 account, who is going to be sweating bullets over each tick? Not only does the first trader already have the feeling that "this trade is going to work out," but now he or she is trapped with the additional pressure of having to manage a position that causes huge equity percentage swings with every tick. Traders relying on their judgment while in a position that is churning their brain with extreme emotions is like trying to row a boat upstream with a piece of Swiss cheese—it simply does not work.

These factors perpetuate a vicious cycle, with the end result being traders who, like bad used-car salespeople, are consistently selling themselves a faulty collection of beliefs that set them up for slaughter. Instead of following a game plan with which to exit a position, traders in this situation spend their time justifying why they are right and will end up closing a position only for one of two reasons. First, the pain of holding becomes so great they cannot "take it" any longer. Once they reach this "uncle" point, they start frantically banging their keyboard to sell (or cover) "at the market" in order to relieve the pain. Second, their broker politely offers to help them out by giving them a phone call, gently letting them know that they should exit their position. This is also called "getting a margin call." This trade is also placed "at the market." In these situations, there is no plan, no thought, and no objectivity. Just a batch of forced sell orders, or, in the case of someone who is short, a batch of forced buy orders, or covering. This act of capitulation, traders exiting a position because they have to, not because they want to, is emotions-based trading at its finest, and this is what moves the market. Whether it is a sustained multimonth move to the downside because of continuous capitulation selling or a quick 10-minute rally because of shorts being forced to cover, these acts are responsible for the major moves in all markets, in all time frames. In the end, markets don't move because they want to. They move because they *have* to.

The pressure of traders trying to act "consistent with their original choice" combined with traders who are trading way too big for their account, leads to more disasters in trading than anything else. Disasters for most people, that is. For every 10 to 20 traders who are blowing up their account, there are typically one or two traders who are making a mint. After all, the money doesn't just disappear. It simply flows into another account—an account that utilizes setups that specifically take advantage of human nature.

# THE CASE STUDY YOU WON'T READ ABOUT AT HARVARD BUSINESS SCHOOL

Figure 1.1 is a chart of an actively traded stock with the name deliberately removed for now. During 2004 it was vigorously bought by one side of the trading community and energetically shorted by the other side. Both parties had plenty of opportunities to make money. On December 29, 2004, this stock made a new 52-week high, hitting $33.45 the next trading day. Over the next five sessions it pulled back to support at point 3, at $27.62, which represented

**F I G U R E  1.1**

a solid buying opportunity, replicating the buying opportunity that took place at point 1, with the same oversold stochastic reading as point 2.

This chart represents a classic case of an inflection point in which a group of traders has to make a decision. A trader who bought the stock as it broke out to new highs will be feeling pain, while the trader who shorted the highs will be feeling euphoria. Traders who are long the stock way back from $10.00 will feel excited and wonder if they should add to their position on this pullback. A trader who is flat the stock is anxious, not wanting to miss the next move, and will be looking to buy the stock here at this pullback to support. Take a moment to look at this chart. What would you do here? Do you short the stock or buy it? What would you be willing to risk? These are questions all traders need to know before they actually place the trade.

Let's work with someone I will call Joe Trader. Joe has been trading for a while and has learned a lot about risk reward levels and about being patient and waiting for high-probability setups. He looks at this chart and sees a decent buying opportunity in this stock. He has a $100,000 account. Near the close he buys 2,000 shares at $27.80, using about half his cash buying power, not even getting close to using any margin. He places a stop limit order at $26.20 and also places a GTC (good till canceled) sell order at $32.60, which is just below the recent highs. He's risking $1.60 ($3,200) to make $4.80 ($9,600), a very comfortable 3:1 risk reward ratio. If he's stopped out, he will lose 3.2 percent of his account's value, which he deems an acceptable risk against making a potential 9.6 percent return on the trade.

The next day, on January 7, 2005, the stock gaps lower, opening at $23.78, well below Joe's stop limit order. (See Fig. 1.2.) This leaves Joe in the stock, and his stop limit order won't fire unless the stock rallies back to $26.80.

Joe doesn't panic. He's been down this road before. He is negative on his trade but it's not terrible, just a dollar over his original stop. He understands that when stocks break down, they will almost always retrace a portion of the move before ultimately moving lower. Also, the daily stochastic is oversold, setting the stock up for a bounce, even if it is just a dead cat bounce. He decides to leave in his limit stop order for this eventual retrace, and he plans to see where the stock ends up near the close.

Fifteen minutes before the closing bell he checks the stock and notices it never reached his stop limit order, but it also bounced off its lows on the day. He thinks there is a good chance that the stock will start to retrace a portion of the move the next trading day. He is calm. He is objective. He decides to hang on. Unfortunately, the next trading day isn't until Monday, and he spends most of the weekend thinking about his stock, not really reacting to the environment around him. On Sunday his wife notices that he has been quiet all weekend, almost listless, and keeps staring at charts on his computer screen. She flips through her latest issue of *Cosmopolitan* magazine to see if she can get any insights into how to cheer him up, but by the time she is done reading the insightful articles, she wonders why she ever married this submissive little mouse of a man in the first place. The guys in the articles are so much more daring and fun! By the time she goes to bed Sunday night, she is angry.

Joe, oblivious, is still up looking at a chart.

Monday morning finally arrives. Joe jumps out of bed early after a restless sleep, just in time to see that the stock is trading lower premarket. It gaps down by almost $3.00 at the open of the regular session. (See Fig. 1.3.) Joe looks at this and shakes his head. How could this have happened?

**F I G U R E   1.2**

16.93 25.59 20.00 80.00

As Joe numbly sips his coffee, he looks at the chart "objectively" and sees all the reasons why the stock should bounce. It's now down by over 40 percent from its all-time highs in only seven days. It's near major support on the daily charts. The daily stochastic is now deeply oversold. He is realistic. He knows this stock is done for, but he also knows that at some point the stock will at least retrace, and he will be able to exit gracefully. He watches the stock all day, chewing his nails, slurping coffee, and getting nothing done. The stock closes at over $6.00 below his stop. Aghast, he decides to hang on for another day, as the stock is way overdue for a bounce.

It is not until he hears the garage door opening downstairs that he remembers he was supposed to drop off his wife's pile of clothes at the cleaners. He grabs them and races out the front door.

On Tuesday, January 11, the stock (okay, its TASR) gaps down yet another 3 points, opening at $17.01. (See Fig. 1.4.) Joe takes a deep breath and grits his teeth. He is dead tired from not being able to sleep last night, and to top it off, his wife has suddenly been acting downright

**F I G U R E   1.3**

hostile. He wonders if she saw his P&L on the computer screen, but he's confident that he's kept that covered up really well, always minimizing his execution platform when he leaves the room. He knows he should talk to her, and he will, as soon as he exits this position and goes flat.

He focuses on the chart. He tells himself not to panic like a stupid newbie and to react like a professional trader. He knows he will never let himself get into a situation like this again, but, in the meantime, he has to keep a cool head and get out of this mess.

He reflects that, over the past four months, he has been able to generate an income averaging $5,000 per month from his trading account. If he closes out his TASR position here at $17.00, he will be down $21,600 just on this one trade. It would take him over four months just to rebuild his capital. He asks himself, "Okay, forget about your original order. Let's say you just entered the trade here. What would be a reasonable target?" He quickly sets up a series of Fibonacci retracement lines on his chart to see where the 50 percent retracement level is of the entire move down. That level is $22.79, well below his original stop, but if the

**F I G U R E   1.4**

TASR - Daily  NASDAQ

stock rallies up to that level, it means $11,580 in profits, leaving him with just a $10,020 loss to make back instead of $21,600. He places his new sell order, confident that this is going to work, and sits back to watch the action.

Amazingly, the stock continues to drift lower during the day. Joe stares at the chart, continually reminding himself to keep a cool head, that the stock is desperately oversold and that it will soon bounce. *Be patient, wait for the retracement, don't be a chump and sell at the dead lows.*

As the markets near the close, TASR breaks new intraday lows yet again, cracking $14.00 a share. Joe pushes back from his desk and yells in disgust. This is impossible. TASR is down by nearly 60 percent in eight days. About to explode with rage, he realizes he simply cannot deal with this any longer. His nervous system is a wreck, and his neck muscles feel like plywood. He sells near the close for $14.02, a loss of $27,560. He still cannot believe how far and how fast TASR has fallen. How much lower can it go? On impulse, he looks at the weekly chart and notices there isn't any support until $10.00 a share. He immediately reverses and goes short 4,000 shares at $14.04, just before the closing bell. Although disgusted with himself, he feels better now that he has taken action, and at least he won't miss out on the remaining down move for this stock. He is anxious to see where TASR opens the next day.

He decides not to tell his wife about any of this, but he does leave a Post-it note reminding himself to pick up the clothes from cleaners the next day.

TASR opens flat the next day, and then steadily starts to rally. (See Fig. 1.5.) Joe is confident the rally will be short-lived. However, he does place a stop just above yesterday's highs. This time he places a stop market order, as it was the stop limit order that got him in trouble in the first place. He feels very confident that this trade is going to work out. This is a good horse!

TASR closes near its highs on January 12, but it does not exceed the previous day's highs, so Joe's stop is not hit. He can't believe his bad luck, and he hopes the stock will gap down the next day. His wife calls to say she is going out with the girls. He grabs a six pack and turns on HBO to see how Tony Soprano is dealing with the problems in his life

**F I G U R E   1.5**

Well, the next day comes around, and the stock gaps up by almost $4.00. Joe's stop order gets him out at the open, as this turns into a market order when the price is above his stop, which is $20.83. He lost $6.79 on the play. On 4,000 shares that is $27,160, nearly identical to that of the loss on his first trade. His $100,000 trading account is now down to $45,280. He needs to make 121 percent just to get back to break even. He is so angry he doesn't know what to do, and eventually he picks up his keyboard and slams it against the wall. About an hour later his wife calls to say that they should seek counseling. Joe pours himself a large whiskey and contemplates the meaning of life.

Joe got the stock long. He used a low-risk entry point, had a great risk-to-reward ratio, and he was risking only 3 percent of his portfolio. He didn't even get a margin call like many traders did in this same situation. The bottom line, it was a great plan, but it turned into a disaster.

But for someone else it was a great trade. This chart of TASR represents a different view. (See Fig. 1.6.) This is a common setup that is created when large funds want to get out of a stock. They push the stock to new highs, sucking in the retail crowd, and then they start unload-

## F I G U R E   1.6

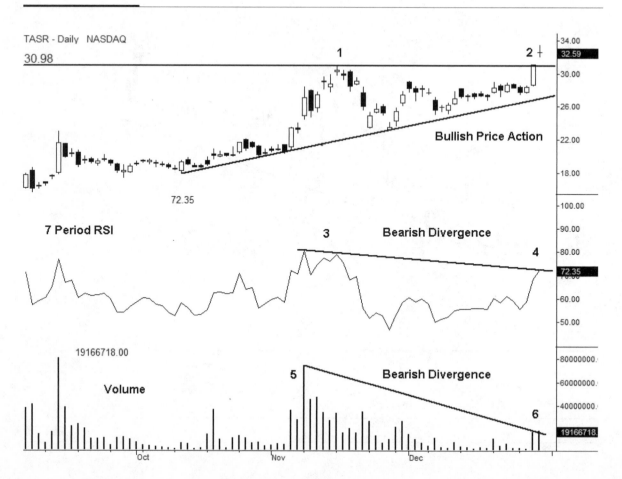

ing. They know the retail crowd will buy the new highs, and they also know the retail crowd will also feel comfortable buying all the way down to support. This gives the institutions ample time to sell their holdings. I call this setup the "fake and break," and I use it as a fade play for swing trades on stocks. (To *fade a market* means to take a trade in the opposite direction of the move.) In other words, if a stock is rallying with this setup, then I'm looking to short it.

## TRADING RULES FOR SELLS/SHORTS (BUYS ARE REVERSED)

These are the rules I use in trading the "fake and break" setup. This is a setup I use on individual stocks.

- **Look at stocks making new 52-week highs:** On December 30, having made new 52-week highs the day before at point 1, TASR gapped up and hit a new all-time high of $33.45 (point 2).
- **For stocks making new highs, look for a bearish divergence using a seven period RSI (relative strength index):** When TASR made new highs on December 30, the RSI hit 72.35 (point 4), well below the level it hit on November 15 when it made its last 52-week high (point 3). When prices make higher highs and, at the same time, the RSI makes lower highs, this is called a *bearish divergence*. The RSI measures the power of the move, and this is telling the trader that the stock is losing power.
- **For stocks making new highs, look for a significant decrease in volume:** When TASR made new 52-week highs, it was on one-fourth of the volume of the last thrust to new highs. This is the equivalent of a car running out of gas. There is no sustained price movement without volume.
- **Short the stock the day after it closes below the previous 52-week high:** On January 3, TASR closes back below $30.98, the previous 52-week high established on November 15. Utilizing this setup, the trader, let's call her Joanne, goes short 2,000 shares at the open on January 4, getting filled at $30.27. She places a stop 25 cents above the all-time highs. Since the all-time highs are $33.45, the stop is placed at $33.70. This is a stop market order, not a stop limit order as Joe used.
- **To exit, use a close backup above the high of the low day while above key support. If key support is broken, stay in the trade until there is a close backup above the high of the low hour on a 60-minute chart.** We take a look at this briefly here, but this is a concept I talk about in much detail later in the book.
- **Don't trail stops.** The exit is the price reversal signal.

After TASR is entered short, the stock never rallies enough to close above the previous day's highs. So Joanne is still in the stock short once it breaks key support on the daily charts in the form of the key uptrend line. Once it breaks this key support level, the selling gets ugly.

Figure 1.7 is a 60-minute chart that shows the increase in volume once TASR breaks key support on the daily charts, at point 1.

**F I G U R E   1.7**

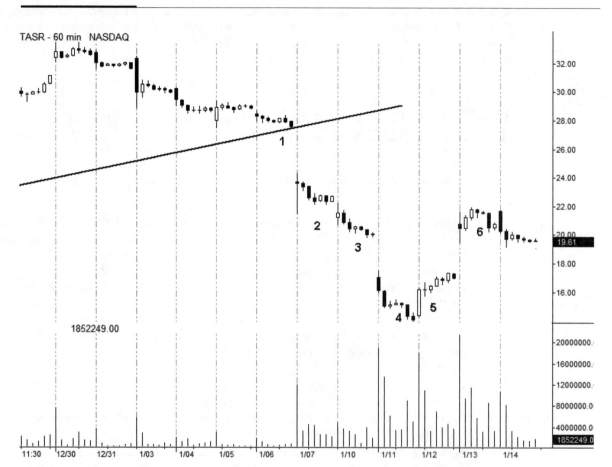

During the three large sell off days, at points 2, 3, and 4, at no time does the market rally enough to close above the high of the low 60-minute bar. The next day, at point 5, TASR rallies enough to close above the previous 60-minute bar, which is the low bar of the entire move down. This close is the signal to cover, and once the next bar opens, Joanne covers her 2,000 shares of TASR at $16.17, pocketing $28,200. She also reverses and goes long 4,000 shares at this same level, using the lows of the move as a stop.

She stays in the move until the 60-minute price action creates a close below the low of the high 60-minute bar. This happens the next day at point 6, and Joanne closes out her long at $20.54 for a profit of $17,480. As Joe is berating himself for being such a stupid fool and sitting through his first day of counseling, Joanne is counting her profits totaling $45,680 and wiring a portion of them out of her account to pay for a one-week vacation to Maui. When a trader loses money, it isn't gone. It has just been moved into another trader's account.

# IT'S NOT THE ECONOMY, STUPID

TASR didn't lose 60 percent of its value in eight trading days because it wanted to. Desperate traders and mutual funds who loaded up on this stock to sell covered calls were the main victims. Covered call writing was one of the most reliable forms of income generation for most of 2004. This is because the market was choppy and didn't go anywhere. Because this method was doing so well, Wall Street announced plans to start a couple of mutual funds that specialized in covered calls. Although there are no guarantees in the markets, here is one "almost" guarantee: As soon as Wall Street announces a special vehicle for trading a particular market or strategy, then that market or strategy is done for. Once the covered call funds got started, the markets roared higher during the last two months of 2004, invalidating this strategy as the best way to take advantage of current market conditions. Another example? In 2004 Wall Street introduced a Holders Trust for Gold, GLD, right when gold peaked at $450 an ounce. The moral of the story? When Wall Street decides to package it up, put a bow on it, and sell it to the public, that move is over. But I digress.

TASR lost 60 percent of its value because a lot of people were caught on the long side, like Joe Trader, and froze. Many of them didn't make a conscious decision to sell the stock. They held on until they couldn't take the pain any longer, or their brokers got them out because of margin calls. It's the margin calls that caused the worst of the selling when TASR closed near $14.00 a share. These forced market orders caused riplike movements in the stock that resulted in even worse fills for traders like Joe who were trying to use their skills to finesse their way out of the trade.

Disgusted with themselves and red in the face, the victims of these trades stalked off to contemplate the insanity of the universe. Meanwhile, as we saw, another group of traders took the opposite side of this "capitulation trade" and made great profits. How does a trader get on the winning side of these trades? To fully understand how to do this, we must first step back and understand how the markets really work, and why traders continually and instinctively sabotage themselves in the first place.

Well, the first part is easy. The markets are not that complex, and they work very simply. Markets rise on a day-to-day basis because current demand exceeds current supply—period. It has nothing to do with being in a secular bear market, a cyclical bull market, high price/earnings ratios (P/E), or Maria Bartiromo's choice of a necklace. (For anyone who actively traded during the dot.com bubble, traders would look for a rally when Maria wore pearls. Very rational, of course.) This has everything to do with what traders are willing to pay for a particular market or individual stock *today*.

It doesn't matter if the demand is falsely created by a hedge fund "taking the street" (buying large amounts of a single stock to drain a market maker of its inventory, forcing it to buy the stock back at a higher price). Or a squeeze that whacks shorts and forces them to cover, or a rumor that a biotech stock is being cornered by Martha Stewart. Demand is demand, and that is what drives markets higher. The inverse is equally true: If there is too much supply in the market, prices will fall. The best source of "too much supply" hitting the markets is generally in the form of margin calls and other means of forced selling, such as the Joe Traders of the world throwing in the towel and dumping their position. This is why markets can erase gains so quickly; they take the stairs up, but ride the elevator down. It is very important for a trader to remember this. Yes, the stock may be acting great and its prospects are bright, but if there are 1.5 million shares being offered for sale all at the same instant and there are only 50,000 shares being sought by buyers, then that stock is going crash. It isn't rocket science. It's supply and demand at its finest.

Trading the long or the short side is very easy, once a trader learns to ignore his or her own personal opinions. This means pushing aside any and all prejudices about the market and focusing on the current supply and demand situation. Once traders understand this, the next thing to work on is their own mental trading outlook and how they process this information, and to fully understand how the human brain naturally and emphatically causes traders to do things that make them lose money in the markets. It could be a whopper of a bad trade like Joe Trader's, or a series of smaller bad trades that grind down an account. Either way, it's the human brain that's letting it happen.

And that is what we discuss in the next chapter.

# 2 CHAPTER

## PSYCHOLOGY 101: WHAT THEY DIDN'T TEACH ABOUT TRADING IN SCHOOL

*Only a fool tests the depth of the water with both feet.*

AFRICAN PROVERB

## EMOTIONS ARE FINE AT WEDDINGS AND FUNERALS

Trading is the most deceptive profession in the world. Do you know anyone who has recently walked into an airport, jumped into the cockpit of a jumbo jet loaded with passengers, and taken off down the runway without any prior training? Yet people will routinely open an account and start trading without any guidance whatsoever. And that is equally insane. Little do they know that their emotions and the natural functions of their brain are against them right from the opening bell.

Just as a chatty masseur is the enemy of a relaxing spa treatment, emotion is the enemy of successful trading. Remember, the markets are set up to naturally take advantage of and prey upon human nature, moving sharply only when enough people get trapped on the wrong side of a trade. This sweeps a burst of fear, frustration, and rage into the markets—and creates fabulous trading opportunities for the prepared trader. To head into this adventure called *trading* without having a firm grasp of how human emotions move markets, and how human emotions sabotage your own trading, is like trying to hail a taxi in Manhattan during a thunder shower. In other words, the overwhelming odds are against you.

The whole idea of this chapter is to lay the groundwork for the setups we discuss later in the book. With this foundation, traders will be able to understand how to control their "inner demon" with respect to trading. This is the creature that mentally blocks traders from following the parameters of a particular setup once they are in the trade. This is very similar to the brain freeze that occurred during the river rafting incident discussed in the introduction. It is also important to remember that every trader has different dominant personality traits that they use to absorb information and relate to the world around them. Some traders are more visual, others more auditory, and still others are more kinesthetic—they relate to the world based on how events make them feel on the inside. These three traits can have a big impact on a person's trading. Traders who are dominantly kinesthetic are doomed from the outset—until they realize that is how they relate to the world and what impact that has on their trading. Near the end of the book there is a chapter on tips for when trading "isn't working for you." In this chapter there is a personality test that helps to determine what type of personality you are and the pros and cons for each personality trait. The cons will work against a trader without their even knowing it—until they learn about it and realize what's going on.

In addition, the trader will realize the importance of utilizing a specific methodology for each setup, because each setup takes advantage of a different aspect of human emotions. *A trader cannot apply the same trading rules to all setups across the board.* This is one of the biggest mistakes I see newer traders make. A two-point stop in the E-mini S&Ps can work well with one setup but cause nearly every trade to get stopped out in another. Trading five lots per $50,000 can work well with one setup but be devastating with another. By understanding the psychology behind the trade, the individual will also then understand the right parameters and the right allocation to use for each setup. Each setup really is unique, and it has to be treated that way.

The end result of this chapter is for you to develop what I call a *professional trading mindset.* Although we discuss setups for most of this book, traders have got to have the trading psychology nailed down or their trading experience will be short-lived and painful.

## SHOW ME A GUY WITH A SYSTEM, AND I'LL SHOW YOU A GUY WHO IS WELCOME IN MY CASINO

This is an old Las Vegas saying that applies equally well to the financial markets. Having a system gives people a sense of security—nothing can go wrong. Every time I walk into Mandalay Bay or Bellagio in Las Vegas, I am reminded that all these fabulous structures were paid for by people who thought they could beat the blackjack tables. The owners of the Luxor borrowed $550 million over 20 years to build their place. They were able to pay it off in less than three. Tell them at the front desk that you have a strategy, and you'll most likely get a presidential suite and a private table.

Why don't the strategies work in Vegas? The reason for this is twofold: The house has an edge with percentages, and as soon as the system falters a couple of times, the human mind gets to work trying to tweak it to make it perfect. This eventually screws up the entire process. In the casinos, as in trading, it takes only one stupid bet to blow the whole wad. Casino owners know this, and this is why they sell the strategy books right there on the property, prominently displayed in their own gift shops. This elevates the concept of the fox guarding the hen house to a whole new level.

It's the same process with the markets. The odds are against the trader surviving because the market has an edge: It doesn't have any emotions. Like the river making its way to the ocean, the markets ebb and flow with total disregard for the objectives of the people hanging on for the ride. Humans have a tendency to try to imprint their will on the markets. This is like trying to get a tornado to shift course by yelling at it.

## THE RIGHT MENTAL OUTLOOK FOR THE MARKETS: DON'T TURN ON YOUR COMPUTER WITHOUT IT

*He who conceals his disease cannot expect to be cured.*

ETHIOPIAN PROVERB

First traders must understand the psychology, and then they can learn about the setup. It's like two pieces of a puzzle, and these two pieces have to snap together snugly in place before the trader can expect to trade for a living without repeating the same mistakes over and over again.

I've spent a lot of my career focused on trader psychology—not only working on myself, but working with hundreds of other traders. I've spent a lot of time in large trading rooms with hedge funds and prop traders, executing orders right alongside hundreds of other traders. I've watched the fear and the elation and the greed permeate a room and a group of traders like a disease. I've literally seen money from accounts on one side of a room flow into the accounts on the other side of the room, as each group of traders focused on different setups and parameters. In addition, I've worked with over 100 traders who have come up to my office to sit beside me and watch me trade, and to have me look over their shoulder while they trade. I'm the first to say that I'm not a shrink, but let's just say my experiences have left me with a clear road map of the process most traders go through when they first start to trade. Every person is unique, but when it comes to money, the differences are quickly stripped away. A herd of thirsty cattle will quickly drop all pretenses and stampede to get to water.

In addition to my experiences in working with other traders, it shouldn't be surprising to hear that I learned a lot of this first hand through the best teacher that the market has to offer: extensive pain and suffering. My stepfather, Lance, a broker with Morgan Stanley, got me started trading options when I was a sophomore in high school. Of course, I'm not sure if he was introducing me to a great career or just trying to generate enough extra commissions to pay the mortgage—but it all worked out in the end.

He noticed that while I was at the mall slinging cookie dough and sodas, I had built up a decent-sized coin collection, had my own mail order business, and was actively engaged in buying and selling rare coins from dealers and individual collectors. This was a small operation to be sure, but the entrepreneurial spirit was alive and well. He said that I could do essentially the same thing with household name stocks, but instead of trading the actual stocks, I could leverage my positions by trading options. I thought about it for about eight seconds and decided to give it a shot. On my first trade I bought 10 out of the money call options on INTC for 50 cents, and I sold them a week later for $1.35, pocketing $850 less the commissions that were going to help pay our mortgage. My monthly expenses as a sophomore in high school amounted to about $150. It didn't take me long to figure out that a person could make a living doing this. My capital became, in a sense, an employee working for me. And it beat working at the mall. My senior year in high school happened to be 1987, which was quite a year for trading. By blind luck, I owned puts during the crash on October 19, when the Dow lost over 22 percent in one day, so I had some money to play with as I headed to college.

I continued to trade actively through college, where I started out studying business in California, used my trading stake to finance a year abroad studying history in Cambridge, England, and eventually graduated from the University of Texas at Austin. During this time, I quickly developed a very consistent approach to my trading: I would routinely turn a $10,000 account into the high 5 or low 6 figures over the course of a year. I would then buy myself a piece of rental property and a couple of nice gizmos. Then I would sit back and decide what other bigger and better things I wanted to buy. Once I figured that out, I would go back to trading. Armed with these visions of "bigger and better things," I would dive back into the markets—and promptly give back the rest of my trading account in less than a month. This happened not once but three times. The most memorable trade happened right out of college, when I was able to give back a $150,000 trading account in less than a week. (That's what happens when you buy 200 OEX puts at $7.20 and sell them a week later for 75 cents). Luckily I did have enough real estate at this point to be able to sell one of the properties to raise a new trading stake.

At this point, of course, I had to sit down and figure out what I was doing wrong. I knew I could make money trading—why couldn't I keep it? My studies in history had a huge impact here. I could clearly see that since the beginning of modern civilization, the world had gone through a repetition of similar events all driven by human decisions. This insight really changed my focus and how I looked for opportunities in the markets. I stopped looking for the next great indicator and started looking for repeatable market patterns based on human nature.

During this time I also came across a book by Mark Douglas called, *The Disciplined Trader*. This book was a real eye opener in that Mark showed how to turn everyday stressful trading situations into "normal" successful trading behavior. His follow-up book, *Trading in the Zone*, is also excellent. His books have had a huge impact on me, and they are required reading for anyone I'm working with. Mark's insights, as well as my long discovery period, finally gave me the answer: Whenever I focused on the setups and not the results, I did fine. *But whenever I focused on the results and not the setups, I got killed.* Why is this? Once I got my hands on a decent-sized trading account, I would start to think of things like, "I want to turn this account into a million dollars." Instead of focusing on the setups, I would focus on making a million dollars. This caused me to jump into the trading habits that ruin all traders: betting it all on one trade, not using a stop because the trade "had to work out," and focusing on making a million bucks instead of waiting for a high-probability trade setup. Sure, it would have been easier to just blame it on my mother for hitting me with a wooden spoon once when I was a kid, but at some point we have to step up and take responsibility for our own actions.

Once this revelation sank in, I started to do two things differently: First, I started wiring any profits out of my trading account at the end of each week. This kept me focused on producing a steady income, as opposed to making a grand killing. I also discovered it was a great way to protect profits—the market can't have them if they are safely tucked away out of reach. Second, I started a competition among the various setups I used. This way I could measure the performance of every one of my setups at the end of each month. The setups that made money I kept using. The setups that lost money, I dumped. This was incredibly important to my trading. The only way I could keep my competition going was to execute my trade setups the same way each and every time. Anytime I deviated from a standard setup, I would mark this down in my trading journal as an "impulse trade." I kept track of the performance on these too. After about six months of tracking my impulse trades (wow, this market is going higher, I have to get in), I realized that they were not making me any money and were in fact preventing me from making a living as a trader.

In working with other traders, I see impulse trading as one of the most common reasons for people getting their heads handed to them. They don't have a plan. They just get long when that feels right, and they get short when that feels right. I've literally had traders in my office who have come up to work specifically on their impulse trades—only to sneak in orders when I wasn't looking. It's that powerful an urge to jump in and be a part of the action. It's like a drug addition, and like most addictions, it never works in the long run. My method for dealing with them is to simply sit next to them and watch them trade—and to do exactly the opposite of what they're doing. At the end of the day, or week, we compare our profit and loss statements, and that usually tells the story. This is a win/win situation because it is a great lesson for the impulse traders—there are actually people out there doing the exact opposite of what they are doing and making money—and it is a profitable exercise for me. The cure for impulse trading is patience. Patience is such an important quality for a trader—both in learning what setups best work for you, and in waiting for those setups to occur. Impulse traders who cannot own up to this bad habit need to stop trading and go to Vegas. The end result will be identical—they will lose all their money. But at least in Vegas the drinks are free.

If people are stuck in a relationship with an individual who berates their best efforts and undermines their dreams, then it is time to leave this individual and move on. It is in this vein that I "broke up" with my impulse trade. I liked my impulse trade. It was fun. It made me feel good. It was exciting. But the bottom line is that my impulse trading undermined my potential and prevented me from realizing my dreams of being a full-time trader. Once this realization took hold, I took immediate steps to cut that cancer out of my life. This included a reward and punishment system that I discuss later in this book, in the chapter on formulating a business plan.

In the end, I stuck with my friends who believed in me—my setups that worked when I gave them half a chance. Once I was able to follow my setups consistently, exactly the same way each and every time, I was able to make the transition to trading full time. A large part of my transition was mental and developing what I call a "professional state of mind."

Before this could happen, however, I went through three very distinct phases in my trading career. I've found that most traders go through these same phases in one fashion or another. Unfortunately, by the time they get through Phase III, they are typically out of money. The three phases are as follows:

- Phase I: Destined to Lose—six months to a year
- Phase II: Fear-Based Trading—two to six months
- Phase III: Search for the Holy Grail—six months to death

Phase IV, of course, represents the time that a trader has become consistently profitable. It is critical that traders understand this process and recognize from which phase they are currently operating. This is obviously important for a trader's own development, but there is a more subtle reason why it's essential to grasp this concept—so a trader can understand how to crush other traders who are still stuck in one of these phases. This is the biggest poker game on the planet, and the money flowing into your account isn't appearing as if by magic. It's coming from someone who is still learning how the markets work, and who most likely followed his or her gut and got suckered into taking the wrong side of the trade.

## PHASE I TRADING: DESTINED TO LOSE— TRAITS THAT MAKE PEOPLE A SUCCESS IN LIFE GETS THEM KILLED IN THE MARKETS

*He that lives on hope will die fasting.*
BENJAMIN FRANKLIN

It has been said that the path to hell is paved with good intentions, and nowhere is this more apparent than in the world of trading. I have yet to meet one individual who went into trading with the goal of losing money. Everybody's intentions are quite the opposite, and the first thing people do when they enter the world of trading is tap into what has worked for them successfully in the past. The problem is that the tactics an individual uses to achieve his or her goals in everyday life do not work in trading, and in fact are one of the main reasons for failure. While good judgment is critical to an individual who wants to climb the corporate ladder or start a business, we have already seen why "good judgment" didn't work in the middle of the TASR trade. This leads us to what has to be the most painful lesson ever inflicted on the optimistic nature of the human species: *The tactics an individual uses to achieve goals in everyday life do not work in trading, and in fact are one of the main reasons for a trader's failure.* The determination, positive thinking, and stubbornness that made people a success in one area of their life simply sets them up for slaughter in the markets. It is these types of traders who obstinately hold on to a losing position, adding to it on the way down, using positive thinking techniques to visualize this fiasco eventually turning into a winning trade. I don't care how many Tony Robbins tapes the employees of Enron listen to; it's not going to get their stock back up to $90 a share. The trader who is unaware of this phenomenon is set up for failure from the very beginning. This doesn't mean that a person shouldn't be positive about their ability to eventually become a successful trader. Far from it. However, a trader will be much better off assuming that every trade they take is going to fail. This way they learn to focus on protecting their downside. The upside can take care of itself. Be positive on life, but pessimistic on your next trade.

Traders who "play the markets" with a mental framework oriented toward how external society rewards and punishes "good" and "bad" behavior are set up to lose from day one. For example, "cutting losses short" is difficult when there is the possibility of the market coming back to the breakeven point. At breakeven, the trader is not a "loser." Thus, according to the benchmarks of society, if traders can exit a position with a gain, they are "successful." This leads to the removal of stops "once in a while" in the hopes of getting out at breakeven—in order to be a winner in the eyes of society (sigh). This can work 10 times in a row, but it is the one time it doesn't work that knocks traders flat on their back. On this particular day, these traders will be among the many who cause a "riplike movement" in the markets as they pound their keys in disgust to get out of a trade that is killing their account. This habit of removing stops, even if it is only once in a while, is reinforced by the societal belief of what defines a winner versus a loser. This habit will destroy a trader's account faster than anything else. By using hard stops and sticking to them, a trader at least has a fighting chance in being able to do this for a living. If they can't at least do that, they will not make it as a trader. Period.

What happens to traders in the beginning is that they naturally end up on a cycle in which they label themselves as a good trader on days that they make money and a bad trader on days that they lose money. This is an ordinary reaction instilled into them based on the principles that apply to general society. After all, straight A's mean a student is a success, while F's mean they are a failure, right? If there is anything I can emphasize in this book, it would be this: *Trading has nothing to do with general society.* In fact, the markets are set up in such a way as to take what most people hold near and dear to their hearts as a means of taking advantage of them. The markets thrive on taking the rules and ideals that govern general society, wadding them up into a ball, lighting them on fire, and then shoving them down a new trader's throat. Any trader who is unaware of this phenomenon is being played like a fish right from the opening bell.

General society tells us that losing money equates with failure and making money equates with success. The trader, after a losing day, unconsciously thinks, "I've lost money. I can't do this. If I would've just removed my stop, the market would have come back and got me out at breakeven, and then I'd still be a contender." So what happens is that the trader starts looking for opportunities to remove his or her stop in order to not end up with a losing trade. Not on every trade, of course. Just on some trades. And how do traders determine when to do this? Easily enough, they just use their "judgment" while in a trade. And this is exactly when professional traders step in for the kill.

This society focus on money traps traders into the very habits that cause their ruination. Removing a stop in the hopes of getting out at breakeven is one of the worst habits a trader can develop. Sure, it will work some of the time, but it has to turn into a disaster only once to wipe out half an account or more. While the rest of the world views losing as a bad thing, in trading, small losses are the best sign of success. Nobody outside of trading will ever understand this, so don't waste a lot of time telling your in-laws how losing only $2,000 yesterday is part of your success plan. Yes, this means you are doing your job, but as long as the sun continues to rise in the east, other people will never get it. The only people who understand traders are other traders. Personally, when I'm at a cocktail party and people ask me what I do for a living, I've found it's just easier to say that I'm a leper. People at least understand that and can empathize.

The biggest issue for newer traders is to reprogram their brains into realizing that, in trading, losing is winning. A professional trader's job is to take small losses. Period. Most traders don't realize that there are only a few days each month where big profits can be made. The rest of the time traders are doing their job if they are keeping their head above water. The idea is to keep the trading account intact for when the big moves come along. If on Monday some traders take three small losses in a row and end up down on the day, they are doing their job and have the chance to be successful professional traders, because they will have maintained the bulk of their account to use on one of the few days when the markets really move. That is what trading is about. It's about traders sticking to the parameters that they have set for themselves and sticking to the setups that they've decided to follow. It's not about gut reactions and chasing the latest sound bite mentioned on CNBC. That is the path to trading annihilation.

I remember getting a call from a guy in mid-2003 who was running a $10 million hedge fund for his family. It was never made clear to me how he qualified for this role, though I think he mentioned something about knowing how to use the Internet. He sent me an e-mail about YHOO, asking me for my thoughts. I looked at the chart. The stock was trending higher on nice volume, and I told him about a couple of different setups I would use to get long the stock. Apparently that wasn't the answer he was looking for, because he called me the next day telling me I was reading the chart wrong. As I listened to him rant on about page views and price earnings (P/E) ratios, a light went on. I interrupted him and asked, "Where did you short this stock?" After a moment of silence followed by a cough, the story emerged. He had shorted it at $12.00 based on a newsletter recommendation. As the stock rallied, the newsletter shorted more, and so did he. By the time I talked to him, he had shorted 400,000 shares at an average price of $16.25 for a total outlay of $6.5 million.

I asked if the newsletter was still short, and he said no. I checked my quote screen and saw that YHOO was trading at $22.50 and had just cracked out new 52-week highs. He asked me if he should short some more to raise his average cost, "so it won't have to go down as much for me to get back to breakeven."

Here he was down $2.5 million on the trade, his family hadn't seen the statements, and he was trying to salvage his career as the family financial guru. There was zero rationality in his thinking. I told him he needed to get out of the trade, or at least buy call options for a hedge. I even said that YHOO was going to keep on rallying until all the people who were short cried uncle and covered. Apparently that wasn't the advice he was looking for either. He ended up shorting another 100,000 shares, and finally caved when YHOO hit $30 for a loss of $6.25 million. It's an excruciating story, but this happens all the time with all types of different account sizes. This guy didn't want to take a small loss because he didn't want to look like a loser to his family. His motto became, "As long as I hold onto this position, it's not really a loss." This is like having blood pour out of your bowels and you choose not to go to the doctor. "As long as I don't go to the doctor, no one will know I'm dying." Trust me, once you are dead, people will figure it out.

Averaging down on a losing position is like a sinking ship taking in more water. When the family fund manager kept shorting YHOO as it made new highs, he may as well have been driving nails into the Mona Lisa. Both are deliberate acts of destruction. Financial planners always talk about *dollar cost averaging*. I call it *dollar loss averaging*. Adding to a winning trade is okay, but adding to a losing trade is insane. If you caught some of your employees stealing from you, would you give them a raise or fire them and find somebody else? This guy trading YHOO would have given them a raise, a housing allowance, and a comfortable pension.

As traders approach the end of Phase I, assuming they still have any capital left, they have some solid experience under their belt. They haven't quite figured out why they are getting hammered by the markets. It's not like they have lost money on every trade. In fact, they've had some great trades. Unfortunately, they've also been knocked down pretty hard on a number of occasions, and their account is under water. They started off optimistically, but now they just want to be a little more careful. And the bottom line is that they don't want to lose any more money. Welcome to Phase II.

## PHASE II TRADING: FEAR-BASED TRADING OR, "EVERYTHING I TOUCH TURNS TO CRAP"

Many traders think that once they become more cautious, their trading will improve. They would be wrong.

When traders decide they don't want to lose any more money, they unwittingly turn themselves into the "late entry" champions of the trading world. They wait and they wait and they make doubly sure that a trade looks good before they take it. In this scenario, the markets start to rally, and by the time the trader is absolutely convinced that this rally is for real, he or she is jumping in near the dead highs of the move. He or she and the rest of the traders who did this just gave the markets the fuel needed to start moving down. Why? Because suddenly the market has a lot of stops being placed beneath it, and like wind on a forest fire, these stops will ignite a sell off. This safe, cautionary entry quickly turns into a loss. The difference this time is that prudent traders religiously stick to their stops. The problem is that this overcautious behavior gives them terrible entries, and their odds of getting stopped out are extremely high. Yes, small losses are good, but if nearly every trade results in a small loss, the account will eventually wear itself down.

Phase II usually doesn't last very long. Traders in this phase generally don't lose a lot of money, but they lose enough. Once traders figure out that they can stick to their stops, but that their entries are suffering, they reach what alcoholics refer to as a "moment of clarity." If the traders' entries are bad, then obviously their indicators are bad. So they go looking for some better ones. And thus begins the search for the Holy Grail.

## PHASE III TRADING: THE SEARCH FOR THE HOLY GRAIL—HOLDING YOUR BREATH IS NOT ADVISED.

The search for that fail-safe indicator that's going to work nearly every time takes a trader down a path littered with corpses, broken dreams, and stuttering fools. Many traders stay on this search for the rest of their lives. The irony is that individuals in this phase think they are developing as traders, when in reality their development as traders is dead in the water, having been stopped faster and with greater intensity than Monica Lewinsky's future in government. Traders in Phase III are stuck in quicksand, entrenched in a losing game that can last years, decades, or longer. The end result is a trader who spends this time repeating the same mistakes over and over again or happily discovering new ones.

The cycle that takes place is one of always looking for the next best thing. It's the search for that oh-so-special indicator or system that is going to give the traders their lodestone reward.

In a typical scenario, this means diving headlong into a couple of different trading programs or ideas and endlessly tweaking them until they reveal their magic. One typical scenario relates to traders who develop a simple set of mechanical rules, which are kept secret, of course, that will help them attain a substantial profit each year with virtually no risk and using only a small amount of capital. They get especially excited when they see that these methods, when carefully applied to select historical data, work amazingly well. The ones that didn't work out could easily have been "filtered out." This type of trader typically dies with a one-page summary of how well the trade works, and a stack of 68 pages that explain when not to take the trade.

Other traders stuck in Phase III will go to seminars and learn about trends, and learn the importance of never fighting the trend. They discover the magic of moving averages and how they cross over when the trend changes. Oh, the power! When the market is trending, they work beautifully. Eventually, though, they get discouraged when they figure out that 75 percent of the time markets are trading sideways, as professionals chop the Holy Grail seekers into mincemeat.

This may lead traders to the world of options and they start looking at spreads to contain risk and writing premium to generate monthly income. This works great when the markets are chopping around, but then when the markets start trending again, these positions can, and often do, get killed.

The list goes on and on. At various stages throughout this journey, after traders have studied a number of systems, strategies, and indicators, one day they sit down and create what they think is the perfect chart with the perfect indicators. Then they start to use it. It may work well during the first couple of days, or even the first couple of weeks, but then the traders gets burned on what they thought was a perfect setup. So, instead of using an MACD (Moving Average Convergence Divergence) with a setting of 12, 26, 9, they read somewhere that a setting of 12, 17, 10 is faster. They go in and reformat all their charts with the new setting and eagerly await the next trading day. Their setups work for a couple of days or a couple of weeks, and then a couple of trade setups don't work out. Back into cyberspace the traders go. They are determined. They are focused. They neglect their family, miss the daughter's softball game, and lose track of time. But it's all worth it, because seven days later, at 3:45 in the morning, they discover what they've been looking for. On their stochastic, they've been using the settings of 14, 3, 3 when they should have been using 15, 3, 1! They put it on a chart and apply it to historical data. It works much better! The traders once again reformat all their charts, and, once again, eagerly await the next trading day.

And when this doesn't work, they go from a 15-minute chart to a 13-minute chart. And when that doesn't work, they switch from trading the E-mini S&P to the E-mini Nasdaq. And when that doesn't work, they learn that the euro is the place to be. And when that doesn't work, they become a gold bug, because, don't you know, it's the only real money? It's always, always, always the next best thing. This cycle repeats itself forever until the trader gets sick of this roller coaster and jumps off at the next stop. Most never figure this out and remain stuck here for the rest of their trading lives. The kids go from diapers to dormitories, and they barely notice because they're still lost, tweaking the next best thing, never realizing they're the chump with the strategy who would be welcomed with open arms in any casino. Like Duluth, Minnesota, in February, it's a terrible place to be.

This whole situation is summed up succinctly by one of the hedge fund characters in Ben Mezrich's entertaining book, *Ugly Americans: The True Story of the Ivy League Cowboys*

*Who Raided the Asian Markets for Millions.* "The whole game of arbitrage is spotting who the asshole is. If you can't spot the asshole—well, then *you're* the asshole."

# SIGNS THAT A TRADER IS STUCK IN PHASES I, II, OR III

Here are a few additional anecdotes and situations that let traders know they are still stuck in these beginning stages of trading.

## Good Till Close

A popular order type for swing traders is called a GTC order, or "good till canceled." This means just what it says: "Keep my order in place until my target is hit or until I cancel the order." My partners and I, as well as many brokers, refer to GTC orders as "good till close." This is because many traders will keep their "good till cancelled" order in place right up until price action gets "close" to their order. What happens is that the stock they are in is rallying hard and approaching their GTC sell order. They start looking at the stock and think, "Wow, this stock is acting great! I don't want to get out of it because it's going to keep heading higher." So they call their broker and cancel their GTC sell order. The stock rallies, pushes up through that order level, and then eventually starts to sell off. The trader has no exit strategy, and the stock continues to fall and turns into a losing trade. This starts off as a greed play and turns into a fear play. When enough of these happen to traders, they start to get really fearful about losing money.

## Size Really Does Matter

When traders get scared and start to put most of their focus on not being wrong, a variety of bad things start to happen. The most common is that the traders get into a new position, and as soon as they see a small profit, they take it. They buy the minisized Dow at 10100, and it goes to 10104. Even though there are screaming buy signals in place and there are zero sell signals, they, miracle of miracles, have a profit, and they'll be damned if they are going to let the market take it away from them. So they pocket the four Dow points, which amount to $20 per contract, or about $14.00 after commissions. Never mind that the Dow goes on to rally another 40 points, and then and only then, does it give an exit signal.

What happens is that traders are taking a four-point profit, a three-point profit, a six-point profit, and then on the last trade of the day it goes 30 points against them. So the traders have three winners out of four but they are down on the day. And it's kind of a typical thing that'll happen for traders who are in this frame of mind of not wanting to have to go through the pain of watching a profitable position go all the way back into the red.

Many brokers actually analyze their client's accounts in order to predict when they are going to blow up. This way they can hedge the traders before the losses actually occur, essentially trading against them. The number one indicator that a trading account is going to blow up is an increase in the frequency of trading combined with the increased use of market orders instead of limit orders. Firms that hedge see this situation develop, begin to lick their chops, and fade their customer's account, taking the opposite side of every trade. In general, traders who suddenly start taking smaller profits are also trading much more frequently than they used to. It is important to realize that some firms will see this activity and take specific action, because 90 percent of the time this means a trader is about to blow up their account. Don't be the trader that comes up on the broker's radar screen as a hedging candidate.

Yes, size does matter. Bigger losses are a lot worse than smaller profits. However, a trader who takes small profits because of fear is not following a plan. A trader who is not following a plan, who is only reacting to internal emotions, is going to get beat. Not maybe. Not probably. *Going to.*

## Greed Is Bad Nourishment for the Brain

There are limitless ways for traders to sabotage their account, but this is a particularly good one. What happens is that traders get into a comfortable routine. Maybe they are averaging $250 a day trading the mini-sized Dow on a $50,000 account. This, for them, is a reasonable goal on the capital they are trading. One night they are at dinner with their spouse who asks how the trading is going. The traders respond that all is going great. The spouse is pleased and says something like, "Well, since your trading is going so well, I've been thinking that I'd really like to get a BMW. Can we go ahead and get one?"

And so the next day the traders wake up and think, "Okay, if I'm going to get this BMW, I've got to step up my trading and start making $750 a day. This way I can set aside a large down payment, and I can get the car in the next six to eight weeks." The very second traders utter those words, a trigger clicks in the remote recesses of their mind, and they have unknowingly entered a period where they will not be able to do anything right. Instead of sticking to their original parameters, they're going to start reaching for more. What used to look like a perfectly good 20-point profit in the mini-sized Dow now looks puny—it certainly won't have much of an impact on the BMW purchase. So the position doesn't get sold as the traders sit back and wait for the market to give them more money. The market inevitably turns and the traders end up getting stopped out for a loss. In this mindset, what once used to look like a reasonable profit becomes too small, and this throws the entire trading plan out the window.

I remember working with one trader who was in almost exactly this same situation. He was a good trader, but had recently entered a losing streak, and he couldn't figure out why. I asked him if he suddenly was trying to trade his way into any big, specific purchases. Yes. Aha. Something for his wife. We talked about this phenomenon for a while, including the story about the fur coat, which is described in *Reminiscences of a Stock Operator* by Edwin Lefevre, a book that is a must read for all traders. My friend paused for a moment, rubbed his chin. "Well, I think I know how to fix this problem," he said. "I'll just divorce my wife."

This is the home run mentality, and it's a downfall to all traders. It's important for the trader to remember that the market is not going anywhere. Like an all-you-can-eat-buffet in Vegas, it's going to be there all the time. There is no reason to try to load up your plate to the max on your first trip through the buffet line. People can grab their plate, mosey on over to the buffet, pick up a couple of pieces of shrimp, and saunter back over to their table and enjoy them. Then, when that's done, they can go back and pick out a few slices of brie. There is no need to be a hog and load up the plate. The buffet is always going to be there. A person can sit there all day and take little nibbles from the buffet all day long. Remember, in the markets, bulls can win and bears can win, but pigs get slaughtered.

## Speaking of Jesse Livermore

Many traders know that *Reminiscences of a Stock Operator* by Edwin Lefevre is a book about Jesse Livermore, the famed trader who made approximately $100 million in 1929 dollars in the stock market crash (about a billion in today's dollars). What many people do not know is that on March 5, 1934, he filed for bankruptcy, and on November 28, 1940, he blew his brains out in the bathroom stall of a hotel. Although this may not sound like a strong endorsement for the book, it is a must read for any serious trader. While this book talks about the trading strategies that made him his fortune, the book *Jesse Livermore, World's Greatest Stock Trader* by Richard Smitten also goes into detail about the years and days leading up to his suicide.

I majored in history and was trained to take pieces of historical data and form an opinion, based on facts, about what really happened in the past. From what I've read of Jesse Livermore's life and eventual demise, my opinion is that he suffered a bout of euphoria after the 1929 crash. This euphoria caused him to trade recklessly and with huge size, and this caused him to lose his fortune in less than five years. Although he had gone broke and made a fortune three times before, the size of this loss did permanent psychological damage, and the pressing weight of "trying to make it all back" is what eventually did him in. Let's take a look at what euphoria can do to a trader.

## Euphoria: Redefining Stupid

Euphoria is the worst emotion for a trader to succumb to, even worse than greed. What happens with euphoria is that traders have such a great day in the markets that they proclaim themselves king of the trading world. Normally let's say they trade 10 contacts. Well now, since they are "king," they are going to start off with 50 contracts, and go up from there if they feel like it. After all, they are now "the world's greatest trader" and can do no wrong.

This happens to traders frequently, and the resulting act of insanity is just like doubling each bet on a roulette wheel. People can sit on red and keep doubling up on each bet until they win. This works great right up until the time that they have maxed out their capital on red, and the color comes up black. Doubling and tripling up on positions just because a trader is feeling confident is yet another sucker's game. What's worse is that this strategy always leads to traders giving back all the fantastic gains that made them euphoric in the first place. This places added pressure on traders—now they have to trade in order to get back to where they were. This, of course, causes a multitude of bad habits.

Increasing trading size just because you are feeling awesome about your trading is like being in a marriage that is going fantastically well. The conversations are sparkling, the mutual adulation adoring, and life under the covers is grand. Happiness abounds in spades.

How can you make this better? Double up! Have an affair. A good idea in theory, but this is only going to turn out one way—very, very badly.

## PAPER TRADING—WHY IT'S MORE WORTHLESS THAN AN IRAQI DINAR

There are a few good reasons for people to paper trade. Paper trading will help a trader learn a new execution platform. This way they can figure out how to use the software through a demo account and save themselves costly errors that arise when they try to place orders on an unfamiliar system. Also, paper trading is good for forward testing a system or strategy to see how it works before committing real money. However, paper trading does have one distinct disadvantage—it can be worthless in a way because it does not take into account how a trader will act when there is real money on the line. That is what makes or breaks a trader. It's ok to trade a smaller size, but without real money on the line, a trader won't understand how they hold up under pressure. This is also a good way for a trader to test how far apart they are mentally from "paper trading vs. real trading." A trader should feel the same trading paper as they do real money. To the extent that they feel extreme emotions when really trading vs. paper trading, it will give them a clue where they are on the psychological trading scale. In other words, how screwed up they are psychologically when they are actually trading real money. When a trader freaks out on a real trade, it is a red flag that they are trading too big for their account size. In this case, a trader should keep trading smaller size until they feel the same emotionally as when they are in a paper trade.

The most dramatic instance I've seen with this is in working with traders in Asia, specifically in Taipei, Hong Kong, Tokyo, and Shanghai. Asians are fantastic gamblers, willing to risk huge sums. This can be a problem with trading and it only takes one bad trade to ruin an account. One guy I worked with was trading 100 lots at a time in a $100,000 account. Each 1 point move in the S&Ps represented $5,000. The first day he made 5 points ($25,000), and the next day he lost 7 points ($35,000). These were normal fluctuations for him, and it showed. He'd get so excited and animated that I thought he was going to implode. I had him cut his size down to 10 lots. At first he was bored, but then a strange thing happened. He wasn't excited, so he traded objectively . . . and he made money. We got him to trade in the same fashion as if he were paper trading, and it made all of the difference. Being able to work with traders overseas is a great win/win for me as I get to learn how other people view the U.S. markets, as well as see how U.S. news is filtered through their local news channels. Being able to put yourself in another person's shoes brings more understanding of how the world really works. That may not help you decide whether or not to take the next trading setup that comes your way, but it does help form a macro view of the world—and it does make life more interesting.

### Good Ideas to Keep in Mind

A trader's relationship with the market is really like a dance, and it's best to let the market lead. It's important not to come into the market with an overly bullish or overly bearish outlook. The stronger a trader believes in an idea, the easier it will be to get suckered into taking the wrong side of a trade. In an upcoming chapter I talk about how to read market internals, and this is a great way to get a read on what's happening in the markets. Instead of coming into the day a raging bull or a roaring bear, I just come in as an interested observer. The "radar screen" that I watch keeps me in the loop and gives me odds on the path of least resistance. As long as we're dancing together, I'd like to know when my partner is going to try to dip me.

And there's a little saying that I always like to remember; it's called "discipline before vision," which is something I first heard from Peter Borish, the former head of research for Paul Tudor Jones. I might think the market is going to crash today, but I'm still going to have a stop in place in case I'm wrong. The vision of being short during a crash is a pleasant one, and the thought of a big move gets traders to do stupid things, like doubling up and adding to losing positions. Disciplined traders live to fight another day. Through most of 2004 and 2005, I've heard many traders who are "staying positioned for the next, inevitable terrorist attack." After the events of September 11, they saw how that impacted on the market, and they want to get positioned for the next attack. (Yes, this is a terrible way to look at a disaster, but this is how traders think. If there is a hurricane in Florida, then it's time to go long lumber because they will have to rebuild a lot of houses). The funny thing is, this vision of being positioned for a crash totally clouds their judgment. The only thing the market hates is uncertainty. The events of September 11 were unexpected, and the market got crushed. However, terrorist activity is now a certainty. It is no longer an unexpected event, and therefore the market has already priced in future terrorist attacks. Sound insane? On July 7, 2005, America woke up to the news of the London bombings. The Dow at one point was down over 200 points pre-market open. All of these people got heavily short. The markets rallied and closed positive on the day, and these "waiting for the next disaster traders" got crushed. Discipline before vision.

It is also important to remember that there is no need to spend wasted years looking for complicated setups or the next Holy Grail. There are very simple setups out there to use. Some of the best traders I know have been trading the same setup, on the same time frame, on the same market for 20 years. They don't care about anything else, and they don't want to learn about anything else. This works for them, and they are the masters of this setup. They have nothing else coming in to interfere with their focus. If a setup doesn't happen that day, then they don't take a trade.

Other successful traders I know have learned to celebrate their losses. When they get into a trade and get stopped out, they jump up and clap their hands. When they get into a trade and it hits their target, they do nothing. They're doing the exact opposite of everyone else, and they're making money. When Jesse Livermore was in the process of making his fortune, one of his favorite quotes was, "If I bought a stock and it went against me, I would sell it immediately. You can't stop and try to figure out why a stock is going in the wrong direction. The fact is that it *is* going in the wrong direction, and that is enough evidence for an experienced speculator to close the trade." Small losses make all the difference, and traders must learn to reward themselves for doing their job in this regard.

It is important to remember that a trader is not trading stocks, or futures, or options. Traders are trading other traders. There is another person or system out there taking the opposite side of the trade. One side is going to be right, and the other side is going to be wrong. Whoever has the better setup on this trade is going to win. Is the trader on the other side of the trade an amateur or a professional? That trader should be wondering the same thing about you. The next time you succumb to greed and chase a trade, remember that there is a professional somewhere else in the world who has been waiting patiently for this setup and is doing just the opposite.

I have found that the most important step to becoming a successful trader is just learning how to accept a loss without any anger or frustration or shame. It's just part of trading. It's not a big deal. I take losses every day, and I do it live in front of people all of the time. It's just part of the process. Okay, this trade just hit its stop. Next. It's like Tom Hanks's character in the movie *A League of Their Own*, who screams at his female player and makes her cry. "Are you crying?" he asks, shocked. "There's no crying in baseball!"

And there's no crying in trading and no throwing your coffee cup against the wall or screaming at your monitor. Losses and missed trades are just part of the deal. On some days things are just not going to come together. If I'm using a setup and I'm stopped out two times in a row, then I just stop using that setup for the rest of the day. For whatever reasons, it is out of sync with the markets on that particular day. No big deal. There is no need to reformat the MACD. It's just part of trading.

The key is to have two specific sets of rules. First there needs to be a trading methodology. For this setup, do the traders go all in or scale in? Do they scale out or get all out at a specific target? Do they trail a stop or leave it? Where is the stop placement in relation to the target? These are all things that have to be set in stone before the trade is placed. Once the trade is placed, there is no room for rational thought. The setup has to be followed the same way each and every time, or the traders will never be able to gauge if the setup is going to help them or hurt them in their trading. Otherwise they are just making impulse trades, and those are the sucker trades. Second, there has to be a money management rule. How many shares or contracts does a trader allocate toward this setup? How much equity is a trader willing to risk on this setup over the course of a day, a week, a month, or a year? After traders do this for a while, what happens is that they develop the habit of following their rules and they eventually learn to trust themselves.

Once traders learn to trust themselves, they can then free their mind to focus on market opportunities that present themselves, instead of being wrapped up tight in a ball of fear, frustration, and doubt. This is where traders make the transition out of the first three phases and begin to really have an opportunity to do this for a living. The transition involves focusing on developing their own trading skills instead of focusing on the money. And the skills are easy—keep the emotions in check and have the discipline to follow the setups. Don't focus on making $1,000. That is what the amateurs do. Focus on developing your skills and executing the setups the same way each and every time. It sounds simple enough, but I've worked with enough traders to know that most of them can't do it over the long haul. They get impatient and don't want to miss out on the action, so they jump in and chase without a clear setup. Once they do this, they go back into the barrel with all the amateurs.

Most of trading involves waiting. First, it involves waiting for a setup. Once the setup occurs, then the professional trader takes it without hesitation. The skill comes in waiting for it to set up and not succumbing to an impulse trade. Then, once in a setup, a trader has to have the discipline to wait for the exit parameters to be hit and not cave and bail out too early. Waiting is the hardest thing for many traders to do, but it's the waiting that separates the winners from the losers. Even for a daytrade, it can be hours before a setup happens or a parameter is hit. And that's the whole key. Just being patient and waiting. The person who chases four rabbits catches none.

Also, it is so important to realize that professional traders are not in every move. It is okay to have the market leave the station without you. Catching every move is impossible, but chasing every move is the mark of an amateur. This is why it is imperative for traders to have a set of rules to follow for both entries and exits, as opposed to relying on their own gut feelings to manage a position. Develop a set of rules and have the discipline to follow them; they exist for your protection.

For me, the biggest difference in my trading occurred when I learned to ignore my brain and just focus on a handful of good setups. Once I learned the setups, the next challenge was to have the discipline to follow them the same way each and every time. No thinking, no hemming, no hawing. I did this by recording my trading activity and grading myself on how well I executed each setup, instead of how much money I was making or losing. Whereas focusing on the P&L automatically encourages the bad habits that plague many traders, a setup-based approach encourages habits that can push a trader into the realm of consistent profitability.

In the end, professional traders focus on limiting risk and protecting capital. Amateur traders focus on how much money they can make on each trade. Professional traders always take money away from amateurs. Amateur traders start to turn into professional traders once they stop looking for the next great technical indicator, and they start controlling their risk on each trade.

*You cannot be disciplined in great things and undisciplined in small things.*
*Brave undisciplined men have no chance against the discipline and valor of other men.*
*Have you ever seen a few policemen handle a crowd?*

GENERAL GEORGE S. PATTON

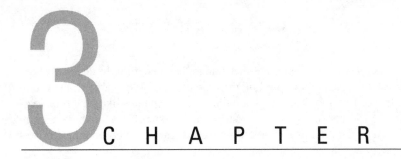

# 3

## CHAPTER

# HARDWARE AND SOFTWARE—TOP TOOLS FOR TRADERS

*Dress a goat in silk and it's still a goat.*

CELTIC PROVERB

## HARDWARE—IT'S ALL ABOUT THE RAM

This chapter is about creating a level playing field for all traders with respect to the equipment and software they are using to tackle the markets. If traders can get this part right, they are at least going to have a fighting chance to compete on a level playing field with everybody else. If traders are behind the technology curve, they are going to be trading at a distinct disadvantage. In trading, people without an edge in terms of equipment, mental outlook, and methodology are like young wildebeest trying to snatch a drink at the edge of a crocodile pond—they're simply not going to make it. Why would people deliberately create a weakness in their trading plan by having trading software or technology that is outdated? It would be like entering the Daytona 500 with a Winnebago. This is the easiest part of a solid trading plan, and it is 100 percent under a person's control.

The amount and type of trading equipment that traders have is going to depend a little on their own financial resources, and a lot based on the type of trading they are doing. Top of the line systems with three or four monitors are available from companies like Dell on a leasing program for less than $150 per month, so cost isn't a huge issue. If traders have a computer that is more than three years old, they need to upgrade some of its components or just get a new one.

The most important component of a trader's computer is the RAM. This is the amount of memory available while the computer is running applications in real time. Traders with an older computer will definitely need a boost here, as this has a major impact on how fast they will be receiving their quotes and other live data. This is also the most expensive part of the computer, though prices continue to drop. As I'm writing this on February 7, 2005, there are three ads on the Internet that boast top-of-the-line computers for $399. These are equipped with a nice 2.4 gigahertz processor, a fat 40 Gigabyte hard drive—and a puny 256 megabytes worth of RAM. This is inadequate for a trader. The RAM on a trader's computer should be at least 1 gigabyte, and nearly all basic systems come with much less than that. Realistically a trader is going to spend about $2,500 for a high-performance computer with at least 1 gigabyte of RAM, multiple flat screen monitors, and a solid multi-monitor-ready graphics card. There are companies out there that market "trader computers" for a lot more money, but exactly the same computer is available at Dell for much less. Dell also has the best customer service I've ever encountered. I've had monitors go out that have been replaced for free by Dell within 24 hours. The same thing happened with another popular manufacturer and the turn-around time was six weeks. The main thing to keep in mind is that a trading computer should be specifically set up for trading and have a minimum of other stuff going on. If there are kids in the house, make sure they have their own computer for Internet surfing and computer games, and tell them not to touch the trading computer under pain of death.

One question I receive a lot from traders is, "How many monitors do I need?" This really depends on what you are trading. I personally utilize 10 monitors for viewing charts, and 2 additional monitors for other tasks such as e-mail, instant messaging, and Internet surfing. These are all set up on four different computers. Most traders do not need this many monitors, and I know of many traders who make a great living with just two. For me, I keep my day trading and swing trading separate, and for these trades I use different accounts, different monitors, and different execution platforms.

Figure 3.1 shows a snapshot of my day-trading execution platform. This keeps a running tally of how I'm doing on the day, for each market and with a grand total. On the day shown in Figure 3.1 the DAX and S&Ps generated a nice upside, while I kept getting stopped out in the euro. The dots on the chart show my entries and exits. All my swing trades are set up on a different execution platform.

This strategy of having distinct accounts for day trading and swing trading helps me to keep the different trade setups separate, because I could be short the mini-sized Dow futures in my swing account, but long the same contract in my day-trading account. These are in different time frames and require different parameters. By keeping them in separate accounts, there isn't any confusion, and the performance for both types of setups is easier to track. Also, because I'm writing newsletters and updates during the trading day, I need access to more data than most traders.

**F I G U R E   3.1**

Strategy Runner (736CTCAR) - Standard

Portfolio  Contract  Strategy  Trade  Settings  Account  Help

16:01:27  Connected

Contracts (11)　　　　　　　　　　　　　　　　　　　　　　　　　　Position: Open　　Total P&L: 37570.00

| Id | Contract | Bid V | Bid | Ask | Ask V | Last | Vol | Exch Tin | Low | High | Open | Prev Cl | Change | #Or | Po | Avg | Points | P&L |
|---|---|---|---|---|---|---|---|---|---|---|---|---|---|---|---|---|---|---|
| 1 | XEurex:FDAX:JUN | 0 | 0.0 | 0.0 | 0 | 3892.0 | 0 | 20:42:0 | 0.0 | 0.0 | 0.0 | 3892.0 | 0.0 | 0 | 0 | 0.0 | 1134.0 | 28350.00 |
| 4 | CME:MINI NSDQ: | 377 | 1417.50 | 1418.00 | 79 | 1418.00 | 3 | 15:01:1 | 1403.50 | 1433.5 | 1432.50 | 1432.0 | -14.00 | 0 | 0 | | 0.00 | 0.00 |
| 5 | CME:MINI RUSSE: | 2 | 560.90 | 561.00 | 28 | 561.00 | 5 | 15:01:1 | 553.70 | 569.4 | 569.10 | 569.30 | -8.30 | 0 | 0 | 0.00 | 23.20 | 2320.00 |
| 6 | CME:MINI S&P:JU | 100 | 1113.00 | 1113.25 | 757 | 1113.25 | 34 | 15:01:1 | 1104.75 | 1122.2 | 1122.00 | 1122.00 | -8.75 | 0 | 10 | 1113.50 | 170.00 | 8500.00 |
| 8 | eCBOT:TNOTE10: | 1260 | 109.250 | 109.255 | 327 | 109.250 | 1 | 15:01:1 | 109.230 | 110.04 | 110.000 | 110.02 | -0.090 | 0 | 0 | | 0.000 | 0.00 |
| 12 | CME:Cd. Dollar:JL | 2 | 0.7250 | 0.7254 | 1 | 0.7253 | 1 | 15:00:3 | 0.7232 | 0.729 | 0.7270 | 0.7266 | -0.0013 | 0 | 0 | | 0.0000 | 0.00 |
| 13 | eCBOT:DJIND 5DI | 5 | 10222 | 10223 | 10 | 10222 | 3 | 15:01:1 | 10154 | 10309 | 10302 | 10305 | -83 | 0 | 0 | 0 | 180 | 900.00 |
| 14 | CME:Euro FX:JUN | 37 | 1.2061 | 1.2063 | 30 | 1.2063 | 1 | 15:01:1 | 1.2050 | 1.2162 | 1.2149 | 1.2156 | -0.0093 | 0 | 0 | 0.0000 | -0.0220 | -2750.00 |
| 18 | CME:J-Yen:JUN04 | 10 | 0.009116 | 0.009115 | 8 | 0.009116 | 2 | 15:01:1 | 0.009111 | 0.0092 | 0.00921 | 0.00923 | -0.000097 | 0 | 0 | | 0.000000 | 0.00 |
| 21 | CME:Sw. Franc:JU | 1 | 0.7792 | 0.7793 | 118 | 0.7793 | 1 | 15:01:1 | 0.7780 | 0.7855 | 0.7859 | 0.7856 | -0.0063 | 0 | 0 | | 0.0000 | 0.00 |
| 22 | eCBOT:TBOND:JU | 357 | 105.29 | 105.30 | 21 | 105.30 | 9 | 15:01:1 | 105.24 | 106.15 | 106.05 | 106.12 | -0.14 | 0 | 0 | 0.00 | 0.08 | 250.00 |

Chart | Completed Orders | Messages | Online | 　buy　sell　market pane

Price Scale  Time  Interval　　　Study Type: None

100%  120  1  Style  Study

Working (0)　Activate | Modify | Cancel | Cancel All

Stat  Action type  Price  Lots  Sent time  Id  Exch

There is a danger for traders in setting themselves up with information overload. I visited one trader who had 25 monitors shooting data at him from all directions. Shockingly, he could never decide when to pull the trigger to get into a trade. It is important to remember that traders don't need to know everything that is going on in the markets. They just need enough information to be able to decide whether or not to take their setup. All of the successful traders I know focus on just a handful of setups. They don't need a confirming move in crude oil in order to take their buy signal on the S&Ps. If traders have found one or two setups that really work for them, then they can, and should, ignore a lot of the data out there. Laserlike focus on a small part of the markets brings expertise and a better understanding of when to take a trade.

**FIGURE 3.2**

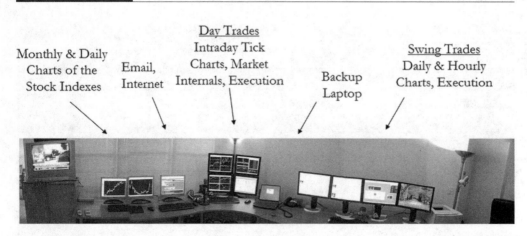

Figure 3.2 shows the computer setup I use for my trading. I do like to have one computer that I use specifically for e-mails, instant messaging, and Internet surfing. This is the computer that is going to get attacked by viruses, so I want to keep it separate from the others. In addition, I also keep a backup laptop in place that is attached to a dial-up modem. Thankfully I rarely have to use it, but whenever the power goes out or my broadband connection goes down, I can still have access to my accounts and current quotes.

## Monitors, Graphics Cards, and Other Gizmos—What to Get and Where to Get Them

The graphics cards that I like the best are the Matrox G200 Multi Monitor Series (MMS) cards. These are available right off their Web site, www.matrox.com, for about $400. They are also available on eBay (www.ebay.com) for about $120. The dirty little secret in the hardware business is that most hardware is available on eBay for half price or less. This used to be where people could buy products at a discount because of inventory clearance or merchandise that falls under the semi-legal arena of being redistributed without manufacturer's approval or warranty. These days, the company itself typically sets up an alias and sells its own products right on eBay in order to tap into the "auction crowd." I've always purchased things like graphics cards right off of eBay, and I've never had a problem with getting ripped off or getting a faulty product. The most important thing to remember when buying something from eBay is to make sure the sellers have great feedback. If they have low ratings, or worse, no ratings, then don't touch them. I'm not a computer guy, but it was really easy to take out my old graphics card and slip in the new one. A trader who is unsure how to do this can look in the yellow pages and find a consultant to do this for a reasonable cost. Have them come to your house or office. Whatever you do, don't take your computer and drop it off at some mass-market, nonspecialist dealer, whose employees often have a lesser degree of computer-specific expertise.

For the actual monitors, one of the best deals out there for big flat screens is (as I'm writing this on March 13, 2005) the Dell UltraSharp 2001FP 20.1 inch Flat Panel LCD Monitor available for $679 each. The LCDs are much lighter in weight than the CRTs, by a factor of more than three to one. Although LCDs cost more than CRTs, the gap is narrowing. Also, for multimonitor setups, LCDs have a thinner "bezel" or rim around the screen which lessens the gap between adjacent monitors. By going down just a little bit in size, a person can save a lot of money. The same models in 19 inches are $269 each and in 17 inches are $169 each. The 19s are a great size for traders, and if resources permit, the larger ones are awesome. The Samsung models are also nice, but they are a little pricier than the Dells. I have both, and I like them both the same. Samsung has a very new 20.1 inch LCD, the model 204T, that is selling only at a few dealers as of this writing for just under $600. This model will be widely available by the time you are reading this. If you like to shop around, then check them both out. If you just want to get a trading computer as quickly as possible, then stick with Dell.

Two great places to find deals on monitors, or anything on hardware for that matter, is www.slickdeals.net and www.techbargains.com. These sites search the Internet for deals and coupons on anything related to technology, including monitors, hard drives, DVD players, and so on. There is always somebody having a sale. Also, public companies like Dell will issue special coupons during the last few days before they close a quarter to boost sales. These always show up on these two Web sites. A few weeks ago I was able to pick up a laptop from Dell using a $750 off coupon code I got from www.slickdeals.net. There is no reason to pay full retail price for anything. This is a good first test for a trader. Don't panic and buy the top.

Another area of interest for traders is setting up multimonitors in such a way that they fit comfortably on a desk, don't take up a lot of space, and are easy to access. One site I like for this is www.lcdarms.com. Here traders can get different wall and desk mounting solutions for their monitors. In terms of desks and chairs, this is really wide open. A door across two file cabinets works really well as a desk. There are desks available from medical supply companies that are interesting in terms of how they are set up. The desk isn't that big of a deal, however. Traders just need a place to put their computer equipment. The chair is a different story. Traders are going to be spending many quality hours with their posterior region planted firmly in a chair. Getting a good one is worth the money. My favorites are the Aeron chairs from Herman Miller.

## TAMING THE TECHNOLOGICAL BEAST: KEY THINGS ALL TRADERS SHOULD KNOW TO KEEP THEIR COMPUTERS ALIVE AND WELL

Once traders have their hardware in place, it is time for them to turn their attention to the software. There are a lot of software choices available for traders, but what this boils down to for most people is a charting program and an execution package. While this is important, there is another category of software that is vital to the trader, and this is software aimed at keeping a computer in top working order. This is by far the most neglected area for traders. Let's take a look at this first, and then we will delve into the trading software. Don't worry, I'm not a techie so this will be easy to follow, and I'll make it quick.

Trading in and of itself can be one of the most stressful occupations on the planet. One day's worth of market activity can determine whether a trader's kids are going to study abroad in Oxford, all expenses paid, or are stuck at the local community college making telemarketing calls part time to pay for their books. Technological problems or disruptions increase the stress factor and cause drains of both real and mental capital. Traders who are stuck behind the technology curve are at more of a disadvantage than those who are up to speed. From software that is outdated to specific tactics used by companies to dump process-clogging spyware on the user's computer, traders who choose technological ignorance are setting themselves up for disaster. Having a trade go wrong because of technological issues is inexcusable for the serious trader who is trying to make a living at this profession.

The bottom line is that traders who want to maintain a competitive edge in this business must first be aware of the technological dangers facing them in today's world. Once aware of the hurdles, determined traders must then take a proactive approach and take the time to attack these issues head on. The three main technological problems for traders today are as follows:

- **Computer invaders:** The PCs are traders' most important trading tool. Being connected to the Internet, the traders' computer is being abused without their knowledge. This causes most malfunctions on computers today, and traders must be aware of how to first remove the "crud" and then block it so it won't happen again.
- **Process cloggers:** Use these steps to maximize computer effectiveness and prevent crashing.
- **General technology problems:** What to do when the technology around the trader fails to deliver—because it will.

Ignoring these preventable issues is like trading without a stop loss. Take the time to take care of this right now and get on the path to smooth trading.


## Strip Away the Crud That Is Slowing Down Your Computer

Traders can have the best software available for trading, but if their computer isn't properly cared for, protected, and maintained, then the greatest trading software in the world becomes worthless. Each day the trader's computer is bombarded and invaded with hidden crud, and it is truly shocking how dangerous some of this stuff is to the trader's PC. For the trader who is serious about making this business a full-time job, neglecting these next steps is the same as a professional football player drinking a 12-pack of beer the night before he is supposed to play in the Super Bowl. That would deliberately put his team at a disadvantage. Why give the other guys out there an edge? In trading, the other guys are trying to take your money. There is no reason to make it any easier for them.

The biggest technical problem facing traders today is one of which most are completely unaware: staying "spyware-free." It is one of the most important things traders can do to keep their PC running smoothly and safely. Spyware will crash traders' computers, ruin their

Internet connection, and make Internet surfing unsafe. Spyware is not a cookie, which I talk more about shortly. In a nutshell, spyware is software that companies place on users' PCs without their permission. Sometimes it is unknowingly with the users' permission, if the users don't read the fine print in the agreement they accept before downloading a software program. This spyware software takes over the traders' Internet browser, and collects data on their surfing habits, generates pop-up ads when the traders visit certain Web sites, and generally slows down their computer. In addition, a lot of spyware is poorly written and can cause incompatibility issues, corrupt important system functions, and threaten the stability of the trader's computer. Traders who want to keep their computer running smoothly, and keep it from freezing up and crashing, must attack back and get all the spyware off their computer—and then prevent it from coming back.

The first time I learned how to do a search for this malicious software, I found over 50 spyware programs on my computer. After they were removed, my computer operated faster and stopped freezing up on me. This stuff is downloaded "behind the scenes," so it is invisible to the computer user. Before I did this, I was certain that I didn't have any spyware on my computer, as I don't do much in the way of Internet surfing. Needless to say I was surprised.

There are two excellent spyware removal applications available, and they are both free, so there is no reason not to use them regularly. The two best applications there are for removing spyware are *SpyBot Search & Destroy* and *Ad Aware*. It is important that the trader use both of these applications, since each one finds what the other misses. Computers are not safe using just one of them. To find out where to download these, just type them into the search field on Google (www.google.com), which will provide a list of sites from which they can be downloaded for free.

Once traders have installed these two "must have" applications, they then need to keep them up to date. I would recommend checking for updates weekly. Similar to antivirus software, the trader needs to stay protected from the latest spyware out there. To update SpyBot, just open the application from the start menu (use the advanced mode option) and select "search for updates." It will then show what updates are available for download. Always install all the updates. Another feature that SpyBot has is called "Immunize." Select this icon and under "Permanent Internet Explorer Immunity" select "Immunize." This works in blocking new spyware. It also gives the trader the option of locking the trader host's file against hijackers, a feature I highly recommend using. To update Ad Aware, just open it and select "Check for updates now."

Anything these applications find is spyware and should be removed. Traders who choose not to remove them have no one to blame but themselves when their computer crashes because of spyware. On a more malicious level, these programs can potentially invade traders' privacy by recording where they buy items online along with their billing and credit card information. I recommend doing weekly scans, and, as I have already said, always remove anything these programs find to keep your PC safe.

Another easy way to block spyware is to stop using Internet Explorer. All spyware programs are written for this browser, since this is what 95 percent of the population uses. There is a newer Internet browser available called Firefox, which is made by Mozilla (www.mozzilla.org). It has more advanced features than Internet Explorer, is faster, and is a lot safer to use.

## Cookies and Spam—It's a Bad Idea for Lunch, and It's a Bad Idea for Your Computer

Another device companies use to track information on the trader's PC is called a *cookie*. This is a small text file that can be good or bad. It's good for visiting a favorite Web site, such as Amazon.com. With a cookie installed, Amazon will remember who the users are, so they don't have to always log in when they visit the site. However, there are also bad cookies placed by companies such as Doubleclick that track site usage, coordinate pop-up ads, and generally invade the trader's privacy. The best thing to do here is to start from scratch and delete all the cookies on the computer. To do this, go to Start, Settings, Control Panel, Internet Options. Under Temporary Internet Files, there is a button that says, "Delete Cookies." Click this. After the cookies are deleted, go to Privacy, Advanced. Once there, check the box that says "Override automatic cookie handling." Below that I check "Prompt" for First Party Cookies and "Block" for Third-Party Cookies. This way when the trader goes to Amazon, a message pops up asking if the trader wants to accept the cookie. I say yes because that is a site I visit often. Any third party cookies like "doubleclick" will automatically be blocked. This will prevent pop-up ads and keep the trader's computer running in top form. If I am asked to accept a cookie from a site I rarely visit, I will say no and the cookie will not be planted on my computer.

Spam is typically a big problem for everyone. Mail Washer Pro (www.mailwasher.net) and Cloud Mark (www.cloudmark.com) used together are the best solution I've ever seen for spam protection. Mail Washer Pro stops spam before it ever hits your mailbox. For stuff that does get through, identify those to Cloud Mark, and they won't get through again. Both these programs together will cost about $80. I use Microsoft's Outlook program to handle all my e-mail, and these programs can work directly with it. I used to routinely get 100 spam e-mails a day. Once I installed Cloud Mark, they all disappeared. It was truly a miracle.

Finally, it is critical that everyone have virus protection software. Norton Antivirus is good, but it takes up a lot of resources. Another one that is good is Trend Micros PC-cillin (www.trendmicro.com) Internet Security. For miscellaneous software, I like Copernic (www.copernic.com) desktop search. This free software provides a great, easy way to search for e-mails and files on a computer. This saves time in trying to find that missing e-mail or file. All a person has to do is type in a word or the name of the file and the software will find it in seconds. This is instead of sifting through e-mails in Outlook or trying to search with the windows function, which takes forever. During market hours, a trader does not have a lot of time to spend on little things like searching for a missing file. This speeds it up.

These are the basics for the general computer software. Let's take a look at how to keep a computer running smoothly, and then we'll start looking at specific trading software.

## TURBO CHARGING THE TRADING COMPUTER

There are three things traders should be doing on a weekly basis to ensure that their computer is running at maximum efficiency. The first two of these involve deleting files on the computer that are unnecessary. To do this, first go to the Recycle Bin, which is an icon located on the desktop. Right click, select "empty recycle bin," and delete the files. Every file the computer user deletes is not really deleted—it is just moved to the Recycle Bin. To really get it out of the computer and free up memory, the trader needs to empty the Recycle Bin.

The second place where memory is gobbled up is in what is called the *cache*. This "catches" all the Web sites the trader visits for faster downloading of the site next time it is visited. With the advent of broadband, this is an unnecessary feature. To "clean the cache" go to Start, Settings, Control Panel, Internet Options. Under "temporary Internet files" click "delete files." A pop-up box will appear asking if the user wants to delete all offline content. This is important to do, so the trader should click the box to indicate yes. Hit "ok" and sit back. If the computer user has never done this, it can take five to ten minutes to delete all the garbage on the computer—or longer. It may appear that the computer is frozen. It's not. Walk away and come back later. The serious trader should do this at least once a week.

Finally, once these two things are completed, the serious trader will want to defrag his or her hard drive. Disk fragmentation slows the computer down and is often the cause of a variety of other problems such as hangs, crashes, and errors. Fragmentation accumulates rapidly through normal computer use, and program access time continues to increase, problems worsen, and the productive life of a computer will be shortened by years. Defragging the hard drive puts all the pieces back together again, making the computer run much more efficiently. Traders should do this weekly, if not daily. Go to Start, Programs, Accessories, System Tools, Disk Defragmenter. Make sure the hard drive is highlighted (usually this is drive C) and click "Defragment." This can take 20–30 minutes if this has never been done before. There is also a program called Diskeeper that eliminates fragmentation automatically so it is never an issue.

## THE BACKUP PLAN: WHAT TO DO WHEN YOUR COMPUTER CRASHES OR THE POWER GOES OUT—BECAUSE THEY WILL

Once a trader's computer is in top working form, there are still other technical problems that can occur. In my experience, there are four main problems that all traders should be prepared for:

1. Black- or brownouts that cut off all electricity.
2. Cable or DSL goes down.
3. Difficulty in contacting a broker.
4. Data feed goes down or the trading platform goes down.

These are problems that can happen at any time. Serious traders can prepare themselves for all these eventualities.

A black- or brownout will occur when it is least expected. The last one happened to me when three other traders had booked appointments to spend the week trading next to me at my office. That is hard to do when there isn't any power. The point is that the timing is never good. I've personally been involved in half a dozen of these through the last two years for a variety of reasons. This can relate to the weather, a power grid going out, or a car accident involving a telephone pole. It can happen out of nowhere, and traders will suddenly find themselves without power, losing their ability to view the market and execute trades. To combat this situation, the serious trader must have the following in place:

- **Battery backups on the computer**: These are available at any major office supply shop. In the event of a loss of electricity, these will give the trader around 30 minutes of power, which is plenty of time to close out positions or reset parameters in case the power is going to be down for a long time. This also gives the trader time to manually shut down the computer, which is much safer than having it go out suddenly because of a power loss.

- **Noncordless phone**: These are the old-fashioned phones that have a cord attached to the headset. When the electricity goes out, so does the cordless phone. With the old-fashioned corded phones, a trader will still be able to make a phone call to his or her broker. Obviously a cell phone would work in this situation—but those things run out of juice at the worst possible moments. Corded phones can be purchased for less than $20 at any department or electronics store.

- **Dial-up backup**: Cable or DSL can go out even when the electricity is still on. This usually happens at the absolute worst time, so the astute trader will want to be prepared. The best way to combat this is to have a fully charged laptop connected to a phone line. This way the trader has Internet connectivity if the DSL or cable goes down—and the trader will also have a backup in case the electricity goes out. By having a laptop that is fully charged and ready to go, attached to a phone line, a few hours of valuable time can be gained.

Another technological trend in the industry is for brokers to let computers do all the work. Although this provides for efficiencies and cuts costs, the bottom line is that if I have a problem, I had better be able to get hold of my brokers right away. If I call my brokers and can't get hold of them, I start foaming at the mouth—a signal that it is time for me to switch brokers. If I want to be on hold, I will call the airlines, not my brokers. My suggestion here is to take advantage of technology and get the broker or brokers hooked up on an instant messaging program. This is an incredibly efficient way to stay in touch throughout the day. If my data feed goes down, I can IM (instant message) my broker for a quote. My expectations for my brokers are that I can contact them via phone or instant message right away. If they are not available, then I have the number and instant message as a backup. In trading, there is no excuse for not being able to get a live person to help out with an order or question right away. What else do we pay them all the commissions for?

If the trader's data feed goes down, much of what already has been discussed will help. Being able to contact a broker to get a quote or place a trade in this situation is imperative. Yahoo Finance is also a great site to get free quotes on stocks, options, and futures.

Finally, the most neglected aspect of any computer user's life is the backing up of data. I recommend getting a Maxtor One Touch drive. These are available at places like Best Buy, or online at www.maxtor.com. Once it is hooked up, all a trader has to do is touch a button and the entire hard drive will be backed up. It seems like a pain to set up until that one day when the computer finally does crash.

Trading successfully requires an edge. Traders who choose to remain in ignorance about what is really going on with their computer, or are "outta luck" when the power goes out, are leaving themselves at a decided disadvantage with traders who are prepared. By staying up to date on the technological front, the trader has an advantage over those who don't. And having an advantage over other traders is the only thing that will make the trader a winner in this business.

## NOT ALL QUOTES ARE CREATED EQUAL

Now that we've beaten the nontrading technical issues to death, let's look at issues geared specifically for trading. This typically comes down to three areas:

1. Quote software
2. Trade execution software
3. Market-related subscriptions and services

Let's look at quote software first. Much of the decision to use a specific charting software package typically comes down to "whatever a person has stumbled across" as he or she began the trading journey. For most traders, this is not a good thing. I remember when I first started trading online in the late 1980s, and I had to hit "refresh" every time I needed a new quote. I was charged a fee each time I hit "refresh" if I didn't trade enough. I stayed with that brokerage for about three weeks, and that was three weeks too long. It is important for the trader to have a quote system that is robust, is in real time, and has the flexibility to easily add a variety of indicators and tools. *The ultimate goal of traders is to develop a trading style that best fits their own personality.* A flexible quote system gives people the ability to try different things until they find the setups and techniques that work best for them. There are only a few quote vendors who fit this bill, and there are many who do not. The bottom line is that good quotes are not free and can easily run a few hundred dollars a month. Skimp on the desk, not on the quotes.

The two main quote systems I use are TradeStation (www.tradestation.com) and eSignal (www.esignal.com). TradeStation makes it possible for me to easily add my own indicators and studies, and I like its chart functionality and ability to back-test specific setups and data. I like eSignal because it has fast reloading time and is robust and easy to use. Although I like having two quote vendors in case one is having problems, for my own trading it is a must. For example, I follow the German DAX market, and I rely on real-time put/call ratios throughout the trading day. As of this writing, eSignal carries data on the German DAX, while TradeStation does not. And, to top it off, Tradestation carries data on the put/call ratio, while eSignal does not. It's important to find out everything a quote vendor offers before signing up. Obviously, if all a trader follows is the DAX, then TradeStation is not going to be a big help. At some point TradeStation will cave in and add it, and who knows, it may have already added it by the time this book hits the shelves. I'll also continue to bug eSignal about adding the put/call ratio, because at some point it will have to bow to pressure from the trading community and offer it up. Interestingly enough, most quote vendors do not offer the put/call ratio, which is a hugely important reading of current market sentiment.

Another good source I use for quotes is the market data available at the Chicago Board of Trade's (CBOT) Web site, www.cbot.com. There are of course other good quote systems available. The key is to utilize a robust and flexible version that best fits a trader's needs. For the most part, traders will get what they pay for in this area. The best way to find a good quote system is to first and foremost ignore any marketing material that is put out by the company itself. This is like believing that a can of soda is good for you because it says "diet" on the label. One of the biggest marketing gimmicks in trading is "free level II data." Level II data are worthless and shouldn't be watched in the first place. Larger traders use Level II to trick and fool smaller traders by putting up fake size and using every method at their disposal to hide what they are really doing. It also causes traders to overtrade, which is the number one way to get out of this business in a hurry. Traders will save themselves a lot of frustration simply by turning this off. In sum, ignore the marketing and ask other traders who have been actively slinging stocks and futures for at least five years.

## A BAD EXECUTION PLATFORM CAN INFLICT CAPITAL PUNISHMENT ON YOUR ACCOUNT

In the late 1990s and early 2000s, it was all about faster executions. A trader who had an execution platform that was faster than the others had an edge. Online Web-based brokers caught on and started out offering "60-second guarantees" on fills. Those of us who were using direct access laughed in their face. Sixty seconds might as well have been a week. Today, nearly every broker has adapted and everybody has lightning fast executions. So what platforms have the edge?

Think back to what I say about trader psychology in Chapter 2. Most of the mistakes traders make are emotional. I've watched traders get flustered, especially in futures trading, and make mistakes with their orders. They go long five contracts of the mini-sized Dow and then make an error in trying to place their stop that ends up liquidating their position. Other times they put a target in place and end up doubling up on their position because of a mechanical error. Or, worse, they don't feel like going through the entire process of placing a stop, then placing a target, and then remembering to cancel the remaining open order once either the stop or the target is hit—so they don't place a stop or a target. These are the traders who "rely on their judgment while in a trade" and create great opportunities for the rest of us when they inevitably freak out. Manual order submission and trade management is a tedious, error prone process. Coupled with heightened emotions, it is a recipe for trader blowout. Maybe not today, and maybe not tomorrow, but that day is always lurking on the horizon.

In addition, some traders simply are not computer savvy. They are not comfortable on computers, and it is easy for them to fumble an order. The best computer users are kids, and it's because they have grown up playing video games on their PCs. Some traders I know have deliberately learned to play "one person shooter" games on their PCs in order to improve their speed on the keyboard. The most popular of these is called "Call of Duty." This game places you in various battles during World War II, and it is literally act fast or die—kind of like trading. By the time people get through this adventure, their eye-hand-mouse-keyboard coordination will have improved exponentially. My trading partners and I have all gone through the game, and it improved our hand-eye coordination considerably. This game is available at stores like Best Buy for $30.

Trading execution software today has evolved to help traders protect themselves from . . . themselves. Think of a typical trade. Let's say I go long 10 contracts of the mini-sized

Dow futures at 10814. I place a 20-point stop, and I want to exit half my position on a 10-point move to 10824, and for the rest of my position I will trail my stop—every time the Dow moves 10 points, I will move my stop up 10 points. This requires active trade management, with the pressing of a lot of keys and many mouse clicks. One mistake and I can turn this winning trade into a loser.

What if, each time I bought the mini-sized Dow, my trading execution platform knew I would be using a 20-point stop and a 10-point target on the first half of my position? If it knew that, then it could place the orders for me automatically, and I wouldn't have to do a thing. What if it also knew that when my first target was hit, I wanted to bring my stop up to breakeven? And it also knew to change the number of contracts in my stop from 10 to 5 when the first target was hit? What if it also knew to then trail the stop? What if I had a target, and it knew to cancel my stop order once my target was hit? All automatically? So all I had to do was get into the trade, and after that I could essentially walk away because the software was managing the trade for me according to my specifications? The purpose of my day would be to sit back, relax, and focus on finding high probability entries, instead of having to scramble around once I'm in the trade and actively manage it—a process that can be mentally straining and cause many emotional fluctuations.

That is the kind of software that is available today. All traders have to do is wait and be patient for an appropriate entry level, take the entry, and then the software can manage the trade for them according to their own specifications. This process removes a lot of the mental stress involved in trading and helps to prevent traders from making the common mistakes that ruin many of them. This type of functionality is not readily available with many brokers, but I'm sure they will catch on and the improvements in this field will continue to roll along. Today this type of software is available through third-party vendors who create the code, and then brokers elect, or not elect, to offer this platform to their customers.

Three of these platforms that I'm familiar with in this category are TradeMaven (www.trademavenllc.com), Strategy Runner (www.strategyrunner.com), and NinjaTrader (www.ninjatrader.com). In my experience they are all fantastic leaps in trading technology. TradeMaven is memory-intensive and can slow down a user's computer, so it is important to have a fast, stand-alone system when using this. Strategy Runner is also good, and I used it for a while, but it does charge a per-trade fee that can quickly add up. NinjaTrader has a low monthly fee and is easy on system resources and also has a small per-trade fee. This is the one that I currently use. Figure 3.3 shows how it works.

Figure 3.3 illustrates a shot of the "Strategy Manager" window, where traders can enter in their predetermined trade entry and exit points. The Strategy Manager is open and the Position Strategies tab is selected. The strategy that is highlighted is called TradeTheMarkets, which is a strategy I created. In the position type box (Pos Type), I have selected the bottom choice (Stop/3T). This means that this strategy will have three profit targets and one stop order. In other words, I can buy six lots of the E-mini S&Ps and scale sell out of my position two lots at a time, at predetermined exit points. The details are entered in the middle of the screen. For this trade, when I get in long or short, the software will automatically place a 2-point stop, and it will automatically place orders so that I can scale out of two contracts when I'm up one point, another two contracts when I'm up two points, and the final two contracts when I'm up three points. In addition, once I am out of my trade, the open stop order is automatically canceled.

**F I G U R E   3.3**

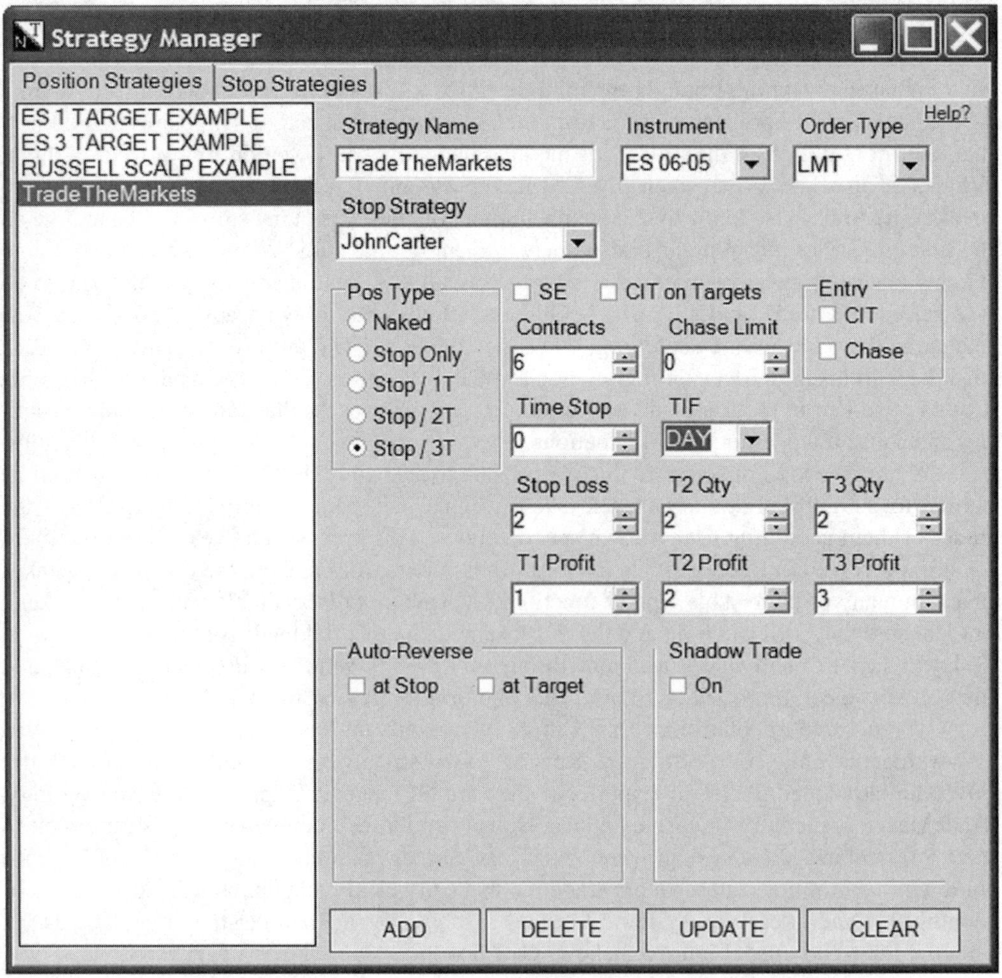

This screen focuses on my "target exit strategy." My "stop exit strategy" is different, and you can see that a stop strategy called "JohnCarter" is selected. (See Fig. 3.4.)

The "Stop Strategies" tab allows the trader to create a single stop or a trailing stop. The trailing stop will automatically move based on the parameters put into this screen. As the various profit targets are hit, the stop loss will move up a specified amount, ensuring that an increasing portion of any profits are protected.

Traders may have just one setup that they use, or they may have half a dozen or more that they have created over the years. Each setup that a trader uses should have a different set of rules for exiting the trade. Some of the setups may utilize a 3:1 risk reward ratio (risking 1 point to make 3) while others utilize a 1:2 risk reward ratio (risking 2 points to make 1). Some of the setups may use trailing stops and multiple targets, and some may have stationary stops and single targets. All the various exit and stop strategies can be created for each setup, on each market in which it is going to be utilized, and matched together. Once these are all created, all traders have to do is tell the software which setup they are about to take, on which market, and then focus on the entry level. Once they enter the trade, the software does the rest of the often very tedious and error-prone work. What is also nice is that a trader can have a couple of plays running simultaneously in different markets and not get frazzled watching after all of them. This type of technology automatically brings discipline and focus into the trader's life and generally makes the trading day smoother and more deliberate, leaving a trader refreshed at the end of the day instead of worn out.

## F I G U R E　3.5

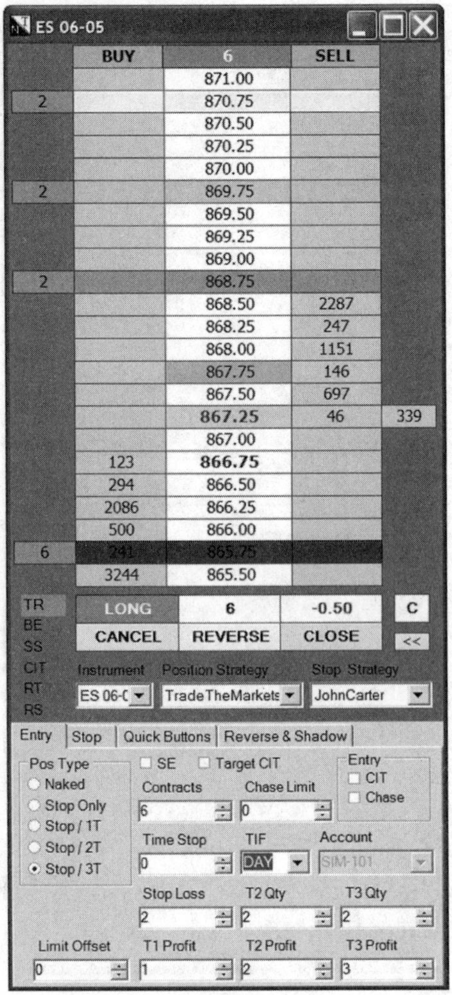

**ES 06-05**

| BUY | 6 | SELL | |
|-----|-----|------|---|
|  | 871.00 |  |  |
| 2 | 870.75 |  |  |
|  | 870.50 |  |  |
|  | 870.25 |  |  |
|  | 870.00 |  |  |
| 2 | 869.75 |  |  |
|  | 869.50 |  |  |
|  | 869.25 |  |  |
|  | 869.00 |  |  |
| 2 | 868.75 |  |  |
|  | 868.50 | 2287 |  |
|  | 868.25 | 247 |  |
|  | 868.00 | 1151 |  |
|  | 867.75 | 146 |  |
|  | 867.50 | 697 |  |
|  | 867.25 | 46 | 339 |
|  | 867.00 |  |  |
| 123 | 866.75 |  |  |
| 294 | 866.50 |  |  |
| 2086 | 866.25 |  |  |
| 500 | 866.00 |  |  |
| 6 | 241 | 865.75 |  |
|  | 3244 | 865.50 |  |

| TR | LONG | 6 | -0.50 | C |
|----|------|---|-------|---|
| BE | | | | |
| SS | CANCEL | REVERSE | CLOSE | << |
| CIT | Instrument | Position Strategy | Stop Strategy | |
| RT | ES 06-C ▼ | TradeTheMarkets ▼ | JohnCarter ▼ | |
| RS | | | | |

Entry | Stop | Quick Buttons | Reverse & Shadow

Pos Type
○ Naked
○ Stop Only
○ Stop / 1T
○ Stop / 2T
⊙ Stop / 3T

☐ SE  ☐ Target CIT

Contracts 6
Chase Limit 0

Entry
☐ CIT
☐ Chase

Time Stop 0
TIF DAY ▼
Account SIM-101 ▼

Stop Loss 2
T2 Qty 2
T3 Qty 2

Limit Offset 0
T1 Profit 1
T2 Profit 2
T3 Profit 3

What is also nice is that, once the trade is placed, all these orders are easy to follow and are marked visually on a screen of the market being traded.

In Figure 3.5 the screen shows that an order was filled for six contracts on the E-mini S&Ps at 868.75. The total number of contracts being traded is displayed at the top of the column. On the left side of the column there are the three profit target orders, two contracts each, placed at one, two, and three points above the entry price (869.75, 870.75, and 871.75, respectively). Down below the entry price is a stop order for six contracts at 866.75, which is two points below the entry price. A single mouse click was used to place the market buy order at 868.75. All these other orders were simultaneously and automatically placed by the software as specified in the selected strategy. In addition, since these are OCO orders (one cancels the other), as each profit target is reached, the stop loss is reduced by the appropriate number of contracts and trailed accordingly.

This represents the new generation of trading software, and all traders should seriously consider such a system. Many brokers do not offer these features. For example, I love TradeStation's charting ability, but its order execution is a little behind the curve in regards to this type of trading technology. They are working on it, to be sure, and they may have caught up by the time this book is released. For now, it is software programs like NinjaTrader that are leading the pack.

## OPINIONS ARE LIKE BELLYBUTTONS; EVERYBODY HAS ONE

This section isn't about recommending good financial market subscription services that are available. It's about how to treat them. There are many market-related services, newsletters, and Internet chat rooms that are operating today. These services typically offer opinions on the markets, and they usually charge a fee for accessing their information. They offer thoughts on market direction and, sometimes, specific market picks. I used to be a newsletter junkie, and still am to some extent. These days I'm much less interested in individual opinions and am more interested in Web sites that offer a quick synopsis of the current state of the markets through a variety of technical data. To that end, one of the best sites on the Internet is Decision Point, run by Carl Swenlin (www.decisionpoint.com). This site allows traders to get a quick feel for the markets and offers an endless amount of drill down detail, which I like to peruse on Sundays. It's the best $20 a month ever spent. I also like to read comments by John Mauldin in his weekly newsletter, *Thoughts from the Frontline* (www.2000wave.com). His writing is lucid, far reaching, and entertaining. My favorite newsletters for staying on top of world economic trends, particularly Asia, are found at www.gavekal.com. The founders are Anatole Kaletsky, Charles Gave, and his son, Louis-Vincent Gave.They have offices in various parts of the world, stay on top of what's going on economically, and actively discuss implications and trends, and they write about all of this in an entertaining and interesting way.

I also find it useful to read and balance the views of the people who think the Dow is going to 3,000 versus the views of the people who think the Dow is going to 30,000. There are both rational and ridiculous arguments for both cases. I personally don't have an opinion where the stock market is going to be by March 27, 2023. I'm more focused on where it is going to be by the end of next week. Also, it is important to take these views with a grain of salt. With Wall Street, if everyone is expecting the same thing to happen, then it's not going to happen. It is certainly important to stay on top of the major trends affecting the world today, namely, an aging population, rising crude oil prices, and the explosive economic growth of China and India. These are real trends that affect nearly everything in our lives. Where there are trends, there are opportunities to make money.

The main thing to keep in mind is that everyone is offering an opinion, especially if it's regarding a specific trade recommendation. The writer may sound absolutely convinced it is the best trade on the planet, and this conviction can easily pass into the brain of the reader. The bottom line is this: If traders take a recommendation from a subscription service, they still have to set appropriate risk parameters and decide how much they are willing to lose on the pick. Just because a guru thinks the market is going to crash doesn't mean that it is going to. I've heard more stories about people blowing out their accounts because "they put it all on a newsletter recommendation." There is a tendency for traders to feel more confident in a trade because it is being recommended by somebody else. A tip! In reality, it's just a trade setup like any other, and it is important that a trader not get lured in with a false sense of security that this particular trade is going to work out exactly as planned. Whether traders found a setup for themselves or whether they are following a trade setup recommended in a newsletter, the ultimate responsibility is on the trader. Don't get overconfident just because you read about something online.

## ESTABLISHING PRIORITIES: IF YOU ARE GETTING INTERRUPTED DURING THE FIRST TWO HOURS OF THE TRADING DAY, IT IS YOUR FAULT

I talk more about this at the end of the book when I discuss the business plan, but it does touch a little on technology here. The bottom line is that a trader needs focus and concentration in order to be successful in this business. The most critical hours in the stock market are generally the first two hours of the trading day. This is where most of the setups occur. It is up to the traders to communicate to colleagues, or, if they are trading from home, to their spouse and children, that they cannot be disturbed. When I am trading, I am not checking e-mail, I am not answering the phone, and I am not accepting uninvited visitors. If my wife wants to be dropped off at the gym before the trading day starts, she knows the deadline. If she lets me know after the deadline, my answer is always the same, "Honey, you know I love you. The trade is on." Click. (I usually remember flowers on those days.)

It can be hard to communicate things like this directly. You'll find it is helpful to write out a fully developed trading plan and then share it with the people in your life. Once they understand that this is important to you and that you are serious, they will generally respect any boundaries that are clearly outlined in what they are reading.

In terms of communicating with people throughout the day, for anyone who doesn't utilize instant messaging software, this is an incredibly efficient way to stay in touch. People can call at exactly the wrong moments during a trade. With instant messaging, people can type in a question and the traders can get back to them at their leisure. Instant messaging was built for traders. This is free software, and I utilize the three most popular programs: MSN, Yahoo, and AOL. I also utilize a software program called Trillian (www.ceruleanstudios.com) that ties all three of these together into one application. The key with instant messaging software, however, is to block everybody except for people traders have specifically permitted to their list. If everyone knows you are online, then everyone will bug you. Instant messaging for traders is appropriate between their brokers and other traders. It is inappropriate for anyone else who could interrupt a trader's workday, and this includes family members and clients. There are very few people who are on my list, but they are all important to my trading day. My wife did make the cut, however, and it has proved to be a useful way to stay in touch when the markets are moving.

## WHY WATCHING *HARRY POTTER* ON DVD AFTER 12 NOON EASTERN IS BETTER THAN WATCHING CNBC

I am bringing this up because I've seen too many traders who quit their jobs and follow what I call the "CNBC setup." They are excited because they are able to finally trade fulltime. They feel they've been at a disadvantage all these years, getting quotes from the Internet, sneaking trades onto their computers in between meetings, and hearing about key news events only after the markets have already closed. So what do they do? They plop a TV down right next to their computers, turn on CNBC, and glue themselves to the screen, looking for trading opportunities.

CNBC has a very specific job: to provide enough entertainment to viewers so they tune in and watch. With a lot of people watching, the network makes more money from the commercials. It's as simple as that. CNBC is fun to watch, and when things get serious, it does a great job of reporting. I found out about 9/11 as it unfolded live before my eyes from Mark Haines. I flipped to some of the other channels, but ended up parking it on CNBC that day because it did, hands down, the best job reporting about it. Who can forget Maria Bartiromo reporting about the event, covered in ash and soot just after the first building collapsed? It was a gut-wrenching experience to watch, and the reporters and the network did a great job.

That said, traders must realize that they cannot make a living "trading the news" off any financial news channel. By the time it appears on television, it is way too late to react. Trading floors have already heard the news, and by the time it makes it to the public, the floor traders are closing their positions, ideally to suckers who just saw the headlines. If anything, CNBC can be used as a fading tool—taking the opposite side of the news. Once it runs out of stories and starts repeating the same things over and over, I turn down the volume and either turn on a commercial-free music radio station or, once in a while, plop in a DVD. Who can get tired of watching *Gladiator*?

Traders who do this for a living spend their days waiting for specific setups to take shape. Yet one of the biggest weaknesses for most traders is a need to be in every move. If the markets start running away, many traders just can't help but jump in, fearing they may be missing something big. This is a fatal flaw that will ruin any traders who can't control this habit. If there is anything I can hammer into your brain as you are reading this book, it is this: It is okay to miss moves. Professional traders miss moves; amateur traders try to chase every move. By listening to music or keeping a DVD on in the background, traders have something to pass the time while they wait for their specific setup to take shape. This makes them less prone to impulsively jump into trades just because they are bored or because they can't stand missing out on a move. The goal is not to catch every move in the market. The goal is to take the specific setups that a trader has outlined as a part of their business plan. Otherwise he or she is just a gunslinger, and sooner or later all gunslingers get killed.

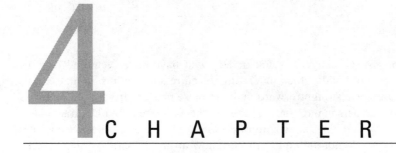

# 4
C H A P T E R

# MARKETS 101—UNDERSTANDING THE BASIC MECHANICS OF THE MARKETS DISCUSSED IN THIS BOOK

*To the brave man every land is a native country.*

GREEK PROVERB

## THE WORLD BEYOND STOCKS AND WHY IT'S IMPORTANT

We've covered why markets move, how traders sabotage themselves, and what to do with your computer. That was the equivalent of prep school. It's time to graduate and start looking at the markets.

I wrote this chapter specifically for stock traders who have never ventured beyond these borders into the world of bonds, stock index futures, currencies, grains, gold, oil, and so forth. My goal is to provide a straightforward guide to these markets from a trader's perspective. I do not try to talk a person into trading these markets—more individual traders get eaten for lunch in these markets than anywhere else (which of course provides numerous trading opportunities). I also do not attempt to discuss how all these markets interact with and influence one another on a global level. That would involve a macro discussion of how the world works and is not within the scope of this book. I just want to show you how I trade them for a living.

For people who are interested in a more macro view of how all the financial markets are tied together, the upcoming trends these interactions are creating, and how to get positioned for these trends, pick up a copy of John Mauldin's book, *Bull's Eye Investing* (John Wiley and Sons, 2005). John shows the trader two important things with this book: first, what to expect in the years ahead and how to prepare for it. He does this with a unique perspective, as his sources of information are extremely far reaching. Second, for people who realize they should have a portion of their funds managed by a professional, John takes the reader through a process of how hedge funds work, finding the right funds, and how to perform due diligence. It's a great book with fascinating research.

For traders who are already readily familiar with these other markets, feel free to skim through this chapter and move on to the next—though I would read the next section as well as the part that compares trading the mini-sized Dow (YM) to the E-mini S&Ps (ES).

Although I say in the introduction I won't be focusing on basic trading terminology such as *uptrends*, I do want to explain the other markets outside of stocks that I reference in this book. The reason for this is that most traders I've met are stock traders only. Some might have a little experience with the E-mini futures, but for the most part the focus is on actual stocks and that's it. To put this in perspective, there are roughly 25 million stock brokerage accounts in the United States. There are only 450,000 futures accounts. For people who are familiar with only stocks, contracts such as the 30-year bond, soybeans, S&Ps, euro, and gold often seem nebulous, scary, and out of reach. But are they?

Figure 4.1 shows a very good reason for knowing how all these various markets work, and that reason is as follows—there are always going to be some markets that are trending and some that are stuck in a trading range. In general, trending markets provide more trading opportunities. While the figure shows a range-bound Dow over most of early 2005, the 30-year bonds were in a clear, tradeable downtrend, and the gold, euro, and soybean markets were in clear, tradeable uptrends. Although the mini-sized Dow (YM) is one of my favorite markets to trade, there are plenty of times when it is stuck in a trading range, going nowhere. Although Figure 4.1 is based on a daily timeframe, this same thing happens on all intraday time frames as well. While one market is chopping, another market is trending. I have setups for both types of markets that I review later in this book. While choppy markets do provide specific setups for traders to take, these are scalp trades only, generate more transactions and thus increase costs, and won't result in a potentially bigger move available in a trending market.

## F I G U R E   4.1

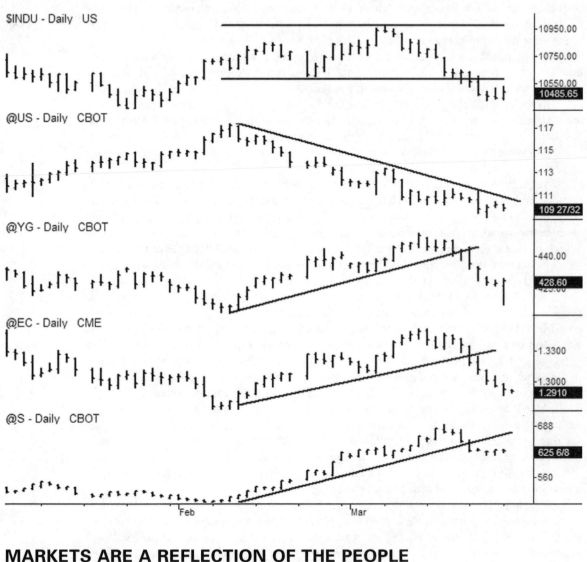

## MARKETS ARE A REFLECTION OF THE PEOPLE WHO TRADE THEM: IS YOUR COMPETITION WIRED ON STARBUCKS OR METHODICALLY FILLING IN A CROSSWORD PUZZLE?

In addition to traders exposing themselves to a wider variety of potential trending markets, it's important to at least understand how these other markets work for three reasons. First, these other markets affect stock prices.

A lasting rally in bonds can force large funds to start buying stocks in order to readjust their allocations. A surge in oil prices can place downward pressure on stocks. Rising lumber and steel costs can hurt some companies' earnings while help others. Second, there are going to be times when the stock market is dead in the water, and these other markets will provide opportunities for traders to continue making a living. Third, each market has its own personality. Traders who have been exposed only to stocks are betting it all that this is the market which best suits their personality. There may be another one out there that fits like a glove, so to speak, which makes the traders' job that much easier.

In the end, all charts and all markets are the same. They always have been and they always will be, because all chart patterns depict the same thing—emotional reactions and decisions made by human beings. Even if it is a mechanical system that is making the trades, it was still written by a human. A trader is always trading other traders, no matter what the market.

Yet each market is made up of different types of traders. What are these traders like? If they are S&P traders, then it's possible they are wired on Starbucks and are super aggressive. If they are trading bonds, it's possible they are busy methodically filling in a crossword puzzle in between trades. If they are trading corn, it is possible that they are napping at their desk. Which type of trader would you rather trade against? Compete against? One of the key differences between most successful traders and unsuccessful traders is this: Successful traders are in markets where their personalities shine.

A stark example of this can be found in a friend of mine who trades 10-year notes. He routinely makes just over seven figures a year trading this market. A few years ago he got bored and decided to start trading the S&Ps. He liked the excitement and the action, and wanted to be a part of that game. Result? It was a struggle from the first trade, and he lost hundreds of thousand of dollars. Licking his wounds, he went back to trading 10-year notes— and making just over seven figures a year. Boring is not necessarily a bad thing. I can't emphasize enough the importance of trading the right market for your personality.

Also keep in mind that many firms realize there are many newer traders out there who are buying the latest software packages in order to "beat the markets." These firms buy the same software and use it to trade against the newbies. This is in addition to these firms having a full-time research staff and access to tons of information. These types of firms usually focus on the S&P futures. Are you prepared to trade against these guys in the S&Ps and make a living off their occasional mistakes and bad judgment?

I started off as a stocks and options trader. I liked these markets, did well in these markets, and continue to trade in these markets. However, I was always curious about the other markets that were available. For a long time I didn't do much about this curiosity. Why? Frankly they seemed scary. Yet I really just wanted to see how these other markets worked and at least to see how I did trading them. Maybe I would find something I liked better than stocks. However, I felt that futures and foreign exchange currency trading (forex) were suited only to traders sitting behind a desk at a large bank or institutional trading firm, so it took me a while to finally venture into these markets. This isn't so much the case today because these markets have become more accessible. Ironically, however, some of these same institutional traders now visit me at my offices to learn the various trade setups I utilize in these markets. They had no problem trading these instruments with the firm's money, but when they left to try it with their own money, the psychological factors kicked in and they struggled.

I eventually worked with some traders in these markets in the mid 1990s, and they helped to strip away the myths, showing me how these markets worked and how to reduce risk and create solid trading opportunities. In my search to understand the futures and forex markets, I had to pull bits and pieces together over the course of several months from different sources to finally understand how all these trading instruments worked. Most of the information was elusive at best—a more apt description would be worthless. I never was able to find a consistent, easy-to-understand summary that told me all I needed to know about trading these instruments, and this process was frankly frustrating and annoying. As a trader, I just want to know the basics—how do I trade them, how much money do I need to trade them, and how does the price movement affect my P&L? I'll use the rest of this chapter to create the summary information I wish I'd had then. In the end, I'm glad I tried these other markets out, as it is these other markets that allowed me to make the jump to trading fulltime for a living.

# FUTURES 101

Think of this as a quick blurb designed to help a trader better understand the futures markets. This account is by no means comprehensive—there are entire books written on the subject. However, to an individual who has traded only stocks, the futures markets are probably a mystery and maybe even a little menacing. Yet traders who have already learned the importance of strict money management will appreciate what futures trading has to offer. Typically, once people try trading futures, they simply stop trading stocks. The ease of entry on both the long and the short sides, ability to focus on a few markets instead of hundreds of stocks, and the lack of market maker games makes them a refreshing change from the world of stocks. Let's begin.

First off, there are many types of futures contracts. A person can trade anything from copper to coffee, from stock indexes to silver, or from pork bellies to palladium. It's not important to worry about most of these contracts in the beginning, but it is important to understand a core group of these contracts and how they work. I know many traders who focus only on one of these contracts and are doing quite well. However, it took them time to find the right market and the right setup within that market that was best suited to their personality. This can be an often long and perilous journey, but once they found the right fit, they never looked back. These are the main futures markets that I follow and trade outside of stocks:

- Mini-sized Dow (YM)
- E-mini-S&P (ES)
- E-mini-Nasdaq (NQ)
- E-mini-Russell (ER)
- Full-sized 100-oz. electronic gold (ZG)
- Mini-sized gold (YG)
- Full-sized 30-year bond (US—pit, ZB—electronic)
- Ten-year notes (TY—Pit, ZN—electronic)
- Soybeans (S)

- Corn (C)
- Wheat (W)
- Euro currency (EC)
- Crude oil (CL)
- Mini crude oil (QM)
- Various single stock futures (referred to later in the book as SSFs)

Note that some of these are mini and some of these are fullsized. The letters in parentheses next to the names represent the symbol that is used to get a quote. There are full-sized contracts on the Dow (DJ), S&P 500 (SP), and Nasdaq (ND) but these are pit-traded and I prefer to trade the smaller mini electronic contracts. Why? Because orders from the pit take longer to process, and market orders often result in fills that, in the real world, would result in a search warrant.

The minis on these stock indexes have huge volume and great liquidity. The new full-sized 100-oz. gold (ZG) contract is a refreshing change from the pit-traded gold (GC) contract. Again, I much prefer to trade the electronic version of these contracts over the pit-traded versions. There are also mini-gold (YG) and mini-silver (YI) electronic contracts which are good to trade. Pit-traded products like the grains are fine to trade. However, the trend is that the volume is flowing out of the pit contracts and into the electronic contracts. The electronics are where the action is, and that is where you want to be trading.

To get charts on these, traders will have to instruct their quote vendor that they want to add quotes from the CBOT (Chicago Board of Trade) (for the mini-sized Dow, bonds, 10-year notes, gold, and grains), CME (Chicago Mercantile Exchange) (for the E-mini S&P, E-mini Nasdaq, E-mini Russell and euro), and NYMEX (New York Mercantile Exchange) if they want quotes on oil and pit-traded gold. There is an "E-mini only" quote feed that is cheaper, but a trader will want the full version to get quotes on the full-sized contracts. It will cost around $80 a month for both full versions of the CME and CBOT. By the way, the word *E-mini* is branded by the CME, which is why the YM is called the *mini-sized Dow* instead of *E-mini Dow* because it trades on the CBOT, which is a different exchange.

## IN A NUTSHELL—WHAT TRADERS NEED TO KNOW

When traders buy a futures contract, they are not physically buying anything. This is simply a way of participating in the price movement of the market of their choice. If they think a market is going to move 10 points, they can buy a futures contract, long or short, and make money on the move if it goes in their direction. They can also obviously lose money on the move if it goes against them. Also, if they own a stock index futures contract that expires, they are not going to get a bunch of stock certificates dumped on their doorstep. The expired contract will be converted to cash, and they will see the cash deposited in their account. Other contracts like soybeans are "deliverables," meaning that a person can be the proud owner of 5,000 bushels of soybeans per contract upon expiration. Is this really a worry? Brokers never like it when a contract expires in a trader's account. They will call and badger a trader to get them to close it out, so there is little worry of forgetting. If for some reason it still happens, there won't be a truckload of soybeans dumped on your doorstep. It's all handled on the brokerage end and people there can get the account back to normal.

For price movement, if a trader has one contract in the E-mini S&P futures, for example, and it moves one point (i.e., from 1032.75 to 1033.75) that translates into $50 on his P&L. For the Nasdaq, a one-point move equates to $20. For the mini-sized Dow, a one-point move is $5. Therefore, if a trader buys three E-mini S&Ps and catches a two-point move, that is $50 × 2 points × 3 contracts = $300. There is leverage here, indeed, but it is more manageable than most people think. Where traders get in trouble is when they trade too many contracts in relation to their account size, something I talk more about later. By the way, when the S&P moves a point, the Dow moves roughly 10 points, so these two contracts are nearly identical to trade. If traders say they just made 50 points in the YM (mini-sized Dow) that is just like making 5 points in the ES (E-mini S&Ps).

Figure 4.2 shows a mini-sized Dow trade with 10 contracts. The chart reflects a 27-point move, which is worth $1,350 to a trader's P&L. I summarize all these contract specifications for bonds, euro, soybeans, and so on, at the end of this chapter. Of course, these price fluctuations go both ways so money management is the absolute key to trading futures. It is imperative that traders know their stop before they enter the trade, and that they stick to it and not play any psychological games. In futures, as in stocks, hoping and praying can, and does, lead to ruin. However, the nice thing about futures is that they are so quick and the fills so clean that a trader can get stopped out, and then a few moments later get right back in. A trader can't be afraid to take small losses, period. Reentry is only a commission away.

In addition, electronic contracts were set up specifically for traders: They are super liquid, and fills are instantaneous. There are no market maker games such as those that happen daily with individual stocks. And with electronic contracts a trader is out of the pit, where outsiders can sometimes be treated little better than a cockroach. Here are a few other things I like about futures:

- If traders think the market is going to break out, they can buy a stock like INTC (Intel Corp) and watch it sit there while the market roars on without them. They were right on the market—but their stock pick didn't move with the market. With the stock index futures, a person is trading the market instead of watching the market. It is what it is.

- A trader can short on a downtick—this makes a huge difference in trying to get filled during a breakdown. If traders try to short the stock KLAC (KLA-Tencor Corp) "at the market" on a breakdown, they may not get filled for 20 cents until it has an uptick. If they short the futures "at the market" on a breakdown, they get a quick fill at the current market price. Recently this is becoming less of an issue as the exchanges continue to see the wisdom of allowing more and more stocks to be shorted on downticks.

- I used to be a big trader of OEX (S&P 100 Index) options for day trades. After trading futures, I stopped trading OEX options. The spreads and premium of OEX options now look ridiculous. Where else can a person be dead right on an intraday move and still lose money? The OEX options market! Although I do use OEX

**F I G U R E   4.2**

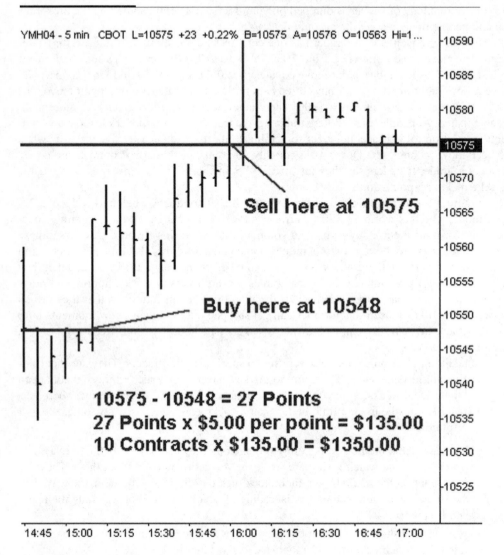

YMH04 - 5 min   CBOT   L=10575  +23  +0.22%  B=10575  A=10576  O=10563  Hi=1...

Sell here at 10575

Buy here at 10548

**10575 - 10548 = 27 Points**
**27 Points x $5.00 per point = $135.00**
**10 Contracts x $135.00 = $1350.00**

14:45   15:00   15:15   15:30   15:45   16:00   16:15   16:30   16:45   17:00

options for swing trading, I wouldn't day-trade them with my mother-in-law's trading account. Not when the mini-sized Dow and E-mini S&P futures are so clean and efficient.

- A person can do most of his trades "at the market" and get good fills, unlike stocks and especially unlike options.
- For stocks, a person needs $25,000 to day-trade. For futures a trader can open an account with $5,000 (or less) and day-trade. There are no day-trading rules or classifications. That said, I recommend that people start with a larger-sized trading

account, but I also realize that everyone has to start somewhere. My first trading account was $2,000. Can people quit their job and open up a futures account with $5,000 and trade for a living? Absolutely . . . not. I talk more about this later.

To buy one of the futures contracts discussed in this book, traders generally need about $2,000 in their account. This varies by broker, and can be lower, but this is an average. This money is called *margin*, and a trader can think of it as placing a 4 percent down payment on a $50,000 house. By placing the down payment, the trader controls the house, so to speak, and benefits from any price increase, and loses on any price decrease, on the house itself. So if traders have a $10,000 account, they can buy five mini-sized Dow contracts (five $50,000 houses) and sometimes more by utilizing lower intraday margin rates. However, for money management purposes, I heartily recommend giving some thought to how many contracts are traded in an account. This is a critical part of your trading plan, and something I discuss in more detail at the end of the book. You can certainly choose to trade five contracts in a $10,000 account. You can also choose to visit India without getting any shots in advance— but that doesn't mean it's a good idea. (My assistant, Priyanka, is from India, and she keeps daring me to visit.)

I typically trade one contract for every $10,000 to $15,000 that is in my account. This way the account swings will not be as severe, and I can trade with a level head. One trader friend of mine trades one contract for every $50,000 in his account. He makes money and is never stressed out. Conversely, I've seen programs that say to take a $5,000 account and trade five contracts, and by doing this a trader can make six figures a year. This is insane, and traders would be better off donating that $5,000 to charity, because they will lose it all trading it that way. There are few guarantees in the futures industry, but losing all of your money trading with this much "maxed out" margin is the one sure bet available today. Other key points about futures:

- There are also now futures available on stocks. Called *single stock futures*, they are great to use as swing trades in combination with index futures. Although some of the symbols have low actual volume, the "real volume" is based on that of the underlying stock. (I talk more about single stock futures in the chapter on propulsion plays.)

- With futures, at the end of the year traders don't have to list each individual futures trade like they would have to do with stocks for their tax return. They get a 1099 form from their broker with their total profit or loss for the year. All they have to put on their tax return is that number on the 1099. That is much easier and much less time consuming than listing every trade. Tax treatment is also favorable. For stocks, a trader has to hold them over a year to get classified at the cheaper "long-term gain" rate. For futures, a trader gets a 1099 that says, for example, $20,000 in gains for the year. Of this, 60 percent of the money is treated as long-term gains (lower tax rate), and 40 percent at the short-term rate. This is the 60/40 rule. This rule holds true even if you go flat at the end of every trading day. This applies to all futures contracts except single stock futures, which are treated as stocks in this regard.

- It is possible to trade futures in an IRA or retirement account through a trust company. I don't recommend this unless traders have already developed a proven track record in their own speculative accounts. And, if this is the case, I recommend that they then allocate no more than 15 percent of any retirement funds to these vehicles. Traders have no business starting out in futures using their retirement funds. This is like deliberately choosing to go into battle without a bulletproof vest, or, for that matter, a weapon.

Each stock index futures vehicle has four contracts that are traded each year: March (H), June (M), September (U), and December (Z). A trader will want to trade the closest month, because that is where the volume is concentrated. For example, if today is February 15, 2005, then the closest month is the March 2005 contract. To get a quote for the March 2005 contract on the mini-sized Dow, a trader would enter in the symbol, month, and year. In this case, that would be YM (symbol), H (month = March), 05 (year = 2005). The full symbol would be YMH05. This is for TradeStation. For eSignal it would be YM H5. Each quote service is a little different. When one contract expires, just start trading the next contract out. The four times a year that the contracts expire are always a little goofy.

Just remember that although the E-mini futures expire the same day as options expiration, on the third Friday of the month they are being traded in, the volume actually jumps into the next contract month on Thursday of the preceding week. For example, in March 2005 options and futures expiration was on the third Friday, which was March 18. The volume jumped into the June stock index futures contracts on Thursday, March 10. Bonds actually switch three weeks early. Each contract is a little different. If traders aren't sure, they just need to ask their broker, write it down, and put it next to their PC. Also, because these are futures contracts, there is always a price difference between two contracts. While the March 2005 contract will say 10686 for the mini-sized Dow, the June contract will say something like 10698. A trader shouldn't be confused by this too much. Futures contracts really are based on "future prices," which accounts for the difference. Just remember that each contract is its own entity.

Also note there is usually a 10- to 20-point difference between the mini-sized Dow futures price and the Dow Jones Industrials cash price. There is a very complicated explanation for this, involving "basis" and "future price projections" and so on that are not really important to the short-term trader. It's just something to be aware of so traders don't think something is wrong with their quote systems.

That sums up the basics with regard to the mechanics of trading futures. The key is just to get comfortable with a futures execution platform and how it works. Buying a mini-sized Dow contract is just like buying IBM (International Business Machines) or GOOG (Google) in terms of mechanics. I also recommend starting off trading one lot at a time. A new futures trader will make mistakes, and a mistake on one lot is much cheaper than a mistake on ten lots or more. A trader who has never used a futures broker before should talk with other traders to check out rates, levels of service, and so forth. On the Web, you can check www.razorfutures.com for a list of different trading platforms and execution systems.

## THE MINI-SIZED DOW VERSUS THE E-MINI S&P 500

Now that we have covered Futures 101, I'd like to review some of the basic differences between the mini-sized Dow and the E-mini S&P. I'm focusing on these two contracts because, in my experience, these are going to be the contracts most of the people reading this either currently trade or will consider trading. I do trade both contracts actively, but the mini-sized Dow does have a few advantages over the E-mini S&P that I want to point out. This applies even more for newer traders.

## THE YM Has Better Spreads Than the E-mini S&P and E-mini Nasdaq

The mini-sized Dow (YM) has the same specifications as the popular E-mini S&P (ES) contract:

- One point in the E-mini S&P equals about ten points in the mini-sized Dow.
- One point in the E-mini S&P equals $50; ten points in the mini-sized Dow equals $50.

Figure 4.3 shows movement on the Dow and S&P over exactly the same time frame. The Dow has moved 13 points lower (from the high at point 1 to the low at point 2), and during this same time, the S&P has moved 1.5 points lower. The Dow moved lower in 13 one-point increments. However, the S&P made a similar move in six quarter-point increments. To break this down more simply, when the Dow moves 10 points, it does so in 10 one-point increments. When the S&P moves an equivalent one point, it does so in four quarter point increments. This is a 60 percent difference in the spread. People who are trading the YM over the ES are putting that spread differential right into their pocket. Commissions and spreads are a cost of doing business, and anything that can be done to reduce costs will improve a trader's bottom line. The spread on the NQ is even wider than on the ES.

Another interesting phenomenon is that nearly all setups on the ES also can be executed identically as the YM. In fact, I often watch the ES for trade setups, and then take them on the YM. However, by using the YM instead of the ES on these setups, a trader will get picked off on stop runs less frequently. Why is this? It goes back to the spread. A 2-point stop on the ES is the same as a 20-point stop on the YM. There are many times when the ES will run 2 points on a stop run, and this moves the YM 18 or 19 points, missing the stop. The YM has 12 extra places to place a stop or target over the ES in a 20-point move. Because of this, I prefer to do my pivot trades almost exclusively in the YM.

## LIQUIDITY IS KING

When the mini-sized Dow first came out, it was trading very little volume. However, the contract caught on fast, and today it trades volume in the six figures nearly every day. The ES is still the big boy when it comes to volume. This is something to consider for some traders. There are traders who are doing a lot of size, or are trading extremely fast, and the extra volume in the ES is going to be a benefit. For most individual traders this is not an issue. Although perfect for the smaller retail trader, the YM has caught fire and now has the liquidity to move size. In trading, volume begets volume, and the YM will continue to expand even more as traders, commodity trading advisers, and managed funds take advantage of the trading advantages of this contract.

## F I G U R E   4.3

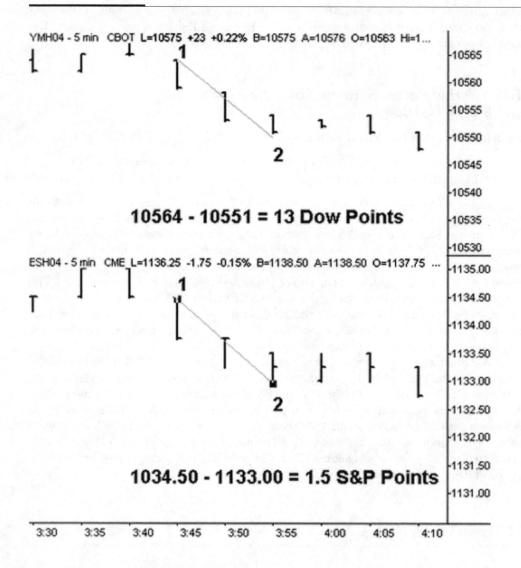

**10564 - 10551 = 13 Dow Points**

**1034.50 - 1133.00 = 1.5 S&P Points**

## Staying on the Path of Least Resistance

A trader can watch the 30 stocks in the Dow to get a very good idea of how the index is acting or is going to act. I like to place all 30 Dow stocks in a window and have them automatically sorted from strongest to weakest each day on a Net % Change basis. Getting a feel for all 500 stocks in the S&P 500 at a glance is impossible. By doing this with the Dow, I can look at my sorter list and see at a glance that, for example, 26 out of the 30 of the stocks are red (down on the day).

Figure 4.4 shows all 30 Dow stocks sorted from worst to best on a Net % Change basis. I can watch the list and see that 4 stocks are up on the day at this moment in time, while 26 stocks are down on the day. Later in the day I might see that 11 are up on the day and that 19 are down on the day, and I can tell at a glance that the Dow is getting stronger—even if the index is still chopping around. If the individual components of the Dow are getting stronger,

**F I G U R E   4.4**

### TradeStation RadarScreen - Dow

|   | Symbol | Last | Net Chg | Net %... ▲ | Description | High | Low | Volume Today |
|---|--------|------|---------|------------|-------------|------|-----|--------------|
| 1 | AIG | 51.20 | -4.21 | -7.60% | Amer Intl Group | 55.80 | 50.16 | 70,463,600 |
| 2 | WMT | 48.85 | -1.26 | -2.51% | Wal-Mart Stores | 50.50 | 48.50 | 29,182,100 |
| 3 | HD | 37.60 | -0.64 | -1.67% | Home Depot | 38.75 | 36.96 | 12,160,300 |
| 4 | GE | 35.47 | -0.59 | -1.64% | General Electric | 36.22 | 35.45 | 20,764,100 |
| 5 | CAT | 90.15 | -1.29 | -1.41% | Caterpillar Inc | 92.25 | 89.83 | 3,183,400 |
| 6 | HPQ | 21.71 | -0.23 | -1.05% | Hewlett-Packard | 22.04 | 21.42 | 16,384,900 |
| 7 | IBM | 90.44 | -0.94 | -1.03% | Intl Bus. Machines | 91.76 | 90.04 | 5,740,800 |
| 8 | JPM | 34.29 | -0.31 | -0.90% | JPMorgan Chase & Co | 35.11 | 33.84 | 20,157,400 |
| 9 | AXP | 50.91 | -0.46 | -0.90% | Amer Express | 51.94 | 50.85 | 4,566,500 |
| 10 | VZ | 35.19 | -0.31 | -0.87% | Verizon Communications | 35.80 | 35.06 | 6,482,300 |
| 11 | INTC | 23.03 | -0.20 | -0.86% | Intel Corp | 23.44 | 22.90 | 68,418,913 |
| 12 | SBC | 23.50 | -0.19 | -0.80% | SBC Communications | 23.92 | 23.45 | 10,542,800 |
| 13 | UTX | 100.87 | -0.79 | -0.78% | United Technologies | 102.18 | 100.21 | 2,011,300 |
| 14 | DD | 50.86 | -0.38 | -0.74% | Dupont(E.I.)Denemours | 51.88 | 50.62 | 3,753,900 |
| 15 | C | 44.62 | -0.32 | -0.71% | Citigroup Inc | 45.70 | 44.40 | 17,256,800 |
| 16 | KO | 41.39 | -0.28 | -0.67% | Coca-Cola Co | 41.95 | 41.29 | 5,868,100 |
| 17 | PG | 52.65 | -0.35 | -0.66% | Procter & Gamble | 53.42 | 52.37 | 5,360,300 |
| 18 | MMM | 85.14 | -0.55 | -0.64% | 3M Co | 86.21 | 85.07 | 2,301,400 |
| 19 | HON | 37.00 | -0.21 | -0.56% | Honeywell Intl | 37.64 | 36.75 | 3,398,100 |
| 20 | DIS | 28.58 | -0.15 | -0.52% | Disney (Walt) Co | 28.89 | 28.51 | 5,202,000 |
| 21 | PFE | 26.15 | -0.12 | -0.46% | Pfizer, Inc | 26.54 | 25.93 | 24,129,200 |
| 22 | MCD | 31.00 | -0.14 | -0.45% | McDonald's Corp | 31.52 | 30.88 | 4,403,700 |
| 23 | AA | 30.27 | -0.12 | -0.39% | Alcoa Inc | 30.83 | 30.18 | 3,607,700 |
| 24 | MO | 65.17 | -0.22 | -0.34% | Altria Group | 66.00 | 65.11 | 5,768,000 |
| 25 | JNJ | 66.94 | -0.22 | -0.33% | Johnson & Johnson | 67.45 | 66.65 | 11,087,600 |
| 26 | MSFT | 24.10 | -0.07 | -0.29% | Microsoft Corp | 24.35 | 24.10 | 64,799,558 |
| 27 | GM | 29.40 | 0.01 | 0.03% | General Motors | 30.19 | 29.15 | 16,649,500 |
| 28 | MRK | 32.50 | 0.13 | 0.40% | Merck & Co | 32.68 | 32.23 | 6,946,600 |
| 29 | BA | 58.84 | 0.38 | 0.65% | Boeing Co | 59.12 | 58.30 | 3,857,000 |
| 30 | XOM | 60.68 | 1.08 | 1.81% | Exxon Mobil | 60.70 | 59.93 | 18,723,600 |

Sectors \ Dow \ Futures \ Internals \ SSF

the entire index will eventually make a run higher. This filter gives me a clean downward or upward bias to the market as I can watch more stocks going red or going green, as the markets start to fall apart or try to improve. This type of "at a glance" analysis is very difficult to do with 500 stocks that make up the S&P 500 index.

Also, with the Dow components, it is easy to see which ones have more weight. If CAT (Caterpillar, Inc), IBM (International Business Machines), MMM (3M Co), and UTX (United Technologies Corp) are all down on the day, this is going to have more of an impact on the Dow than if INTC (Intel Corp), SBC (SBC Communications Inc), PFE (Pfizer Inc), and HPQ (Hewlett-Packard Co) were all down on the day.

Figure 4.5 shows a listing of all of the Dow stocks and the current percent weighting each has within the index. Again, this would be very difficult to do with all 500 stocks of the S&P 500.

## Easier to Trade Than Stocks

If traders currently are in an individual stock, they can have all kinds of outside influences move the price. Maybe insiders are dumping their own stock. Maybe an analyst has just issued an upgrade while the analyst's trading department is dumping shares off to an unsuspecting public. Maybe the company is giving positive forward guidance as its last hope to stave off bankruptcy proceedings. The factors affecting an individual stock are endless.

However, when investors in general want to sell stocks, the Dow reacts by heading south. If they want to buy, the Dow spurts green. The "Dow effect" encompasses individual investors, hedge funds, program traders, and arbitrage traders. In addition, the Dow moves actively in all buy and sell programs. It is supply and demand at its finest, and this is what makes the mini-sized Dow futures contract such a great instrument to trade. Even better, while an individual stock may be halted, the YM trades on. Even on days where the YM could reach a daily price limit—which is currently a 10 percent move in the entire index—this could still be offset in the cash market using the Dow Exchange Traded Funds (DIA). If traders have a stock halted that they own, there is nothing to do but wait—generally for pain.

## Newer Traders Do Better with the YM

It is not an assumption that new traders do better with the YM. This is based on my observation of watching hundreds of traders go through a process in which they move from trading stocks and jump into the futures markets. They start trading the ES, and they lose money. Then they switch to the YM, and things start taking shape and they make money. I've even watched newer traders start off in the YM, and then try the ES, then the NQ, and then the ER—and they always come back to the YM. Why is this? Part of the reason is psychological—it just sounds better to take a 13-point profit as opposed to equivalent 1.25 points in the ES. I've watched ES traders let a "small" 1.25 profit turn into a loss, whereas a YM trader with an equivalent 13 points will automatically and unhesitatingly sell off a couple of contracts in order to cash in some profits. Finally, it is important to realize that the best traders in the world are trading the ES. As a newer trader, it is not the best idea to

**F I G U R E   4.5**

| | COMPANY NAME | SECTOR | SYMBOL | % WEIGHTING |
|---|---|---|---|---|
| 1 | 3M Co. | Diversified Industrials | MMM | 6.0455 |
| 2 | Alcoa Inc. | Aluminum | AA | 2.1499 |
| 3 | Altria Group Inc. | Tobacco | MO | 4.6293 |
| 4 | American Express Co. | Consumer Finance | AXP | 3.6151 |
| 5 | American International Group Inc. | Full Line Insurance | AIG | 3.6186 |
| 6 | Boeing Co. | Aerospace | BA | 4.1747 |
| 7 | Caterpillar Inc. | Commercial Vehicles & Trucks | CAT | 6.4027 |
| 8 | Citigroup Inc. | Banks | C | 3.1691 |
| 9 | Coca-Cola Co. | Soft Drinks | KO | 2.9389 |
| 10 | E.I. DuPont de Nemours & Co. | Commodity Chemicals | DD | 3.6101 |
| 11 | Exxon Mobil Corp. | Integrated Oil & Gas | XOM | 4.3005 |
| 12 | General Electric Co. | Diversified Industrials | GE | 2.5192 |
| 13 | General Motors Corp. | Automobiles | GM | 2.0867 |
| 14 | Hewlett-Packard Co. | Computer Hardware | HPQ | 1.5419 |
| 15 | Home Depot Inc. | Home Improvement Retailers | HD | 2.6705 |
| 16 | Honeywell International Inc. | Diversified Industrials | HON | 2.6279 |
| 17 | Intel Corp. | Semiconductors | INTC | 1.6342 |
| 18 | International Business Machines | Computer Services | IBM | 6.4233 |
| 19 | Johnson & Johnson | Pharmaceuticals | JNJ | 4.7479 |
| 20 | JPMorgan Chase & Co. | Banks | JPM | 2.4325 |
| 21 | McDonald's Corp. | Restaurants & Bars | MCD | 2.2017 |
| 22 | Merck & Co. Inc. | Pharmaceuticals | MRK | 2.2948 |
| 23 | Microsoft Corp. | Software | MSFT | 1.7131 |
| 24 | Pfizer Inc. | Pharmaceuticals | PFE | 1.8573 |
| 25 | Procter & Gamble Co. | Nondurable Household Products | PG | 3.7365 |
| 26 | SBC Communications Inc. | Fixed Line Telecommunications | SBC | 1.6804 |
| 27 | United Technologies Corp. | Aerospace | UTX | 7.1691 |
| 28 | Verizon Communications Inc. | Fixed Line Telecommunications | VZ | 2.4993 |
| 29 | Wal-Mart Stores Inc. | Broadline Retailers | WMT | 3.4794 |
| 30 | Walt Disney Co. | Broadcasting & Entertainment | DIS | 2.0298 |

go up against these people. If you are just starting out in Tai Kwon Do, do you want to spar with a beginning white belt or an advanced black belt? The YM doesn't have the same intensity of the ES crowd. Remember, traders are not even trading a market—they are trading other traders.

This may seem like I'm knocking the ES—I'm really not. It's an awesome contract to trade, and later in the book there are plenty of setups in which I utilize this contract. However, this is a contract for professionals, and I do think it is better for newer and intermediate traders to stick with the YM in order to improve their odds of success.

# CONTRACT SPECIFICATIONS—WHAT A TRADER NEEDS TO KNOW TO TRADE KEY MARKETS

I want to spend a little time going into the contract specifics for some of the markets I just discussed. The most confusing thing about futures contracts for newer traders is that, unlike stocks, each futures market has different pricing specifications and trades in different months. This makes it tricky to figure out how much a move is worth to a trader's P&L, and it is a pain to try to figure out how to bring up a quote. (Note that I have listed all the month codes in the chapter on propulsion plays, but I will also review some of them here.)

If a stock trader is buying IBM or RIMM, each still works the same, even though they are different stocks. A move of $1 in either stock has the same impact on a trader's P&L. Unfortunately, that's not how it works in the futures markets. Again, if you are already familiar with these, feel free to skim. My intention for newer traders is that you'll be able to use this as a quick reference guide now and down the road as you look at trading additional contracts. *Please note that all times discussed are based on the Eastern Time Zone.*

**Mini-Sized Dow (YM)**—the YM trades on the CBOT until 5:00 p.m. and reopens again for trading a little over 3 hours later at 8:15 p.m. The contract months are March (H), June (M), September (U), and December (Z). The YM moves in increments of one point, which equals $5 per contract. Catching a 30-point move using one contract would equal $150. Traders need around $2,000 in their account to be able to trade one YM contract. Although this contract trades nearly 24 hours, I usually focus on it only during the regular cash market session from 9:30 a.m. to 4:15 p.m. Quotes on TradeStation for 2005 contracts: YMH05, YMM05, YMU05, YMZ05. @YM is the continuous symbol. Quotes on eSignal for 2005 contracts: YM H5, YM M5, YM U5, YM Z5. YM #F is the continuous symbol. On eSignal there is actually a space in the quotes as indicated. *Continuous* means that the contract will automatically change from March to June to September, and so on, on rollover days. For 2006, just change the 05 to 06 for TradeStation and 5 to 6 for eSignal, and so on for following years.

**E-mini-S&P (ES)**—the ES trades on the CME until 4:15 p.m., then reopens 15 minutes later at 4:30 p.m. to start the next session. There is also a shutdown period from 5:30 p.m. to 6:00 p.m. The contract months are March (H), June (M), September (U), and December (Z). The ES moves in increments of 0.25 points, which equals $12.50 per contract or $50 for a full one-point move. A three-point move in the ES using one contract would equal $150. Traders need around $2,000 in their account to be able to trade one ES contract. Although this contract trades nearly 24 hours, I usually focus on it only during the regular cash market session from 9:30 a.m. to 4:15 p.m. Quotes on TradeStation for 2005 contracts: ESH05, ESM05, ESU05, ESZ05. @ES is the continuous symbol. Quotes on eSignal for 2005 contracts: ES H5, ES M5, ES U5, ES Z5. ES #F is the continuous symbol.

**E-mini-Nasdaq (NQ)**—the NQ trades on the CME until 4:15 p.m., then reopens 15 minutes later at 4:30 p.m. to start the next session. There is also a shutdown period from 5:30 p.m. to 6:00 p.m. The contract months are March (H), June (M), September (U), and December (Z). The NQ moves in increments of 0.50 points, which equals $10 per contract or $20 for a full one-point move. A three-point move in the NQ using one contract would equal $60. Traders need around $2,000 in their account to be able to trade one NQ contract. Although this contract trades nearly 24 hours, I usually focus on it only during the regular cash market session from 9:30 a.m. to 4:15 p.m. Quotes on TradeStation for 2005 contracts:

NQH05, NQM05, NQU05, NQZ05. @NQ is the continuous symbol. Quotes on eSignal for 2005 contracts: NQ H5, NQ M5, NQ U5, NQ Z5. NQ #F is the continuous symbol.

**E-mini-Russell (ER)**—the ER trades on the CME until 4:15 p.m., then reopens 15 minutes later at 4:30 p.m. to start the next session. There is also a shutdown period from 5:30 p.m. to 6:00 p.m. *One of my favorite ways to use the Russell is as a leading indicator.* It will often time break down or break out before the other three indexes discussed above. The contract months are March (H), June (M), September (U), and December (Z). The ER moves in increments of 0.10 points, which equals $10 per contract or $100 for a full one-point move. A three-point move in the ER using one contract would equal $300. Traders need around $2,000 in their account to be able to trade one ER contract. Although this contract trades nearly 24 hours, I usually focus on it only during the regular cash market session from 9:30 a.m. to 4:15 p.m. Quotes on TradeStation for 2005 contracts: ER2H05, ER2M05, ER2U05, ER2Z05. @ER2 is the continuous symbol. Quotes on eSignal for 2005 contracts: AB H5, AB M5, AB U5, AB Z5. AB #F is the continuous symbol. I have no idea why these quotes are so different from one another on these quote vendors. This contract is attractive as it has the largest daily P & L range of the four electronic stock index contracts.

**German DAX**—I want to include a brief note on this index, because I've seen a lot of press on this contract in recent months. (I'm writing this on March 29, 2005.) This is the German equivalent of the Dow. This is a good market to trade, but it is not for beginners. I've seen many traders who normally trade 10 YM or 10 ES lots, which are interchangeable, jump in the DAX and also trade 10 lots. They heard it was like the Dow, because it has a trading range similar to the Dow, and it's made up of 30 big stocks like the Dow, so they go ahead and use a 20-point stop, just like they would on the Dow. When their stop is hit, they think they should only have lost $1,000 but it ends up being $6,500. The bottom line is that the DAX is a large contract. It trades in a similar range as the YM, but instead of $5 a point, it's worth 25 euros a point. Today (March 29, 2005) the exchange rate is 1.2937, which makes each point worth $32.34. This is like trading a little over 6 YM or ES contracts. In the 10-lot example, it would be the equivalent of trading 65 lots on the YM or ES. This is obviously important to know. The DAX trades from 2:00 a.m. until 1:00 p.m. EST in the winter. With daylight savings that changes from 3:00 a.m. to 2:00 p.m. EST. To get quotes on this contract, you have to sign up for Eurex with your data feed, which runs about $9 a month. The contract trades March, June, September, and December. Currently quotes are not available through TradeStation. The symbol for the June 2005 contract in eSignal is entered in as follows: AX M5-DT. The CBOT is considering launching a $25 per point electronic Dow product, which would make a nice replacement to the DAX.

**Full-sized 100-oz. electronic gold (ZG) and pit-traded gold (GC)**—I've talked a lot about the stock indexes futures, so let me talk briefly about gold. By trading gold, you will be in good company. No other market in the world has the universal appeal of the gold market. For centuries, gold has been coveted for its unique blend of rarity, beauty, and near indestructibility. Nations have embraced gold as a store of wealth and a medium of international exchange, and individuals have sought to possess gold as insurance against the daily fluctuations of paper money. Gold is also a vital industrial metal, as it is an excellent conductor of electricity, is extremely resistant to corrosion, and is one of the most chemically stable of the elements, making it critically important in electronics and other high-tech applications. That's all well and good, right? But as a trader, all I really care about is if the market in question provides good trading opportunities. Over the last several years gold has become a great market to trade with plenty of volatility and trending price action. The electronic contract trades on the CBOT and the pit-traded contract trades on the COMEX (Commodity Exchange Center Inc) division of the New York Mercantile Exchange (NYMEX). I personally switched over to the electronic contract when it opened for trading in late 2004, but it is important to know when the pit session is going strong. The pit starts trading at 8:20 a.m. and ends at 2:00 p.m. The CBOT electronic version, on the other hand, trades from 8:16 p.m. to 5:00 p.m., Sunday through Friday. The contract months for gold can get complicated. The official months are "the current month, the next two months, and any February, April, August, and October falling within a 23-month period and any June and December falling within a 60-month period." For the setups I'm using, I'm looking at the front month or the next month out, which means that every month is in play. The rest of the available trading months are for people looking at hedging many years into the future. I like to establish trades in this contract during pit session hours. Gold moves in increments of 10 cents, and each 10 cents is worth $10 per contract. A full $1 move in the price of gold is worth $10 per contract. Traders need around $2,000 in their account to be able to trade one contract. Quotes on TradeStation for 2005 continuous contracts are: @ZG and @GC.P. Continuous quotes on eSignal for 2005 contracts are ZG #F and GC #F. Note that to get quotes on the pit-traded contract, traders have to be signed up for COMEX data through their quote vendor.

**Mini-sized gold (YG)**—this is the same as regular gold, except that there isn't a pit-traded contract. YG trades on the CBOT and is one-third the size of the regular contract. A 0.10 move is worth $3.32 per contract. A full $1 move is worth $33.20 per contract.

**Full-sized 30-year bond (US—pit, ZB—electronic)**—interest rate futures were pioneered by the CBOT in 1975 in response to a growing market need for tools that could protect against sharp and frequent swings in the cost of money. U.S. Treasury bond futures were introduced first, followed by futures on 10-year, 5-year, and 2-year U.S. Treasury notes. Over the past two decades, contract volume has exploded, reflecting the growth of the underlying instruments and profound changes in the marketplace. If you focus primarily on the stock market, it is critical that you become familiar with bonds. The bond market dwarfs the equity markets. Therefore, it is important to know when money is flowing out of bonds or into bonds. The bond markets and the stock markets also have an interesting relationship. Sometimes they move directly opposite each other, during periods of portfolio reallocation. This happens when huge funds have to sell stocks and buy bonds to readjust the percentage of capital invested in each. During these times, new highs in the bond market lead to new lows in the stock market, and thus bonds become a great leading indicator. The pit contract trades from 8:20 a.m. to 3:00 p.m., Monday through Friday. The electronic version trades until 5:00 p.m. and reopens 3 hours later at 8:00 p.m., Sunday through Thursday. I always trade the electronic version. The contract months are March (H), June (M), September (U), and December (Z). The bonds move in increments of 1/32, which is called a *tick*, and are worth $31.25 per contract. 32/32 equals one full point, which is $1,000 per contract. Traders need around $2,000 in their account to be able to trade one bond contract. Quotes on TradeStation for 2005 contracts: USH05, USM05, USU05, USZ05. @US is the continuous symbol. Quotes on eSignal for 2005 contracts: ZB H5, ZB M5, ZB U5, ZB Z5. ZB #F is the continuous symbol.

**Ten-year notes (TY—pit, ZN—electronic)**—10-year notes trade on the CBOT and are the same as the 30-year bonds in terms of trading hours and trading months. The notes move in increments of 1/64, which are called a *tick*, and are worth $15.625 per contract.

Traders need a little less than $2,000 in their account to be able to trade one note contract. Quotes on TradeStation for 2005 contracts: TYH05, TYM05, TYU05, TYZ05. @TY is the continuous symbol. Quotes on eSignal for 2005 contracts: ZN H5, ZN M5, ZN U5, ZN Z5. ZN #F is the continuous symbol.

**Soybeans (S)**—my appreciation of the grain markets came about as an accident. I own a 1,000 acre farm in Palisade, Nebraska, and because of that I started watching the grain futures prices. I liked how they traded, and, once I learned about the contract specifications, I realized they trade very similarly to the E-mini S&Ps and mini-sized Dow. Soybeans trade in the pit from 10:30 a.m. to 2:15 p.m., Monday through Friday. There is also an electronic session that runs from 8:31 p.m. to 7:00 a.m. The symbol for this is ZS, but I don't watch this session or trade it. This is one of the few contracts I trade in the pit. Soybeans move in increments of ¼ cent, and each ¼ cent is worth $12.50. A full cent is worth $50. This is just like the E-mini S&Ps where they move in quarter-point increments worth $12.50, and a full point is worth $50. An 8-cent move in soybeans is just like an 8-point move in the ES or an 80-point move in the YM and is worth $400. To buy one contract, a trader needs a little more than $2,000. Quotes on TradeStation and eSignal are just like the E-mini S&Ps, except they use S instead of ES. Soybeans trade in September (U), November (X), January (F), March (H), May (K), July (N), and August (Q). There are also mini-soybeans (YK), but I don't trade them as they are very small and illiquid. Soybeans are the most volatile of these three grains. They generally trade in a range equal to 1½ times the ES and YM.

**Corn (C)**—everything with corn is the same as with soybeans except the contract months are December, March, May, July, and September. This is the quietest of the three grains. A one-cent move is worth $50, just like soybeans. To buy one contract, a trader usually needs less than $1,000. Quotes on TradeStation and eSignal are just like the E-mini S&Ps, except they use C instead of ES. It's generally a very steady market that trends well, and its daily range is generally half that of the ES and YM. There is a saying in trading circles that goes, "If you can't make money trading, then trade corn."

**Wheat (W)**—everything with wheat is the same as with corn, and a one-cent move in this market is also worth $50. One contract usually costs under $1,000. Quotes on TradeStation and eSignal are just like the E-mini S&Ps, except they use W instead of ES. The volatility in this market is right in between soybeans and corn. There are other, smaller U.S. exchanges that also trade wheat, but I just trade the CBOT contract. Note that all quarter-cent moves in grains are recorded as eights. So a price of 3414 actually means 3.41½ (3.41 and 4/8) and 3416 means 3.41¾ (3.41 and 6/8).

**Euro FX (EC)**—this contract is traded on the CME, as are futures in the British pound, Japanese yen, Swiss franc, and other currencies. I just focus on the euro. This is not the same as trading the euro in the forex markets, which I talk about in a moment. Also, I discuss the euro and compare euro futures to forex in later chapters. For now, all a trader needs to know is that there is a pit-traded session from 8:20 a.m. to 3:00 p.m. and an electronic session that is 24 hours, shutting down from 5:00 p.m. to 6:00 p.m. The euro FX moves in increments of 1/100 of a cent which are called *ticks,* and each tick is worth $12.50. The euro FX trades in March, June, September, and December. Quotes on TradeStation for 2005 contracts: ECH05, ECM05, ECU05, ECZ05. @EC is the continuous symbol. Quotes on eSignal for 2005 contracts: 6E H5, 6E M5, 6E U5, 6E Z5. 6E #F is the continuous symbol. Note that you can get a quote on eSignal using EC, but this will be the pit-traded contract only, while using @EC on TradeStation does capture the electronic volume.

**Crude oil (CL)**—oil has become a big focus for stock prices ever since it shot above $40 a barrel and kept on going. This is not a market for beginning traders, but it is helpful to understand how it works from a trader's perspective. This contract trades on the NYMEX (New York Mercantile Exchange). Oil moves in increments of 1 cent. A 1-cent move equals $10 per contract, so a full $1 move in the price of oil equates to $1,000 per contract. The pit opens at 10:00 a.m. and closes at 2:30 p.m. After hours trading starts at 3:15 p.m. and goes through until 9:30 a.m. There are contracts for each month for many years out.

**Mini-crude oil (QM)**—the contract for mini-crude oil is the same as for the big contract, except a 1-cent move is worth $5 per contract, and a full $1 move is worth $500 per contract. For oil, be aware that contracts expire early—a September contract will expire in August.

**Various single stock futures**—these are discussed in detail in the chapter on propulsion plays. One contract represents 100 shares of stock, so a 1-point move with one contract represents $100 to a trader's P&L.

That is the basic information for the trader on these futures contracts. One important thing to keep in mind is how all these contracts translate in terms of price movement with respect to the risk management techniques traders choose to utilize in their own trading plan. Let's take a look at an example stop loss taken in the NQ.

Figure 4.6 shows a 12- point loss that was taken in the NQ, which equates to a loss of $240 per contract. If a trader wants to use a monetary stop of approximately $240 for every trade in every market, then it is helpful to create a reference sheet of how this translates into other markets. This way a trader will be less prone to making a pricing error when it comes to figuring out appropriate stop losses in various futures markets. In this chart, we can see that a 12-point stop in the Nasdaq is equal to a 4.75-point stop in the S&Ps, which is equal to a 48-point stop in the YM, which is equal to a 2.40-point stop on the Russell, which is equal to an 8-tick stop on the 30-year bonds, which is equal to a 19-tick stop on the euro. This also equals a 24-cent stop on crude oil, a 48-cent stop in mini-crude oil, a 2.40 stop on gold, a 7.20 stop on mini-gold, and a 4¾-cent stop on the grains.

Easy enough? Let's take a quick peek at the forex markets.


## Forex for Newbies

Again, this section is geared toward traders who are not familiar with the forex markets, so experienced forex traders should feel free to skip ahead, though the part on "How to Hedge Your Own Life in the Forex Markets" might be of interest. This section started off very, very long—as any section that starts with the phrase, "In the beginning" will inevitably be. A fellow forex trader, Todd Gordon, helped me to go through this several times and cut it down to the bare essentials.

The Foreign Exchange market, also referred to as "forex" or "FX" is the largest financial market in the world, with a daily average turnover of well over 1 trillion dollars—30 times larger than the combined volume of all U.S. equity markets. "Foreign exchange" is literally the simultaneous buying of one currency and the selling of another. Currencies are traded in pairs; for example, euro/U.S. dollar (EUR/USD) or U.S. dollar/Japanese yen (USD/JPY). The most liquid of these currencies are called the *majors*,

**F I G U R E   4.6**

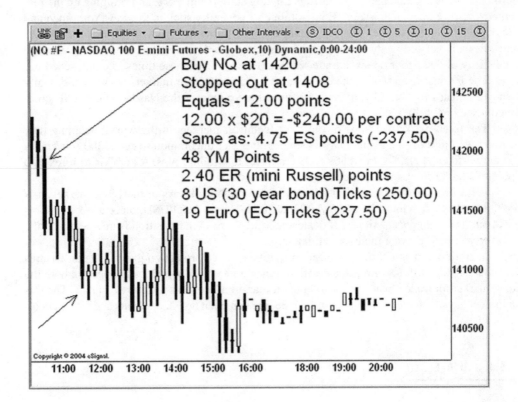

and make up more than 85 percent of all daily transactions in this market. The majors are made up of the following:

USD = U.S. dollar
JPY = Japanese yen
EUR = euro
GBP = British pound
CHF = Swiss franc
CAD = Canadian dollar
AUD = Australian dollar

Forex trading begins each day in Sydney, and moves around the globe as the business day begins in each financial center, first to Tokyo, then to London, and finally to New York. This is truly a 24-hour market, and investors can respond to currency fluctuations caused by economic, social, and political events at the time they occur—day or night.

One thing I like about the forex markets is that the 24-hour trading day includes four major market opens that offer the same volatility and liquidity found in the one-time-per-day

9:30 a.m. EST stock market opening. First is the Japanese open at 8:00 p.m. EST, then the Eurozone opens at 12:00 a.m. EST, third is London at 3:00 a.m. EST, and bringing up the rear is the New York open at 8:30 a.m. EST. Although I generally stick to the New York open and sometimes the Japanese open, there are many traders I know who trade all the opens or whose schedules are dictated by their work, which for some people can include odd hours. With the availability of these four opens, a trader can fit at least one of these times into any schedule.

The FX markets are also the deepest, most participated-in markets in the world. Daily turnover equates to over $1.2 trillion, 16 times the volume of the Nasdaq and NYSE combined. (See Fig. 4.7.)

The forex markets are one of the most technical markets in the world, meaning they respond well to most technical analysis studies. It is not uncommon to see a 300-pip breakout move stop and change trend at a technical level to within 5 pips. A "pip" is to forex as a "point" is to the stock index futures.

A trader also doesn't have to worry about contract rollovers in the forex market. It is possible to buy a few lots of the EUR/USD, GBP/USD, and AUD/USD, place a stop, and forget about it for months at a time. FX dealers atomically roll your position from one day to the next for you as to prevent the event of delivery.

In addition, most FX dealers offer a negative balance protection guarantee that ensures that your account will never reach a position of negative equity, which can happen in both the stock market for traders who are maxed out on margin as well as the futures market. There is an interesting way to take advantage of this. People can open up FX accounts at different deal-

**F I G U R E   4.7**

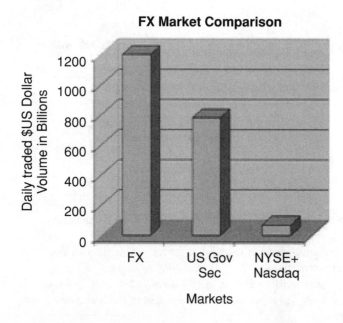

FX Market Comparison

ers and deposit a small portion of their overall trading capital. They can go long a currency in one account, short the same currency in another account, and just leave both accounts alone, with no stops or targets. While the two positions are open, they will offset each other equally, so it's a perfect hedge. If the currency then gets into a prolonged move, one of the accounts will get closed when the account equity gets to zero. At this point the trader is still breakeven on the trade because the losses in one account are offset by gains in another account. If the currency then continues to trend in the open account, the trader benefits from already being "in the move." I don't do this personally, but a few traders I know have done this and have had instances where accounts in the neighborhood of $20,000 have turned into accounts in the neighborhood of $400,000 on the backs of a couple of great moves. The key is they take the positions and literally forget about them for six months. The currency just has to trend one way or the other. This obviously involves some luck, and I wouldn't call it a "core strategy of any wise retirement plan." My favorite reason for trading the forex markets is that they trend better than any other markets. Once a market gets going, it can easily trend for weeks and months in a nice steady march higher or lower. Unlike the stock market, which has been consolidating for the past few years, there are real trends happening all of the time in the forex markets. Stock market traders talk of missing the big moves of the dot.com days. Today the dot.com moves are happening in the forex markets.

The biggest complaint I've heard people say about forex is that the FX dealers are taking the other side of their trade. I usually hear this from people who have overtraded their account and have lost all their money. This is really true in any market—somebody is always taking the other side of your trade. In my experience with forex, however, it is the high-frequency day traders who don't last. On the other hand, the traders who place smaller positions and let them work out over the course of a few days to a few weeks or longer do well. As in any trade, market makers can mess with a position in the very short term, but over the course of a swing trade they have no power. When George Soros was short the British pound and was told that the British government had allocated the equivalent of 20 billion U.S. dollars to stabilize the currency, he shrugged and said, "That will help them for 30 minutes. Then what are they going to do?" He made over a billion dollars on that trade.

## THIS IS HOW MOVES ARE MEASURED

Forex trading, like many new things, is confusing yet simple. If a quote for the EUR/USD is 1.23, it simply means that 1 euro is equal to 1.23 U.S. dollars. A quote for the USD/JPY at 109.50 simply means that 1 U.S. dollar is equal to 109.50 Japanese yen (see Fig. 4.8).

Forex markets move in what are called *pips*. A pip (price interest point) is the smallest unit of price for any foreign currency.

- EUR/USD trading from 1.2300 to 1.2301 = a gain of 1 pip
- USD/JPY trading from 108.01 to 108.09 = a gain of 8 pips
- GBP/USD trading from 1.8302 to 1.8311 = a gain of 9 pips
- EUR/USD trading from 1.2300 to 1.2401 = a gain of 101 pips

A full one-cent move in the currency is equal to 100 pips.

**FIGURE 4.8**

# Quoting Examples

<u>USD base currency quote</u>

## USD/JPY 109.50/55

<u>Non-USD base currency quote</u>

## EUR/USD 1.2815/18

Bid      Ask

Bid      Ask

In this example, if you 'hit the bid' you will sell US$1 and buy 109.50 Yen

In this example, if you sell 1 Euro (€), you will buy US$ 1.2815

If you want to buy dollars and sell Yen, you will 'lift the offer' and pay 109.55 Yen for US$1

If you want to buy Euros and sell dollars, you will pay € 1.2818 for US $1

## Calculating Pip Values

First, we start with the complicated way of how pip values are calculated, which is as follows:

- (One pip, including decimal point/current exchange rate) × (notional amount)
- For the EUR/USD this translates into:
  (.0001/1.2935) × (E 100,000) = Euro 7.73096
- But, we want the pip value in U.S. dollars, not euro, so we go one step further:
  7.73096 × current exchange rate (1.2930) = $10.00 per pip.

What this boils down to is this—any forex contract that ends in USD is worth $10 per pip, or $1,000 for a full one-cent move (100 pips). The euro, for example, moves in a range of 80 to 150 pips per day. This $10 per pip calculation would include the euro (EUR/USD), pound (GBP/USD), etc. These are the contracts most people trade. It gets a little trickier when this is not the case. For example, on March 29, 2005, a USD/JPY contract and any additional contracts that end in JPY are going to be worth $9.35 per pip. On this same day, any contract that ends in CHF is going to be $8.29 per pip. The EUR/GBP is going to be

$18.70 per pip, and so on, based on the various exchange rates. Again, most traders seem to focus on currencies that end in USD, so the $10 per pip has become a universal number when talking about forex. There is also a mini-version of these contracts in which each pip is worth $1.

## What Happens to Currencies When Prices Change

If a quote for the USD/JPY is at 108.00, it means that it takes 1 U.S. dollar to buy 108 Japanese yen. If the price moves to 109.00, this means that the yen has weakened against the dollar, because it now requires more yen to obtain the same one U.S. dollar. If the EUR/USD is trading at 1.20, this means that one euro can buy 1.23 U.S. dollars. A move to 1.22 means that the euro has strengthened against the U.S. dollar because it requires more USD to obtain the same one euro.

# HOW TO HEDGE YOUR OWN LIFE
# IN THE FOREX MARKETS

There are many trade setups for forex that work in smaller time frames, and I talk more about these setups later in the book. However, the fascinating thing about the forex market is traders' ability to participate in world events on different scales and essentially "hedge their life."

For example, my wife and I visited Spain, France, and Italy from December 18, 2003, through January 14, 2004. (Yes, it's colder then, but there aren't any lines.) Excluding airfare, I added up estimated costs in euros. On the day we booked this trip on September 30, 2003, the exchange rate was 1.1675. Based on this rate, I estimated that the trip would cost U.S. $15,000. This cost would fall if the euro fell, but would increase if the price of the euro also increased. I pulled up a chart (see Fig. 4.9).

In this figure, point 2 shows where the market was trading on the day we booked the trip. Point 1 shows the all-time highs at 1.1932 that were hit on May 27, 2003. For our trip, I wanted the euro to fall so our costs would also fall. However, just because I wanted the euro to fall didn't mean that it would. If the euro took off, our trip could get considerably more expensive. Since a regular contract represents $100,000 worth of U.S. currency, it was much too large to use as a hedge. The minis each represent $10,000 worth of U.S. currency, so this is where I looked to set up a position.

Looking at the chart on this day, I decided to place a buy stop order for two mini EUR/USD contracts at 1.1933, one pip above the all-time highs. This buy stop order means that I will get into the market only when it trades up and through 1.1933. Instead of getting stopped out of a short position, I would be getting stopped into a long position since I was currently flat.

I decided to do this at this higher level, instead of at the immediate price, in case the euro did roll over and fall. If it fell from when we booked our tickets, it would be a plus for us, as our trip would get cheaper with each decline. However, if the euro broke out to new highs, it could ignite a huge rally and really inflate our trip budget. One mini-contract represents $10,000, so I

**F I G U R E  4.9**

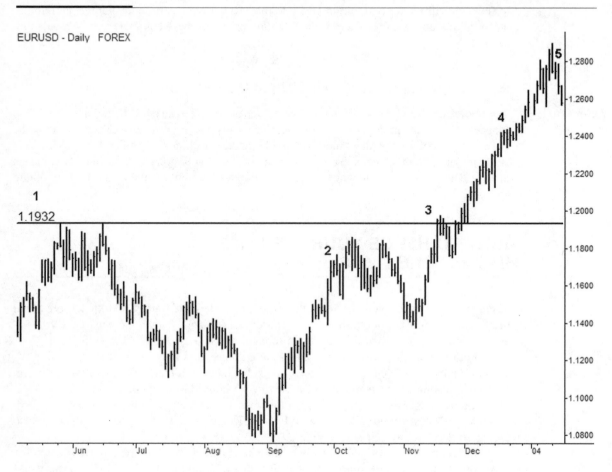

EURUSD - Daily  FOREX

was essentially hedging $20,000 in U.S. currency with the two mini-contracts. Since I underestimated how much the trip would cost, this actually worked out perfectly in the end.

On November 18, almost two months later, my buy stop was hit at point 3. By the time we left for our trip at point 4, the euro had moved over 500 pips from my entry. By the time we got home at point 5, I closed out the position at 1.2665, a gain of 732 pips. Two mini-contracts equaled a gain of $1,464, which paid for the increased exchange rate we had to pay while we were over there. Had the euro hit my buy stop and then sold off to 1.10, I would have lost money on the trade, but this would have been offset by the money saved during the trip because of the more favorable exchange rate. Had I set this up as a "normal" trade using five regular-sized contracts, a 732-pip move would have equaled $36,600.

There are many other ways people can "hedge their life" in the forex markets. For people who think the value of the U.S. dollar is going to continue to decline and are worried about the value of their savings deteriorating against other world currencies, they can hedge their savings account by going long the EUR/USD. If a person has $240,000 in savings, he or she can buy two regular contracts and four mini-contracts, and have a perfect hedge.

## FOR TRADERS, THIS IS ALL YOU NEED TO KNOW

The biggest question traders always ask is, "How much money do I need to buy one contract, and what happens after I buy it?" For forex, it can vary based on your broker, but in general to buy one regular-sized contract, a trader will need about $1,000, and to buy a mini-contract, a trader will need about $100. This depends on the leverage being offered by the broker. A typical scenario is that traders will open up a small mini-account with $500 and get 200 to 1 leverage. They will then buy two mini EUR/USD contracts, and this will cost them $130. Their $500 account now has $371 in available equity, after the $129 in margin has been deducted. In the worst case scenario (which can happen), the trade goes completely wrong. It will have to move 185 pips against the traders (which wipes out their $371 in equity) before their position is closed out by the dealer—provided they have zero balance protection. The $130 in margin that was used to establish the position is returned to the account, bringing the balance down from $500 to $130. If the trade works out and gains 55 pips on two mini-contracts and is sold, then this $110 profit is put into the account, along with the initial margin, and the total balance then becomes $610, less transaction costs. If a trader is using the big contracts in this scenario, everything is the same except it is times 10.

How much does this cost in terms of transaction fees? Well, the spread is typically three pips wide in the EUR/USD for most FX dealers, which is what the trader pays instead of commissions. It's still a transaction cost—anyone who calls this "commission free" trading should be hanged. For the minis it equates to $3 per side, and for the regular contracts its $30 per side. The spreads will continue to narrow, and this will get cheaper. This isn't much different from trading the ES. In this case, the spread is $12.50. Add, say, an $8 round turn cost and now you are really trading $20.50 a round turn. A trader should always add the spread into their transaction costs.

I personally spend most of my time watching the following 8 currency pairs. In parenthesis I have listed their TradeStation quote symbol, eSignal quote symbol, and the nickname many traders use when referring to the contract:

1. EUR/USD (Euro) TS: EURUSD eSignal: EUR A0-FX

2. GPB/USD (Cable) TS: GPBUSD eSignal: GBP A0-FX

3. AUD/USD (Aussie) TS: AUDUSD eSignal: AUD A0-FX

4. USD/JPY (Dollar Yen) TS: USDJPY eSignal: JPY A0-FX

5. USD/CHF (Swissy) TS: USDCHF eSignal: CHF A0-FX

6. USD/CAD (Loonie—reference to the Loonie Bird on the $1.00 Canadian coin) TS: USDCAD eSignal: CAD A0-FX

7. EUR/GBP (Euro Sterling) TS: EURGBP eSignal: EURGPB A0-FX

8. EUR/JPY (Euro Yen) TS: EURJPY eSignal: EURJPY A0-FX

Although there are many other minor currency pairs, these eight will provide plenty of trading opportunities, and all tend to move together. It is also important to have a chart of the dollar composite index ($DXY on TradeStation, $DXC on eSignal). In general, if the dollar index is moving higher, then USD/JPY, USD/CHF, and USD/CAD are also moving higher. This action will push EUR/USD, GPB/USD and AUD/USD lower. When the financial news networks mention that "Warren Buffett is short the dollar" he is really long EUR/USD, GPB/USD and/or AUS/USD as well as short the USD/CHF, USD/JPY, and/or USD/CAD. If the dollar goes lower, then the first three currency pairs will move opposite of the dollar and go higher, and the last three currency pairs will move with the dollar lower. There isn't a straight "dollar currency" to go long or short. They all trade in pairs against each other. For more advanced information on the forex markets and how they work together, visit www.tradethemarkets.com or www.razorforex.com.

Now that we understand how all these different markets work and the trading opportunities they represent, let's jump in and review what I start looking at with the opening bell of the regular stock market session.

# 5
## CHAPTER

# THE STOCK MARKET IS NOW OPEN—SEVEN KEY INTERNALS TO GAUGE INTRADAY MARKET DIRECTION

*Unless you enter the tiger's den you cannot take the cubs.*

JAPANESE PROVERB

## MUSICIANS KNOW HOW TO READ MUSIC; TRADERS MUST KNOW HOW TO READ THE MARKETS

For anyone who trades individual stocks, ETFs (exchange traded funds) such as the QQQQ (Nasdaq 100 Trust), DIA (Dow Diamonds Trust) or SPY (Standard & Poor's Depositary Receipts for the S&P 500), or stock index futures intraday, this is probably the most important chapter in the book. Not understanding this chapter and then going on to trade these instruments intraday is like not knowing how to swim and then trying to qualify for the 100-meter backstroke. Although I will swing trade almost anything, a large percentage of my intraday trading is confined to instruments that reflect the movement of the stock indexes. There is a good reason for this—there is a ton of data available during the trading day that will show a trader what is happening behind the scenes in the stock markets. By understanding how to read and interpret these data, a trader will have a better feel if the predominant pressure in the markets is on the buy side or the sell side and can make trading decisions accordingly. There are plenty of traders out there who have only the vaguest idea of how to interpret these tools, and an even larger group of newbies that has no clue they even exist. This represents a large pool of cash that is ripe for the plucking, and knowledge of this information gets traders closer to the front of the handout line.

There is another critical reason for thoroughly understanding this material. Every single trading day is going to present setups on the long side as well as setups on the short side. By understanding how to accurately interpret these internals, a trader will know the following:

- Which days to ignore all short setups.
- Which days to ignore all long setups.
- Which days to focus on setups that do best in choppy markets.
- Which days to focus on setups that do best in trending markets.

This knowledge is critical and has a big impact on whether a trader is going to have a winning day or a losing day, and, as the weeks and months progress, an upward trending equity curve or something, well, less amusing. Let's get started.

## TICKS—THEY CAN RUN, BUT THEY CAN'T HIDE

The NYSE (New York Stock Exchange) ticks (TradeStation symbol $TICK) summarize the number of stocks on the NYSE that are increasing in price versus those that are decreasing in price from the previous price quote. Many times this is not purely buying and selling as an uptick may represent only that the ask was hit, while a downtick may represent only that a bid was hit. This type of information is like learning that Britney Spears might be pregnant. In other words—who cares? Yet I've watched traders stare at the ticks, mesmerized by a move from −300 ticks to +200 ticks, and think this was a positive thing for the markets. In reality, this type of move is not positive—it's immaterial, and the information is useless. This brings us to the first rule I follow when watching the ticks:

*Any tick reading that is below +400 or above −400 is noise and should be ignored.*

I start paying attention to the ticks on any readings that are over +600 or under −600. These types of moves tell me that there is sustained buying or selling pressure hitting the markets. This doesn't signal any actions on my part, but it does give me a heads-up. If the ticks continue and hit +800 or −800, this does trigger specific action on my part, because only a sustained buy or sell program can move the ticks to this level. This brings us to my next rule in using the ticks for day trading:

*If I'm long intraday and my stop hasn't been hit and the markets generate a –800 tick reading, I will close out my position at the market. Conversely, if I'm short and the markets generate a tick reading of +800 and my stop hasn't been hit, I will close out my position at the market.*

Readings this high are telling the traders loud and clear that, on an intraday basis, they are either right or wrong, depending on their position. If I'm short, and the market is telling me I'm wrong with a +800 tick reading, I take the hint and close out my trade. This also has the nice benefit of increasing a trader's risk to reward ratio, as it is possible in many instances to get out of trades early that would otherwise have been stopped.

I want to make one thing perfectly clear before I move on: *I never exit a trade early just because "I think I'm wrong."* I have learned the hard way over many years of doing this to stick to my original parameters—unless I have designated a specific, measurable event that alerts me to get out of the trade early. A reading of +800 or –800 ticks is one of these specific events. My deciding to get out of a trade early has nothing to do with gut feel or interpretation—I've already discussed in Chapter 2 how woefully inadequate human beings are at making objective decisions while in a trade. Luckily, there is no way around a tick reading of +800 or –800. The markets either hit that level or they don't. There is no emotion involved.

I'm emphasizing this point because I've had the opportunity to sit next to many traders who come to visit me at my trading office. We trade next to each other, side by side, for one week. For the first two days it's straightforward and low key. I do my trades; they do their trades. It may seem relaxed and laid back, but there is a very specific reason I do this—I can learn more about people in one day watching them trade live, with their own money, than I can learn about them through normal conversations over the course of five years. In mere talking, people put their best face forward—the image that they think they are or should be. However, with their money on the line, this façade lasts about 12 minutes, and the underlying, dominant personality springs forth. Sometimes this ain't pretty.

In working with this many other traders, I've seen firsthand the reason most people never make it in this business. In the final analysis, most traders are atrocious at managing their exits. This is indisputably the one thing that prevents most people from making a living as a trader. To put it simply, many traders manage their exits by how they feel about the trade. Worse, if they are down on the day, they will manage trades differently from the way they do when they are up on the day, and they don't even realize this. To illustrate this point, there are also many times when I will take a trade, and they will take it with me. We will get into the same trade at exactly the same time, and five minutes later I will see them selling out half their position. Of course, I'm perplexed by this because they said, "JC, I'm going with you on this next trade." The ensuing conversation goes something like this.

ME: Steve, I thought you said you were going to follow me on this one. Did you just sell some of your position?

STEVE: Uh, well, no, I . . .

ME: I heard the software execution platform say "sell."

STEVE: Oh, that, yeah, well, I'm selling some here to book gains.

ME: Why?

STEVE: Didn't you say it was a good idea to scale out of your position as it goes your way?

ME: Yes, but I said only if you had to have a specific exit strategy. You can't exit a trade based on your gut feelings. So why did you sell?

STEVE: Uh, the ticks were going higher, and I wanted to sell into strength.

ME: The ticks are only at +300.

STEVE: But they were at +284.

This goes on for some time. As a matter of faith I let these traders try to convince me they are justified in their actions, but my eventual goal is to get them to admit to what they are doing—selling because they are nervous or scared or excited or whatever, and that surge of emotion is what made them push the button. In other words, there was absolutely no rational reason to take the action that they did.

Trading is an extremely private world for most people, with friends and spouses kept totally in the dark of the emotional ups and downs that traders feel and experience each and every trading day. Getting a trader to admit to what's really going on internally is like trying to pry open a walnut with your fingers. It's challenging because most traders are masters at masking what they are really feeling. Whether a trader is up $25,000 or down $25,000, many times the outside world will never know. I've been there and know the feeling. Armed with this knowledge, I go on the "friendly attack" and eventually get most of them to fess up. I don't pull any punches. I tell them that no one is ever going to understand their trading journey like another trader. Speak now or be stuck in your rut forever. Usually this works, and it gets traders to open up and confront their trading demons—trading therapy 101. Let's look at the rest of the tick reading rules I follow.

The next thing I'm looking for in the ticks is if they hit +1000 or −1000. This is the most important reading of the day for two reasons: First, this usually represents the maximum amount of sustained buying or selling pressure the market can handle. It's like a sprinter getting to the end of a 100-yard dash and having to stop and gasp for breath. Second, it represents a specific new trading opportunity. These extreme readings set up a "fade" play that I follow. If we get a reading of +1000 ticks, I will set up a short. If we get a reading of −1000 ticks, I will set up a long. I discuss this play in detail in Chapter 9.

This brings me to the next rule I use with the ticks:

> *If I am long and the markets hit +1000 ticks,*
> *I will use that as a signal to exit the remainder of my position.*
> *If I am short and the markets hit −1000 ticks,*
> *I will use that as a signal to exit the remainder of my position.*

Figure 5.1 is a snapshot of the ticks from March 29, 2005. This is how I have them set up on my TradeStation charts. I use a five-minute chart, but the interval is not important—the key for me is I want to be able to see a full trading day's worth of data. (Side note—all the charts you see in this book have a white background. This is for printing purposes. When I'm watching these on the screen, I set the background to black, and the chart colors are usually blue or green on up moves and red on down moves.)

**F I G U R E   5.1**

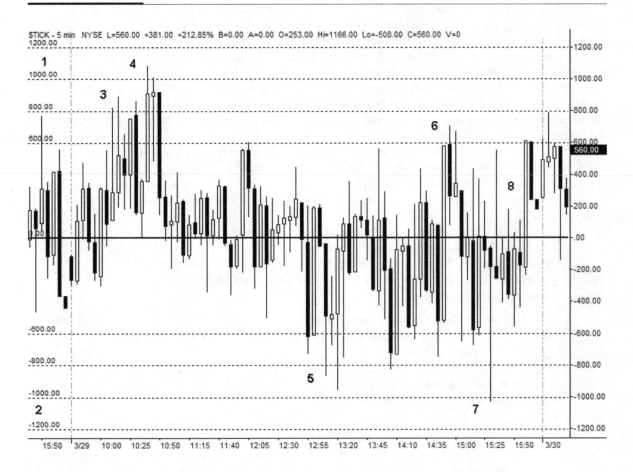

In this chart we can see at points 1 and 2 that there are horizontal lines placed at +1200, +1000, +800, and +600 ticks, as well as at –1200, –1000, –800, and –600 ticks. These horizontal lines serve a very specific purpose, which brings me to my fourth rule in using ticks:

*I set up audio alerts at all the key tick levels.*
*This way I don't have to stare at the chart, and I never miss a move.*

These audio alerts are a key part of my trading plan. I can be on the phone, down the hall, or in the bathroom, and I will hear if the ticks make a move. Remember that at the 800 and 1000 levels I take action, so I don't want to miss them, no matter what I'm doing. Yes, there have been times when I've had to initiate a new trade with my pants around my ankles, as I'm stumbling out of the bathroom. I spend a lot of time staring at computers, so I like to make these alerts halfway entertaining. When ticks hit +1000, I hear Daffy Duck screaming "I'm rich! I'm rich!" and when the ticks hit –1000 I hear the Wicked Witch from the *Wizard of Oz* crying, "I'm melting! I'm melting!" Visiting traders raise their eyebrows when these alerts first start to hit, but they get their attention—which is the whole idea.

I want to point out that I specifically use a bar chart or candlestick chart for anything having to do with audio alerts. Another popular chart, the "line on close," is also good when watching the ticks, because it helps to show a trader when they are rolling over or "hooking." However, these types of charts can, and do, miss many audio alerts because the line is literally created on the close of the bar, and misses the high and low fluctuations—which is what sets off the audio alerts.

In this chart we can see that at point 3 the ticks hit +800. On this day I had a short in the mini-sized Dow with a 20-point stop. When the ticks hit +800, I covered my short for a nine-point loss. When the ticks hit +1000 ticks 25 minutes later, I heard the audio alert for this level, and I set up a new short in the YM. (This is a trade setup that is covered in Chapter 9.)

Between about 10:30 a.m. EST and 12:30 p.m. EST nothing happened. The ticks were twitching back and forth like a freshly caught tuna on a boat deck. At around 1:30 p.m. the action picked up enough to the point where the ticks registered a reading of –800, and they even hit –1000 later in the day. Let's take a look at this same chart with the actual market action overlaid on top of it (see Fig. 5.2).

1. The ticks are usually quiet at the open, and at point 1 we can see that the ticks just flopped back and forth for the better part of an hour. The markets did a whole lot of nothing during this time.

2. By 10:25 a.m. we get the first notable tick reading at +600, and this drives the markets higher with ticks eventually hitting +1000. (Remember, this is a shorting opportunity that is discussed later in the book.)

3. The mini-sized Dow futures hit 10542 when the ticks move over +1000, and this ends up being their dead highs of the day.

4. I like to watch how the markets react when the ticks start stair-stepping and making higher highs or higher lows. The ticks shot up to +600 at around 12:00 noon, EST, but the markets did not move higher. Yet when the ticks started making lower lows, so did the market. This is key information. If high ticks of over +600 can't move the markets higher, then that is a tip-off that the selling pressure is predominant.

5. This series of lower lows in the ticks leads to an eventual steep sell off. The market generally works up to "abrupt" rallies or sell offs—the ticks can clue a trader in which way the "out of the blue" move is likely to be.

6. Here we see the ticks make higher highs, forming an uptrend.

7. Yet when the ticks made higher highs, the YM made lower highs. This is a bearish divergence and a signal that the rally can be sold because there isn't enough "juice" to get things rolling.

There are rare days in which the markets rocket higher and keep on going, or gap down and keep on selling. On these days consistent extreme tick readings are generated, usually in

**F I G U R E   5.2**

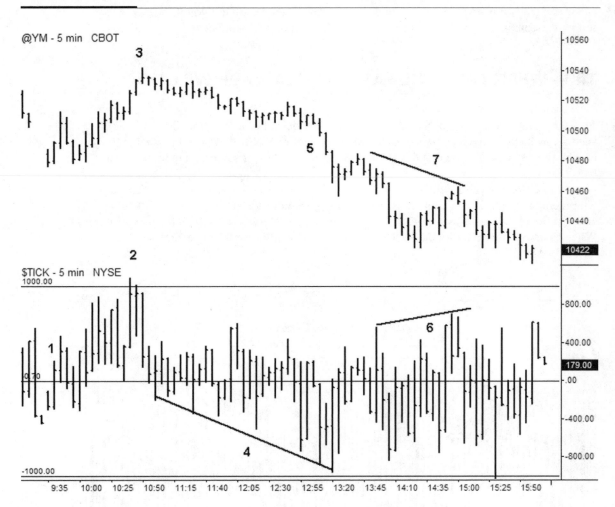

the neighborhood of 1200 to 1400. These consistent high readings are rare, but when they happen, I don't fight them. This brings me to my last rule regarding the ticks—this is something I take into account after 10:30 a.m. EST and watch throughout the day:

*When the ticks spend 90 percent of their time above zero*
*with repeated extreme high tick readings,*
*I ignore all day trading short setups and focus on longs.*
*When the ticks spend 90 percent of their time below zero*
*with repeated extreme low tick readings,*
*I ignore all day trading long setups and focus on shorts.*

The ticks are a great way to see what is going on "underneath" the price action. The charts can tell you if prices are going higher or lower, but they can't tell you if the buying or selling pressure is merely fleeting or unrelenting. Leave that job to the ticks.

## TIKI—WHEN ONLY THE FASTEST HEADS-UP WILL DO

The tiki (TradeStation symbol $TIKI) is similar to the ticks, but it measures the net upticks versus downticks on the 30 Dow stocks instead of the entire NYSE. Because this reading follows only 30 stocks, it is the first thing that fires off when a buy or sell program hits the markets. (See Fig. 5.3.)

Tiki charts are filled with noise and at first glance they look useless to watch. The key with them, however, is to set up alerts in the same fashion as the ticks. On the tiki, I set up alerts to fire off at +26, +28, and +30 on the upside, and −26, −28, and −30 on the downside. When buy or sell programs hit the markets, these alerts fire off instantly. In general, small pro-

**F I G U R E   5.3**

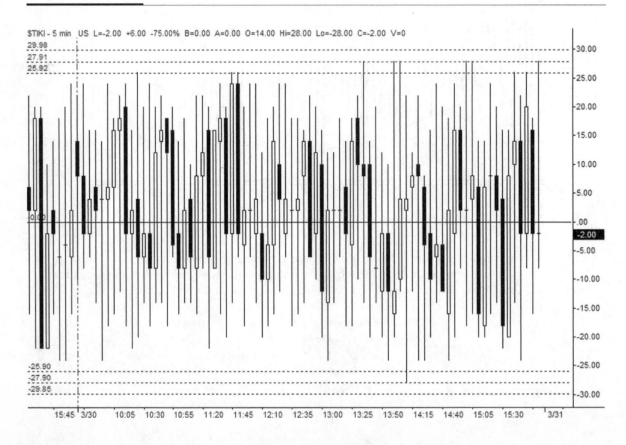

grams generate the 26 levels, medium programs hit the 28 levels, and massive programs hit the 30 level—meaning that all 30 Dow stocks are moving in the same direction. These readings are rare and highlight significant and sustained periods of buying or selling.

Surprisingly, I don't use these signals for any actionable exit strategies. If I'm short, and a +28 tiki level is generated, I'm probably wrong on the move, but I will wait until the ticks get to +800 before I exit. This is because a buy or sell program can be swift and over in a blink, causing the tiki movement to be erratic. This brings me to my first rule with the tiki:

*For exits, tiki readings are only the heads-up; ticks are the confirmation.*

Figure 5.4 shows the tikis on March 29, 2005. When comparing this to the ticks, the first thing that is evident is that the tiki looks like it's all over the place and hard to read. However, upon closer inspection, immense value can be found.

**F I G U R E   5.4**

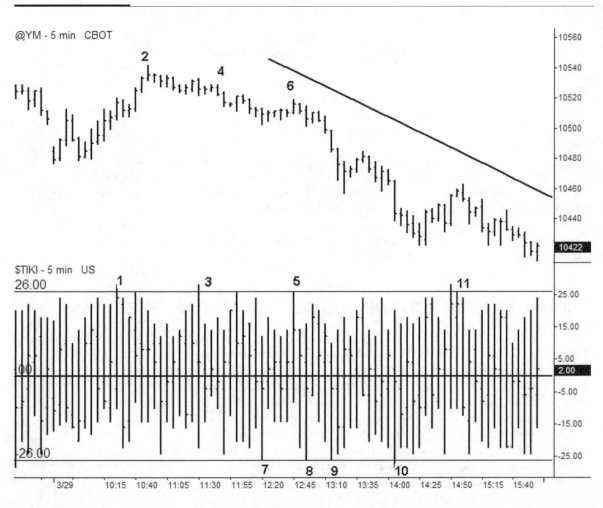

1. I always like to see what type of program hits the market first—a buy or sell program. This represents the first real "try" of the day, and I want to see how it pans out. In this chart, the first program of the day is a buy program that hits at 10:25 a.m. EST.

2. This sends the Dow to new highs.

3. The next program is also a buy, and it hits at 11:30 a.m.

4. However, this time the Dow does not make new highs and in fact continues to drift lower. This is a heads-up that "even a buy program" is not able to move the market higher.

5. There is another buy program at 12:45 p.m., and this one is after the first sell program hit the markets.

6. This buy program causes a small pop in the markets, but this buying dries up quickly.

7. At points 7, 8, 9, and 10 a series of sell programs hits the market, and each time a sell program hits, the markets make new lows. When this happens, the next opposing signal is a fading opportunity.

8. At point 11 there is an opposing signal with a buy program—an opportunity to go short.

This brings me to the next and last rule I use in following the tiki:

*If buy programs are driving the markets to new highs,*
*then the occasional sell program is a buying opportunity.*
*If sell programs are driving the markets to new lows,*
*then the occasional buy program is a shorting opportunity.*

I like to see where most of the programs are hitting. Are they mostly buy or mostly sell programs? This is important because most of the time markets are doing nothing. They are chopping back and forth. If most of the programs on the day are buy programs and these programs are pushing the markets up to new highs, then I want to use the quiet selling opportunities to get long. This way I'm getting into the market when it's quiet, *before the next move higher*, instead of chasing it higher. A good example of a setup that works well in this situation is the pivot plays I discuss in Chapter 7.

## TRIN—LIKE HIGH SCHOOL, IT'S ALL ABOUT PRESSURE

The trin (TradeStation symbol $TRIN), also known as the Arms Index named after its creator Richard W. Arms, measures the relative rate at which volume is flowing into advancing or declining stocks on the New York Stock Exchange. To calculate the trin, the following formula is utilized: (advancing issues/declining issues)/(advancing volume/declining volume). If more volume goes into advancing issues than declining issues, the Arms Index falls below 1.0. If more volume goes into declining stocks than advancing stocks, the Arms Index rises above 1.0. Most educational material on "how to use the trin" tells traders that "over 1.0 is bearish, so consider shorting, and under 1.0 is bullish, so consider buying." That statement is annoying and misleading, and it brings me to my first rule when using the trin:

*I don't care what the current reading is.*
*I only care about the current reading in relation to where it has been.*

In other words, what I care about is not the trin reading itself, but the trend of the trin. A reading of 1.50 might seem bearish, but if the reading started the day at 2.00 and we are now an hour into the trading day and 1.50 is the low, this is bullish. This means that volume is flowing into advancing issues and that there is sustained buying pressure in the markets. Conversely, a reading of 0.85 might seem bullish, but if the reading started the day at 0.45 and we are now two hours into the trading day and 0.85 is the high, this is bearish. This means that volume is flowing into declining issues and that there is sustained selling pressure in the markets. Let's take a look at Figure 5.5.

**F I G U R E   5.5**

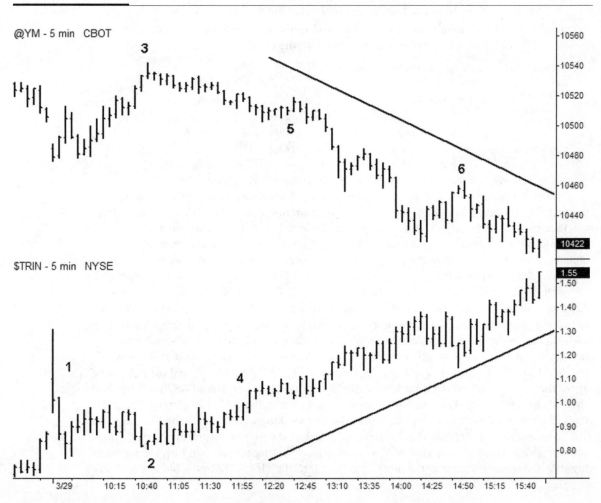

1. Figure 5.5 is a shot of the mini-sized Dow on March 29, 2005, the same day we used for the tick and the tiki. At point 1 we can see that the trin started the day near 1.40. The first 15–20 minutes are volatile as listed issues open on a delayed basis on the NYSE. Because of this, I dismiss the first five-minute bar but I like to note the opening levels based on the start of the second five-minute bar.

2. The trin settles in, and by 10:40 a.m. it is trading near its lows of the day at 0.81.

3. The YM hits its highs of the day in correlation with the low trin reading.

4. By 12:00 noon the trin has been in a steady uptrend, making new highs on the day (having discounted the first five-minute bar).

5. The YM is quiet and choppy, and it is trading in the middle of the day's range. However, even though the markets are quiet, the trin continues to rally. This is the key action I'm looking for—which way is the trin trending? A trend higher indicates that volume is flowing into declining issues, and this means that when the market actually does break, the odds are strong that it will be to the downside. As we can see on the chart, a little later in the day the market breaks down.

6. The YM tries to rally here, but it is in vain as the trin is staying in a nice uptrend. The YM soon rolls over and drifts down into the close.

This brings me to my next rule for the trin:

*If the trin is trending higher and making higher highs on the day,*
*I will ignore all long setups.*
*If the trin is trending lower and making lower lows on the day,*
*I will ignore all short setups.*

Let's take a look at another multi-day chart and the trin action (see Fig. 5.6):

Figure 5.6 shows a good overall representation of what various trin patterns mean. On the first day, February 22, 2005, the trin started off low. Some would call this bullish. Yet the trin then proceeded to rally all day long, and the Dow fell more than 120 points. The rule of "no longs on this type of day" serves a trader well. Conversely, if I am in a short and the trin is making new highs, I realize there is no reason to cover, as the eventual market break has a high probability of being in my favor.

On February 23, 2005, the trin started off high, but then proceeded to trend lower all day long. Although many traders will get caught up in the previous day's selling and use this initial strength as a shorting opportunity, they would realize the folly of this idea if they knew to follow the trend of the trin. With the trin heading lower, the markets stabilized early in the session, and a modest rally ensued. Because the trin continued to make lower lows on the day, I just focused on long setups. On February 24, 2005, the trin started off high once again then proceeded to spend the rest of the day grinding lower. Based on this, I ignored short setups on the day. The YM broke nicely higher later in the day. On February 25, 2005, the trin once again started off high and spent the day working lower. Finally on February 28, 2005, the trin started off high—but moved higher. While it was making new highs on the day, I ignored long setups and focused only on short setups. During the last two hours of the trading day, the trin reversed and the markets rallied into the close. The most bullish days are

**F I G U R E   5.6**

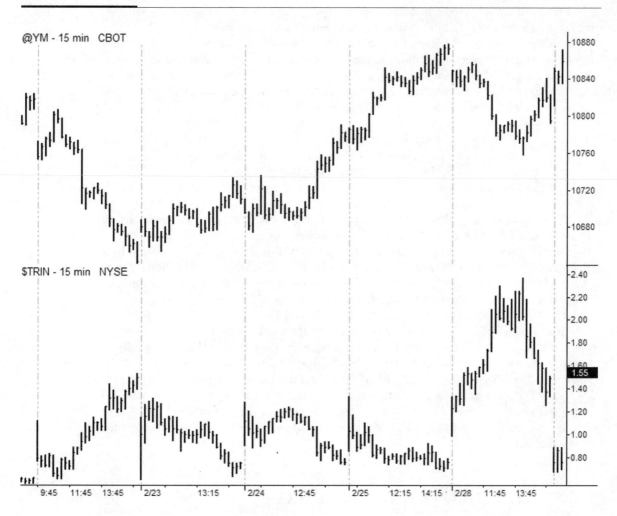

gap ups where the trin starts off low, say around 0.50, and stays at that level all day long. On this day it doesn't trend lower because it can only go so low—it won't make it to a zero reading. The sustained lower reading looks like a consolidation pattern on a chart, and is extremely bullish. On these types of days, I ignore all short setups, and a breakout to new highs is a buying opportunity.

The key with the trin is to watch to see if it is making new highs on the day or new lows on the day. Whenever this is happening, I just ignore the opposing setups. I've read where some people recommend to use levels such as 1.50 as "oversold" and start looking for a bounce, or 0.50 is "overbought" and start looking for a sell off. I am not a fan of oversold or overbought, and I generally ignore this with most indicators, and the trin is no exception intraday. The biggest rallies take place when the trin hovers under 0.50 all day long. Just because something is overbought doesn't mean its going to reverse. For reversals, I will look only at price action, and I discuss these types of setups in later chapters.

Although I'm not a big fan of overbought and oversold in general and I don't worry about overbought or oversold readings intraday on the trin, I will pay attention to where it closes on the day. This closing number actually is valuable when it comes to gauging an extreme overbought or oversold reading. These readings are rare and happen about a dozen times a year, and this brings me to my next rule when using the trin:

*If the trin closes above 2.0,*
*the market has an 80 percent chance of rallying the next day.*
*If the trin closes below 0.60,*
*the market has an 80 percent chance of selling off the next day.*

The moves the next day won't necessarily be big moves, but they will generally be opposing moves. I will keep this in mind as I'm viewing my setups the next trading day. If the previous day's close was over 2.0, then the next day I'm going to focus more on long setups and ignore short setups. Here's where it gets interesting—if after a 2.0 reading the markets can't rally the next trading day, then the markets are in deep trouble and are setting up for a major slide. This happened during the first week of July 2004 (see Fig. 5.7).

On this daily chart of the trin and the mini-sized Dow, the trin closed on July 1, 2004 with a reading of 2.80 (point 1). The next day the markets tried to rally early in the session but ultimately collapsed and ended lower on the day. This is always an ominous sign, and the Dow went on to lose 673 points before bottoming out on August 6, 2004. On July 6, 2004, the trin closed at 2.12 (point 3) and the Dow managed to rally the next day (point 4) but the bulls' moment of glory was short lived. This same scenario unfolded during the second trading day of 2005 on January 4, when the trin closed at 2.53. The next day, the markets couldn't rally, and they ended up selling off 410 points through the rest of the month.

## TRINQ—THE TRIN FOR THE NASDAQ

The trinq (TradeStation symbol $TRINQ) is just like the trin, except that it's for the Nasdaq. The same rules apply here—all I'm interested in is the trend of the trinq.

Figure 5.8 is the same chart we were looking at on March 29, 2005, but I've added the trinq as well as the Nasdaq. With the trinq going higher, the Nasdaq is going lower. In general I place more weight on the trin, but I like to see what is happening in the Nasdaq as well. There are times when the trinq will be the leading mover, making new highs or new lows before the trin. On days where the trinq is mixed and the trin is trending, I will pay more attention to the trin. The strongest moves in the market occur when both the trin and the trinq are moving more or less in alignment.

**F I G U R E   5.7**

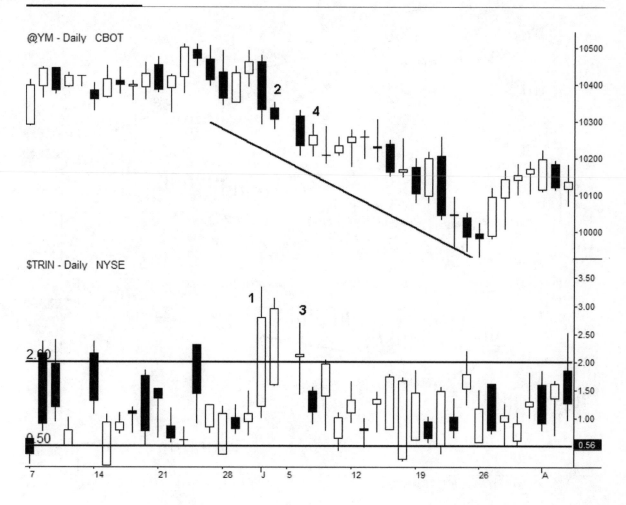

## PUT/CALL RATIO—THE KEYS TO THE KINGDOM

As a trader, what would you give to be able to know what the rest of the market participants are doing at any given time? If a broker told me he or she could provide me that information each and every day, I'd be so appreciative I might even let him or her charge me $25 a round turn for an E-mini futures contract. While a secret report is not going to magically appear in your in-box, the put/call ratio (TradeStation symbol $WPCVA and referred to during the rest of this section as PC) is as close to actually having this information as a trader is going to get.

**F I G U R E   5.8**

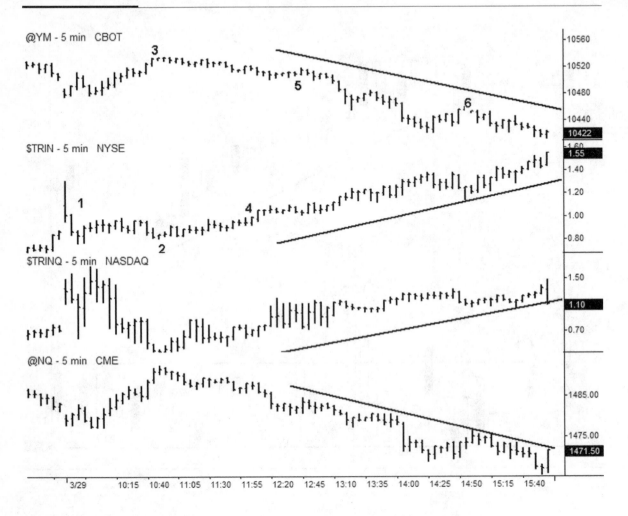

The PC ratio measures how many put options are bought versus call options. The formula is very simple to calculate—take the volume for puts and divide by the volume for calls. (For anyone who is not familiar with options, buying a put is making a bet that the market is going to fall, and buying a call is making a bet that the market is going to rise.) If there are 50,000 puts sold and 100,000 calls, the ratio is 50,000/100,000, or 0.5. If there are 125,000 puts sold and 85,000 calls, the ratio is 1.47.

There are three main PC ratios that are generated throughout the day—the equity PC ratio, the index PC ratio, and the combined equity/index PC ratio. The equity PC ratio is generally very low, which reflects a retail crowd that has a tendency to favor the long side (more call buying). The index PC ratio is usually very high (more put buying), which reflects an institutional mindset that wants to stay hedged for any unexpected move lower. The combined equity/index PC ratio reflects both of these groups and gives a trader the best gauge of what the overall market participants are thinking, and, more importantly, where they are placing their bets. It is this combined equity/index PC ratio that I watch during the trading day.

To illustrate how I use this indicator, let's assume that the market is made up of exactly 100 participants. Let's further assume that all 100 of these people are bearish on the markets, and because of this prevalent feeling, they have established short positions in stocks, ETFs, and index futures, as well as through the buying of puts. With all 100 market participants bearish and now short, a very interesting turn of events takes place—there is nobody left to sell. With nobody left to sell, the markets don't have any downward pressure, and they start to drift higher. This drifting eventually hits the first set of stop orders placed in the market by the 100 market participants who are short. Within any given group of traders, some will be using tight stops, some medium stops, and some wide stops. The group of tight stops gets hit first, and this generates fresh buying pressure in the form of short covering that drives the markets higher, right into the next range of stops. This next series of stops kicks off yet another short covering spree, which, once triggered, drives the markets even higher into the next range of stops, and so on until all the stops are taken out.

At this point the 100 market participants get bullish, and start buying stocks and index futures, as well as call options. Once they all scramble to establish their positions, a very curious thing takes place—there is nobody left to buy. With nobody left to buy, the markets begin to drift lower and take out the first set of tight stops, which in turn creates enough selling pressure to drive the markets down to the next set of stops, and so forth. It's a vicious cycle.

Obviously this is a simplified scenario, and in the real world not every single market participant is going to be bullish or bearish at exactly the same time. However, the amount and intensity of bullish and bearish bias does fluctuate regularly, and this shift in attitude causes markets to move in a fashion related to the "oversimplified scenario" just described. This brings me to my first rule regarding the PC ratio:

> *If the combined equity/index PC ratio gets over 1.0 intraday,*
> *I will ignore all short setups and start looking at long setups.*

A PC ratio of over 1.0 represents extreme bearishness and put buying, and, as a result of the scenario described above, places a floor in the markets. Not an immediate floor. The ratio doesn't go to 1.0 and suddenly the markets stop declining and then immediately rally. It's a process, and a visible support level does take shape because of the simple fact that there are too many bears in the market—and lots of buy stops sitting overhead, just waiting to be taken out. These 1.0 readings usually happen when the markets have fallen for a number of days in a row, or bad earnings or economic data hit the tape, suddenly infecting many market participants with a bearish outlook. In fact, many times a market will continue falling until the PC ratio gets over 1.0. The opposite extreme is also true, which brings me to my next rule:

*If the combined PC ratio falls under 0.60 intraday,*
*I will ignore all long setups and start looking at short setups.*

A PC ratio of under 0.60 represents extreme call buying and puts a ceiling in the markets. This represents a scenario in which there are too many bulls and very few people left to buy. Now there are lots of sell stops sitting beneath current levels, just waiting to be hit. This usually happens after the markets have rallied for a number of days in a row, or seemingly great earnings or economic news hit the tape. Also, people who have missed the move start chasing in the fear of being left behind. In fact, many times a market will continue rallying until the PC ratio gets under 0.60.

Figure 5.9 is a 15-minute chart that shows the mini-sized Dow overlaid on top of the equity/index PC ratio. On February 22, 2005, the PC ratio stayed low most of the day, dipping

**F I G U R E   5.9**

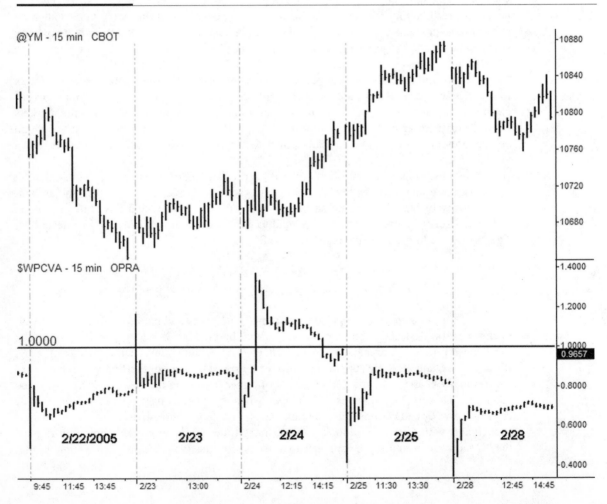

below 0.60. This represents a bullish outlook and the buying of stocks, index futures, and calls. This placed a lot of stops below the markets, and the Dow subsequently sold off over 120 points to clear them out. On February 23, the PC ratio spent a little time over 1.0, which represents a bearish outlook, the establishment of short positions, and the buying of puts—and the placing of many stops above the market. This was enough to kick start a modest rally into the close as the overhead stops provided the fuel for the market rally. On February 24 the PC worked itself to an extreme high reading, while the markets gapped down and stayed under pressure early in the session. However, with so many people bearish and with so many buy stops sitting above the markets, the market had little choice but to rally. On February 25 the PC started the day low but quickly rallied and stayed near 0.80 for most of the day. On February 28, the PC started off low and spent nearly an hour under 0.60. This means that everyone was excited and buying calls because of the rally on February 25, and now, with so many sell stops in the market resulting from all the fresh long positions, the markets drifted lower and took them out.

To reiterate, the main thing I'm looking for in the PC ratio is whether or not it is at an extreme range. This indicator doesn't spend a lot of time in the extreme ranges, but they are hit enough to have an impact on the markets. What about when the PC is not generating an extreme reading?

The PC actually spends a lot of time in what I call "neutral" territory. This is between .070 and 0.90. During these periods, the PC is generally a nonfactor in my trading decisions. However, there is another aspect to the PC that I will watch during the day, and that is the "trend" of the PC. And this brings me to my next rule:

*If the market is rallying, I want to see the PC rallying to confirm the move.*
*If the market is falling, I want to see the PC falling to confirm the move.*

If the PC is rallying, this means that more people are getting bearish, and they are shorting stock, shorting indexes, and buying puts. This means people don't believe in the rally, and they are using the strength to establish short positions. Little do they know that their act of shorting merely adds fuel to the next leg higher, as the market now has a series of stop orders sitting overhead, just waiting to be ripped through. If, however, the market is rallying and the PC is falling, this is because people believe in the rally and are chasing it—a sign that it has run its course. Naturally, the opposite is also true. If the market is falling and the PC is falling, this means that more people are bullish and they are using the market weakness to buy stocks and buy calls. They are merely providing fuel for the market to continue on its downward path in the form of new sell orders placed below the market. If the market is falling and the PC is rallying, this means that people are getting scared and are chasing the market lower—a sign that the decline is about to end (see Fig. 5.10).

1. On March 29, 2005, the mini-sized Dow futures gap down and try to push lower.
2. The PC rallies as people scramble to establish short positions and buy puts.
3. This increases put buying. Even though it doesn't push the PC above 1.0, it is enough to get the markets to reverse course and take out the overhead stop orders.
4. Traders view this rally in the YM as a positive thing, and they start buying calls as the market pulls back. This call buying intensifies, driving the PC ratio to under 0.65.

**F I G U R E   5.10**

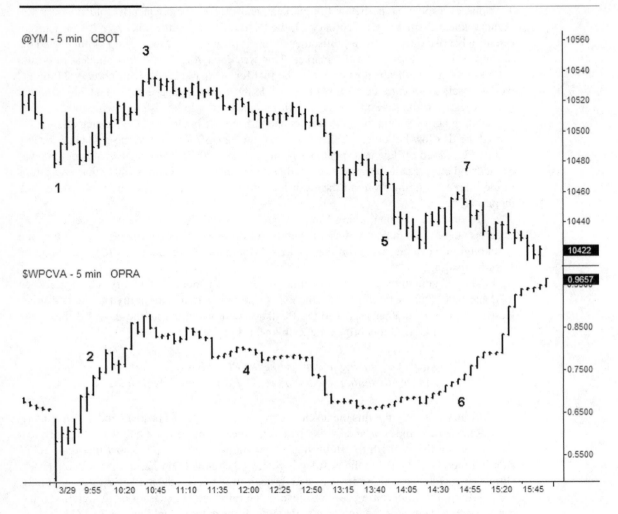

5. With the aggressive call buying, the YM drifts lower for a few hours, and then
   cracks, falling over 120 points.

6. With the decline, traders start to worry that they are going to miss the down move
   and they start shorting stock and buying puts. This drives the PC ratio to its highs
   on the day.

7. Although the markets don't rally into the close, they stabilize, as a high PC ratio
   starts to establish a floor in the markets.

Figure 5.11 shows the markets the next day. With the markets closing near their lows
on March 29, people get bearish the next morning, and on the gap up they start shorting
aggressively and buying puts for the "inevitable" move lower. The PC ratio gets very high as

## FIGURE 5.11

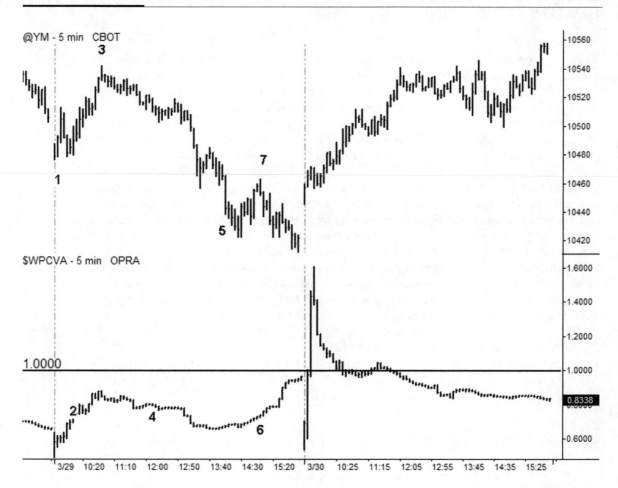

the traders race to get positioned on the short side. How does the market respond? By closing over 140 points higher than that of the previous day's close.

I do want to point out that I largely discount the PC ratio until after 10:00 a.m. EST. There are a lot of listed stocks that take time to get opened, as well as a lot of overnight option orders that take time to get executed. This causes a lot of erratic movement in the PC ratio. Also, I ignore the reading on options expiration day, as it tends to get out of whack with all the specific options-related activity.

The PC ratio is a valuable intraday trading tool. As of this writing, there are many data feeds that do not carry this indicator. On TradeStation, you have to be permissioned for "opra" in order to receive the PC ratio. For example, while it is available on TradeStation, it is currently not available on eSignal. More quote vendors will supply this information if their customers ask for it. Also, this information is available for free at www.cboe.com in its "Market Data" section. These numbers are updated every half-hour.

# SECTOR SORTER LIST—
# BEAUTY IS NOT ONLY SKIN DEEP

The sector sorter list (SSL) is a simple tool I use to gauge what is going on "beneath the indexes." I list all the key sectors and have them sorted automatically every few seconds through the trading day based on their Net % Change. This tells me at a glance which sectors are leading the markets higher or lower, and this brings me to my first rule regarding the sector sorter list:

*Any move without the banks (BKX), brokers (XBD),*
*and semiconductors (SOX) is suspect and most likely will not last.*

On April 1, 2005, the only sectors up on the day, for the most part, were energy, housing, and gold. (See Fig. 5.12.) One of the worst sectors of the day was the semiconductors, and not far behind them were brokers and banks. I like knowing where these sectors are in the mix for three reasons: First, the giant money center banks represent the biggest (or almost biggest, depending on current prices) market capitalization sector in the market. The markets need participation from this index if they hope to make any headway. Second, brokers are a great market proxy. As go the brokers, so go the markets. Third, everyone participates in the semiconductor stocks. They have a strong following by both retail and institutional investors alike. If I see a decline with these three sectors leading the way lower, I am confident that the decline is going to last. The reverse is also true.

The other way I like to use this list is when the markets are quiet and choppy. Often there are stealth moves in the markets. This happens when the overall indexes are restricted in a tight range, but underneath the surface a couple of key sectors are deteriorating or firming. This often is not picked up in the index itself. This brings me to my next rule:

*During these quiet periods in the market, the more sectors that go red,*
*the greater the odds are that, when the market finally does break, it will be to the downside.*
*Conversely, the more sectors that go green, the greater the odds are that,*
*when the market finally does break, it will be to the upside.*

Like a doctor's relationship to a patient's medical chart, the sector sorter list helps a trader gauge the overall health of the current market environment.

# THIS IS HOW YOU KNOW
# IT'S GOING TO BE A CHOPPY DAY

One of the most frustrating things for traders is dealing with a tight range, choppy day in the stock indexes. Choppy days occur when the stocks indexes spend most of the day trading in a slow, narrow range, providing minimal volatility. Most traders don't realize that the trading is choppy until about halfway through the day. They can tell by looking at the chart, and they

**FIGURE** 5.12

| | Symbol | Last | Net Chg | Net %Chg ▽ | Description |
|---|---|---|---|---|---|
| 1 | $OSX.X | 142.28 | 2.97 | 2.13% | Phlx Oil Service Sector Index |
| 2 | $XNG.X | 333.76 | 6.86 | 2.10% | Amex Natural Gas Index |
| 3 | $XOI.X | 870.23 | 17.75 | 2.08% | Amex Oil Index |
| 4 | $HGX.X | 481.75 | 3.21 | 0.67% | Phlx Housing Sector Index |
| 5 | $UTY.X | 393.85 | 1.86 | 0.47% | PHLX Utility Sector Index |
| 6 | $GSO.X | 157.45 | 0.61 | 0.39% | Gsti Software Index |
| 7 | $XAU.X | 94.01 | 0.26 | 0.28% | PHLX Gold And Silver Sector In |
| 8 | $GIN.X | 155.94 | 0.01 | 0.01% | Gsti Internet Index |
| 9 | $BMX.X | 111.79 | 0.00 | -0.00% | Phlx Computer Box Maker Sector |
| 10 | $HMO.X | 1357.03 | -0.81 | -0.06% | Morgan Stanley Healthcare Payo |
| 11 | $DFX.X | 261.06 | -0.24 | -0.09% | Phlx Defense Sector Index |
| 12 | $INX.X | 183.89 | -0.82 | -0.44% | CBOE Internet Index |
| 13 | $XCI.X | 672.76 | -4.10 | -0.61% | Amex Computer Technology Index |
| 14 | $GSV.X | 132.64 | -0.84 | -0.63% | Gsti Services Index |
| 15 | $IIX.X | 146.07 | -1.01 | -0.69% | Amex Interactive Week Internet |
| 16 | $CYC.X | 741.75 | -5.15 | -0.69% | Morgan Stanley Cyclical Index |
| 17 | $MSH.X | 452.24 | -3.19 | -0.70% | Morgan Stanley High-Technology |
| 18 | $BKX.X | 95.84 | -0.71 | -0.74% | PHLX  KBW Bank Sector Index |
| 19 | $TRAN | 3686.61 | -29.36 | -0.79% | Dow Jones Transportation Index |
| 20 | $DRG.X | 312.31 | -2.53 | -0.80% | AMEX Pharmaceutical Index |
| 21 | $IXF.X | 2634.55 | -22.28 | -0.84% | Nasdaq Financial-100 Index |
| 22 | $GHA.X | 301.12 | -2.69 | -0.89% | Gsti Hardware Index |
| 23 | $CMR.X | 572.08 | -5.73 | -0.99% | Morgan Stanley Consumer Index |
| 24 | $XBD.X | 144.12 | -1.52 | -1.04% | Amex Securities Broker/dealer |
| 25 | $NWX.X | 202.80 | -2.18 | -1.06% | AMEX Networking Index |
| 26 | $BTK.X | 486.83 | -6.02 | -1.22% | AMEX Biotechnology Index |
| 27 | $GSM.X | 203.35 | -2.82 | -1.37% | Gsti Semiconductor Index |
| 28 | $SOX.X | 411.22 | -5.77 | -1.38% | Phlx Semiconductor Sector Inde |
| 29 | $RLX.X | 424.02 | -6.16 | -1.43% | S&p Retail Index |
| 30 | $XAL.X | 47.96 | -0.99 | -2.02% | AMEX Airline Index |

TradeStation RadarScreen - Sectors

Sectors  Dow  Futures  Internals  SSF

can tell by the amount of losing trades they have taken. In addition, there are specific trade setups that work great in choppy markets. If a trader relentlessly pursues a setup that works best in trending markets, they are going to get killed. Two of my favorite choppy market strategies are described in Chapters 7 and 9 (pivots and tick fades).

My goal is to identify what type of market it is going to be as early as possible in the trading day. To do this, I set up a five-minute chart of the E-mini S&P 500 futures, and the only indicator I place on this chart is volume. Once this is done, I place a horizontal line at the 10,000 level on the volume chart (or as close to 10,000 as I can place it).

In Figure 5.13 we can see that the trading during the first hour had the vast majority of volume bars going over 10,000. This means that over 10,000 contracts were traded every five minutes. The range on this day was wide, in the neighborhood of 14 points (or 140 Dow points). In Figure 5.14 we can see that volume was at or under this 10,000 market right from the opening bell, with one spike higher that took place in response to a news report. The resulting range for most of the trading day was confined to between 1209.00 and 1206.00, a range of three points (or 30 Dow points). This brings me to my rule for watching this volume chart:

> *If the first six bars on a five-minute ES chart have most of the volume*
> *at or well under 10,000 contracts, expect a choppy, tight range session.*
> *If the first six bars on a five-minute ES chart have most of the volume*
> *at or well above 10,000 contracts, expect a more volatile session with better trends.*

**F I G U R E   5.13**

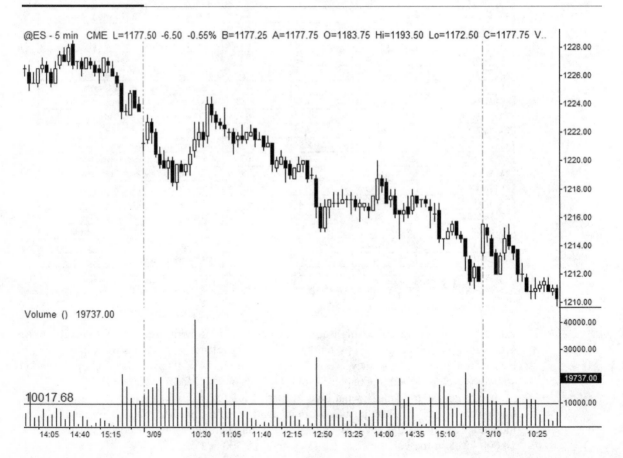

**F I G U R E   5.14**

This is a simple way to determine early on if the markets are going to be choppy or more volatile on the day. This allows traders to choose the setups that are more appropriate for these types of markets early in the day.

## PUTTING IT ALL TOGETHER—SIZING UP THE TRADING DAY FROM THE OPENING BELL

It is easy to get overwhelmed by too much data, and the key for reading all of these data is to do it in such a way that your brain can take in the information as quickly and as efficiently as possible. I do this by looking at this data in a certain order, in two columns, top to bottom, left to right.

Figure 5.15 shows how I tie all this information into a single screen. The trin and the trinq are in the upper left, and these are what I look at first. Then my eyes go below this to the PC ratio, which is what I look at second. After this I look at the ticks, which are at the bottom left of the screen. From here my eyes jump to the upper right and to the sector sorter list. Finally, I look at the tiki. I don't even have to look at a chart to know that the market has been selling off steadily all day.

Figure 5.16 shows these key indicators against the backdrop of a strong market. At a glance I can see that the trin and trinq are trending lower, and that the PC ratio started off well at over 1.0 on the day. I can see that the ticks are spending a lot of quality time above zero, and that most of the sectors are in positive territory. I can also see, with the tiki, that there have been a lot more buy programs than sell programs. On this type of day, I want to focus on long setups and ignore short setups.

› **F I G U R E   5.15**

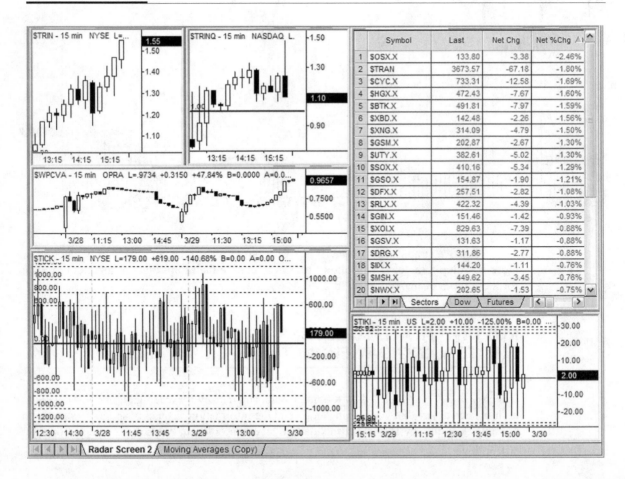

## F I G U R E   5.16

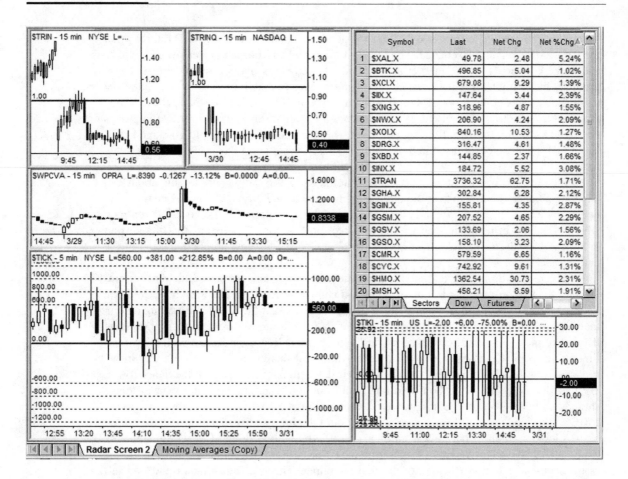

In addition to being able to get a solid feeling for whether the market has upside or downside pressure, this will also help a trader understand when the markets are in "chop mode." This will happen when these different indicators conflict with one another. For example, the trin is making new highs (bearish), but the ticks are spending all their time above zero (bullish). One of my favorite ways to see whether or not we have a choppy market is also the most simple. I look at the sector sorter list, and if about half the sectors are green and half the sectors are red, well, it can't get more neutral than that.

I don't include the ES five-minute volume chart on this layout simply because there is not enough room. I watch this on another screen.

I created this layout in TradeStation. You can recreate it by looking at Figures 5.15 and 5.16, or by going to www.tradethemarkets.com and downloading a copy complete with all the audio alerts.

# LISTENING IN ON THE FLOOR—THE VALUE OF PIT NOISE

There are feeds available from people who are standing just outside of the S&P futures pit at the Chicago Mercantile Exchange. They will sit there and call out the current bid/ask prices and make comments on the market action. I like to have this playing quietly in the background. One of my trading partners, Hubert Senters, likes to play it loud as he pays attention to all the nuances coming out of the pit. Hubert introduced me to pit noise and the first few months I listened to it, the noise drove me crazy and I hated it. So I turned it off. After 3 days I realized I was struggling in figuring out which way the market was going to go—and I realized I had subconsciously taken in the pit noise. These days I won't day trade the stock index futures without it. Here is how it works and how I use it:

First off, it's important to understand what the people in the pits are talking about. All day long a trader is going to hear the bid/ask being quoted, and it typically goes like this, "six twenty by a half, six twenty by a half," and so on. This is a quote for the big S&P contract, which is quoted in tenths instead of quarters like the E-minis. This means that the current bid/ask is 1136.20 by 1136.50. The quotes just focus on the last few numbers instead of the entire price.

The person doing the talking will frequently refer to "paper versus local." Paper coming into the market means it is a retail order and can be placed by brokers such as Goldman Sachs, Merrill Lynch, and so forth. "Local market" means that the locals are trading among themselves; this happens when the action is slow and the volume is light. Hubert and I have listened to many pit broadcasters and by far the best one is Ben Lichtenstein with www.real-timefutures.com. He absolutely loves what he does and this comes across each day in his broadcasts. In July 2005, Hubert and I held a four-day seminar in Chicago at the Sears Tower. We had Ben come in for an hour and talk about how he reads the tape and what listeners should key in on. Then, the next day, we took the group of 50 seminar attendees down to the CME so they could watch Ben in action calling out the pit noise live. They saw exactly what he was looking at and what he was calling out and why he was doing it. It was an amazing experience, and we received permission from the CME to bring in a film crew and capture the floor event—in addition to filming the entire seminar. This was amazing in and of itself because the CME is notorious for not allowing film crews on their floor, and I have thanked them profusely for letting us capture the event on film. Of course, the guys in the pit gave Ben hell because he led the floor tours—and part of that was captured on tape as well. By the time this book reaches the shelves, there will be a DVD available of the entire seminar, and a separate DVD available that focuses on Ben, pit noise, and the visit to the CME. For people who attended the seminar, it was the experience of their trading lives. We now work closely with Ben. Anyone who wants to sign up for his service, you can mention that you were referred by me and receive a 40 percent discount from the price listed on his website. I have no financial ties with Ben's subscription business. I just love his service and am more than happy to tell people about it. Let's look at more things to key in on when listening to pit noise.

A "thin top" means that there are not a lot of bids at these levels—look for the market rally to fail. If Ben mentions a scale buyer or scale seller, I pay attention to what the seller is doing and at what levels.

When Ben mentions a "top tener" this means one of the 10 biggest guys in the pit is doing something. Once in a while you will hear that a "top tener" is stuck short, and these provide great opportunities to jump in on a trade as they are forced to cover hundreds of the big S&P contracts to get out of their position. This is information you can't learn from watching a chart.

I also like to listen to the overall noise level. Is it quiet and slow, or loud and fast? If the noise explodes, it is almost like the ticks reaching the +1000 level. This level of activity is unsustainable, and the markets will reverse. If the sound is quiet and then it gradually gets louder, I will go in the direction of the market until the noise "explodes," and then I'll get out.

My favorite way to use the noise from the pit is to listen and figure out if the noise is louder on the up moves or the down moves. If a market is rallying, and the pit noise is loud, and then the market pulls back and the pit noise is quiet—this is a crystal clear signal that the momentum is higher and I will aggressively buy all pullbacks on these days. The reversal is also true. Once I got used to this, I found it very hard to look at a chart without having this "pit noise indicator" in the background.

There are many other ways to use pit noise. If someone is above or below the market with size and the locals fill it, go in the direction of that move. This means the locals are pushing the markets instead of fading the markets.

If the pit moderator tells you what the low is and that low is below the lows of the day you see on your charts, the market is going lower and is about to make new lows on the day. If the pit moderator says look for a stop run at 1136, pay attention to that number if you are below it.

The most important thing with pit noise is not to get caught up in the excitement. It is easy to think this is the Holy Grail when you first get it. But it's not. It's just another tool. Traders who get caught up in the excitement of the pit buy the highs and sell the lows, just like any other amateur.

It will take about two months of solid listening to get used to it. After you get used to it, it's hard to trade without it. We put together the DVD to shorten the learning curve, and on it we explain in a lot more detail about how to use this tool. Information on the DVD is available at www.tradethemarkets.com.

It is important to realize that the markets spend the majority of the day consolidating and resting. Traders who wait for a move and then have to chase it will always be at a disadvantage with traders who get in before the move takes place. The way to do this is to watch these internals and look for clues as to the path of least resistance. When the markets are quiet, get positioned for the next move in this direction. Once the move takes place, the amateurs will chase it and you can sell your position to them.

# Two

## Specific Intraday and Swing Trading Setups for Futures, Stocks, Options, and Forex

*Be not afraid of going slowly;*
*be afraid only of standing still.*

CHINESE PROVERB

CHAPTER

# THE OPENING GAP: THE FIRST AND HIGHEST PROBABILITY PLAY OF THE DAY

## TRADING WITHOUT A SPECIFIC SETUP IN MIND IS LIKE HIKING IN THE AMAZON WITHOUT A COMPASS

Before we jump into the first of the setups, the opening gap play, I want to quickly review one absolute truth about this business. That truth is as follows—when it comes to trading for a living, all investors fall into one of three categories:

1. Those who have a system they follow each and every day.
2. Those who are developing a system and are on the lookout for the Holy Grail.
3. Those who never believed in utilizing a specific system and trade just on instinct— and are still explaining to their spouse how they lost all their trading capital.

The point of this, of course, is to emphasize the importance of facing each trading day with a game plan and of establishing a trade setup from a three-pronged approach. In addition to the actual setup, there also needs to be a foundation from which to operate the setup. This foundation consists of the following: the trading methodology, the money management technique, and the knowledge of the best markets to trade for that particular setup. In other words, it's a lot more than just "what's the entry?" Do traders scale into a trade or go all in? Do they scale out or go all out? Is it better to use a tight stop and bigger size, or a wider stop and smaller size? Does this trade work better on the mini-sized Dow or the euro? Each market is unique. Each setup is unique. Each timeframe is unique. Without these additional data, traders are destined to fail, and are only kidding themselves into thinking they can do this for a living. They may have a lot of fun for a few months or a year, and they may get an incredible high out of a great trade, but it won't last over the long haul. The idea is to create a situation that allows a person to do this for a living—each and every day.

This section focuses on a series of setups for the active trader, and is a collection of strategies that I currently use in my own trading. Specific markets are highlighted with exact entry, exit, and stop loss levels, focusing mostly on intraday setups. Swing trading setups are also discussed, and these are noted as such. In general, any setup that is used on the stock index futures can also be used on individual stocks. Exceptions to this guideline are noted. I like to use day-trading strategies in one account and swing-trading strategies in another account. This keeps everything separate and easy to track. I chose to show setups that had a successful resolution in order to demonstrate how to manage the exits on these setups. In instances where these setups get stopped out, and that does happen, that is an easy exit to manage—the stop was hit. As a trader, it is important to realize that not every trade will work out. It is quite possible to get stopped out two or three times in a row before catching a successful move. This is a normal part of trading, and it is important that a trader not get frustrated. A typical scenario I've witnessed with traders is that they get stopped out of a setup, and then hesitate to take the next one, which of course turns out to be a winner. Or they get stopped out of a setup, so the next time it occurs they take profits too fast. The point of this is that a trader needs to become like a machine and just do the setups. On any given day, I will take five intraday setups. One of these will get stopped out, two will be scratched, and two will be winners. On days where my first three trades are winners I will usually stop for the rest of the day and book my gains.

I utilize a variety of specific setups in my daily trading routine. I started off trading stocks and stock options, so most of the setups focus on some aspect of the stock market, whether it's through individual stocks or the mini-stock index futures. There are also setups in other markets I discuss, particularly in the euro and bonds, as well as some forex setups. Some of these I developed myself, and some of these have been developed by other people whom I trade with. The purpose of this section is to give you specific setups that you can utilize the next trading day. It should also give you a blueprint for developing and tweaking your own setups. For me, the biggest difference in my trading occurred when I learned to ignore my brain and just focus on a handful of good setups. Once I learned the setups, the next challenge was to have the discipline to follow them the same way, each and every time. I did this by recording my trading activity for over a year and focusing on the results *for each setup.* If I deviated from the setup, if I tried to outthink it and got out too early or in too late, I noted this in my data and marked it as an "impulse play." After a while I noticed that these impulse plays didn't make me any money. I saw the light, so to speak, and suddenly my trading focus took a dramatic shift. Instead of focusing on the potential gains of a trade or worrying about missing a move, I focused on executing a flawless setup. That is the key between a trader who can do this for a living and a trader who lives a life of quiet frustration. It is very hard to do. But it's the difference between life and death.

It's like quitting smoking. Either people choose to light up another cigarette or they do not. They take it one day at a time. For each day they don't light up, the better the odds they will never smoke again. It is no different in trading. For each day traders can actually be totally disciplined and follow their setups exactly as planned—even if it means standing aside when the market is racing away without them—the better the odds they will make it in this business. If you want thrills, go to Disneyland.

Although I can't stand over your shoulder and help you with your discipline, I can show you the setups that I use to trade for a living. I have loosely organized these in the order that I look at them throughout the trading day. As you try these out on your own, you will find that you naturally gravitate toward some rather than others. Key in on this, as a trader will tend to move toward setups and markets that seem to fit their personality. Let's jump right in with the first setup and one of my favorites—the opening gap play.

## NOT ALL GAPS ARE CREATED EQUAL

I find gap plays to be the best way to start off my trading day. Not only are they the first trades of the stock market session, but, more importantly, they can also tell a person a lot about the upcoming market action for the day. Because of this, I spend more time talking about this setup than the others.

Gaps are contrarian plays, or "fade plays" as I like to call them. Opening gaps create a lot of excitement and emotion in the market participants, and I like to step in and take the opposite side of this emotion. The play is completely against the crowd, which I like, and is one of the lowest-risk trades available. What exactly is a gap? *Gaps* occur when the next day's regular cash session opening price is greater or lower than the previous day's regular cash session close, creating a "gap" in price levels on the charts, similar to that space we see each night between David Letterman's two front teeth. It is important to note that traders will not see this gap on their charts unless they specifically set up a "gap" chart. With a 24-hour chart, traders will not see the gaps. This is discussed in more detail shortly.

When it comes to gaps, not all markets are created equal. Gaps in "single item" markets do not act the same as gaps in "multi-item" markets. Examples of single-item markets include bonds, currencies, grains, and individual stocks. These gaps typically fill at some point, but not necessarily on the same day. For this play, I'm specifically interested in gaps that have a high probability of filling on the same day they are created. For these single-item markets, a news item controls the entire order flow for that day, instead of affecting just a small portion of an entire index.

This is especially true of individual stocks. Individual stocks are like politicians, in that each day they can produce a fresh skeleton from the proverbial closet. Earnings announcements, corporate scandals, and insider deals can create gaps in price that never get filled. Ken Lay and Bernie Ebbers certainly wish their Enron and Worldcom stock would fill their overhead gaps. Unfortunately, the odds of this happening are about the same as getting the European Union to agree on a unified constitution. In other words, it's never going to happen. Because of the unpredictable nature of individual stocks, they make poor candidates for gap fills. The exception to this is gaps on individual stocks that are gapping with the market and not on any particular news. How does a person tell this? If a stock is gapping 10 cents for each one-point move on the S&Ps and there isn't any news on that stock, then that stock can be played as a gap play. For example, if KLAC (KLA Tencor Corp) gaps up 42 cents and the S&Ps are gapping up 4.00 points and there isn't any specific news on KLAC, then it can be played as a gap play. It's just moving with the overall market.

As compared with single-item markets, a multi-item market such as the E-mini S&Ps or the mini-sized Dow futures, as well as their equivalent ETFs (exchange traded funds) via the Spiders (SPY) and Diamonds (DIA), make great candidates for gap plays. This is because there are individual components of these indexes that will respond differently to various news items. Good news for oil companies is bad news for transportation companies. Good news for defense stocks can be bad news for travel-related stocks, and so on. This means that, although the market may gap up on a news item, there will be individual stocks within the index that will either ignore the news or sell off on the news. This weighing down, coupled with an initial pullback in the strong issues that are gapping up, weighs down the entire index, creating an opportunity for the market to fill its gap. In addition, many fund managers watch the open gaps. They've been doing this a long time and know that the markets hate to leave "messy charts" in the form of open gaps. If the markets gap up, they will generally wait to start committing to the long side until the market has pulled back and filled its gap. In this way it is also like a self-fulfilling prophecy.

What about the Nasdaq or the Russell? I've watched these markets as well, and although they do fill their gaps a large percentage of the time, that percentage is lower than the Dow and the S&Ps. In the end, my favorite gap plays are in the mini-futures and ETFs representing the Dow and the S&P 500.

## The Magic of Premarket Volume

The great thing about gaps is that they are like an open window, and like all windows, at some point they are going to be closed. The key, then, is to be able to accurately predict when the day's gap (window) is going to be filled (closed). What is as important as analyzing the gap itself is analyzing the *market conditions* that produce the gap. The reason for the gap is immaterial. Upside earnings surprises, terrorist threats, takeover announcements, economic reports—each morning the markets are bombarded with news. It's not the actual news, but how the markets respond to that news that is important. To understand how the markets are really reacting to the news, all a person has to do is look at the premarket volume. In addition to news gaps, which are more or less fishing expeditions, there are also professional gaps. Professional gaps are designed to keep the retail investor out of the market. These occur when the Dow gaps up 100 points and then trades in a tight range for the rest of the day. The move essentially happened before the market opened. The professionals who were positioned for the move benefit, while the average retail investor is left with nothing and no opportunity to participate in the move. Again, premarket volume can tell a trader if the gap is going to be a professional breakaway event or is going to lead to price action that has a high probability of filling the gap on the very same day it was created. A professional gap with high premarket volume can take weeks to get filled. Much more common are gaps that are news reactions or fishing expeditions. These are smaller in nature, are highlighted with low to moderate premarket volume, fill quickly, and can be faded regularly.

The question, then, is if I ignore the reason for the gap, what is it that I'm looking for that determines whether or not I will take the setup? Premarket volume in what, exactly? The key action I am watching is the premarket volume in a specific set of cash stocks. I like to look at all the cash stocks that also trade single stock futures (SSFs). The list of these stocks is available at www.oncechicago.com. As of this writing there are about 120 stocks—they are all the big stocks that trade a lot of volume. Note that I'm not watching the volume of the SSF contract, I'm watching the volume of the actual underlying cash stock. I particularly like to watch KLAC (KLA Tencor Corp), MXIM (Maxim Integrated Products Inc), NVLS (Novellus Systems Inc), and AMAT (Applied Materials Inc). I like these stocks because they are traded actively in the premarket session and are traded aggressively by both individual traders as well as fund managers. Even though these components are not part of the Dow, they still provide a clear map as to how the market is handling any particular news that is out on the day. If the volume on these stocks is heavy, then it is obvious that the market is taking this news very seriously. If the volume on these stocks is light, which is more common, then the market is either not interested in the news or, more likely, has already priced it in. It is on these days that the gaps have a very high probability of filling on the same day in which they were created.

What I'm looking for is the premarket volume in these stocks as of 9:20 a.m. Eastern, 10 minutes before the regular cash session opens. The premarket session opens at 8:00 a.m. Eastern, so these are data on 1 hour and 20 minutes worth of trading. If these stocks are trading under 30,000 shares each at this time, the gap (up or down) has an approximate 85 percent chance of filling that same day. However, if it jumps up to 50,000 shares each, the gap only has about a 60 percent chance of filling that same day. On these particular days, however, the midpoint of the gap has an 85 percent chance of being hit, so I do take this into account and adjust my target accordingly. For example, if the gap is 50 points on the Dow and the premarket volume is moderate, then my target is going to be 25 points from my entry instead of the full 50 points, which would constitute a gap fill. Finally, if the premarket volume jumps to over 70,000 shares each, the chances of the gap filling that same day drop to 30 percent. These are typically the days that involve a professional breakaway gap. On these days I don't fade it. I typically stand aside and wait for one of my other setups to unfold.

Why does this premarket volume indicator work? Think about it as driving a car uphill on an empty tank of gas versus a full tank of gas. If the market is really set up to move, then there will be real volume coming into the cash market to propel that car "up and over" the hill. If the market is just setting up a head fake, then the volume in the cash market will be low, as there won't be any real conviction in the move. Ignore the news and follow the money. Table 6.1 shows how I use this information to manage my trades:

## T A B L E   6.1

| Pre-Market Volume in Key Stocks | Position Size | Trade Target |
|---|---|---|
| Less than 30,000 | Full size | Exit entire position at gap fill |
| Between 30,000 and 70,000 | 2/3 size | Exit half at 50 percent of gap fill, half at gap fill |
| Above 70,000 | No fade trade | No fade trade |

There are many days when three of the stocks are trading under 30,000 shares and another stock will be trading 95,000 shares. In these cases, I will first check to see if there is specific news on that stock. If there is, I will throw it out. If there isn't, I will then take an average and call this a "moderate" gap and play it accordingly—meaning that my target on the first half will be 50 percent of the gap fill instead of holding onto the entire position for a full gap fill. For moderate gap plays, I do not trail down the original stop, even when I get out of half my position.

## The Best Days of the Week to Take This Trade

One of my trading partners, Hubert Senters, has compiled data over the last 4½ years based solely on the raw gap data, disregarding any readings on premarket volume. In Table 6.2, these data are sorted by day of the week and show what percent of the time the markets filled their opening gaps on the same day in which they were created.

As is evidenced by these data, gaps in and of themselves have a very high probability of filling on the same day in which they are created. If a person could get these same odds at a blackjack table, Las Vegas would be put out of business in three months. That said, it is important to note that Mondays are the days with the lowest percentage of filled gaps. The main reason for this is that most breakaway gaps happen on Mondays—there are a lot of developments that can happen over the weekend. On Mondays I will still take low-volume gaps, but if the volume is moderate, I will pass on gaps that are over 50 Dow points or 5 S&P points. Finally, I've noticed that expiration day (the third Friday of every month) and the first trading day of the month have low probabilities in the range of 55 to 60 percent. I generally pass on fading the gaps on these two days. The only exception is if the premarket volume is very low. The bottom line is that if the premarket volume gets confusing and a trader doesn't understand the reading on any given day, the odds are still there and the trade is worth taking.

## TRADING RULES FOR GAP DOWN BUYS (GAP UP SELLS ARE REVERSED)

The set of rules for gap down buys is based on a low premarket volume gap. If the volume is moderate, then I will do exactly the same thing, except I will take off half my position when the markets reach the price level that represents 50 percent of the gap fill. If the premarket

**TABLE 6.2**

| Day | Percentage of Gaps Filled |
|---|---|
| Monday | 65% |
| Tuesday | 77% |
| Wednesday | 79% |
| Thursday | 82% |
| Friday | 78% |

volume is high, then I pass on this trade setup. Remember, this is a fade play. I will buy a gap down, and short a gap up. The following set of rules is for a gap down:

1. I first set up a special intraday gap chart that starts collecting data at 9:30 a.m. Eastern and stops at 4:15 p.m. Eastern. This is so I can view the gaps. These gaps won't appear on charts that carry 24 hours worth of data or as "regular session" data on the futures markets.

2. A gap must be at least 10 YM points or 1 ES point—otherwise I will pass.

3. If a gap is over 70 YM points or 7 ES points, I pay careful attention to the pre-market volume. Most breakaway gaps are big gaps. However, if the premarket volume is low to moderate, I will still take these.

4. With a gap down, when the regular cash market opens at 9:30 a.m. Eastern, I buy the YM or ES at the market. The DIA and SPY can also be used. It doesn't really matter which market is utilized, with two exceptions: If one of the stocks in the Dow is "out of whack" then I will play the gap in the S&Ps. By this I mean that if a stock like IBM is up 10 points on earnings, then this index is going to be "out of whack" with the rest of the markets. The other exception is if I am specifically using the Dow in another setup, say the squeeze or a pivot play (these are discussed in upcoming chapters). Then I will take the gap in the S&Ps. This way if I am still in the gap play when this next setup fires off, I can just take it in the Dow and leave my gap trade on.

5. Once filled, I set up a protective sell stop with the following parameters:
   - For gaps that are under 40 YM or 4 ES points, I use a 1½:1 risk reward ratio. (Example, for a 20-point gap, I use a 35-point stop).
   - For gaps that are over 40 YM or 4 ES points, I use a 1:1 risk reward ratio. (Example, for a 45-point gap, I use a 45-point stop).

6. My target is the gap fill itself. If yesterday's closing price was 1058.50 on the S&Ps, then that is my target for the gap fill. For a moderate volume gap, I will split this order up, having half my target at 50 percent of the gap fill, and leaving on the remaining half for a potential full gap fill.

7. I don't trail stops for this setup.

8. If I'm stopped out, then the gap play is over for the day.

9. If neither the target nor stop is hit by the closing bell, I exit my position at the market.

10. For the gap play, there is only one potential setup per trading day.

## WHO IS GETTING A SPANKING AND WHY?

One of the most important steps for traders is to understand why they are making money in a particular trade—which also means understanding who exactly is losing money on the other side of the trade. Who is getting hurt and why?

When markets gap down, there are generally two groups that are going to get hurt. First, there are the people who are long from the day before. When the markets gap down, they are either getting stopped out or they are panicking and selling. Second, there are people who are flat, see the gap down, think it is the end of the world, and start shorting. In this setup, I want to be on the opposite side of the trade from both these groups, because both of them are having a strong emotional reaction to the market, and this emotion is causing them to get into a trade. Therefore, when they are selling, I am buying. These same groups will provide the fuel for the rally through, in the case of the first group, panic buying in trying to make back their early losses, and, in the case of the second group, short covering via the stops they placed when they put on their short trade. Let's take a look. The charts that follow are numbered in specific places where price action is taking shape. Each of the lists that refer to the chart are numbered so that the text following "2" describes point 2 in the chart to which the text is referencing.

## SPECIFIC EXAMPLES OF TRADING THE GAP

### Mini-Sized Dow—December 2003 Contract, October 15, 2003

1. The mini-sized Dow contract closes at 9717 on October 14 (see Fig. 6.1).
2. On October 15, the opening trade at 9:30 a.m. Eastern is 9762, producing an opening gap of +45 points. I "fade the gap" right at the open and short the YM at the

**F I G U R E   6.1**

market. My protective stop is 45 points away from my entry, at 9807, and my target is the gap fill, which is the previous day's close at 9717.

3. The gap fill is complete once the price levels reach the previous day's close. This occurs 35 minutes after the opening bell. This is a relatively smooth trade. I refer to these quick fill gaps as "Bahamas Gaps" because they are relatively smooth, quick, and stress free. This trade nets a profit of $225 per contract.

## Mini-Sized Dow—December 2003 Contract, October 16, 2003

1. The market closes at 9704 on October 15 (see Fig. 6.2).

2. The opening trade at 9:30 a.m. Eastern on October 16 is 9645, creating a 59-point gap down. I buy at these levels and place a stop at 9586.

3. Many people who play gaps would get stopped out right here at point 3, as they trail up their stop to break even to protect gains. For these people, the gap play is now over.

4. Yet by holding onto this play with parameters that were made especially for gaps, I end up staying in profitable trades that shake many other traders out (see Fig. 6.3). The reason for this is that the other traders are using blanket types of parameters

**F I G U R E   6.2**

**F I G U R E   6.3**

for every play, instead of utilizing specific parameters that are tailored for specific plays. Although many gaps fill within the first hour, many can take a couple of hours or more. I like to set the parameters and focus on something else while the market "does its thing." I refer to this type of gap as "Somalia Gaps." Unlike Bahamas Gaps, they tend to cause a lot of stress in the people who are watching them. It's okay to feel stress; professional traders simply don't act on it, maintaining the parameters they have set for themselves. This trade nets out a profit of $295 per contract.

Note that one of the best signs of an amateur trader is a person who only uses tight stops or a 3:1 risk reward ratio on every trade. Most beginning traders are taught by their brokers to use this tight stop formula, risking one point to get three points. As the traders wonder why they always get stopped out just before the market turns, their broker is tallying up commissions generated on the day. In general, wider stops produce more winning trades. They key with wider stops, of course, is to play only setups that have a greater than 80 percent chance of winning. The gap play I'm describing, with the parameters that I use, has a greater than 80 percent chance of winning with the risk-to-reward ratios I utilize. By using a tight stop on a gap play, the probabilities of the trade working out fall dramatically—less than 30 percent. In essence, one of the reasons many traders fail to make it in this business is because they are using stops that are too tight. This might seem like a contradiction, but if almost every trade is stopped out, it's tough to make any money.

What is also important to remember for gap plays is that an active program of trailing stops will negatively affect your win/loss ratio. Once the parameters are set in place, the best thing a trader can do is to walk away and let the orders do their job. Although tweaking is a good thing to do when giving a car a tune-up, tweaking the parameters of a gap trade won't work.

## Mini-Sized Dow—September 2004 Contract, August, 2, 2004

I've found that most traders get too caught up in the reasons for the gap. In reality, the reason is meaningless. Gaps happen because a flurry of emotion hits the tape at the opening bell. However, the reason for the gap has little significance on whether or not the gap fills. On Sunday, August 1, 2004, the U.S. government issued a terrorist warning claiming that there was chatter on the airways about a plan to blow up a large financial institution. The markets got nervous and the markets gapped down in a big way on Monday morning, August 2 (see Fig. 6.4).

**F I G U R E   6.4**

1. On Friday, July 30, 2004, the mini-sized Dow futures closed at 10142.

2. On Monday, August 2, 2004, the markets open for trade at 10091, down 51 points. I buy here right at the 9:30 a.m. Eastern open. I place a stop at 10040. The markets spend a good part of the day chopping around, and I talk with other traders who are nervous about the terrorist threat news. Do I let this "nervousness" get into my own trading? Should I listen to the reasons for the gap?

3. Later that same day, the markets grind higher and I am out at the gap fill (see Fig. 6.5). Gaps are the ultimate contrarian play; don't get caught up with the crowd. This trade nets a profit of $255 per contract.

## E-mini S&P—September 2004 Contract, August 24, 2004

1. On August 23 the ES closed at 1097.00 (see Fig. 6.6).

2. The next morning the 9:30 a.m. opening trade prints at 1101.00, four points above its close. I short at the open, placing a stop at 1105.00.

**F I G U R E   6.5**

**FIGURE 6.6**

3. A little over an hour later, my target is hit as the E-mini S&Ps fill their gap for a total gain of $200 per contract.

## E-mini S&P—September 2004 Contract, August 4, 2004

1. On August 3, the ES closes at 1097.50 (see Fig. 6.7).
2. The next morning, the market gaps down and opens at 1094.25. This gap is 3.25 points, so I use a 1½:1 risk-to-reward ratio, and place my stop at 1089.25.
3. I buy at the open. The market chops up, and then pushes down to new lows. A little over an hour later, the market has firmed, and I'm out of my position at the gap fill. The markets spend a good portion of the day in a tight, choppy range, only rallying in the final half-hour of trade. On many days, the gap play is not only the safest, but it is really the only trade to take. We call the market *choppy* when it trades in a narrow, low volume range because it chops up newer traders to death. This trade nets a total of $162.50 per contract.

**F I G U R E   6.7**

## E-mini S&P—September 2004 Contract, July 14, 2004

1. On July 13 the E-mini S&Ps closed at 1114.75 (see Fig. 6.8).
2. The next morning the market opens down −5.75 points at 1109.00.
3. I buy at the open and place a stop at 1103.25.
4. The gap fills in a little under an hour. This is another example of a "Bahamas Gap," as it is very relaxing to trade with a minimum of false moves. This trade nets a total profit of $287.50 per contract.

## WHAT TO DO WITH UNFILLED GAPS

One important thing to remember: If 80 percent of these plays win, that means 20 percent of them lose. I actually like losing trades for one main reason—this leaves an "open gap" in the markets. An open gap is like a black hole or a tractor beam, eventually sucking prices back to their opening gap levels. Whenever the markets leave an open gap, I mark that level on a Post-it Note and place it on my computer. Let's look at this example (see Fig. 6.9):

**FIGURE 6.8**

@ES - 5 min  CME  L=1116.75  -1.25  -0.11%  B...

Let's get a little more specific on how to play this using a $100,000 account, and utilizing nine contracts for a full position, approximately one contract for every $11,100 in the account. Yes, a person can trade a lot more contracts than that in a $100,000 account, and many brokers will encourage a person to trade more than that. With some brokers a trader can get enough leverage to trade 100 contracts on a $100,000 account. This is, purely and simply, insane. Just because people can do something, doesn't mean they should. The leverage here is far too much. Traders who are using a modest two-point stop on the S&Ps could get stopped out four times in a row. Where does this leave them? 2 points × $50 × 100 contracts = $10,000. Four stops in a row = $40,000. I've seen more than my fair share of people do this, and it is just inexcusable. There are many things people can do in life. They can drink one glass of wine or the whole bottle. They can drink one cup of coffee or the whole pot. They can go to the gym each day or sit and watch TV. It all comes down to choice. Just because people can do something, doesn't mean that it's a good idea. Choose with your best interests in mind. Let's go back to the example.

On August 18, we gapped up a modest 44 points in the Dow prior to some economic numbers. I short at the open. We rallied, sold off into the economic numbers, and then shot higher once the numbers were released. I had a 44-point stop, and the markets rallied just through that level, producing a loss of $220 per contract, or $1,980.

**F I G U R E   6.9**

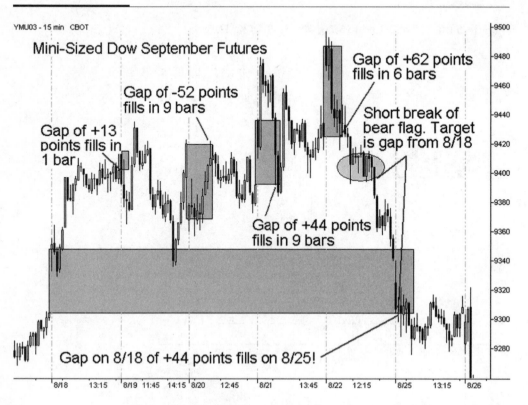

YMU03 - 15 min   CBOT

Mini-Sized Dow September Futures

Gap of +13 points fills in 1 bar

Gap of -52 points fills in 9 bars

Gap of +62 points fills in 6 bars

Short break of bear flag. Target is gap from 8/18

Gap of +44 points fills in 9 bars

Gap on 8/18 of +44 points fills on 8/25!

I head into the next trading day knowing there is now a "black hole" gap below. I can actually hear the sucking sound. The next day we have a modest low volume 13-point gap higher that works out quickly, for $65 per contract ($585). The day after, we get a nice 52-point gap lower that takes a few hours to fill, but creates few headaches, for $260 per contract ($2,340). The next day we get a 44-point gap higher that is on moderate volume. It comes close to our stop but eventually fills the gap for $255 per contract on four contracts. I covered the first five contracts when we got to 50 percent of the gap fill level, which is 22 points. 4 contracts × 44 points × $5 = $880, and 5 contracts × 22 points × $5 = $550 for a total of $1,430 on the play. Finally on August 22 we get the "sucker gap" when Intel announces "cautious upside earnings revisions." The market explodes and gaps up 62 points, right into key resistance—on low premarket volume.

I short the gap. Six bars later, my target is hit for 62 points or $310 per contract ($2,790). *The sucking sound of the black hole below is getting louder.* During the afternoon session we get a bear flag consolidation. I set up a sell stop at 9392 to let the market take me into a breakdown of that flag formation. I get the fill and set my stop above intraday resistance at 9455. My target is the 8/18 black hole open gap at 9304. The market spends the rest of the day on its hands and knees, dry heaving, trying to hold back the internal pressure. This pressure proves to be too much, and, like a freshman college student during his first year away from home, the market eventually falls over and vomits. The gap fills for an 88-point gain or $440 per contract ($3,960).

When there are open gaps left in the market, I always write them down and mark them on my chart. The markets will take them out eventually, usually within 5 to 10 trading days.

## STRATEGIES FOR THOSE WHO CAN'T TRADE FULL TIME

Gaps are one of the best strategies for people who are holding down a full-time job. On the West Coast this is particularly easy as the markets are open well before most people have to head to the office. The main consideration to keep in mind is that a person will want a system like NinjaTrader (see Chapter 4) that will automatically cancel a stop once the target is hit. Another, often overlooked alternative is to have a broker who can be called with the parameters. Typically these brokers will cost a little more in commissions, but it is worth it to have someone watching out for the trade. The biggest advantage of doing this trade as a part time trader is that you won't be prone to making the very mistakes most full-time traders make while watching the trade progress. They get antsy, they get fidgety, and they end up bailing out too soon. Someone who is at the office and doesn't have time to watch the trade actually has a big edge over most of the traders who haven't learned to control their emotions.

Another alternative is to have this setup "auto-traded" by a broker. There are a number of brokers who will trade these setups automatically based on parameters that are given to them. Additional information on this option is available at www.tradethemarkets.com.

## POSITION SIZING WITH A $100,000 ACCOUNT

One frequent question I get is "How many contracts or shares are you trading with this strategy?" These same plays can be executed in five different markets. There are the mini-sized Dow and E-mini S&P futures, the SPY and DIA ETF shares, and there are also futures available on the DIA through One Chicago. The table following shows the different instruments and the number of shares or contracts I would trade on a $100,000 account using this setup. The DIA futures are nice if a trader is using a smaller account. They are a happy medium between having a lot of leverage with the mini-Dow and E-mini S&P futures and no leverage with the DIA and SPY stock. The example shown in Table 6.3 is with a gap that occurred on July 24.

## SUMMING UP THE GAPS

Gaps are the one moment of the trading day where all the players have to show their poker hand, and this creates the single biggest advantage for the short-term trader. Understanding

**T A B L E   6.3**

| Quantity | Market | 7/23 Close | 7/24 Open | Gap: Points | Stop | Profit |
|---|---|---|---|---|---|---|
| 9 | mini Dow | 9,169.00 | 9,233.00 | 64 | 9,329 | $2,700 |
| 9 | E-mini S&P | 987.00 | 993.50 | 6.50 | 1,003.25 | $2,925 |
| 20 | DIA futures | 91.96 | 92.58 | 0.62 | 93.51 | $1,240 |
| 500 | DIA | 91.91 | 92.50 | 0.59 | 93.38 | $295 |
| 500 | SPY | 99.29 | 99.99 | 0.70 | 101.04 | $350 |

the psychology behind the gaps is paramount to playing them successfully on a daily basis. The gaps are so powerful that many traders make a nice living playing these setups alone. The key is to know how they work and to develop a solid methodology and set of rules to trade them.

After reading about this setup and understanding the specifics behind the setup, the serious trader will have a better foundation for a plan to trade the markets successfully on a full-time basis: a proven setup to play, markets that best fit that set-up, and a plan of action to maximize the play. That is pretty much all a trader needs to survive and thrive in this greatest of professions.

# 7
## C H A P T E R

# PIVOT POINTS—GREAT FOR TRENDING DAYS AND EVEN BETTER FOR CHOPPY DAYS

## BEATING INDICATOR-BASED TRADERS TO THE PUNCH

One of the simplest and most effective position entry techniques I use is based on what I call the multipivot levels. This is a setup that can be used on a variety of markets, though I typically use them on the mini-sized Dow (YM), E-mini S&P (ES), E-mini NASDAQ (NQ), and E-mini Russell (ER) futures contracts, as well as some individual stocks. They can also be used on the corresponding stock index ETF via the DIA, SPY, QQQQ and IWM.

The main advantage of this system is that it is price-based as opposed to indicator-based. By the time most indicators generate a buy or a sell signal, the move is already well under way. By following this price-based methodology, I will get into a trade before the indicator-based traders, and I usually end up handing off my position soon after a buy or sell signal is being generated on a stochastic or other oscillator type of system. This is especially true on choppy days. Just as the Johnny-come-latelies are jumping in, I'm closing out my position and looking for the next setup. On choppy days, it's the indicator-based traders who get taken out back and shot. Their buy signals get them in at the top of the move and their sell signals get them in at the dead lows, leading to a frustrating day with a negative P&L Pivots are set up to naturally take advantage of their mistakes, essentially siphoning money from these trading accounts into your own.

This is also a good system for traders who don't have time to stare at the charts all day long, or, not surprisingly, for traders who have a bad habit of chasing the market higher and lower. Playing the pivots automatically creates trader discipline, because the entries and exits are determined before the trading day even starts.

The other thing I like about the pivots is that they can be used as a tool to quickly determine what kind of trading day it's going to be. On a trending day, markets will move to a pivot level, consolidate for 15–20 minutes, and then continue to march in the direction of the trend. On these days I wait for the move through the pivot level and then buy the first pullback to that level. On choppy days, however, the markets will move up to a pivot level, hang around for a short time, and then drift back in the direction from whence they came. Many traders get "chopped up" during these types of trading days, losing money and making their brokers rich in the process. The pivots are naturally set up to be faded on these days and are one of the few profitable ways to trade the low volume, narrow range chop.

There are two very easy ways to tell if the market is trending or chopping. The first is to look at how the markets react to the pivot levels once they reach them. The second is to set up a five-minute chart of the E-mini S&Ps and see what kind of volume is coming into the market after 10:00 a.m. Eastern (see Chapter 5). If the volume is over 10,000 contracts on each bar, then the market has power and volatility behind it. These types of days usually have wide ranges and strong trends. However, if the volume after 10:00 a.m. Eastern is consistently below 10,000 contracts on a five-minute chart, then there is little power to move the beast, and the end result will be a slow, choppy day. On the first type of day, I wait for the markets to move through pivot levels, and then I set up an order to get in on the first retracement. On the choppy days, I place open buy and sell orders against the pivots and have standing orders to fade these moves throughout the day. There is nothing to watch on these types of days, so I generally let my orders do the work for me while I spend some quality time at the driving range.

## NOT ALL PIVOTS ARE CREATED EQUAL

So what exactly are the pivots? There is no big mystery or secret to them, and many readers will have heard about them and have used them in their own trading on a regular basis. For the uninitiated, I explain how I set them up and why they work, and then we can jump into the setups that I use with them.

Pivots are readily available and have been around for a long time. They are support and resistance levels calculated by floor traders using a simple mathematical formula. These levels became widely known and have moved off the floor. Today many traders are aware of them and try to use them, but in my experience they are using them incorrectly. To add to the confusion, there are different formula versions and different time frames that are used when calculating pivots. So, to get started, let's look at what I use, which is one of the standard pivot formulas:

$$\textbf{R3: } R1 + (\text{High} - \text{Low})$$

$$\textbf{R2: } \text{Pivot} + (\text{High} - \text{Low})$$

$$\textbf{R1: } 2 \times \text{Pivot} - \text{Low}$$

**PIVOT:** High + Low + Close/3

**S1:** 2 × Pivot – High

**S2:** Pivot – (High – Low)

**S3:** S1 – (High – Low)

Once a trader has this formula, then the key data needed are the high, low, and close of the previous session. For my own trading, I like to utilize 24 hours' worth of data to capture the highs and lows. However, it is absolutely imperative to use the settlement price for the close, as this is the only closing price that matters. Often a 24-hour setting on a chart means "midnight to midnight," and that will destroy the validity of the data. We will go over this in more detail shortly.

Once I get this high/low/close, I plug these into an Excel spreadsheet with the formulas listed above. This information generates seven important levels for the next trading day: a central pivot, then three levels above (R1, R2, and R3) and three levels below (S1, S2, and S3). The central pivot has the most weight of the seven levels. In addition to these daily levels, I also utilize the midpoints between these levels. Finally, I like to know where the weekly and monthly levels are located. These are calculated by taking the high/low/close of the previous weekly or monthly bar. While the daily pivots change each day, the weekly pivots change only once a week, and the monthly pivots once per month.

It is important to note that it is extremely rare for a stock index to hit its daily R3 or S3 levels. This is important to know because if a market rallies to R2 or a sells off to S2, that usually ends up being the dead high or the dead low of the day. This knowledge will help temper a trader's emotions and keep them on track to follow this system.

## HERE'S EXACTLY HOW I SET THEM UP ON MY CHARTS

I'm going to go through the process of how I update the pivots on my charts each day. I'm doing this on Saturday, March 19, 2005, and I want to calculate the updated pivot levels for when the market reopens again on Monday. To calculate the daily pivot numbers, I use the following data to generate my high, low, and close numbers:

- YM: Start Thursday at 8:15 p.m. ET; end 5:00 p.m. on Friday
- ES: Start Thursday at 4:30 p.m. ET; end 4:15 p.m. on Friday
- NQ: Start Thursday at 4:30 p.m. ET; end 4:15 p.m. on Friday
- ER: Start Thursday at 4:30 p.m. ET; end 4:15 p.m. on Friday

This range of data gives me all the price action for when these markets are trading, allowing for both pre- and postmarket price action to be factored into the next trading day's numbers. The times are slightly different on the above contracts because of the times they were traded on the exchange. The settlement price is the key. If traders are ever unsure about the settlement price, they can check it on the YM at www.cbot.com and go to market data, then settlement prices. For the ES, NQ, and ER, a trader can go to www.cme.com and go to trade CME products, market data, historical data, view more, settlement prices, equity index. It's kind of a maze to get there on the CME website. The direct link is http://www.cme.com/trading/dta/hist/daily_settle_prices.html?type=idx.

The easiest way to get an accurate high/low/close is to just set up a daily chart with the timeframes listed for each contract. In TradeStation this is very easy to do. Just enter the continuous symbol, such as @YM or @ES, and set it on a daily chart. The data will default to the "regular session" which refers to the times listed above. With many other charting programs a trader has to go in and set this up manually, as many of them default to the regular stock market session from 9:30 a.m. to 4:00 p.m. Eastern. Once the chart is setup, just wait until after 4:15 p.m. Eastern on the ES, NQ, and ER and wait until after 5:00 p.m. Eastern on the YM. After these times, just take the high/low/close reading on the daily bar generated for that trading day to get the correct numbers. This closing price will almost always match the settlement price, though I like to check to make sure. For Monday, then, I want the high/low/close for Friday. Let's take a look (see Fig. 7.1):

On Friday, March 18, 2005, we have a daily bar on the YM that started at 8:15 p.m. ET on Thursday, March 17, and ended at 5:00 p.m. ET on Friday, March 18. This range gives us the following numbers:

- High: 10679
- Low: 10579
- Close: 10635

By changing the chart to a weekly time frame, I can also take the high/low/close of the completed weekly bar and get the numbers I will use for the weekly pivots.

### FIGURE 7.1

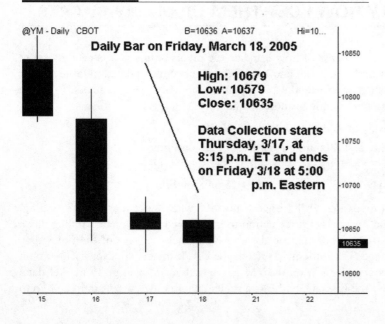

- High: 10870
- Low: 10579
- Close: 10635

On Monday the daily and weekly close will be identical, since they are both based on Friday's close. In this instance the lows are also identical because the lows on Friday were also the lows of the week. The process can be repeated with the monthly levels, but I won't need new monthly inputs until the first trading day in April.

Now that I have my key levels, I want to figure out the key pivot points that I'll be using for Monday, March 21, 2005. The first thing I do is take these high/low/close figures and plug them into the formula. To figure out the daily pivot, I take the high + low + close and divide by 3. 10679 + 10579 + 10635 = 31,893/3 = 10631. We now have our pivot point for the day. To figure out R1, which is the next level above the pivot, I multiply the pivot by 2, and then subtract the low. So we take 10631 × 2 = 21,262 – the low at 10579 = 10683.

We complete this process until we are done, and we come up with the following levels:

- R3: 10783
- R2: 10731
- R1: 10683
- Pivot: 10631
- S1: 10583
- S2: 10531
- S3: 10483

Once I have these levels, I place them on my chart. I also like to note the midpoints between the daily pivot levels. These are calculated very simply as they are literally the midpoint. The pivot is 10631, and R1 is 10683, 52 points away. Half of 52 is 26. I add that to the pivot, and I get a midpoint of 10657. These are all formulas that can be set up in Excel, making this a very quick and easy process. I don't calculate the midpoints for the weekly and monthly levels.

With the chart created and the appropriate pivot levels added, the first thing I will note is where the daily pivot is in relation to where the market closed. The daily pivot is at 10631, and the market closed at 10635. The second thing I will be watching for is where the markets are trading at 9:30 a.m. Eastern on Monday. How far away are they from the daily pivot? This will work in relation to the gap play. The markets test their daily pivot level 90 percent of the time at some point during the day. I will always fade the first move to the daily pivot. For example, if the markets are trading above the central daily pivot, and they sell off to this level, I will "fade" the move by buying it when it reaches the pivot. I will talk about specific entry methods in a moment.

By setting up these formulas in an Excel template, I can quickly obtain all the key levels for the YM, ES, NQ, and ER. I did that, and all I do today is just enter the high, low, and close. Once this is done, the spreadsheet fills in the rest of the numbers for me automatically. It takes me just a few minutes to look up, and then plug the high, low, close into this spreadsheet. I then instantly have my levels for the next trading day. Of course, I have to update the weekly pivots only once a week, and the monthly pivots once a month. The spreadsheet for the chart we are working on is shown in Figure 7.2.

**F I G U R E   7.2**

| Daily Futures Pivots & Midpoints | | | | |
|---|---|---|---|---|
| | **S&P** | **DOW** | **NASDAQ** | **RUSSELL** | |
| High | 1197.00 | 10679 | 1503.50 | 626.60 | High |
| Low | 1186.50 | 10579 | 1483.00 | 619.90 | Low |
| Close | 1190.75 | 10635 | 1491.00 | 622.00 | Close |
| R3 | 1206.83 | 10783.00 | 1522.50 | 632.47 | R3 |
| Mid | 1204.38 | 10757.00 | 1517.75 | 631.00 | Mid |
| R2 | 1201.92 | 10731.00 | 1513.00 | 629.53 | R2 |
| Mid | 1199.13 | 10707.00 | 1507.50 | 627.65 | Mid |
| R1 | 1196.33 | 10683.00 | 1502.00 | 625.77 | R1 |
| Mid | 1193.88 | 10657.00 | 1497.25 | 624.30 | Mid |
| Pivot | 1191.42 | 10631.00 | 1492.50 | 622.83 | Pivot |
| Mid | 1188.63 | 10607.00 | 1487.00 | 620.95 | Mid |
| S1 | 1185.83 | 10583.00 | 1481.50 | 619.07 | S1 |
| Mid | 1183.38 | 10557.00 | 1476.75 | 617.60 | Mid |
| S2 | 1180.92 | 10531.00 | 1472.00 | 616.13 | S2 |
| Mid | 1178.13 | 10507.00 | 1466.50 | 614.25 | Mid |
| S3 | 1175.33 | 10483.00 | 1461.00 | 612.37 | S3 |
| Weekly Pivots | | | | |
| | **S&P** | **DOW** | **NASDAQ** | **RUSSELL** | |
| High | 1216.25 | 10870 | 1532.00 | 637.70 | High |
| Low | 1186.50 | 10579 | 1483.00 | 619.90 | Low |
| Close | 1190.75 | 10635 | 1491.00 | 622.00 | Close |
| R3 | 1238.92 | 11101.33 | 1570.00 | 650.97 | R3 |
| R2 | 1227.58 | 10985.67 | 1551.00 | 644.33 | R2 |
| R1 | 1209.17 | 10810.33 | 1521.00 | 633.17 | R1 |
| Pivot | 1197.83 | 10694.67 | 1502.00 | 626.53 | Pivot |
| S1 | 1179.42 | 10519.33 | 1472.00 | 615.37 | S1 |
| S2 | 1168.08 | 10403.67 | 1453.00 | 608.73 | S2 |
| S3 | 1149.67 | 10228.33 | 1423.00 | 597.57 | S3 |
| Monthly Pivots | | | | |
| | **S&P** | **DOW** | **NASDAQ** | **RUSSELL** | |
| High | 1214.75 | 10864 | 1565.00 | 641.50 | High |
| Low | 1179.50 | 10467 | 1490.50 | 615.90 | Low |
| Close | 1204.00 | 10778 | 1513.00 | 634.70 | Close |
| R3 | 1254.58 | 11336.00 | 1629.67 | 671.10 | R3 |
| R2 | 1234.67 | 11100.00 | 1597.33 | 656.30 | R2 |
| R1 | 1219.33 | 10939.00 | 1555.17 | 645.50 | R1 |
| Pivot | 1199.42 | 10703.00 | 1522.83 | 630.70 | Pivot |
| S1 | 1184.08 | 10542.00 | 1480.67 | 619.90 | S1 |
| S2 | 1164.17 | 10306.00 | 1448.33 | 605.10 | S2 |
| S3 | 1148.83 | 10145.00 | 1406.17 | 594.30 | S3 |

I also like to note where the extreme levels are, because it is very rare when the stock indexes hit their R3 or S3 levels. This is important to know because if the markets rally to R2 or a sell off to S2, that usually ends up being the dead high or the dead low of the day. This knowledge will help temper a trader's emotions. When a market is going up, it is easy to think that it will go up forever. On this same note, when the market is heading down quickly, it is easy to assume it's the end of the world. The emotion of greed is, of course, a disaster to any-one who succumbs to it because of the surge of adrenaline that runs through the body. By understanding the odds of a move above and beyond these outer levels, a trader will be able to stay more objective and take the money away from the people who are panicking.

The pivots help to keep a trader grounded. Instead of getting overexcited and hoping for a market crash, the pivot trader knows there is a 90 percent chance that the markets will not close above R2 or below S2 on any given day. A move to that level signals a time for the trader to take profits instead of pyramiding into a bigger position that will lead to disaster.

Let's take a look at the pivot levels that we calculated for Monday, March 21, 2005, on a five-minute chart (see Fig. 7.3):

This chart looks very busy with the daily pivot levels labeled on the left, the midpoints of the daily levels in the middle, and the weekly pivot levels on the right. For sake of space, I left the monthly levels off. I like to take a look at this wide view first in order to see where

**F I G U R E   7.3**

the extreme levels are located for Monday's trading. Once I've done that, I will then reduce the chart to a more manageable level (see Fig. 7.4).

In this chart I've zoomed in so that I can see where the key close levels are for Monday's trading.

## THE PSYCHOLOGY BEHIND THE PIVOTS— WHO IS GETTING BURNED

Before I jump into the rules and specific setups that I use to trade the pivots, I want to cover briefly why they work. The first, and most obvious, is that a lot of traders watch these daily

**F I G U R E   7.4**

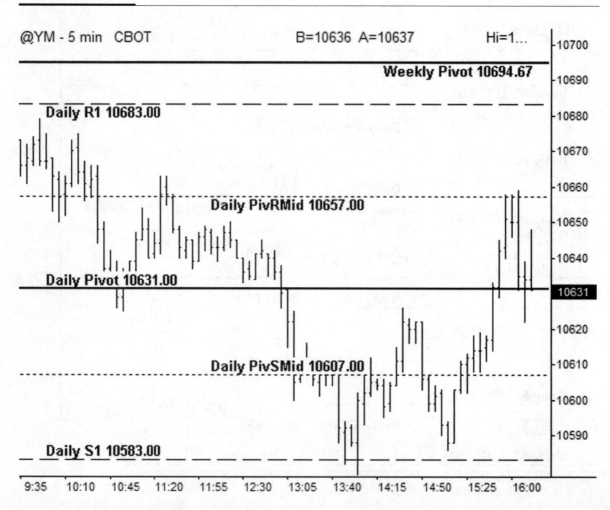

levels, so there is a self-fulfilling prophecy involved. The same can be said for Fibonacci Levels, but they do not hold nearly as well as the pivots. Why? I elaborate on this in the next two points.

On the floor, it is generally a trader's goal to grab smaller moves, typically two points in the S&P 500, which is about 20 points in the Dow, or smaller depending on what is going on in the pit. The floor traders all operate in a big circle, with the brokers standing on the first step that surrounds the pit. This gives them the best view of all the locals so they can get the best price for their customers. Since it is easier to trade with someone right in front of you, the prime space for locals to stand is just inside the top rail that separates the top step brokers from the locals. Experience, politics (who you know), and the ability to take orders of all sizes (not just 1 lots) can get a local a prime position near the top step brokers. Usually this space is determined by how long the local has "held the spot" and his ability to continue to make markets. New traders must find space where available. This is usually the farthest point from the brokers, which is the center of the pit. Because of this layout, there are several different scenarios being trading at one time. The locals on one side of the pit are making markets based on order flow coming from the brokers on their side of the pit. If a broker in one corner was selling size (a very large position) while a broker on the other side of the pit was buying, the two brokers don't always hear each other or even know what the other side is doing. It would be very easy for them to do their trade together if they knew that they could meet each other's needs. Instead, locals near the broker who is buying start "racing" the broker by buying from other nearby brokers and then turning around and selling their contracts to him. This causes many price fluctuations throughout the day and often results in the public getting stopped out before the action settles down again. In its purest form, the traders on the outside will get in on a trade, let's say it's a long, and then sell their position to the guys on the inside of the circle who can't really see what is happening way out on the top steps. What happens is that the traders on the inside, by the time they see the market moving, are the last ones in the pit to get in on the move. If they are lucky, they will then be able to turn around and sell it to the public. As the guys on the inside are selling to the public and closing positions, the guys on the outside are also selling to the public but they are opening new short positions, essentially fading a public that is chasing the up move. And the cycle renews itself like this throughout the day. This causes a specific dynamic in the markets, generating specific cycles of speed and rest on an intraday basis. They focus on the pivot levels to base their entries and to also gauge market action. The pivots play on this in that they are spaced out to catch these "patches of momentum." A Dow pivot is usually 30–50 points apart, and this is the type of movement that perpetuates the cycle I just described. The floor traders in the center of the circle are catching half this move, dumping it, and waiting for the next level to be hit. The key is to get in when the market is quiet and get positioned for the next round of activity.

One of the main reasons these pivots work has to do with the vast majority of inexperienced traders out there. The floor traders start a trade, and the inexperience of most traders causes the momentum that finishes a trade. How? Because average traders rely on a lot of different "indicators." They are getting in and out of their positions far too late, which causes losing trades and a specific cycle of market movement as their stop placement slowly and steadily increases the velocity of market movement in the direction of their stops. Indicators are just that, an "indication." This is like your significant other slapping you across the face, and you taking it as an "indication" that this person might be angry with you. If it takes a slap across the face to realize this, then you are following the wrong indicators. By the way, all market indicators are the wrong indicators, because they are all lagging. Price action is pure. This overreliance on indicators by the majority of traders is what helps this system to work. By the time the average trader gets a buy signal, the pivot play is almost over and users of this system will be selling their position to the indicator-based trader. Then the subsequent reversal that takes place is because of all the stop losses sitting out there, like trout sunning themselves on top of a lake— easy targets for the hawks who come swooping down from overhead. The market pauses, drifts down, and picks up steam and rips through all the stop losses, pausing when the run is over. This pause generally happens at a pivot level. It's where the floor traders are beginning to accumulate their next position for the next cycle of play.

Let's jump into the trading rules and look at some setups:

# TRADING RULES FOR PIVOT BUYS ON TRENDING DAYS (SELLS ARE REVERSED)

1. Unlike the gap charts, I want to see 24 hours' worth of data, so I can view any overnight highs and lows. Each day I update the appropriate pivot levels on the charts to reflect the previous day's action. On Monday's I also update the weekly pivots, and on the first trading day of a new month I update the monthly pivots.

2. The first pivot play is done in conjunction with the gap, if there is one. If there is a gap down, then I buy a decline into the closest pivot level. If there isn't a playable gap (over 10 YM points or 1 ES point), then I will wait until 9:45 a.m. Eastern to initiate the first play.

3. If the volume on the five-minute ES chart is over 10,000 contracts, then I'll wait for the markets to penetrate a pivot level, moving up at least a quarter of the way to the next pivot level. Once this happens, I will then set up a bid to buy the first retracement back to the violated pivot level.

4. I enter my trades with limit orders only. I place orders "just in front of" the pivot. For the YM I use 3 points; the ES 0.25 points; NQ 0.50 points; ER .20 points; and for individual stocks .05 cents. For example, if I'm trading the YM and the pivot level is 10000, then I would buy a decline to 10003 and short a rally to 9997. Sometimes the pivot will be an odd number, such as 1117.38 on the ES. In this case I always round in the direction of the trade. So, if I'm bidding for a long, I will round 1117.38 to 1117.50, and my bid will be 1117.75. If I'm offering a short, I will round 1117.38 down to 1117.25 and place my offer at 1117.00. My stops and targets, then, would be "just in front of" these appropriate long and short levels.

5. Once filled, I place an order to close the first half at the next pivot level, and the second half at the pivot level after that, using the same "just in front of" parameters.

6. I place a 20-point stop for the YM, 2 points for the ES, 4 points for the NQ, and 1.50 points for the Russell. For stocks, I will use a stop based roughly on the price of the stock. If the stock is under $10 a share, I will use a stop of 20 cents.

If it is between $10 and $20, I will use a stop of 30 cents, between $20 and $30 I will use a stop of 40 cents, and so on, adding another 10 cents for each $10 increment in price. (So a $75 stock would have an 80-cent stop, etc.)

7. If the first target is hit, I will then move up the stop to my entry level pivot, minus the "just in front of" fractions discussed in rule 3. For example, if I get in a YM long at 10003 and the pivot is at 10000, then my new stop would be 9997 once the first target is hit.

8. If I am in a trade at the market close and neither my stop nor my target has been hit, I will close my position out "at the market" at 4:10 p.m. Eastern for futures, and at 3:58 p.m. Eastern for stocks.

9. I don't initiate any new positions after 3:30 p.m. Eastern, but I will manage existing positions into the close.

10. The markets rarely have a sustained move above R3 or below S3. If I trade to those levels, I will always fade the move.

11. After two losers in a row, I'm done with pivots for the day.

## TRADING RULES FOR PIVOT BUYS ON CHOPPY DAYS (SELLS ARE REVERSED)

The rules for choppy days are identical except for the targets. On choppy days, I just focus on the YM and the ES. My first target is mechanical, 10 points for the YM and 1 point for the ES on half of my position. Once this is hit, I will trail up my stop in the same way I would for a trending trade. The second target becomes the "just in front of level" for the actual next pivot level. In working with other traders, I've found that they grasp the concept of the "choppy day" setup easily, but struggle with the "trending day" setup. Therefore I focus most of the examples on the trending day setups, and we go through those first.

### Specific Examples of Trading the Pivots

### E-mini S&P—September 2004 Contract, September 10, 2004

1. The S&Ps gap down into daily S1 (see Fig. 7.5). I have a limit order to buy placed at 1114.00, just above daily S1. The market comes very close to this level, but not close enough. I am not filled, and the market rallies away without me. Once the market pushes up through the midpoint, I move my bid to buy the next pullback to the midpoint. The midpoint is at 1115.88, so I get a little in front by placing an order to buy at 1116.25. I am filled quickly at this level. I place an initial two-point stop at 1114.25, and my first target is "just in front of" the next pivot. The pivot is 1118.00, so my first target is 1117.75.

2. My first target is hit, and I move my stop up to 1115.50 (just below the midpoint where I entered the trade). Shortly thereafter my second target is hit at 1119.75, and I am out of the trade.

**F I G U R E   7.5**

3. I place an order to buy a pullback to the pivot at 1118.25. I am filled and place a two-point stop at 1116.25. My stop is hit. The market rallies back through the pivot, and I place another order to buy a pullback to 1118.25. I am filled and place the same two-point stop at 1116.25.

4. My first target is hit "just in front of" the next pivot level at 1119.75.

5. I move my stop up on the second half of my position to 1117.75, which is just below the pivot where I entered my trade.

6. I exit the second half of my position at 1122.00, just in front of the next pivot level. Once the market pushes decisively through this pivot level, I place a bid to buy at 1122.50, just above R1. I am not filled, and the market goes on to make new highs. At this point it is past 3:30 p.m. Eastern, and I am done with my pivot plays for the day.

## E-mini S&P—September 2004 Contract, September 9, 2004

1. The S&Ps gap open, and I place an order to short just below the midpoint at 1121.00 (see Fig. 7.6). I am filled, and place a two-point stop at 1123.00. My first target is just in front of the next pivot level at 1120.00. This target is hit, and I move my stop down to 1121.75, which is just above the pivot level I used for my entry. My second target is just in front of the next pivot level at 1118.00.

**F I G U R E   7.6**

2. My target is hit on the second half of my position. The market bounces and starts to move up to the daily pivot, and I place an order to short at 1119.25. I am not filled, and the market rolls over and moves quickly into daily S1.

3. I move my order to short down to the next pivot level, and my order is now 1117.25. I am filled and place a stop at 1119.25. My first target is 1116.00. This target is hit, and I move my stop to 1118.00.

4. My second target is hit at 1114.25, and I place an order to short a rally back to S1 at 1115.25.

5. I am filled and place a two-point stop at 1117.25. I get stopped out as the market rallies hard.

6. I'm filled at 1118.00. I place a stop at 1116.00.

7. The market rallies to the next pivot level, and I'm out half at 1119.25. I move up my stop to 1117.25. My next target is quickly hit at 1121.00.

8. Normally I would place an order to buy the next pullback here at 1120.00. But I don't. Why? Because I'm following the rules. It is now past 3:30 p.m. Eastern, and I'm not initiating any new trades!

9. This trade would have been stopped out.

## E-mini S&P—September 2004 Contract, September 8, 2004

1. The markets gap down and I place an order to buy at 1118.75 (see Fig. 7.7). This order is not filled. When the markets rally through the daily pivot, I raise my bid to 1120.75. I am filled and place a stop at 1118.75. My first target is 1123.00.

2. My first target is hit. I move up my stop to 1120.25.

3. I am stopped out of my second half, and I wait for the next setup.

4. The market continues to trend down, so I want to short the next move to the overhead pivot.

5. The market rallies, and I get short at 1120.25. I place a stop at 1122.25, and my first target is 1118.75.

6. My first target is hit, and I move my stop to 1120.75. Shortly thereafter my second target is hit at 1116.75. I place an order to short the next rally to an overhead pivot, and I am filled at 1118.25. I place a stop at 1120.25. My first target is hit at 1116.75, and I move my stop down to 1118.75. The market rallies into the close, and I am stopped on the second half.

**F I G U R E   7.7**

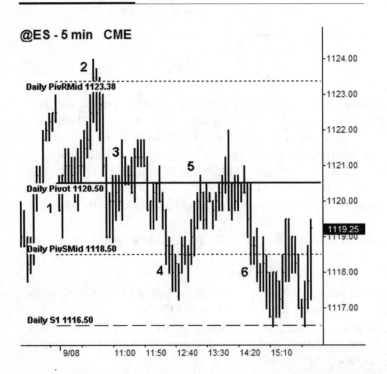

## E-mini Russell—September 2004 Contract, September 10, 2004

1. The Russell 2000 futures gap down, and I place a bid at 561.90. (see Fig. 7.8). I am filled and place a stop at 560.40. My first target is 563.80, and this is filled quickly. I moved up my stop to 561.50.

2. My second target is hit at 566.50, and the market continues to rally through this midpoint.

3. Once the market pushes through the midpoint, I place a bid at the pivot below at 564.20. The market never comes down to this level and in fact makes new highs. Once this happens, I move up my bid to the next pivot level, and my new bid is 566.90. I am filled close to 2:00 p.m. Eastern. I have been bidding long for 3½ hours. With pivots, patience is a virtue!

4. I place a stop at 566.40, and my first target is 569.30. My first target is hit, and I move my stop up to 566.50. The market hangs around this same level into the close. Since neither my stop nor my target is hit, I exit "at the market" at 4:10 p.m. Eastern and get out at 569.40.

**F I G U R E   7.8**

## E-mini Russell—September 2004 Contract, September 2, 2004

1. The Russell 2000 opens flat and pushes higher, right into daily R1 (see Fig. 7.9). I set up a bid to buy the next pullback to the midpoint at 554.90. I am filled and place a stop at 543.40. My first target is the next pivot level at 557.20. This level is hit, and I move up my stop to 554.40.

2. The markets spend the next four hours consolidating, then finally push up and hit my second target, once again showing how patience with the pivots pays off.

3. The market pushes through the midpoint and starts to pull back. I place a bid at 560.10. The market comes close, but I am not filled. The Russell pushes through daily R2, and I move up my bid to 562.60. I get filled here and place a stop at 561.10. My first target is 564.90.

4. My first target is hit. I move up my stop to 562.10. The market approaches the close without hitting either my stop or my second target. I exit at the market at 4:10 p.m. Eastern and get out at 566.30 on the second half of my position.

## E-mini Nasdaq—September 2004 Contract, September 3, 2004

1. The Nasdaq gaps down, and I place a bid at daily S1 at 1380.50 (see Fig. 7.10). This isn't filled, and when it moves up through the midpoint, I raise my bid to

### F I G U R E   7.9

**F I G U R E   7.10**

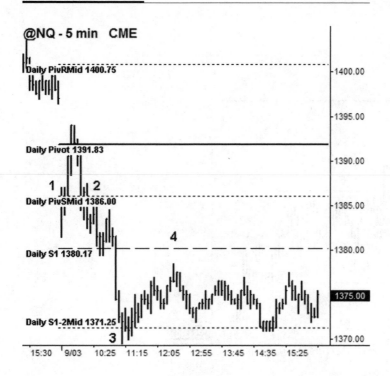

1386.50. I get filled and place a stop at 1382.50, with my first target at 1391.00. The first target is hit, and I raise my stop to 1385.50.

2. I'm stopped on the second half. The market goes on to make new lows, and I place a short at 1385.50. I don't get filled.

3. The market continues to fall and slams into the next pivot level.

4. I move my short bid down to the next level at 1379.50. I don't get filled and nothing else sets up for the day. A good day to rearrange the sock drawer.

## E-mini Nasdaq—September 2004 Contract, August 5, 2004

1. The Nasdaq has a slight gap up into the midpoint, and I short at 1383.50 (see Fig. 7.11). I place a stop at 1387.50, and my first target is at 1379.50.

2. My first target is hit, and I move my stop down to 1384.50. The market rallies, and I am stopped out on my second half.

3. The Nasdaq sells off through the next pivot level.

4. Once it is through this level, I place an order to short a rally back up to this level at 1373.50. I get filled and place a stop at 1377.50 with my first target at 1369.50. The first target is hit quickly, and I move my stop down to 1369.50. My target on the second half is 1364.50.

**FIGURE 7.11**

5. My target on the second half is hit, and I am now flat.

6. I place an order to short a rally to the above pivot level at 1368.50. I am filled and place a stop at 1372.50. My first target is the pivot below at 1364.50. This gets hit, and I move my stop down to 1369.50.

7. My second target is hit at 1359.50. I place an order to short a rally to the next overhead pivot level at 1364.00. I come right up to this level but am not filled, and that is the last pivot play that sets up for the day.

## Mini-Sized Dow—September 2004 Contract, August 5, 2004

1. The mini-sized Dow futures open mixed and begin selling off early in the session (see Fig. 7.12). I place an order to short the next rally to midpoint at 10118, but I don't get filled. Once I break down through the daily pivot, I move my order to short down to 10091. This time I get filled, and I place a stop at 10111 and an order to cover half my position at 10069. I'm filled on the first half of my order, and I then move my stop down to 10097. My next target is 10041.

2. My next target is hit, and I'm now flat.

3. The market continues to move lower and tests the next pivot level. I place an order to short at the pivot level above, right at 10035. The market is acting really slowly. I put

**F I G U R E   7.12**

my orders in place and go grab some lunch. By the time I get back, I'm still not filled, which is why I absolutely love the low volume August trading. It takes a couple of hours, but I end up getting filled later in the afternoon. I place a stop at 10055, and my first target is 10015. This target is hit quickly, and I move my stop down to 10041.

4. My second target is hit at 9988, and I'm now flat. Since the market continues to trend lower, I place a bid to short at the next overhead pivot level and I place an offer at 10008.

5. The market trades right up to this level, but I don't get filled. When the market collapses, I move my offer down to 9982, but this doesn't get filled either.

## Mini-Sized Dow—September 2004 Contract, September 2, 2004

1. The markets open mixed and rally into the midpoint at 10189 (see Fig. 7.13). I set up to buy the first pullback, and I place an order at 10163. I come very close to this level but not quite, and I don't get filled. The market rallies through the next pivot level, and I move my bid up to 10192. The market doesn't even look back and keeps on going, moving up through yet the next pivot level.

2. I move up my bid again to 10221. This time I get filled and place a stop at 10201, and my first target is 10238. The first target is hit quickly, and I move up my stop to 10215.

FIGURE 7.13

@YM - 5 min   CBOT

3. My second target is hit at 10261, and I am now flat.

4. The market rallies, and I place an order to buy at 10267. I don't get filled, and the market closes near its highs.

## Mini-Sized Dow—September 2004 Contract, August 25, 2004

1. The Dow gaps down, and I place in a bid at 10077 (see Fig. 7.14). I get filled and place a stop at 10057 with my first target at 10090. My first target is hit, and I move up my stop to 10071.

2. The Dow continues to rally, and my second target is hit at 10104.

3. I place an order at 10096 in order to buy the next pullback. I get filled and place a stop at 10076. The market slows to a crawl for the next hour and nothing happens. Then momentum begins to pick up, and I'm out of my first half at 10104. I raise my stop to 10090.

4. My second target is hit at 10118.

5. The Dow continues to rally to the next pivot level. I place an order to buy a pullback at 10124. I don't get filled.

**F I G U R E   7.14**

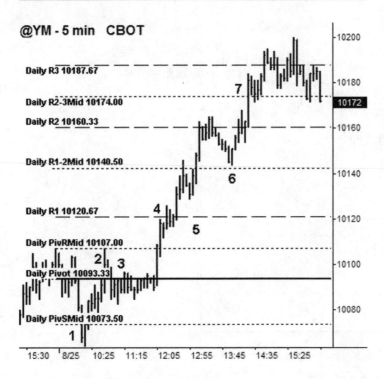

6.  The market pushes higher to the next level, and I raise my bid to 10144. I get filled and place a stop order at 10124 with my first target at 10157. My first target is hit quickly, and I raise my stop to 10138.

7.  My second target is hit at 10171, and I am now flat. The market continues to rally to daily R3. This is a rare event. The markets hardly ever get through R3, and I always fade initial moves to these levels. I place an order to short at 10185. I am filled and place a stop at 10205. The market pushes up to 10200 and fades into the close. Since neither of my parameters is hit, I cover at 4:10 p.m. Eastern at 10176.

## KLAC (KLA Tencor Corp), September 10, 2004

1.  KLAC gaps down on this day, and I place an order to buy at 38.48 (see Fig. 7.15). I am filled, and I place a stop at 37.93. My first target is hit at 38.89, and I raise my stop to 38.38.

2.  The stock continues to rally, and my second target is hit at 39.39.

3.  I place an order to buy the first pullback at 38.99. This order doesn't get filled, and the stock runs away.

**F I G U R E   7.15**

KLAC - 5 min  NASDAQ

**4.** When it breaks the next pivot level, I raise my bid to 39.49. It takes a while, but I get filled and place a stop at 38.99.

**5.** My first target is hit at 39.72, and I raise my stop to 39.39.

**6.** By the time the market approaches the close, neither of my parameters is hit, and I close out at the market right at 4:00 p.m. Eastern at 39.78.

## Trending versus Choppy Markets

For the most part, the setups we just went through cover trending markets. I also wanted to take a look at choppy markets to show how the pivots work under those circumstances. Figure 7.16 shows the mini-sized Dow on a day where it stayed locked in a confined, narrow trading range through the majority of the day. In fact, most of the initial move down happened before the 9:30 a.m. Eastern open for the cash markets. I also inserted some basic indicators onto this chart to show how far they can lag behind on a choppy day versus a setup that is based purely on price. The indicators I'm looking at are basic exponential moving averages as well as an RSI index. This doesn't mean these indicators don't have any value—it's just important to keep in mind that, for the most part, an indicator-only based trading approach is a lagging approach, and this fact is heightened on a choppy trading day.

**F I G U R E   7.16**

1. As the markets chop along and the volume on the ES chart continues to run under 10,000 contracts, this becomes the appropriate time to set up the pivot plays in the following "chop-enhanced" manner (see Fig. 7.17). At point 1 the YM is quiet, and I am looking to fade a move to the nearest pivot level. I don't want to sit and stare at the markets while this mind-numbing action unfolds. Therefore, I place a buy limit order at the nearest pivot level below current price action, plus three points, so I'm just in front of the pivot. I also place a sell limit order at the next level above current price action.

2. The sell limit order is hit first. I came close to the buy limit order but didn't quite make it. Once the sell limit order is hit, I place a 20-point stop. My first target is a mechanical 10 points away from my entry, and my second target is the next pivot level below. It is a weekly pivot level at 10532, so I would set up a buy limit order at 10535 to cover the second half of my short.

3. Both of my targets are hit, and I am taken out of the trade. Note that when the moving averages finally crossed over, the markets were almost at our final target. Indicators like moving averages work amazingly well on trending days, but they are a killer on choppy days. Price rules on the choppy days.

**F I G U R E  7.17**

YMH04 - 5 min  CBOT  L=10575 +23 +0.22% B=10575 A=10576 O=10563 Hi=1 ...

RSI (Close,7,30,70,Cyan,Red)  48.15 30.00 70.00

This example shows something that traders will notice quite often when they trade this system: They will be trading exactly the same levels multiple times during a given day. The level at which a person would get long on a decline is also the level where a trader would close out a short, and vice versa.

Let's take another look at the same chart (Fig. 7.17), but we'll look at all the setups that occurred that day.

1. At point 1, the YM falls to one of the weekly levels, but doesn't quite touch it. I manage to get into the market long because my limit buy order is the weekly level +3 points. The weekly level is 10532, so my limit buy order is placed at 10535. I'm out for +10 points quickly on the first half and then bring my stop up to "pivot −3" which is breakeven −6.

2. At point 2 we come up and ease just through the daily midpoint. I am out of the second half of my long on a limit order to this level. Note that the moving averages have barely crossed higher only when the markets have reached the target. I try to reverse and short, but the market moves too quickly, and I miss the short.

One way around this is to keep a resting order in for the stop as well as a new position. If traders are long 10 contracts and want to reverse and go short when they exit, then they just set sell limit order for 20 contracts. This way traders will exit their long and establish a short position simultaneously.

3. For point 3 I am bidding long for a decline back at the weekly level +3 points. The weekly level is 10532, so my bid is that plus 3 points, which is 10535. When two levels like this are close together (by at least 10 points—in this case a weekly level and the daily pivot), I will place my bid with the level closest to the price action. I am filled on my long. The market eases through and trades around this level for half an hour. My stop is not hit, though it comes close. My initial target for "half at 10 points" is hit quickly, and I trail my stop. It is not until a couple of hours later that my second target is hit at the midpoint. This is an important note: Some of these trades will last a few hours in duration, while others can last 10 minutes. The key is to wait for the levels to be reached and not try to hurry things along or get out because of anxiety or boredom. Although human emotions are a good idea in building relationships with other people, in trading, they have to be ignored.

4. I am out of the second half of my long over three hours later, at a daily midpoint level. Since this is a choppy day, I just reverse and go short, placing the target on the first half of my position 10 points away from my entry. My second target is the next level below + 3 points.

5. The market actually moves quickly, and I'm out of the first half in 15 minutes and the second half another 15 minutes after that. I reverse and go long and set up the same parameters, +10 points on the first half, and back to the other pivot on the second half.

6. I'm out of the first half quickly for +10, and the market continues to trek higher into the close. The market doesn't quite reach my second target, and I end up getting out "at the market" at 4:10 p.m. Eastern, a few points below my target. Note again that by the time the moving averages crossed higher, I was already out of half my position.

## TRAILING STOPS IN THIS FASHION IS THE KEY

I'm not a big fan of aggressively trailing stops. By this I mean that if the market moves in my favor 1 YM point, I will keep my stop static instead of then trailing it up by one point. This auto-trailing stop strategy generally will stop a trader out on the first normal retracement, and these are moves I'm willing to sit through. However, if I've established multiple targets and my first target is hit, then and only then will I generally move up my stop to protect gains on the entire trade. For pivot plays, I treat stop movement the same on both trending and choppy days. I'm just waiting for my first target to get hit. Once that happens, then and only then will I move up my stop.

1.  Here we have our original 20 stop from our long entry on a decline to the weekly
    pivot + 3 points (see Fig. 7.18).
2.  If this was a trending day, then I would wait until my first target—the next pivot
    level—is hit. At that point I would trail up my stop. On a choppy day, my first tar-
    get would be +10 points on the YM, so in this example that would mean that my
    stop would have been moved up sooner, right after my first lower target was hit.

## TIPS AND TRICKS FOR USING THE PIVOTS

The key with this setup and all the setups I use is that the trader gets everything prepared on
his or her charts in advance of the opening. Once it is set up, all the trader has to do is watch
and wait, or better yet, utilize audio alerts to give the trader a heads up that a setup is either

**F I G U R E  7.18**

forming or firing off. With respect to pivots, traders can place orders in advance, as the exact targets, entries, and stops are known before the trade is entered. This way the traders can also focus on other things if they come up. When the traders hear the alerts going off, they know that it is time to go back to their charts and see what is going on. There is no chasing. The orders will either get hit or they will not. This system, as well as all the systems I use, is constructed in such a way as to naturally enforce the mindset of a professional trader, which is the only consistent way to make money in the financial markets.

The important thing to know about midpoints is you don't need to use them all the time. I use them on days when the distance between two YM daily pivot levels is greater than 40 points. This is a general rule, and it is okay to use them if the pivot level is only 30 points. If the pivots are closer together than 30 points, the midpoints don't play as much of a role because the markets will move straight to the next pivot since they are so close together.

On my charts I typically use a black background, which can't be shown in the context of this book. I then make the daily pivots yellow, the weekly pivots light blue (cyan), the monthly pivots purple, and the midpoints white. I also make the central pivots solid lines and the rest of the pivots dotted or dashed lines. This way it is very easy to pick out what the markets are butting up against.

The use of pivots has gotten a lot easier over the years. I used to calculate these manually by using a calculator, and then eventually switched to an excel spreadsheet where all I had to do was enter the high/low/close, and the spreadsheet did the rest. However, I still had to manually draw the horizontal lines on my charts each day, and this took the good part of half an hour. There is software that will calculate the pivots for a person automatically, but it generally uses the wrong timeframes and can create errors because of bad ticks. I'm anal-retentive when it comes to this, and I have to manually enter my pivots each day—I want to make sure they are correct. I finally found a programmer who could help me out on this, and the end result is a piece of software that I use now for both eSignal and TradeStation. The software is set up with the colors I like, it labels the levels accordingly as daily, weekly, midpoint and so on, and I can manually enter the high/low/close. Once these numbers are entered, the software will place all the pivots where they are supposed to go in seconds. For more information on this and other trading software visit www.trade-themarkets.com.

## WHAT ABOUT FIBONACCI NUMBERS?

One question I frequently receive in regards to the pivots is how they relate to Fibonacci retracement levels. For the uninitiated, Fibonacci numbers are used by traders to determine support and resistance levels, with the most commonly used retracement levels being .382, .50, and .618. In my experience, sometimes these work great, and sometimes the market doesn't even know they exist and blows right through them. However, I do like to see where the Fibonacci cluster numbers are on any given trading day. These are more accurate than regular Fibonacci numbers because of the use of more data points and the way the Fibonacci ratios are calculated. To get these numbers takes a lot of work, and for a while I calculated them myself. Then I discovered Carolyn Boroden's work at www.syncmt.com and from then on I just subscribed to her service, as this is her area of expertise. She works on both the time and price axis of the markets using the confluence of Fibonacci ratios. For price she runs retracements of prior swings using the ratios of .382, .50, .618, and .786. She also runs price extensions of prior swings, which are essentially retracements beyond 100 percent. For extensions she uses the ratios of 1.272 and 1.618. Carolyn also runs price projections comparing swings in the same direction. For projections she uses 100 percent and 1.618. In doing this she runs all possible levels from the key swing highs and lows in a chart and looks for the confluences. When she sees a confluence, these become the key levels in the markets to buy and sell against.

For me, I'm interested in the bigger levels found on 60 minute and daily charts, and I use these mostly for swing trading. However, there will be days when these clusters line up with some of the daily pivot levels, and of course on these days those particular levels become that much stronger. I also like to look at these Fibonacci cluster levels on other markets, as they provide key levels across all markets. Let's look at a few examples from Carolyn Boroden's work.

## Mini-Sized Dow—June 2005 Contract, April 6, 2005

Figure 7.19 is on the 15-minute Mini-Sized Dow Futures contract. You can see the obvious uptrend that developed from the April 4 swing low. For this reason, we wanted to focus on setting up clusters on the buy side of the market. We saw a nice zone develop between 10489 and 10492. This zone included the coincidence of a 1.618 price extension, a .50 percent retracement, a 0.382 retracement of another swing, and a 100 percent price projection of a prior corrective decline. The initial low was made directly within this cluster zone at the 10489 level. From there, we saw a rally to 10578 or 89 points.

## Euro FX—June 2005 Contract, April 27, 2005

In the 5-minute euro currency example in Figure 7.20, we found a confluence of 3 key Fibonacci price relationships between 1.2970 and 1.2971. This included a 0.618 retracement of the 1.2961 low to the 1.2988 high, a 0.786 retracement of the 1.2966 low to the 1.2988 high, and a 100 percent price projection of the 1.2984 high to the 1.2966 (swing) low. The actual low was made at 1.2972. The initial rally took you to 1.2990.

## Mini-Sized Dow—June 2005 Contract, April 4, 2005

For entries into the market, we ideally want to set up "price clusters" in the direction of the trend in the timeframe we are trading. We sometimes use "counter trend" clusters for exits or

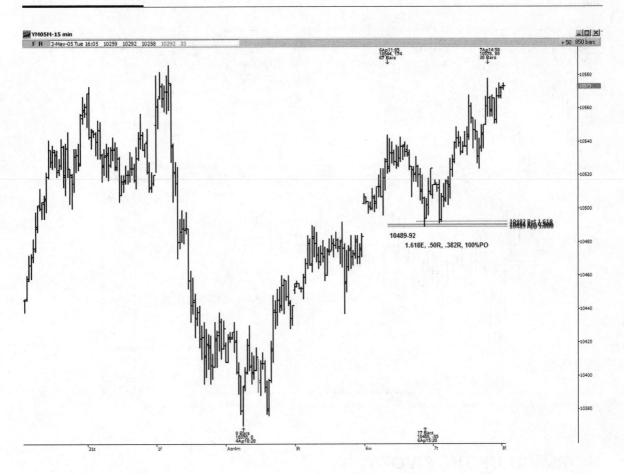

to tighten up stops on a position. The example in Figure 7.21 in the Mini-Dow futures contract shows a confluence (clustering) of at least 5 Fibonacci price relationships between the 10132–10141 area. The focus of these levels came in between the 10132–10136 area. In this case the actual low was made at 10140. A "trigger" for an entry against this zone could be as simple as taking out a prior bar high. At that point your initial stop could be placed either below the low made prior to the "trigger" (10140) or below the low end of the cluster zone (10135). The initial move off this cluster was 58 points.

These examples for Carolyn's work show how these Fibonacci clusters act as support and resistance levels in the markets, and I use them intraday just as I use the pivot levels. They can also be used to initiate swing trades on larger timeframes, as these can be used on any timeframe, from a 3-minute chart to a weekly or even a monthly.

**F I G U R E   7.20**

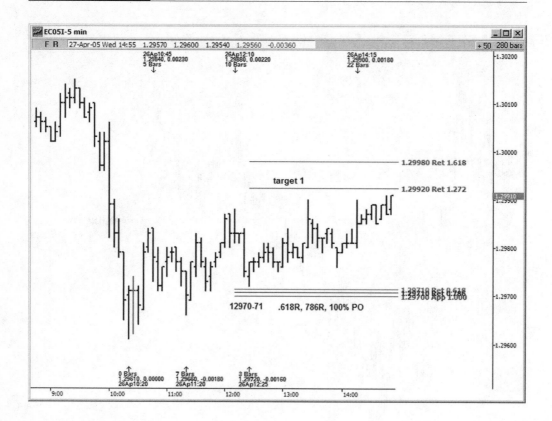

## SUMMING UP THE PIVOTS

The pivot levels work mainly because of the psychology pain/pleasure cycle that perpetuates the markets each day. Traders who follow only indicators will chase a position when it is already halfway to three-quarters the way off its pivot, and it is these traders who provide the stop losses to perpetuate the next cycle of market movement. If you rely on only indicators for your entries, instead of using the price action of the pivots, you will get in and out of these cycles too late, and you won't make any money trading.

What is nice about this system is that traders don't have to watch it very closely once they are in a position. I'm not an aggressive trailer of stops. I like to get in a position, set my parameters, and then focus on other things. Depending on the traders' work situation, they could do this at the office, especially on the West Coast, and especially if they had an order system that automatically bracketed trades. This way they can place the parameters and then go to the next meeting or appointment. *Let the parameters babysit the position*. This is much better as well because it takes human emotion out of the equation.

**F I G U R E   7.21**

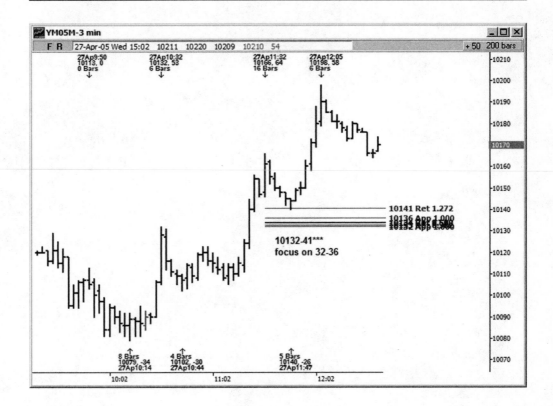

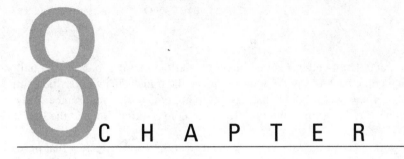

C H A P T E R

# SCALPER BUYS AND SELLS— WHEN ONLY A QUICK CONFIRMATION WILL DO

## IDENTIFYING AND PROFITING FROM CHANGES IN TREND WITHOUT CATCHING A FALLING KNIFE OR STEPPING IN FRONT OF A FREIGHT TRAIN

In watching the markets over the years I've observed that most reversals take place after three consecutive higher closes or three consecutive lower closes, and this tendency is valid for all times frames. The key to this setup is that it is based on consecutive closes and not just intraday or daily high and low price action for an individual price bar on a chart. In other words, the highs and lows are not important. I'm not interested in three higher price highs or three lower price lows. I want to see where the action settles or closes, because that is where the rubber meets the road.

The hard way to follow this play, especially intraday, is to stare at the charts and keep track of consecutive lower or higher closes until you get three in a row. This can cause a person to go bug-eyed, as well as insane, and is recommended only for those who get a thrill from "the little things in life." I'm not a big fan of staring at charts and would be a prime candidate for the mental hospital if I did this with the naked eye. Instead, I've developed a simple indicator in TradeStation that will "paint" the first bar in the sequence after the third bar has met the criteria for a signal. Once I see the paint bar, I just place a market order, and I'm in the trade. Even better, I set up an audio alert so that if I'm down the hall, I'll hear the signal and come back to my computer to place the trade. This works when I'm on the phone with my wife as well, though she has yet to appreciate the importance of the signal and my urgent need to hang up in the middle of our conversation. Such is the life of a trader.

Here is how it works: I am watching the charts and I get three bars in a row that make higher closes. At the close of the third consecutive bar, my paint bar appears on the chart, and it is marked over the first bar in the sequence of three bars. I place an order to go long at the market. To get out of this long, I just wait for three consecutive lower lows to occur, and that will be my signal to exit the trade and potentially go short. Although this is a very easy trade to execute, it may not make sense right out of the gate. Don't worry, if this sounds a little unclear, we will be looking at some charts soon enough.

I use this signal in various timeframes. For scalping the E-mini S&Ps, I like to use a 233-tick chart, because the signals are very fast. On the mini-sized Dow, I will use a 144-tick chart for scalping and a five-minute chart to catch the one or two reversals that set up on any given day. For swing trades, I will use both 60-minute and daily charts. I like to use this primarily on the stock index futures, and the major currency pairs, but it works just the same in any market, in any time frame. It is simple and is based solely on the price action. I will also use this signal for individual stocks that I am following.

## TICK CHARTS ARE BEST FOR SCALPING

Let's quickly review what a 233-tick chart is for anyone who hasn't used one before. This type of chart forms a new bar every time there are 233 trades executed. It doesn't matter what the size of the trade is, just so long as 233 trades cross the tape. When the action is fast and furious, bars will be formed at an accelerated rate. When the action is slow, it will take longer for an individual bar to form. I like to use these charts when I'm scalping for two reasons: First, they are faster than regular time charts when it really matters—when the trade frequency accelerates. In comparison, a two-minute chart is going to form a bar every two minutes, regardless of how fast or slow the trading is. With a tick chart, when the trade frequency slows down, so do the signals that are firing off in this timeframe—thus these charts naturally keep a trader out of the market when there is nothing going on. Second, traders in the pit have no concept of time with respect to a two-minute or a five-minute chart. They are focusing on the actual frequency of trades, and a breakout on a two-minute chart means nothing to them. Why do I use a 233-tick chart versus say a 235-tick chart or a 287-tick chart? There is a simple explanation for this—I like to use tick charts that are lined up with the Fibonacci numbers. Does this mean that a 233-tick chart is better than a 235-tick chart? I seriously doubt it. The Fibonacci numbers are clean, useful and make sense, and that's why I use them. A couple of example plays with tick charts are shown below.

## TRADING RULES FOR BUYS (SELLS ARE REVERSED)

1. Set up a 24-hour chart on intraday charts so the overnight activity can be accounted for in this indicator setup. This can be used in all timeframes. The larger the timeframe, the larger the parameters and potential move. For daily charts I will use the regular session hours.

2. After three consecutive higher closes, I go long at the market, at the close of the third bar in the sequence.

3. The trade is valid until three consecutive lower closes occur, at which point I exit the trade. If the market is still open for an intraday trade, I will simultaneously exit a long and establish a new short position. I don't use a stop loss on this for intraday chart trades because the reversal signal is my exit strategy, whether it is a loss or a gain. For daily charts I will place a stop at the low of the bar that caused the signal to fire off, which is the first of three in the sequence of closes.

4. If I'm in an intraday trade (15-minute chart or smaller) and the market closes before giving an exit signal, I will exit at the market at 4:10 p.m. Eastern.

5. For timeframes that are 60 minutes and above, I will stay in them overnight and exit at the next signal. This could be the next day for a 60-minute chart, and it could be a month later for daily charts.

## SPECIFIC EXAMPLES OF SCALPER BUY AND SELL SETUPS

### E-mini S&P—December 2004 Contract, October 3, 2004

1. Figure 8.1 is a 233-tick chart of the E-mini S&Ps, which is one of my favorite timeframes for taking quick scalp trades in the market. The spot marked 1 on the chart is a little to the right of the painted bar in question. The "paint" is added by TradeStation and it is the thick black mark that covers the bar. This bar is painted because it is the first bar in a series of three with consecutive higher closes.

2. When I see the paint bar signal, I go long at the market. I am filled at 1133.25, which is where we closed at point 2, which is the close of the third bar of this series of higher closes. (This will get easier, I swear.)

3. I am now in the trade until I get a signal that a reversal has developed. Later in the trading session, I get the next paint bar signal, which indicates that a series of three lower closes in a row have taken place. I place an order to sell my long position at the market. Note that the next signal will not show unless it is a reversal. There are a series of many higher closes during this rally, but none of them constitutes a reversal, so they are ignored because the original signal has already fired off.

**F I G U R E   8.1**

4. I am out at 1138.50, which is the close of the third bar in the series of lower lows at point 4 on the chart. The gain on the trade was +5.25 S&P points, or $262 per contract. It is interesting to note that during this trade all the oscillators were measuring overbought near the 1135.00 level, which would have gotten some traders out and caused other traders to start going short. Using this setup, the only thing that matters is the price, which, in reality, is the only thing that matters.

## E-mini S&P—December 2004 Contract, October 5, 2004

1. On October 5, 2004. I got a short reversal signal near 1:00 p.m. Eastern on the 15-minute ES chart, and I entered at the market right after the signal fired off (see Fig. 8.2).
2. I am filled at 1137.00. I'm now waiting for the next reversal signal to cover my short and go long.
3. As we approach 3:00 p.m. Eastern we get a signal, and I cover my short and also go long at the same time.
4. My fill is 1134.00. I'm out for +3.00 points on the S&P play, and I have established a new long position.

**F I G U R E   8.2**

5. There isn't another reversal signal until near 8:00 p.m. Eastern. However, because this is off an intraday chart (15 minutes or less), I exited this position at the market at 4:10 p.m. Eastern, and I was filled at 1133.75 for a loss of –0.25 points.

6. Some traders I know like to watch the action 24 hours a day, and they would stay in the trade until point 6. They would have gotten out at 1136.50 for a gain of +2.50. I don't recommend this. The market action in the stock index futures after hours is slow and irritating, and there are many other things I'd rather do with my time. If you want to actively trade after 4:00 p.m. Eastern, then by far the best liquidity and opportunities are in the currency markets. I prefer the forex cash markets in this regard because there is more liquidity in the various currency pairs during this post 4:00 p.m. timeframe. When markets are active and liquid, they are tradable. When they are quiet, let them be.

## E-mini S&P—December 2004 Contract, September 30, 2004

1. At 12:30 p.m. on September 30, 2004, I got a signal on the 60-minute ES chart, indicating that a reversal was in place (see Fig. 8.3). The bar that is painted is the 10:30 a.m. bar. Remember, even though the 10:30 a.m. bar was painted, the signal

**F I G U R E  8.3**

didn't actually fire off until the close of the third bar at 12:30 a.m. (the 10:30 bar is the first bar, the 11:30 bar is the second bar, and the 12:30 bar is the third bar).

2.  At 12:30 p.m. I go long at the market, and I'm filled at 1114.75. I am now awaiting the next reversal signal in order to exit my position.

3.  I get my next signal a few days later on October 4.

4.  I exit at 1136.50, for a gain of +21.75 S&P points, or $1,087.50 per contract. The 60 minute chart is great for catching swings that last anywhere from 2 to 5 days. This is a great setup for people who are holding down a full-time job and don't have time to stare at the markets all day. In addition, this is a great setup for people who are day trading and are currently losing money. This 60-minute setup forces discipline and prevents a trader from over-trading, which is by far the number one reason why most traders fail to make money in this profession.

## E-mini S&P—September 2004 Contract, June 28, 2004

1.  On this daily chart of the S&Ps, a signal fires off on June 28, 2004, which paints the June 24 daily bar (see Fig. 8.4). (June 26 and 27 were the weekend.)

2.  I go short at the close of the third day, which is what triggered the signal. I'm in the trade at 1132.50. I will now stay in the trade until I get a reversal signal. For a

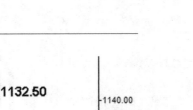

stop I use 1153.50, which is the high of the June 24 bar. In my experience the actual stop is rarely hit because a reversal signal will fire off before the markets reach that level.

3. On July 28, a month later, I get a reversal signal that paints the July 24 bar.

4. I exit at the market on July 28 at the close. I'm out at 1096.00 for a gain of +36.50 S&P points, or $1,825 per contract. Again, this setup is great for people who are working and don't have time to stare at the markets all day. I also think it is important for full-time traders to have two accounts, one for day trading and one for swing trading. During a time when a trader's day trading isn't going well, it is possible to catch a good move in the swing trading account using setups like this.

## Mini-Sized Dow—September 2004 Contract, August 10, 2004

1. On this daily chart of the mini-sized Dow futures, a long signal occurs on August 10, 2004, which paints the August 6 bar (see Fig. 8.5).

2. I go long at the close of August 10, and I'm filled at 9916. I'm now waiting for the next reversal signal in order to exit the trade. The low of August 6 is 9809, which is where I place my stop.

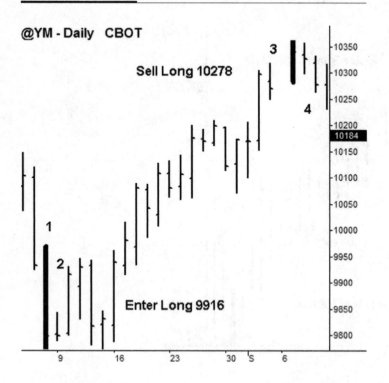

3. The next signal hits on September 7, nearly a month later.

4. I'm out at 10278 for a gain of +362 YM points, or $1,810 per contract. One of the things I like about these swing trades is that they tend to take care of themselves. Compared to the active and sometimes frantic pace of intraday trading, it's almost like buying a rental property and turning the maintenance over to a management company. The type of trading a person chooses to do really is a reflection of their personality. Someone who is inherently a swing trader will have a tough time at day trading.

## KLAC (KLA Tencor Corp), April 5, 2004

1. On this daily chart of KLAC, a reversal signal setup on April 5, 2004 (see Fig. 8.6).

2. I took a short at the close and got in at 52.51. My plan is to now stay in the trade until I get the next reversal signal. My stop is the high of the signal bar, which is 53.97.

3. About a month later, on May 3, I get a reversal signal.

4. I cover my short at 42.96 for a gain of +9.55. For traders who just focus on stocks, this is a great setup to use on the daily charts to catch reversals.

FIGURE 8.6

## Light, Sweet Crude Oil—September 2004 Contract, September 9, 2004

1. It is important to note that this setup is based purely on price action, and therefore works in all markets (see Fig. 8.7). On September 9, 2004, a reversal signal was painted on crude oil.

2. The resulting long was entered at 43.60.

3. On September 28 the reversal paint bar was in.

4. I'm out of the trade at 49.50, for a gain of 5.90. Note that this exit bar also became an entry signal to get back into the trade long as the market reversed right away and made three higher closes. If you are not familiar with crude oil, a one-dollar move on the big contract is worth $1,000, and on the mini-contract it is worth $500. So a move of 5.90 equates to $5,900 per contract on the big (symbol = CL), and $2,950 per contract on the mini (symbol = QM). The quote feed a person needs to get live crude oil prices is Nymex. There is an option for this in eSignal and TradeStation, and it's also available through most of the other robust quote vendors.

**F I G U R E   8.7**

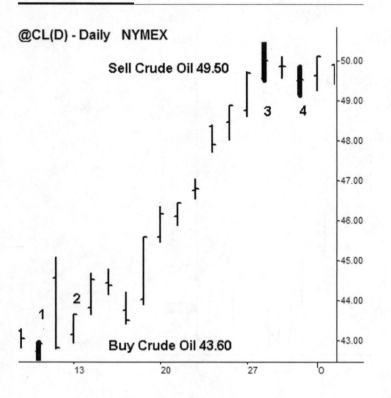

@CL(D) - Daily   NYMEX

Sell Crude Oil 49.50

Buy Crude Oil 43.60

## Mini-Sized Dow—December 2004 Contract, October 6, 2004

1. I wanted to use this example to show how I flow in and out of positions intraday, going both long and short (see Fig. 8.8). This is best done on lower-value intraday charts such as five-minute charts or a tick chart like 233. The first signal on October 6, 2004, in the YM was painted at 10:35 a.m. Eastern.

2. This means, of course, that I am going short at the close of the last bar in the sequence of three bars, which is 10176.

3. The next reversal is noted on the chart at point 3.

4. I cover at 10169 and simultaneously go long. The easy way to do this is to double the number of contracts you are trading on your exit order. So, if you are long 10 contracts, then you place an order to sell 20 contracts in order to exit your 10 long contracts, and at the same time establish a new position that is short 10 contracts.

5. The next signal occurs at point 5.

6. I go long at 10186 and simultaneously go short at this same level.

7. The next signal occurs at point 7.

8. I cover my short at 10173 and go long at the same level.

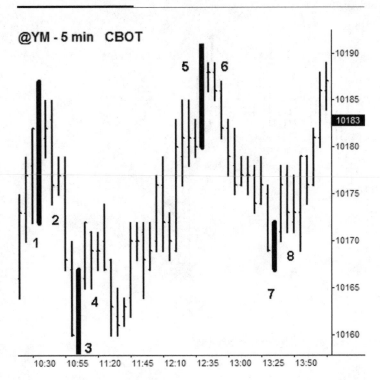

**FIGURE 8.8**

I'd like to share some examples of this same setup in the forex currency markets and continue to add commentary regarding the trading of these instruments. Let's start with a market that most traders are familiar with, the euro currency as it trades against the U.S. dollar.

## Forex Markets—EURUSD, October 15, 2004

1. On the daily chart of EURUSD (see Fig. 8.9), a long signal fires off on October 15, 2004. I go long near point 1 at 1.2469. Remember, the stop is the lows of the signal bar.

2. The market has a steady move higher off this level, pausing to consolidate for a week in early November. However, there aren't any reversal signals given during this time, so there is nothing to do but sit on my hands and stay in the trade. EURUSD resumes its rally and shoots up hard into the end of December. At this point the market rolls over and many people in this trade start taking profits. Again, however, there are no sell signals using this setup. Finally, on January 3, 2005, nearly two and one half months after the initial buy signal, a sell signal is generated at point 2. I exit at 1.3467 for a gain of 998 pips. At $10 per pip, that is $9,980 per

**F I G U R E   8.9**

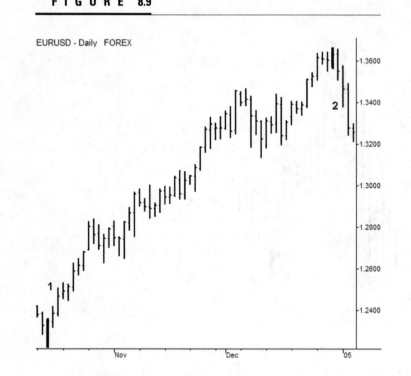

EURUSD - Daily  FOREX

individual lot that is being traded. For each lot, a trader needs to have $1,000 in their account. This is part of the large attraction of the forex markets—the ability to establish specific stops while using leverage to ride out a potential trend until it turns. Forex traders often talk in terms of the dollar value of the contract they are trading. One lot (contract) represents $100,000 worth of currency, 10 lots represents $1,000,000 worth of currency, and so on. Being long 10 lots is referred to as having a "buck" (i.e., a dollar). If I'm long 35 lots of EURUSD and I need to call my broker to change my order, he or she will refer to my position as "three and a half bucks." Also, catching 1 full cent, or 100 pips, is referred to as catching "one large." So on this play, we caught almost "10 large" which is, of course, a huge play. In the interbank market, which is where all of the institutions and large funds trade currencies, the smallest trade size is 1,000,000, or the equivalent of trading 10 lots through your retail forex broker.

## Forex Markets—GBPUSD, May 9, 2005

1. On this daily chart of GBPUSD (see Fig. 8.10), a short signal sets up on May 9, 2005 at point 1 and I go short at 1.8837.

2. The market sells off steadily, and on June 3, 2005 it fires off a reversal signal at point #2. I cover my position at 1.8148 for a gain of 689 pips or $6,890 per contract. Or, in forex trader speak, almost seven large.

**F I G U R E  8.10**

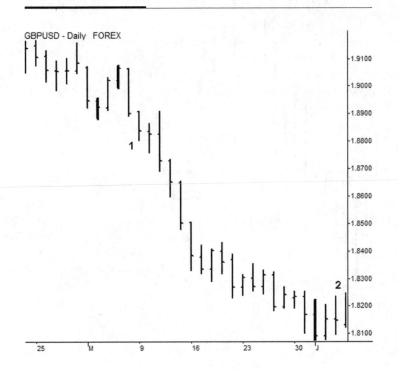

GBPUSD - Daily  FOREX

## Forex Markets—GBPUSD, August 2, 2005

1. While this signal works well on daily charts for the forex markets, it also works well on intraday charts for day trading. On this 5-minute chart (see Fig. 8.11) of GBPUSD, a long signal sets up on August 2, 2005 at point 1. The entry is 1.7696.

2. About an hour later, the corresponding reversal signal fires off at point 2. This is the heads up to close out this position. The price level is 1.7724, a gain of 28 pips or $280 per contract.

## Forex Markets—AUDUSD, July 31, 2005

1. On July 31, 2005 (see Fig. 8.12) AUDUSD sets up a long signal on the 60-minute chart at point 1. The long entry is at 0.7560.

2. The next day on August 1, 2005, a reversal signal is given at point 2, and we exit the play at .7604, for a gain of 44 pips. Remember, any currency pair that ends in "USD" is worth $10 per pip, so the gain on this trade is $440 per lot being traded. The three main currencies I trade that end in "USD" are the euro (EURUSD), pound (GBPUSD), and aussie (AUDUSD). If a currency ends in "USD" this means that it will generally move in the opposite direction of the U.S. dollar

GBPUSD - 5 min   FOREX

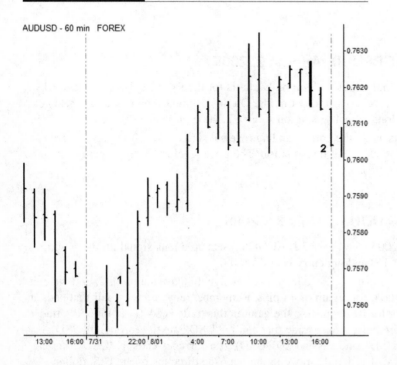

AUDUSD - 60 min   FOREX

index. If the dollar is moving higher, then euro, pound, and aussie are selling off. Within these three currencies, the euro and pound are most closely correlated to the dollar. The Australian dollar is also tied in closely to commodity prices, as Australia is a huge exporter of various commodities. Because of this, the Aussie at times doesn't move in direct correlation with the U.S. dollar. Let's take a look at the other main currency pairs.

## Forex Markets—USDCHF, July 21, 2005

1. On July 21, 2005 (see Fig. 8.13) USDCHF sets up a long signal on the 60-minute chart at point #1. The long entry is at 1.2855.
2. A few days later, on July 24, a reversal signal is given at point #2, and we exit at 1.2971, for a gain of 116 pips. Since this currency pair does not end in "USD" the valuation of the pip will be slightly different than the previous examples. When this play was taken, the value of a pip was around $7. So, in this case, 116 pips equates to a gain of $812 per lot being traded. This currency, the Swiss Franc, trades very closely with the U.S. dollar. If the dollar is going higher, so is swissy.

### F I G U R E   8.13

## Forex Markets—USDJPY, July 20, 2005

1. On July 20, 2005 (see Fig. 8.14) USDJPY fires off a short at point 1 on the 120 minute chart. The short entry is at 112.85.

2. The next day, on July 21, the market gives a reversal signal for an exit at 110.40 at point 2, a gain of 245 pips. Pip value on the USDJPY at the time of this writing is around $8, so this translates into a gain of $1960 per lot being traded, or two and a half large. The Japanese Yen also moves very closely with the dollar.

## Forex Markets—USDJPY, July 22, 2005

1. On July 22, 2005 (see Fig. 8.15) USDJPY fires off a long signal at 111.12. The market quiet downs shortly thereafter, but has a steady grind higher.

2. About a week later, on July 28, a reversal signal shows up on the chart at point 2, signaling an exit at 112.10. This is a gain of 95 pips or $784 per retail lot. All "lots" discussed in these forex trades are based on the retail "standard" lot, which is worth $100,000. This is as opposed to the "mini," which is worth $10,000.

**F I G U R E   8.14**

**F I G U R E   8.15**

## Forex Markets—USDCAD, July 21, 2005

1. On July 21, 2005 (see Fig. 8.16) USDCAD fires off a long signal at point 1. The entry is 1.2169. The market consolidates for a few days, and almost stops the play out—but a sell signal is never given. In this situation, there is nothing to do but wait for a signal to exit the trade. We've already established why human emotion makes a poor "exit signal."

2. Nearly a week later, on July 27, a reversal signal is given at point 2 and we are out of the long at 1.2360, a gain of 191 pips—almost two large. The rate for pips on this currency pair during this play were about $6, which translates into a gain of $1146 per lot being traded. After reviewing this play, we've now covered the six major currency pairs that most traders focus on. There are other currency pairs that are also good to trade, and I will focus on two of my favorites next.

## Forex Markets—EURJPY, August 2, 2005

1. On August 2, 2005 (see Fig. 8.17) EURJPY—euro/yen—fires off a short signal at point 1 at 136.66 on the 15-minute chart. The market chops around for about an hour before breaking down and selling off.

## F I G U R E  8.16

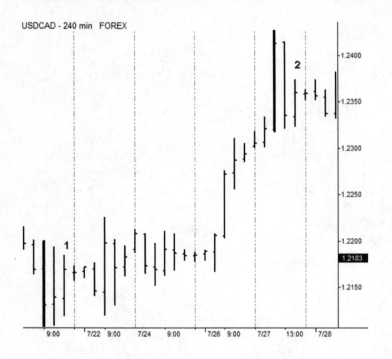

## F I G U R E  8.17

2. Nearly two hours later, a corresponding reversal signal is given at point 2, and I exit the trade at 136.18, for a gain of 48 pips. The pip value on this currency pair was around $8 at the time of this play, which translates into a gain of $384 per lot being traded.

## Forex Markets—EURGBP, July 19, 2005

1. On July 19, 2005 (see Fig. 8.18) EURGBP—euro/pound—fires off a long signal at 0.6912 on the 240-minute chart. The market grinds higher.
2. Two days later, we get three lower closes in a row and the signal fires off at point 2. The exit on the long is 0.6970, or 58 pips. On this currency cross each pip is worth about $18, which makes the payout on this play $1044 per lot. This is actually a very quiet currency, but when it does move, it is very steady and it tends to act like nothing can stand in its way. Because of this trait, we nicknamed this currency pair "the tank."

**F I G U R E   8.18**

## SUMMING UP THE SCALPER BUYS AND SELLS

Scalper buys and sells are especially useful for traders who like to try to buy bottoms or short tops. While it is foolish to short a market just because its "too high" or buy a market because its "too low," its fine to short that high flyer or buy that all-out loser once you get a reversal confirmation with this signal. It doesn't mean that the dead highs or the dead lows are in place, but it does mean that there has been a temporary shift in power, and it is a valid signal to step in and establish a position. Whether this is an intraday reversal on a five-minute chart, or a total market reversal off a daily chart, the concept is exactly the same. In addition, this play is based on pure price action, and I appreciate its simple and effective nature.

## INCREASE PROBABILITIES OF SUCCESS THROUGH MULTI-SETUP COMBINATIONS

One theme that a trader will find in my setups is that they all work well together. I particularly like to combine the pivots with the scalper buys and sells on a 233-tick chart for the ES and a 144-tick chart for the YM. On days when I'm not sure what the market is going to do, I can wait for a scalper confirmation against a pivot level, as this is a trade that has a very high probability of success. Even better, I will get into a pivot trade, and shortly thereafter I get a scalper confirmation in the direction of the trade. I can also use the scalper sell reversal to get out of my long pivot trade. I talk about this more in the chapter on developing a business plan, but the idea is to find what makes sense to you and your personality and mix and match accordingly.

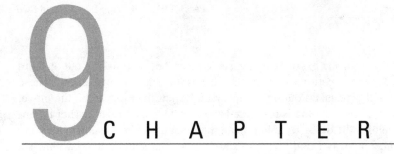

# CHAPTER 9

# TICK FADES: TAKING THE OPPOSITE SIDE OF THE NEWBIES

## THE NUMBER ONE ACTION ALERT AVAILABLE TODAY

The markets spend the majority of their time backing and filling. That is, they drift up to a resistance level, then turn around and drift back to a level of support, not really doing much of anything. For most of this time, there isn't much for a trader to do except wait, and that usually involves extreme patience. Many traders fail in this regard. After all, they are traders, right? They should be taking a trade or managing a trade, not just sitting around doing nothing. This is and will always be one of the biggest misconceptions about trading—the thought that a trader has to be in a trade nearly every minute or every hour of the day. In reality, there are always three positions traders can be in at any given time. They can be long, short, or flat. Being flat, meaning not having any trades on, is the best course of action 60 percent of the time. Cats don't chase the first bird they see. They crouch and wait, sometimes for hours, for the right time to pounce. And so it should be for the active trader. When something interesting actually does happen, such as a buy or sell program hitting the markets, this creates a great scalping opportunity for the alert trader. The key for traders is to be patient, sit on their hands, and wait for these moments to occur.

There is no easier way to do this than watching the ticks, or, I should say, "listening" for the ticks. When the ticks get over +1000 or −1000, this represents extreme buying or selling, and at this stage of the move most of the bullets have already been fired. Many amateur traders get caught up in the froth and excitement, get scared that they are missing out on a big move, and jump onboard in the direction of the move—just as it is starting to peter out. These are the bag holders that will get shaken out on the reversal. Rather than join in on the move, I like to wait until an extreme tick reading is registered and then fade the move. Earlier I mentioned that I liked to listen for the ticks. By this I mean that I set up audio signals to alert me when these levels are hit. This way I don't have to stare at the charts and potentially miss a move if I'm not paying attention. I can be down the hall, hear the alert, and know exactly what is going on.

Getting down to specifics, whenever I see or hear readings of over +1000 or −1000 ticks, I fade the move by placing a market order. If we get a +1000 tick reading and I am flat, I short the move at the market. If I am already long based on another signal, I start exiting that move and initiating a short position. The reverse is also true. If the markets are selling off and traders are jumping in on the move down to the point where a tick reading of −1000 is registered, I want to step in and buy. There isn't any cleaner way to get on the opposite side of amateur traders chasing the market. I've been shown a couple of different renditions of this setup by other traders. The ticks have been around for a long time, and many people who have been doing this for decades have a portion of their trading tied into the ticks.

## TRADING RULES FOR SELL FADES (BUYS ARE REVERSED)

1. I have studied three different setups that I have learned from other traders and have modified them to fit my own trading plan and style. Let's look at the parameters I use for this "extreme emotion" play. I take trades only between 10:00 a.m. to 3:30 p.m. Eastern. A lot of sporadic action can happen during the first and last half hour of trading. I like to let the markets settle in before taking trades.

2. I play tick fades in two markets, the E-mini S&Ps (ES) and the mini-sized Dow (YM). These can also be played in the SPY, DIA, E-mini-Russell, E-mini Nasdaq, and any stocks that are mirroring the action of these indexes.

3. When the ticks reach +1000, I short at the market. I like to set audio alerts for +1000 and −1000 readings. That way I don't have to stare at the chart. If the ticks get to +988 and fall back, I don't take the trade because I won't hear my audio alert. This keeps the setup clean and very specific, and not subject to trader interpretation.

4. For the YM I use a 30-point stop and a 20-point target. I also set a time limit on this trade of 35 minutes. If my stop or target isn't hit within the 35-minute time span, then I exit my position at the market. I like to use a timer with a beep so I'm aware of when the 35-minute time limit has passed. Most traders have very little sense of time when they're in a trade.

5. For the ES I use a three-point stop and a two-point target, as well as the same time limit.

6. If I am stopped out twice in a row on this trade, I am done with tick fades for the day. By "stopped out" I mean if my physical hard stop is hit, as opposed to the time stop.

7. If by 12:00 noon Eastern the ticks have spent over 85 percent of their time above zero, I will pass on all other tick plays for the day. This shows an extreme level of buying in the market, indicating that funds are accumulating stocks. These "power days" are rare, but they do happen about once every four to six weeks. They are accompanied by many extreme tick readings above 1000, typically between 1200 to 1400 ticks. In addition, if it is past 10:00 a.m. Eastern and the ticks have all been one-sided, for example, all positive on the day, I will wait until the ticks have spent some time in negative territory before setting up the first tick fade play.

## SPECIFIC EXAMPLES OF TICK FADE SETUPS

### Mini-Sized Dow—September 2004 Contract, September 1, 2004

1. Shortly after 10:00 a.m. Eastern on September 1, 2004, the ticks move up through +1000 (see Fig. 9.1). I short the mini-sized Dow at the market and am filled at 10192. I place a stop at 10222 and a target at 10172. I also set my timer for 35 minutes.

2. The markets drift lower, but after 35 minutes neither my target nor my stop is hit, so I exit at the market. I am filled at 10182 for +10 points.

3. The ticks hit +1000 again at point 3, and I short at the market. I am filled at 10194. I place a 30-point stop and a 20-point target.

4. The markets roll over, and my target is hit 20 minutes later at 10174 for +20 points on the trade.

5. The markets sell off hard, and the ticks get down to –1000. I buy at the market and am filled at 10118. I place a stop at 10088, 30 points below. I place a target at 10138, 20 points above my entry.

6. My target is hit within eight minutes, and I am out for +20 points.

7. The ticks reverse and quickly hit +1000, and I short at the market. I am filled at 10168.

8. The markets roll over quickly, and I am out at 10148 for +20 points.

9. The ticks hit +1000, but it is 3:50 p.m. Eastern, so I don't take the trade. Remember, according to my trading rules, I don't take any new tick fade trades after 3:30 p.m. Eastern.

**F I G U R E  9.1**

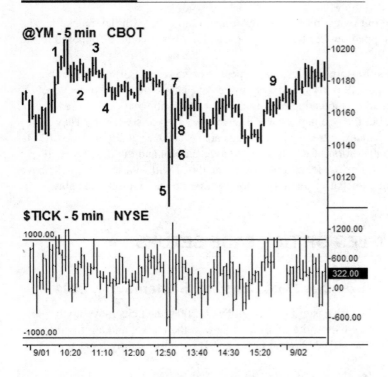

## Mini-Sized Dow—September 2004 Contract, September 10, 2004

1. On September 10, 2004, the ticks hit +1000 shortly after 10:00 a.m. Eastern (see Fig. 9.2). I short at the market and am filled at 10252. I place a 30-point stop and a 20-point target from my entry level, and I set my timer.

2. Thirty-five minutes pass, and my timer goes off so I exit at the market and am out at 10257, a loss of –5 points.

3. The ticks ramp up again and hit +1000, so I short at the market and am filled at 10262.

4. Time flies when you are having fun. My timer goes off after 35 minutes, and I exit at the market. I'm out at 10252 for a gain of +10 points.

5. The ticks head north of +1000 in the middle of the day. The only reason I'm aware of this is that my audio alert goes off. At the time, I was on the phone. I drop it and run over to the computer, short at the market, and am filled at 10264. I set my parameters, set my timer, and go back to my phone call.

6. I hear my timer go off again, and I come back to my computer to see I am still in the trade (that is, my stop or my target has not been hit), and I exit at the market. I get out at 10255 for +9 points. I don't try to finesse these timer exits—I just get out.

**FIGURE 9.2**

7. The ticks push past +1000, and I short at the market. I'm in at 10257. I place my stop and place my target.

8. The ticks continue to push higher, and the market rallies. My hard stop is hit for a loss of –30 points.

## Mini-Sized Dow—September 2004 Contract, September 9, 2004

1. Around noon on September 9, 2004, the ticks hit +1000, and I short at the market (see Fig. 9.3). I am filled at 10283. I place my stop and my target, and I set the timer.

2. Thirty-five minutes pass, and I exit at the market at 10272 for a gain of +11 points.

3. The ticks push up again past +1000, and I short at the market. I get in at 10306, and place my parameters.

4. The market drifts down, and after 25 minutes my target is hit at 10386 and I am out for +20 points.

5. The ticks pop up again, and I short at the market. I am in at 10297.

6. Fifteen minutes later my target is hit at 10277, and I am out for +20 points.

**F I G U R E  9.3**

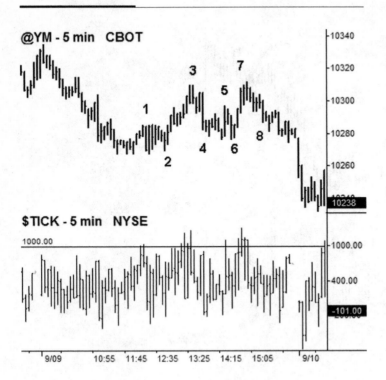

7. The markets shoot higher on ticks of +1000, and I short at the market. I'm filled at 10308.

8. The markets roll over, and my target of 10288 is hit for a gain of +20 points. In the end, this beats working for a living.

## Mini-Sized Dow—September 2004 Contract, September 8, 2004

1. On September 8, 2004, the ticks register a +1000 reading shortly after 10:00 a.m. Eastern, and I short the YM at the market, getting filled at 10355 (see Fig. 9.4). I place my stops and targets and kick back. Once I get into these trades, there is nothing to do but wait.

2. The market rolls over quickly, and my target at 10335 is hit in 10 minutes for +20 points.

3. About 40 minutes later the ticks act up again, and I short at the market, getting in at 10337.

4. The markets go into chop mode, and 35 minutes later my timer goes off and I exit at the market, getting a fill at 10335 for a whopping +2 points.

5. A few hours later the ticks start getting "jiggy with it," and I short and get filled at 10346.

**F I G U R E   9.4**

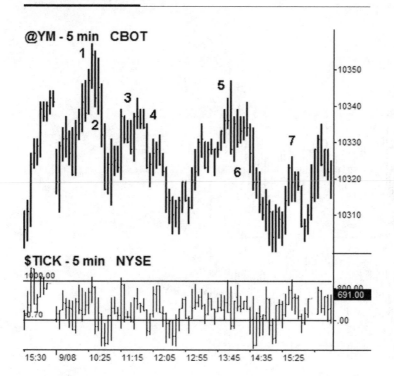

6. About 15 minutes later my target is hit at 10226, and I'm out for +20 points.

7. The ticks ramp up again, but I pass on this trade because it is now past 3:30 p.m. Eastern. The trade would have worked out at a +20 point trade, but I have found that tick plays in the last half hour tend to be less reliable.

## Mini-Sized Dow—September 2004 Contract, July 26, 2004

1. On July 26, 2004, the market action starts off weak, but there aren't any extreme tick readings until just after 11:00 a.m. Eastern (see Fig. 9.5). At this time I get a −1000 tick reading, and I buy the YM at the market, getting a fill at 9912. I place my orders for my stop and target, and I set my timer.

2. After about 30 minutes into the trade, the market firms, and I get out at my target of 9932 for +20 points.

3. The market is quiet for most of the day, and then as it approaches 3:00 p.m. Eastern, we get a +1000 tick reading. I short at the market and get filled at 9932.

4. About 20 minutes later my target is hit at 9912, and I am out for +20 points.

5. There is another extreme reading in the markets, but it is past 3:30 p.m. Eastern, so I sit on my hands and do nothing.

**FIGURE   9.5**

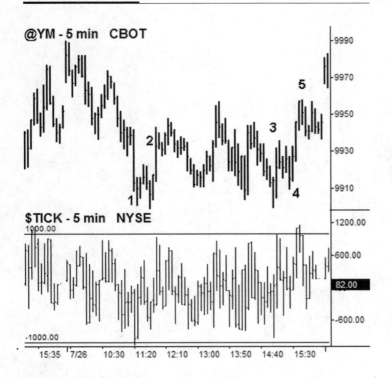

@YM - 5 min   CBOT

$TICK - 5 min   NYSE

## E-mini S&P—September 2004 Contract, September 7, 2004

1.  On September 7, 2004, I get an early +1000 tick reading (see Fig. 9.6). I'm
    watching the E-mini S&Ps, and I'm tempted to short, but I look at the time and it
    is near 9:50 a.m. Eastern. This is before my parameter of 10:00 a.m. Eastern, and
    I pass on the trade. Although this trade would have worked out in my favor, I
    have found that tick trades in the first 30 minutes of trade are haphazard at best.

2.  I wait for the next setup, and it hits the tape near 11:30 a.m. Eastern with a
    +1000 tick reading. I place an order to short the E-mini S&Ps at the market, and
    I get a fill at 1119.75. I place a three-point stop at 1122.75, and I place a target at
    1117.75. Of course, I also set my timer to buzz me when 35 minutes elapse.

3.  Thirty five minutes pass by rather quickly, and the only thing interesting that has
    happened is that my two-foot long arrowana (a tropical fish from the Amazon
    that looks like a Tarpon) tried to jump out of its tank, causing me to jump like I'd
    been hit with a cattle prod. Regardless of this distraction, I hear my alarm go off,
    and since neither my target nor my stop has been hit, I execute an order to get
    out of my position at the market. I am out at 1121.25 for a loss of –1.50 points

**F I G U R E   9.6**

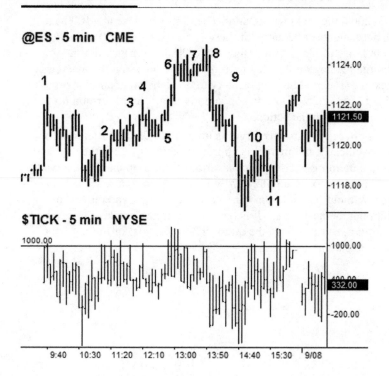

4. Soon thereafter an episode of "ticks gone wild" hits the tape, and they move back up to +1000. I short at the market and am filled at 1122.00. I place my stop and target and set my timer.

5. My timer goes off while I'm enjoying a smoked turkey breast sandwich from Panera Bread Company. I exit at the market at 1121.50 for –0.50 points.

6. The markets pop higher on a +1000 tick reading, and I short at the market. I'm filled at 1123.50. I set my parameters, kick my feet up, and watch the action.

7. Thirty-five minutes pass by swiftly, and at the sound of my buzzer I execute an order to cover at the market. I'm out at 1123.50 for a scratch trade.

8. The ticks hit +1000 again, and I short at the market. I am filled at 1124.75.

9. This time the markets roll over, and my target is hit at 1122.75 for +2.00 ES points.

10. As we move into the last hour, the ticks dare to hit +1000 yet again. I short at the market and am filled at 1119.75.

11. The market rolls over, and I am out at my target at 1117.75 for +2.00 points.

## E-mini S&P—September 2004 Contract, September 3, 2004

1. On September 3, 2004, the pickings are slim. The ticks get close to +1000 and close to –1000, but they never actually hit these levels (see Fig. 9.7). I don't mess around with these kinds of plays. Either they hit 1000 ticks or they don't. We don't hit an extreme reading on this day until the final hour when the markets register a +1000 reading. I leap at this opportunity to do something, and I short at the market. I am filled at 1117.25. I set my stop and my target, and I turn on my timer. I kick back and watch the action.

2. About 30 minutes after my entry, my target is hit at 1115.25, and I am out for +2.00 points. Conveniently, the market is approaching its close for the day, and I can now do something more exciting such as arrange the soup cans in the pantry alphabetically. This is a good example of why it is so important to have a specific setup to wait for. Without one, a trader can spend a day like September 3 over-trading and chopping themselves up. It is tempting at times to take a trade just to alleviate the boredom. But this begs the question—is the goal of trading "not to be bored" or to make money?

**F I G U R E   9.7**

## E-mini S&P—September 2004 Contract, August 26, 2004

1. The ticks approach an extreme reading early in the day, but they don't quite get there, registering a high of +978 (see Fig. 9.8). Since this is not a game of grenades or horseshoes, I stand aside and wait until we get an actual reading of over +1000.

2. Again, we come close to 1000 ticks, but we don't quite cut the mustard. I stand aside and do nothing. This actually isn't as hard as it may seem. I don't stare at the tick chart; I'm only taking action if I hear the audio alert.

3. Finally, we get a reading of over +1000. I short at the market, and I'm filled at 1106.75. I set my parameters and await the action—having done nothing all day at this point in regards to this setup.

4. About 30 minutes later my target is hit at 1104.75, and I'm out for +2.00 ES points.

**F I G U R E   9.8**

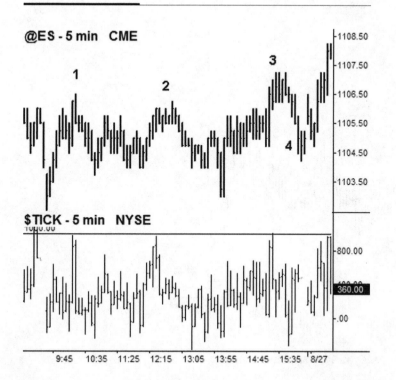

## E-mini S&P—June 2004 Contract, May 24, 2004

1. On May 24, 2004 the markets gapped higher and registered a +1000 tick reading early in the session (see Fig. 9.9). This was before 10:00 a.m. Eastern, so I treated it just like a phone call that pops up as "out of area" on caller ID—I ignored it. Closer to 10:30 a.m. we got another +1000 reading, and I shorted this action with a market order. I am filled at 1098.50, and I set my parameters.

2. About 20 minutes later my target is hit, and I'm out at 1096.50 for +2.00 ES points.

3. Most of the rest of the day is quiet, but as we approach the last few hours, we get an extreme tick reading, and I take a short at 1096.50.

4. About 25 minutes later my target is hit, and I'm out for +2.00 ES points.

5. The ticks get wild and crazy again, hitting +1000, so I short, and I'm filled at 1096.00.

6. The markets remain choppy, and my time buzzer goes off. I cover at the market, and I'm out at 1095.50 for a gain of +0.50 ES points.

7. The markets pop higher again and register an extreme tick reading. However, it's past 3:30 p.m. Eastern, so I don't take any action on this signal.

F I G U R E  9.9

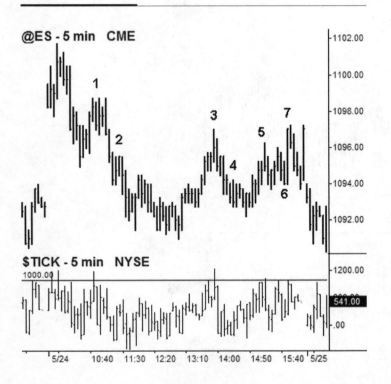

## E-mini S&P—June 2004 Contract, June 7, 2004

1. The markets gap up, and the ticks spend the vast majority of their time over the zero level (see Fig. 9.10). If at 12:00 noon Eastern the ticks have spent over 85 percent of their time above zero, then I pass on any further tick fades on the day. Remember, it is on these days that there is serious buying taking place. Only consistent and steady fund buying can keep the ticks above zero all day long. That hasn't happened yet, but it's in the back of my mind.

2. At around 11:00 a.m. Eastern the ticks register an extreme reading, and I short at the market. I'm filled at 1134.25, and I set my parameters. I take this short because at this point we haven't passed the 12:00 noon Eastern deadline. Also, in the rules I mentioned that if the ticks have spent all of their time above zero by 10:00 a.m. Eastern, I'd like to see at least one move below zero before taking a trade. In this case, we did get some moves just below zero. These aren't ideal conditions but they do pass the test.

3. Time passes by quickly, and my time stop expires. I exit at the market and I'm out at 1133.00 for +1.25 ES.

**F I G U R E   9.10**

4. A little after 1:00 p.m. Eastern the ticks register another +1000 reading. I ignore this reading because the ticks have spent over 85 percent of their time above zero, indicating massive fund buying.

5. This happens again near 3:30 p.m. Eastern, and I ignore this signal for the same reason. The markets are "on fire" today as is evidenced by the consistent high tick readings, with hardly anything dipping below the zero level. I therefore pass on fading these extreme tick readings. Although these days are rare, it is important to know what they look like so they can be avoided in terms of a "tick fade" day.

## SUMMING UP THE TICK FADES

As I state in the introduction, the financial markets are naturally set up to take advantage of and prey upon human nature. When traders see a market running away without them, their natural instinct is to jump onboard and participate in the run. Although this makes sense on paper, this feeling of "missing the move" causes more trading errors than almost anything else. This blinding urge forces amateur traders to jump into markets based solely on the fear that they are missing out on a lot of profits—as opposed to entering the market as a result of a specific setup that they have mapped out and are patiently awaiting to set up. This extreme panic buying and selling is measured accurately by the ticks, and extreme tick readings provide traders with the opportunity to jump into the markets and teach the amateurs a valuable lesson.

# THE SQUEEZE: GETTING POSITIONED FOR THE BIG MARKET MOVES

## DAY TRADING VERSUS SWING TRADING

The squeeze, in addition to the scalper buys and sells, is a setup that I use for both day trading and swing trading. I'd like to take a moment and discuss both of these trading styles. I like to focus a portion of my trading on scalp plays, where I'm jumping in and out of the market with a little piece of profit here, and a little piece of profit there. I call these my bread and butter trades, and my primary focus with these trades is the creation of monthly income. However, I also like to focus a part of my time looking for trade setups that are longer term in nature. By longer term I'm referring to positions that I will be in for a few days to a few weeks, or possibly even a few months. Any fund manager who is reading this is grinning—a few weeks is still extremely short term for them. However, this is one of the great benefits of being an individual trader. There is much more flexibility concerning getting in and out of positions in a shorter timeframe.

The benefit of these types of swing trades is that a person is "in" the market and already positioned for the move. The markets spend a lot of time in trading ranges, building up energy for their next major move. By the time the move fires off, it is usually out of the blue and violent, leaving many day traders behind. This includes the times when a market will gap open and then spend the rest of the day stuck in a narrow range, totally bypassing the day traders.

That's why we call this move a "gap and crap." By keeping some exposure in positions on a swing type basis, I will frequently participate in larger moves that leapfrog over many of the day traders. The secret to swing trading is realizing that "being positioned" is half the battle, and not stressing out over a position that is not working out right away. The markets never break when they are expected to, and they will do so only when they are good and ready, usually when the greatest number of people are unprepared. Sometimes "being positioned" means waiting for weeks for the move to finally unfold. This requires patience and the ability to step aside and not obsessively stare at the charts all day. This is a huge problem for most traders. They sit back, they watch the charts, they get emotional, and they get faked out and close the trade. Typically, once that process has completed itself—faking out as many traders as possible—the markets will make their move. If everybody is expecting a move, then everybody is already positioned for it. If everybody is positioned for a big down move, then everybody is already short and there is no one left to sell. It's a great system. It's also how the markets always have worked and always will work.

One of the best trading books I've ever read on managing "swing trader anxiety" is called *How I Made Two Million Dollars in the Stock Market* by Nicolas Darvas. This book was written a few decades ago and remains one of my favorites. It's a quick, easy read and very entertaining. For anyone who has trouble hanging onto swing positions and jumping out too early, this book is a must read.

It is important to position size correctly for swing trades. In general, if traders cannot sleep because they are worrying about their overnight positions, then they are trading too large in relation to their account size. Swing trades have larger stops, and position size must be reduced accordingly. There is a very easy way to manage this—establish a monetary stop and work backwards from there. For example, if traders are not willing to lose more than $500 on a trade, then all they will have to do is look at the parameters for the setup and do the math to figure out the position size. Using $500 as a benchmark, a day trade that requires a 20-point stop in the mini-sized Dow futures would equate to a position size of five contracts. However, if a swing trade in the mini-sized Dow called for a 100-point stop, then these same traders are going to use one lot. Monetarily these stops are identical because of the reduced position size on the swing trade.

## REDEFINING VOLATILITY—HOW NARROW IS NARROW?

The squeeze takes advantage of quiet periods in the market when the volatility has decreased significantly, and the market is building up energy for its next major move higher or lower. This indicator was introduced to me by my trading partner, Hubert Senters, and it has become an integral part of my own trading plan.

For students of Bollinger Bands, periods of low volatility are identified as the times when the bands "move closer together." This is always great in hindsight, but in real time, how does a trader know that the current narrowness is really narrow enough to qualify as low volatility? This setup answers that question by adding the Keltner Channels as well as a momentum index oscillator.

For readers who are unaware of how these indicators work, I'll take a few moments to explain them here. *Bollinger Bands* are a type of envelope that is plotted at standard deviation levels above and below a moving average. This produces an effect of having the bands widen during periods of higher volatility and contract during less volatile periods. During periods of lower volatility, in sideways moving markets, the bands contract toward the moving average. *Keltner Channels* are based on a standard moving average. The actual band lines are offset by a positive and negative standard deviation value from the central moving average value, to provide upper and lower bands. While the Bollinger Bands expand and contract as the markets alter between periods of high and low volatility, the Keltner Channels stay in more of a steady range. The momentum index oscillator is used to estimate the direction, velocity, and turning points of market movements. Make sense? If not that's fine. I don't understand how electricity works, but I know when I plug my computer into an electric outlet, it will turn on. Now let's look at how I use all this for a setup.

The quiet periods I'm looking for are identified when the Bollinger Bands narrow in width to the point that they are actually trading inside of the Keltner Channels. This marks a period of reduced volatility and signals that the market is taking a significant breather, building up steam for its next move. The trade signal occurs when the Bollinger Bands then move back outside the Keltner Channels. I use a 12-period momentum index oscillator to determine whether to go long or short. If the oscillator is above zero when this happens, I go long; if it is below zero, I go short. These are all canned studies that come with most charting packages. For the parameters, I just use the default settings on TradeStation. These readings are 20 and 1.5 for the Keltner Channels and 20 and 2 for the Bollinger Bands. My partner Hubert also took an extra step and turned all these into an indicator, which makes it easier to read on the chart, which I explain in a moment.

## GETTING THE HEADS UP FOR A POTENTIALLY LARGER MOVE BEFORE IT OCCURS

I use the squeeze signal on various timeframes, as I like it for both day trading and swing trading. On the mini-sized Dow, for example, a squeeze on a two-minute chart can move the market 10–20 YM points, on a five-minute chart 30–50 points, and on a daily chart, several hundred points. The kicker, of course, is that the smaller the timeframe, the more frequent the signals. A two-minute chart may fire off three to five signals in a day, while the daily chart will fire off six to seven signals over the course of an entire year.

Although I spend a large amount of my trading day focused on the E-mini S&Ps and the mini-sized Dow, there are also plenty of times when these indexes are dead in the water. On days when the indexes are trading in a range that is narrower than Paris Hilton's outlook on life, I look to the currencies and bonds for my next setup. My two favorite setups in the currencies are the squeeze play and what I call the box play—a setup that comes up in a later chapter. For currencies, I execute these on the eight currency pairs I've already mentioned, and I prefer to do these in the forex markets. However, the EC on the CME also responds well to this setup. Let's take a look.

# TRADING RULES FOR BUYS (SELLS ARE REVERSED)

1.  Set up a 24-hour chart so the overnight activity can be accounted for in this indicator setup.

2.  The "heads up" on this indicator is the first black dot. This is not a trade signal, but a heads up that a trade signal is setting up. This indicates when the Bollinger Bands are trading inside the Keltner Channels.

3.  The signal on the indicator is the first gray dot after a series of black dots. This indicates that the Bollinger Bands have come back outside of the Keltner Channels. This is shown in detail in the charts that follow.

4.  Once the first gray dot appears after a series of black dots, I go long if the histogram is above zero. Once the signal fires, I just place a market order. This is a momentum play, and I don't want to be messing around with limit orders that may not get filled.

5.  For day trades, I place the following minimum money management stops. If the stop is also near a key price support level, I will take that into consideration and adjust accordingly. For example, if my entry is 1104.00 on the S&Ps and the daily pivot is at 1101.75, I would move my stop to just below that pivot level to 1101.50, for a stop of 2.50 instead of 2.00. I find that nine times out of ten, I just use the default stop.

    - YM: 20 points
    - ES: 2 points
    - NQ: 4 points
    - ER: 1.50 points
    - EC: 20 ticks
    - EURUSD: 20 pips
    - US: 7 ticks
    - Gold: 1.50
    - Stocks: 50 cents

6.  For swing plays and position trades (taken off the daily charts), I place the following stops. I take into consideration the same key levels as discussed in item 4.

    - YM: 150 points
    - ES: 15 points
    - NQ: 25 points
    - ER: 8 points
    - EC: 100 ticks
    - EURUSD: 100 pips
    - US: 35 ticks
    - Gold: 10.00
    - Stocks: $2.50

7.  My target is based purely on the momentum of the trade. Once the momentum index signal starts to weaken, I get out of the trade at the market.

8.  I don't trail stops.

## Mini-Sized Dow—September 2004 Contract, August 18, 2004

1. Figure 10.1 shows how to set up the elements of this play in whatever timeframe a
   trader wishes to view. For intraday trading, I like to watch the five-minute chart. The
   one- and two-minute charts are good for scalping, but these signals are not as powerful as the five-minute chart, though they are tradable. The Keltner Channel is the pair
   of thick black lines and is set at the default parameters of 20 and 2 on TradeStation.
   The Bollinger Bands are the thinner, gray lines and are set at the default settings of
   20 and 1.5. At the bottom is a 12-period (on the close) momentum index oscillator. At
   point 1, the Bollinger Bands have gone inside the Keltner Channels. This indicates that
   the market is going into a quiet period, and it is a heads up. This is not a signal—just a
   heads up that when the Bollinger Bands pop back out, it will be time to take a trade.

2. Here the Bollinger Bands have come back outside the Keltner Channels. It is time
   to take a trade.

3. If the momentum index oscillator is above zero at this point, I go long. If it is
   below zero at this point, I go short. I don't mess around with limit orders. I just
   jump it at the market. This is just an example of what triggers the entry and exits.
   I look at specific plays in a moment.

### F I G U R E   10.1

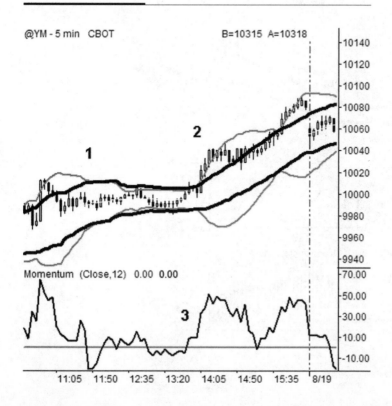

## Mini-Sized Dow—September 2004 Contract, August 18, 2004

1. One of the things my trading partner Hubert did was turn all the things in the first chart into an easy-to-read indicator, which is what I use (see Fig. 10.2). He developed this for both TradeStation and eSignal. When the Bollinger Bands go inside the Keltner Channels, the dots turn black. This is a heads up that the markets have entered a quiet period.

2. At this point the Bollinger Bands come back out of the Keltner Channels.

3. Since the momentum index oscillator is above zero, this is a long signal.

4. On the indicator, this is measured by when the dots turn back to gray after being black. When I see that first gray dot, I know it is time to take a trade. If the histogram is above the zero line, I go long, and if it is below the zero line, I go short. Again, this is just to show you how the indicator works. In the next examples I go over some actual plays. I prefer to take off all the "clutter" that is on the price chart and just use the indicator. But now you know how the indicator works.

**F I G U R E   10.2**

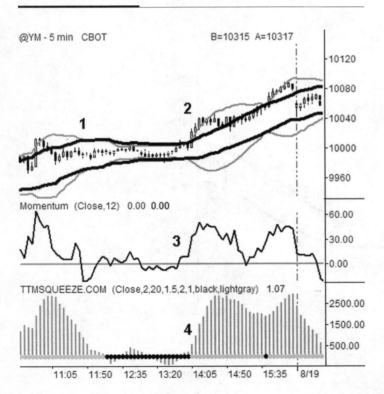

## Mini-Sized Dow—September 2004 Contract, August 20, 2004

1. On this two-minute chart of the mini-sized Dow, we get a black dot a little after 10:00 a.m. Eastern (see Fig. 10.3). This is a signal that the Bollinger Bands have narrowed and are now trading inside the Keltner Channels. I know when I get the next gray dot, I will have a trade signal. In this case, the gray dot happens right away. Usually there is more than one black dot, but once in a while it will just have the single instance, and that's okay. Common sense dictates that the more black dots there are, the more powerful the potential move would be. In my experience this is not true, as I have seen one-dot signals that have bigger moves than twenty-dot signals on numerous occasions. I find it is best to just take the signal when it comes. Humans tend to mess up their trading when they try to outthink their positions. When the next gray dot appears, the histogram is above zero, so I place an order to buy the YM at the market. I am filled at 10164. I place a 20-point stop at 10144. My target is open, as I'll be waiting for the momentum index to falter as my exit signal.

**F I G U R E   10.3**

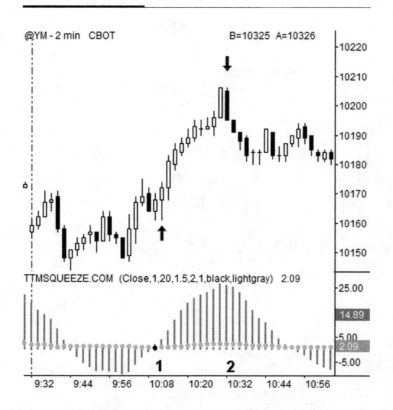

2. The market pushes higher, and I'm watching the histogram. As long as it makes higher highs, I stay in the trade. When it makes its first lower high, I will get out. At 10:30 a.m. Eastern we get a lower high on the histogram, and I exit at the market. I'm out at 10198 for a gain of +34 points.

## Mini-Sized Dow—September 2004 Contract, June 28, 2004

1. On June 28, 2004, the markets trade in a tight range all morning, creating a long series of black dots on the five-minute YM chart (see Fig. 10.4). Remember, the black dots indicate that during this timeframe, the Bollinger Bands are trading inside of the Keltner Channels, marking a period of very low volatility. A little after 1:30 p.m. Eastern, the first gray dot appears in the sequence. The histogram is below zero, so I take a short at the market. I'm filled at 10426, and I place a 20-point stop at 10442.

2. The goal is to stay in the trade as long as the histogram is making lower lows (or in the case of a long, higher highs). It makes its first higher low nearly two hours later, and I exit at the market. (If you were just watching the momentum index oscillator, you would exit as it starts to turn higher.) I'm out at 10325 for a gain of +101 points,

**F I G U R E   10.4**

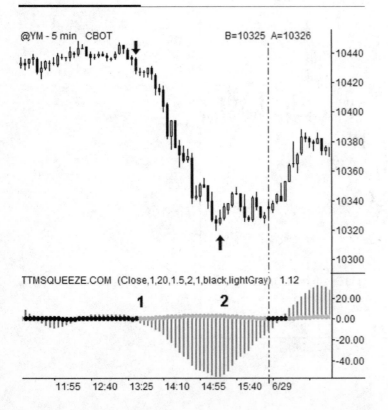

or $505 per contract. A very smooth, low-stress, and profitable trade. This is a great example of a trade where it pays to sit on your hands until you are given a clear exit signal. In fact, part of my reward system isn't focused on profits—it's focused on my ability to follow a setup from entry to exit. Every trader should have a reward system like this. Not for making money, but for hanging in there and following the setup—staying in the trade until you get a specific exit signal.

## Mini-Sized Dow—September 2004 Contract, September 10, 2004

1. On September 10, 2004, the five-minute squeeze on the YM fires off (see Fig. 10.5). About an hour earlier there was a single gray dot, and I went long here. However, the very next dot went back to black. This means that the Bollinger Bands came out of the Keltner Channels, and then went right back in. This is a rare occurrence, but when it happens, I just get out and wait for a solid signal. In that case I was in and out and lost six YM points. About 50 minutes later we get the setup again, and the dots turn gray. For this next trade, with the histogram above zero, I go long and place a 20-point stop. I am in at 10263, and I place a stop at 10243.

### F I G U R E  10.5

**2.** The histogram continues to move higher until 1:30 p.m. Eastern, at which point it starts to lose momentum. I cut the position loose at 10309 for a gain of +46 points.

## Mini-Sized Dow—September 2004 Contract, July 1, 2004

**1.** A little after 10:00 a.m. Eastern on July 1, 2004, the first gray dot appears on the five-minute YM chart (see Fig. 10.6). The histogram is below zero, so I go short at the market. My entry is at 10402.

**2.** The markets drift down, and the histogram begins to level off. The markets continue to make lowers lows, and suddenly the selling accelerates, pushing the histograms down deep into their range. They begin to bottom out at around 11:20 a.m. Eastern, and I cover at the market. I'm out at 10312 for a gain of +90 points.

**F I G U R E   10.6**

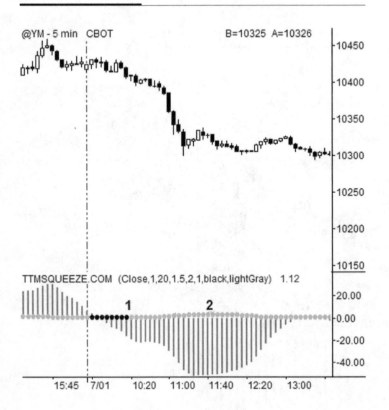

## Mini-Sized Dow—September 2004 Contract, September 2, 2004

1. On September 2, 2004, the five-minute YM chart goes into alert status at around 1:15 p.m Eastern (see Fig. 10.7). Six black dots appear, showing that the Bollinger Bands are trading inside the Keltner Channels. When the next gray dot appears at 1:50 p.m., the histogram is above zero, so I go long at the market. I am filled at 10183. I place a 20-point stop at 10163.

2. The market cruises higher, and the histogram begins to start making lower lows at 3:30 p.m. Eastern. I exit at the market and am out at 10278 for a gain of +95 points. Not every five-minute squeeze ends up with a big move like this, but I've found that when there is a big move, it is generally kicked off by a squeeze on the five-minute chart. I have a rule in trading that says, "Never fight the direction of the five-minute squeeze!" It supersedes all my other intraday trading rules and setups. Remember when I talked about all these plays working in conjunction with one another? If there is a five-minute-long squeeze in place and we are rallying up to a pivot level, then I'm not going to place a short at that pivot level. Never fight the five-minute squeeze.

### F I G U R E   10.7

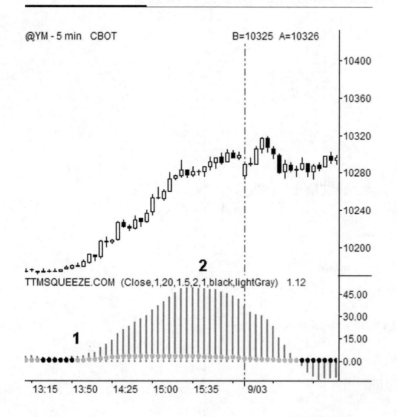

## Mini-Sized Dow—September 2004 Contract, August 25, 2004

1. On August 25, 2004, the five-minute squeeze goes into alert status at around 11:45 a.m. Eastern as evidenced by the first black dot (see Fig. 10.8). About 20 minutes later the dots change back to gray. The histogram was above zero, so I take a long at the market. I was filled at 10113 and I immediately place a stop at 10093 and leave my target as open.

2. About an hour and a half later the histogram starts to make lower highs, and I get out at the market. I'm out at 10149 for a gain of +36 points.

## Mini-Sized Dow—September 2004 Contract, August 20, 2004

1. I like this example because it clearly shows the power of an intraday consolidation move (see Fig. 10.9). It's like a chart of the young wife's life played by Geena Davis in *Thelma and Louise*. There is the narrow consolidation of life energy for a while, and then Thelma busts out and nothing can hold her back. Her personality explodes, and she finally experiences life. Just like the squeeze. The first gray dot appears just after 2:00 p.m. Eastern, and the histogram is above zero, so I go long at the market. I'm filled at 10172, and I place a 20-point stop.

**F I G U R E   10.8**

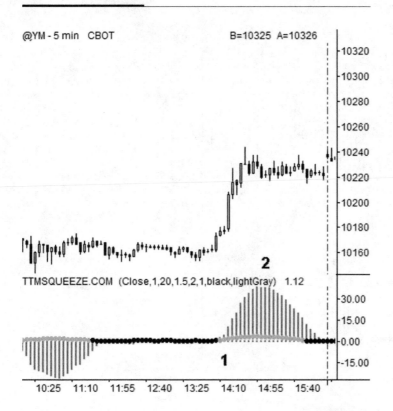

2. The market pops higher, and a little under an hour later the momentum starts to slide. I exit at 10221 for a gain of +49 points.

## Mini-Sized Dow—September 2004 Contract, August 18, 2004

1. On August 18, 2004, the market spends most of the morning consolidating, and, as the volatility comes out of the market, the Bollinger Bands contract and start to trade inside the Keltner Channels (see Fig. 10.10). This shows up in the form of black dots. When I get the first gray dot, the histogram is above zero, and I go long at the market. I'm filled at 10003, and I immediately place a 20-point stop at 9983.

2. The markets push higher and start to lose momentum. I exit at 10034 for a gain of +31 points.

3. A few hours later we get a single black dot that is quickly followed by another gray dot. I take the signal. Since the histogram is above zero, I go long at the market, and I'm filled at 10056. I place a 20-point stop.

4. The histogram is strong right into the close. I stay in the trade until 4:10 p.m. Eastern and exit at the market. I'm out at 10082 for a gain of +26 points.

**F I G U R E   10.10**

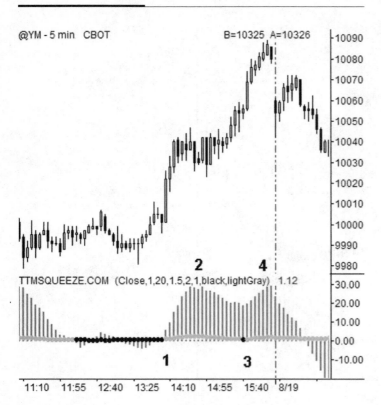

## Mini-Sized Dow—September 2004 Contract, July 28, 2004

1. On July 28, 2004, the YM creeps higher for most of the day, and then a little after
2:00 p.m. Eastern I get a black dot (see Fig. 10.11). Shortly thereafter we go back
to gray, and since the histogram is above zero, I go long. I'm filled at 10028, and
I place a 20-point stop at 10008 and leave my target as open.

2. A little over an hour later the histogram makes a lower high. I exit at the market,
and I'm filled at 10103 for a gain of +75 points.

## 30 Year Bond—September 2004 Contract, August 18, 2004

1. I love using the five-minute squeeze on the YM, but it works on other markets as
well. Figure 10.12 is a chart of the 30-year bonds. At around 11:30 a.m. Eastern
the dots turn black, signaling that we are entering into a period of very low volatility. About 90 minutes later we get a gray dot at point 1, and since the histogram
is above zero, I go long at the market. I'm filled at 111 9/32. I place a seven-tick
stop at 111 2/32. (If you aren't familiar with bonds, one tick is $31.25. So if you
lose seven ticks, that equates to $218.75, or approximately 44 YM points.)

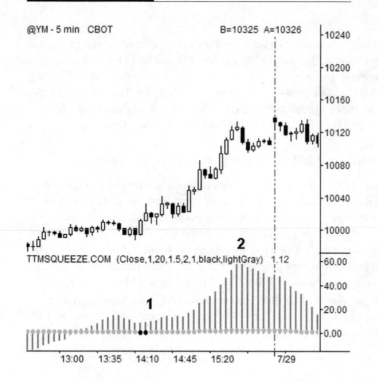

2. The momentum starts to peter out about 40 minutes later, and when the histogram makes a lower high at point 2, I exit at the market. I'm out at 111 11/32 for a gain of +2 ticks. At one point I was up 10 ticks on the trade (the equivalent of 63 YM points), but the market rolled over quickly, which can happen. The key to successful trading is to stay in the signal until it ends. This way when a big move does take place, a trader will be able to stay in the trade and let the profits run.

## 30 Year Bond—September 2004 Contract, August 10, 2004

1. On this five-minute chart of the bonds, we go into black dot territory at around 10:45 a.m. Eastern, and I sit back and wait for the next gray dot to appear (see Fig. 10.13). This happens a little after 12 noon at point #1, and since the histogram is below zero, I short at the market. I'm filled at 110 30/32. I place a stop at 111 5/32. Remember, one full point in the bonds is composed of 32 ticks. When it goes to 32/32, it becomes a new point. For example, when bonds are at 110 31/32 and they move up one tick to 110 32/32, this reads as 111, and so on.

2. The momentum to the downside builds and bonds sell off. Once the histogram makes a higher low at point 2, I cover my short at the market, and I'm out at 110 26/32 for a gain of +4 ticks.

### FIGURE 10.13

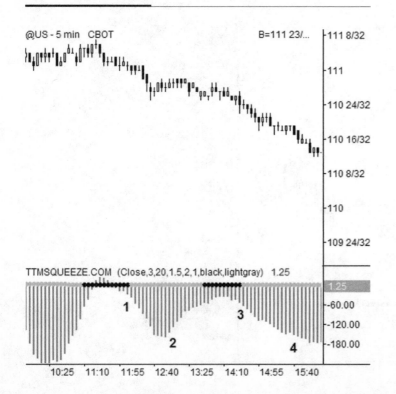

3. At around 1:30 p.m. Eastern we go back into black dot mode, and I prepare for my next trade. About 45 minutes later we get our first gray dot at point 3, and since the histogram is below zero, I short at the market. I'm in at 110 21/32. I place a stop at 110 28/32.

4. Bonds sell off and move lower into the close. I cover at the first higher low at point 4, and I'm out at 110 16/32 for a gain of +5 ticks. The market rolls over again quickly thereafter and closes on its lows.

## 30 Year Bond—June 2003 Contract, April 30, 2003

1. On this daily chart of the bonds, we can see that these markets consolidated heavily for nearly a month during most of April 2003 (see Fig. 10.14). When the first gray dot appears after this consolidation at point #1, I go long and am filled at 113 13/32. Because this is a daily chart, I give the trade more room and use a 35-tick stop at 112 10/32. Bonds rally through the entire month of May, finally losing momentum in June.

2. Bonds get nearly as high as 122 before crashing on economic news at point 2. This kicks off a lower histogram reading, and I exit at the market at the end of that day, getting out at 119 31/32 for a gain of +6 18/32, or $6,562.50 per contract. This is the same as catching a 1,1,312-point move in the YM.

**F I G U R E    10.14**

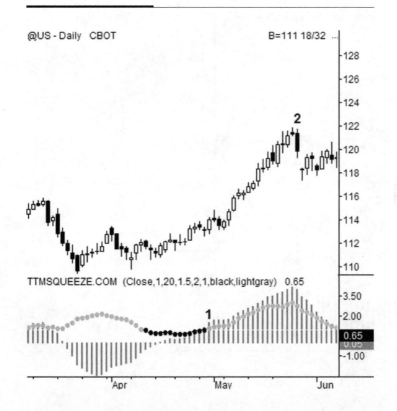

## E-mini S&P—December 2003 Contract, December 2, 2003

1. On this daily chart of the E-mini S&Ps the markets start to consolidate near the end of November 2004 (see Fig. 10.15). On December 1 we get a gray dot. The histogram is above zero, so I go long the next day. There is no magic on the entry formula. I wake up, look at the chart, and if it tells me to take action, I take action. I just get in at the market, very near the open. I'm in at 1062.50 (point 3). I place a 15-point stop at 1047.50.

2. The histograms peak out and start making lower lows during the first week in January. I get out on January 9 at 1129.50 (point 4) for a gain of +67 points, or $3,350 per contract. The market continues to move another 30 points higher. This is all about "being positioned" in the market when it's setting up to make a big move. Note, in the third week of December this contract expired so I closed out my postion in the December contract, and reopened it in the March 2004 contract, which was the next front month. I literally sold the December futures, then turned around and, because the signal was still valid, bought the March futures in order to stay in this play. This is called "rolling over" your position.

**F I G U R E   10.15**

### E-mini S&P—September 2004 Contract, July 8, 2004

1. On this daily chart of the ES, we go into a period of consolidation at the end of June 2004 that lasts into the first few trading days of July (see Fig. 10.16). On July 8 we get a gray dot, and, since the histogram is below zero, I go short about 15 minutes after the open of the regular session. I am filled at 1118.25 (two bars to the right of point 3). I place a 15-point stop at 1133.25.

2. The markets move lower, and toward the end of July they start to run out of momentum. At point 2, I exit near the open at 1092.25 for a gain of +26 points (point 4).

### Mini-Sized Dow—December 2003 Contract, December 1, 2003

1. We've looked at a lot of five-minute squeezes on the YM, so I want to look at a daily squeeze as well on this contract. At the end of November 2003 the daily YM went into black dot mode, and I awaited the next gray dot (see Fig. 10.17). We got it on December 1, and, since the histogram was above zero, I went long shortly after the open and got filled at 9804. I placed a stop at 9654, 150 points below.

**FIGURE 10.16**

**F I G U R E   10.17**

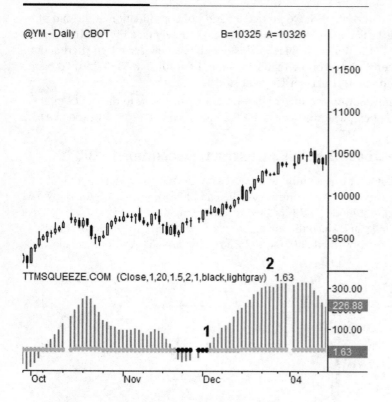

**2.** The YM rallied into early January and started losing momentum during the second week of the new year. I exited on January 9 soon after the open at 10506 for a gain of +702 points, or $3,510 per contract.

## Forex Markets—EURUSD, August 23, 2004

**1.** I like to use the squeeze on the various currency pairs in the forex markets as well. I normally like to use the 60-minute charts and 5-minute charts, but it also works on the daily charts. On August 23, 2004, I woke up to see that the euro had just fired off a short squeeze on the 60-minute chart (see Fig. 10.18). I went in and shorted at the market, getting filled at 1.2252. I place a 20-pip stop at 1.2272. (Remember, one pip in this currency pair equals 1/100 of a cent and equates to $10 on your P&L.)

**2.** The market sells off considerably, and the momentum on the histogram never lets up. I stay in the trade all day, exiting at 4:00 p.m. Eastern at point 2, when the U.S. stock markets close. The main reason I do this is that this started off as

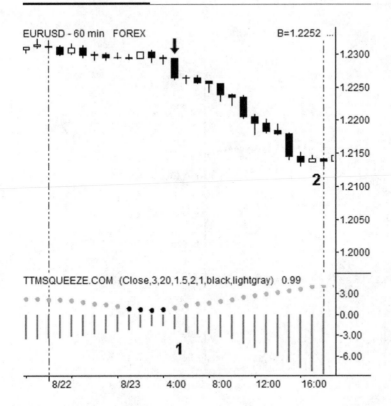

**FIGURE    10.18**

an intraday play, and I generally get out of the office after the stock markets close to go clear my head. I exit at the market and am filled at 1.2146 for a gain of 106 pips, or $1,060 per contract. This is like making 212 points on the YM.

## Forex Markets—EURUSD, September 8, 2004

1. On this five-minute chart of the euro currency we go into black dot territory a little before 10:00 a.m. Eastern on September 8, 2004, and 25 minutes later we get our first gray dot at point 1 (see Fig. 10.19). The histogram is above zero, so I go long at the market, and I'm filled at 1.2054. I place a stop at 1.2034.

2. The market rallies steadily for the next 90 minutes and starts to lose momentum just before 12:00 noon, at point 2. I exit at the market and am filled at 1.2153 for a gain of +119 pips.

**F I G U R E   10.19**

EURUSD - 5 min   FOREX                    B=1.2248 ...

TTMSQUEEZE.COM  (Close,3,20,1.5,2,1,black,lightgray)   1.90

## GOOG (Google Inc), September 9, 2004

**1.** I like to watch the squeeze on various stocks as well, especially on daily time
frames since most of my stock trading involves swing trading. I also use the daily
squeeze on individual stocks for in the money option plays. I talk more about how
I play options in the chapter on the "8/21 EMA for Swings" setup. That said, I
will use the 5-minute squeeze on volatile stocks for potential intraday trading
setups. On this five-minute chart of Google (GOOG) we can see the price action
shortly after its IPO (Initial Public Offering—see Fig. 10.20). On September 9,
2004, the stock went into a squeeze setup at the end of the day, and this carried
into the beginning of the next day. Very soon after the open we get our first gray
dot, and, since the histogram is above zero, I take a long at the market. I'm filled
at 102.33, and I place a stop at 101.83.

**2.** The momentum builds quickly and begins to fade near 11:00 a.m. Eastern. I get
out at 105.45 for a gain of +3.12. Another squeeze play sets up later in the afternoon and fires off right after 12 noon. On this play the histogram is negative, and I
would normally short, but since it is an IPO, shares were not available to the general public to short at this time, so I obviously pass on this trade.

**F I G U R E   10.20**

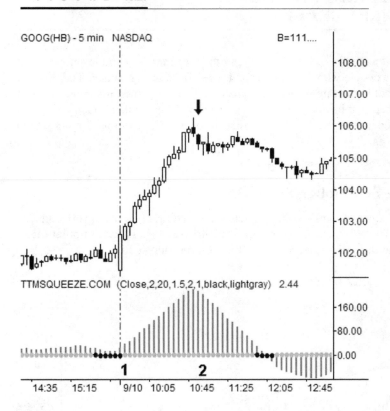

## SUMMING UP THE SQUEEZES

Squeezes show me when the markets go into quiet mode. The only reason markets go into quiet mode is that they are building up energy for their next major move. I like to be on the alert for this, and of course on the alert for the direction of the move. With the squeeze I have a clear indication of when to take the trade. And once I'm in, I just don't mess with the trade. When it starts to lose momentum, it is pretty clear, and that is the signal I use to get out.

Many day traders I talk to ask about the wisdom in swing trading. The biggest question I get involves the risk in being exposed to an overnight position. The most common question is, "What if there is another terrorist attack?" After trading the markets for nearly 20 years, there is one thing I am absolutely convinced of—there is always somebody who knows about the upcoming market move and this person is in the process of getting positioned for it. After the crash on 9/11, one of the ways the government tracked down terrorist cells was to look at all the brokerage accounts that showed heavy short selling in the weeks before the attack. This led to multiple arrests, as people who knew about the upcoming attacks had been shorting insurance companies and airlines aggressively. Out of the blue? Let's look at a few market crashes and just see how "out of the blue" they really were.

# THE KEY TO GETTING POSITIONED
# BEFORE A MARKET CRASH

I don't mean to belittle the events of 9/11 by viewing them as merely a "trade setup." I lost friends, and know many people who lost friends and loved ones in that attack. The point of this is that the event should not scare us and make us cower in the corner. It should not keep us from taking risks, whether it involves getting on a plane, visiting another country, embracing people from other ethnicities, or having exposure to overnight positions. Living scared can hardly be called living.

## Dow Cash Index—September 11, 2001

1. This is a daily chart of the Dow Jones Industrials leading up to the terrorist attack on the World Trade Center on September 11, 2001 (see Fig. 10.21). At point #1, we can see that the daily squeeze fired off a short on August 30.

**F I G U R E   10.21**

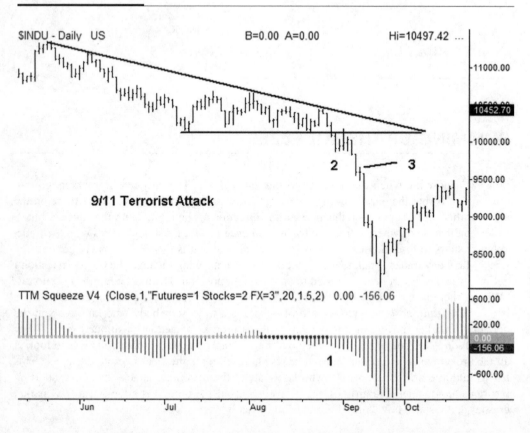

2. The very next day, the markets break through support on a descending wedge pattern. There are now two solid short signals in place. There is no reason to be long this market.

3. Six trading days later it is September 10. The markets make new intraday lows, and the momentum on the squeeze is still strong. There is no reason to be long; there is no reason to cover shorts.

   After 9/11, the markets were closed and didn't reopen until September 17. The Dow closed at 9605 on September 10, and after the next trading day closed at 8920.70, down nearly 700 points. Again, leading into this, there was no reason to be long in this market. Even though we didn't know what was about to happen, somebody did. The charts do not lie.

## Dow Cash Index—October 19, 1987

1. There was another big crash on October 19, 1987 (see Fig. 10.22). This is the year I graduated from high school, and one of my fondest trading memories is having

**F I G U R E   10.22**

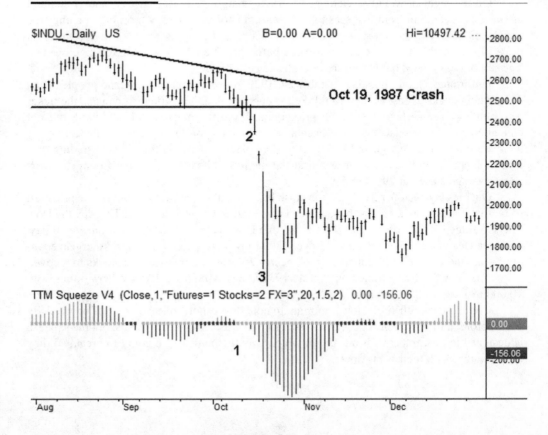

owned puts on IBM during the crash. I wish I could say that I saw the crash coming, but it was pure luck. I had a bunch of calls, read something about hedging, and bought puts on IBM. The puts saved my bacon and then some. If I'd had the squeeze at this time, I would have noted that the daily squeeze fired off a short signal on October 9, 10 full days before the crash.

2. Then on October 14 the markets broke down from a descending wedge pattern. There are now two reasons not to be long in the markets.

On October 19 the markets crash. Those who are already positioned for the move have a nice trading day. Those that don't have the squeeze to guide them experience new variations of the meaning of pain.

## Dow Cash Index—the Crash of 1929

The crash in 1929 was no picnic, either. I talked to one trader who was there when it happened. He is over 90 years old now and still actively trades. To him, nothing has changed, and it's all the same game. Remember in the first chapter when I talk about markets not moving because they want to, but because they have to? We talk about TASR in that example. Along these same lines, here is the quick narrative of the crash of 1929:

On the night of Monday, October 21, 1929, margin calls were heavy, and Dutch and German calls came in from overseas to sell overnight for the Tuesday morning opening (see Fig. 10.23). On Tuesday morning, out-of-town banks and corporations sent in $150 million of call loans, and Wall Street was in a panic before the New York Stock Exchange opened. The selling was heavy, but the influx of cash staved off a crash.

Unfortunately, on Thursday, October 24, 1929, more margin calls hit, and people began to sell their stocks as fast as they could. Sell orders flooded the market exchanges, the ticker was running over an hour behind on price quotes, and the markets sold off hard, but not enough to be considered a crash. The exchange directed all employees to be on the floor since there were numerous margin calls and sell orders placed overnight for the next trading day. Extra telephone staff was also arranged at the members' boxes around the floor. The Dow Jones average closed at 299 that day.

On Tuesday, October 29, 1929, the crash began. Within the first few hours, the price fell so far that it wiped out all gains that had been made the entire previous year. This day the Dow Jones average would close at 230. This is like the Dow losing 2,400 points in one day today. Between October 29 and November 13 over $30 billion disappeared from the American economy—and these were 1929 dollars. It took nearly 25 years for many of the stocks to recover.

The Dow finally bottomed out in July 1932 at near 40. That is like the Dow going from 10,000 to 1,100 in the year 2005.

Coming back full circle, it is important to note that a short squeeze fired off on the daily chart before the 1929 crash. Yes, terrorist attacks and crashes are scary things, but the squeeze is designed to give traders a heads up on which way the markets are going to break, so they aren't caught with their pants down.

**F I G U R E   10.23**

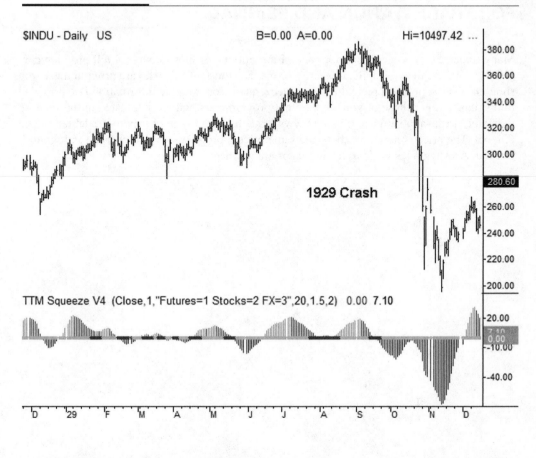

## STRATEGIES FOR THOSE WHO CAN'T TRADE FULL TIME

The squeeze on a daily chart is one of the best ways I know to trade part time. This can be used on individual stocks, and there is no reason to scan thousands of charts. I just sort through the 120 or so stocks that trade single stock futures. These are all of the big, liquid stocks with lots of volume, and the list of stocks is available at www.onechicago.com. Once I see a stock fire off, I will place an order for the trade. These types of trades do not need to be managed intraday. Even though I watch the markets full time, I do not watch my swing trades intraday. There is no point. My parameters are in place, and the only thing I'm going to do by watching my position is try to outsmart it, which never works in the long run. In addition to individual stocks this can be used for sectors, ETFs, and options on these same instruments. For options, I always go in the money with the premium making up no more than 30 percent of the price.

# A NOTE ON THE SQUEEZE INDICATOR
# FOR TRADESTATION AND ESIGNAL

Many traders are also good programmers. I am not one of those traders. I tell programmers what I want, and they make the indicator for me. For those of you who are programmers, you shouldn't have a problem recreating the squeeze indicator from the information I've provided in this chapter. For those of you who are not programmers and are interested in the squeeze indicator, it is available for purchase at www.tradethemarkets.com for both TradeStation and eSignal. The price is nominal, about the same price a programmer will charge to program it for you. Any upgrades made to the indicator are also free.

# BRICK PLAYS—LETTING THE MARKETS STACK UP

## USING BRICKS TO CAPTURE INTRADAY REVERSALS IN THE MINI-SIZED DOW

My trading partner, Hubert Senters, uses the brick play every day, and he uses it exclusively on the mini-sized Dow. He was very helpful in sending me chart examples of brick plays that he had taken while I was working on this part of the book.

The best intraday trades take place when a trader is able to catch the major portion of an intraday reversal. One of the best ways to do this is with a specific price pattern that we call *bricks*. We call them bricks because the price pattern that is formed looks like a bunch of building blocks that have been placed on top of a regular bar chart. These building blocks are formed on the chart because of specific price action. A series of three consecutive higher closes will form an "up" brick, and a series of three consecutive lower closes will form a "down" brick.

If you have a hard time pulling the trigger, this is a good play to use with buy stop and sell stop orders, as you will see in a moment. If you don't have a hard time pulling the trigger, then you can just wait for the signal and go in at the market. This is one of those plays that is difficult to explain, but easy to show. In this case, a picture is worth at least 1,000 words, if not more, so let's go through the trading rules and then go over a couple of actual plays.

## TRADING RULES FOR BUYS (SELLS ARE REVERSED)

This is a momentum reversal confirmation play.

1. Set up a 24-hour time frame on an intraday chart so that the overnight activity can be accounted for in this indicator setup. This is best used on smaller timeframes, typically under five minutes, though it can also be used for swing plays on daily charts.

2. Once a market shifts direction, which is denoted by the bricks changing color, count backwards to the third brick in the formation.

3. Then draw a horizontal line across the top of this third brick back.

4. Once the price action breaks above this horizontal line, go long.

5. Hubert and I use this setup on the mini-sized Dow, and we both manage this trade differently, so I will go over both of our methods. For Hubert, he places a 10-point stop from the entry. Then when he is up 10 points, he sells half his position and moves his stop to breakeven −3. (So if his entry was 10545, then his new stop is 10542.) If the market goes up another 10 points, he sells a quarter of his position and then moves up his stop six points to breakeven +3. (So if his original entry was 10545, his new stop is 10548.) He then hangs onto his last quarter of the position to exit at his discretion. This typically means that he will hold onto this last part of his position until the bricks signal an opposing sell signal.

6. I will get into the same trade and use a 20-point stop. I will exit half my position at +15 points and then stay in the trade until there is a brick that has formed in the opposite direction—an opposing sell signal. I don't trail the stops. Both methods have worked well for us, and this is a good example of how different traders can take the same setup and modify the trading methodology to fit their own particular personality.

Let's take a look at some actual plays:

## Mini-Sized Dow—March 2005 Contract, February 25, 2005

1. On this five-minute chart of the mini-sized Dow futures on February 25, 2005, a long signal occurs at around 10:00 a.m. Eastern (see Fig. 11.1). This takes place when the price action reverses and crosses above the horizontal line created by the third brick back in the series. The first brick in the series is the black brick labeled point 1, the second as point 2, and the third as point 3. The entry price is 10696. This horizontal line is drawn in manually. Originally it started on the brick above where the line is currently drawn at point 3. This horizontal line was sitting near 10710. However, as the market continued to push lower, additional down bricks were formed, and the horizontal line was trailed 3 bricks back accordingly. This line, representing the entry point for a long, continues to be trailed down as long as new down bricks are formed. It is only when the markets can cross back above the third brick back in the series that a trade signal occurs. On a color chart, the up bricks are blue, and the down bricks are red. On these charts, the up bricks are light gray and the down bricks are black.

**2.** In this instance, once the trade is entered, the YM rallies to almost 10790 before rolling over. A reversal signal is generated shortly thereafter at point 4 at a price of 10778, for a total move of 82 points.

I want to also discuss three different ways this setup could be played. The first and most straightforward way would be to stay in the entire trade from entry to exit, capturing the entire move. In this type of play, I start off with a 20-point stop and then stay in the trade until the reversal signal occurs. The downside of this is that the market could rally 18 points and then roll over and stop out the trade.

Another way to play this is to exit half the position at a purely mechanical price target. This is how Hubert and I play this. We execute this trade slightly different from each other, and the mechanics of each of our styles will be explained shortly. By exiting half of your position at mine or Hubert's predetermined mechanical levels for the first half of the trade, some profits would already have been taken. This can mean the difference between a losing trade and a scratch trade. So the second way to play this is to start off with a 20-point stop and then exit the first half of the position at a mechanical level, such as 15 points, and then exit the second half upon a reversal. This is typically how I play the bricks.

The third way to play this is how Hubert plays it, where he uses a 10-point stop and then starts peeling out of the position almost immediately. In this case he sold half when he was up 10 points, sold a quarter of his position when he was up 20 points, and held onto the rest until the reversal. Note that these exit strategies can be used on all the intraday plays discussed in this book.

**F I G U R E   11.1**

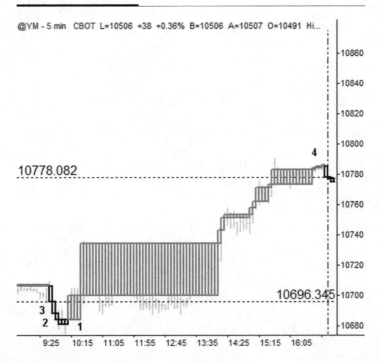

These are all valid exit methodologies for this setup. It is important for a trader to recognize that every setup can be played differently and to find the way that best suits his or her own personality. For the rest of the examples, I focus on the actual reversal points as entries and exits.

## Mini-Sized Dow—March 2005 Contract, March 3, 2005

1. On this three-minute chart of the mini-sized Dow on March 3, 2005, a long reversal signal fired right around 1:00 p.m. Eastern, as the third brick back in the series was penetrated (see Fig. 11.2). The entry on a buy stop order was 10817.

2. For the exit, we are now waiting for a down (black) brick to form, and once that happens, we will use a trailing three-brick stop utilizing the up bricks. By doing this, the trade is exited at 10871, for a gain of +54 points.

## Mini-Sized Dow—March 2005 Contract, March 9, 2005

1. On March 9, 2005, this five-minute chart of the YM fired off a brick short just before noon Eastern (see Fig. 11.3). The entry took place using a sell stop order at 10916.

### FIGURE 11.2

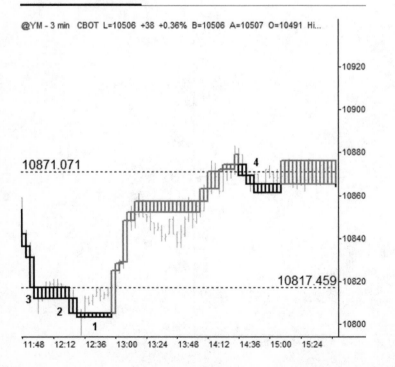

@YM - 3 min  CBOT  L=10506  +38  +0.36%  B=10506  A=10507  O=10491  Hi...

2. For the exit, the goal is to wait for an up brick, and once that occurs, to trail a stop three bricks back. The stop is hit at 10830 for a gain of +86 points. What I like about this is that the setup keeps a person in the trade all through the choppy noise and false rallies that occur between 1:00 p.m. and 3:00 p.m. Eastern. This goes back to the importance of having a specific exit strategy—and only a specific exit strategy—to get out of a trade.

## Mini-Sized Dow—March 2005 Contract, March 10, 2005

1. On March 10, 2005, the YM three-minute chart fired off a brick long just before noon at 10829 (see Fig. 11.4).
2. The setup reversed a few hours later, setting up an exit signal at 10880 for a gain of +51 points.

## Mini-Sized Dow—March 2005 Contract, March 11, 2005

1. On this two-minute chart of the YM on March 11, 2005, a reversal short brick signal fired off at 10864 at around 11:00 a.m. Eastern (see Fig. 11.5).

**F I G U R E   11.3**

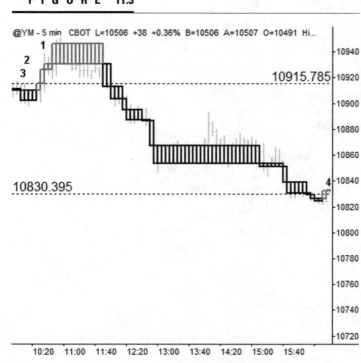

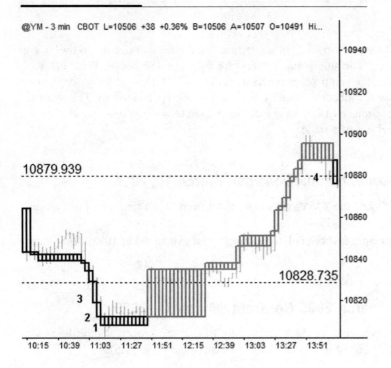

2. The play continued to work lower until the last hour of trade, generating an exit signal at 10806 for a gain of +58 points. Again I would like to point out all the noise in this chart that occurred between 11:30 a.m. and nearly 2:00 p.m. How many traders got chopped up in this? How many chased it higher? How many shorts panicked and covered? A trader who follows a specific setup, with a specific set of parameters, is at a huge advantage over all the people out there who are "trying to rely on their judgment while in a trade."

## Mini-Sized Dow—March 2005 Contract, March 16, 2005

1. On this two-minute chart of the YM on March 16, 2005, a reversal short brick signal fired off at 10699 in the latter part of the trading day a little after 1:00 p.m. Eastern (see Fig. 11.6).

2. The markets continued to sell off, and the bricks stayed in sell mode until about 20 minutes before the close, when a reversal signal hit, stopping the trade out at 10657 for a gain of +42 points.

## Mini-Sized Dow—March 2005 Contract, March 22, 2005

1. On this two-minute chart of the YM on March 22, 2005, the YM fired off a short signal late in the trading day, and a sell stop order was hit at 10622 (see Fig. 11.7).

**F I G U R E    11.5**

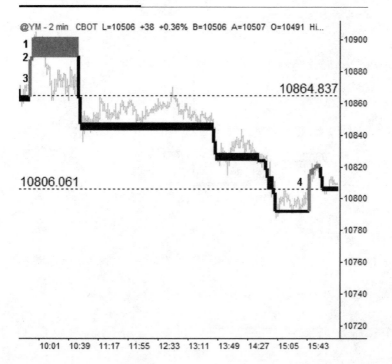

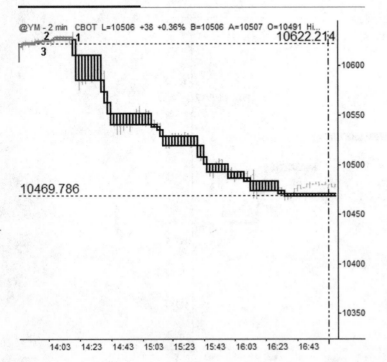

234

2. The markets drifted lower into the close, and there was actually not a reversal signal given to exit this trade. In this case, we just use the 4:15 p.m. Eastern close on the ES to get out of the trade. Although the YM continues to trade until 5:00 p.m., the liquidity really dries up after the ES market closes. In this case, exiting on the close generated an exit at 10469 for a gain of +153 points. Why the big sell off? This was FOMC (Federal Open Market Committee) day, and the markets sold off after the news hit about another quarter-point rate increase. This ties into one of my biggest beliefs about trading the markets—economic reports mean very little in the scheme of things. The market is going to do what the market is going to do. The key is to focus on the setup and ignore the rest of the noise.

## Mini-Sized Dow—December 2004 Contract, October 27, 2004

1. On this daily chart of the YM, a swing play was generated on the bricks near the end of October 2004 (see Fig. 11.8). The entry on this play was 9927.

2. The daily bricks stayed in buy mode until the end of November, when a sell signal was generated at 10575, for a gain of +648 points. When the market reversed in late October there were a lot of bears. This again points to the fact that it doesn't really matter what people think about the market and what they feel it *might* do. What matters is what the market is actually doing. Trade setups like the bricks remove all the emotion.

**F I G U R E   11.8**

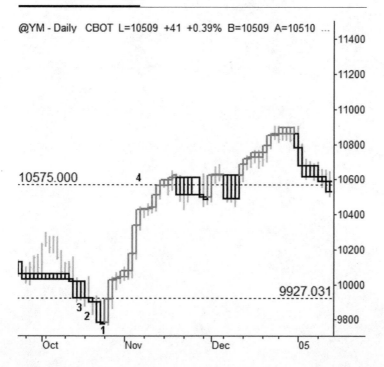

## SUMMING UP THE BRICKS

The brick setup is great when you're trying to catch an intraday reversal. Too many traders try to do this but end up getting burned. They short the market, and it just keeps going higher. Or they buy the market, and it gets flattened. There is no reason to try to catch the exact high or the exact low in a market move. That involves too much risk and has a low probability of success. With this confirmation signal, a trader will be made aware of when the move has petered out and has started its reversal, and although they won't be able to catch the exact highs or the exact lows, they will still be able to catch the "meat of the move."

CHAPTER

# THE PING-PONG PLAY: BATTING THE MARKETS BACK AND FORTH . . . ALL DAY LONG

## A TRADING CHANNEL THAT MOVES AND ADAPTS TO THE MARKETS IN REAL TIME

The Ping-Pong play is a channel play with a twist: This channel is always present and is continually adjusting itself to the market action. There isn't any need to draw a couple of parallel lines and wait for two tests of the highs and two tests of the lows to confirm that a channel is in place. This channel is always hanging around, waiting for a trade to setup.

This setup was discovered by accident by Hubert Senters, one of my trading partners. He spent a couple of years watching KLAC (KLA Tencor Corp) on a two-minute chart and a five-minute chart. He noticed that when KLAC broke up through the 200 simple moving average (SMA) on a two-minute chart, it would head right up to the 200-period SMA on a five-minute chart. To make life easier, he eventually figured out that he could do this all on one chart, by setting up a new two-minute chart that had both a 200 SMA and a 500 SMA. The 500 SMA on a two-minute chart plots just the same as a 200 period SMA on a five-minute chart. Once this play was converted to one chart, it was easy to see that a live, moving channel was in place as the 200 SMA and 500 SMA moved together in an almost graceful dance.

Hubert uses this setup almost exclusively on the stock KLAC. We've also found that it works well for other high-volatility, high-volume stocks that tend to attract a lot of the day-trading crowd.

# TRADING RULES FOR BUYS (SELLS ARE REVERSED)

The Ping-Pong play can be both a momentum play and a fade play, depending on the initial move against one of the moving averages. When prices are trading inside the channel, this is a fade play. When prices break into the channel, this turns into a momentum play.

1. I set up a two-minute chart on a 24-hour time setting. I want the pre- and postmarket activity to be taken into account for the moving average calculations.

2. I like to use candlestick price charts on this play, but it is not critical because I'm not looking for any specific candlestick patterns such as Dojis, Hammers, Shooting Stars, and so forth. If you are unfamiliar with candlestick patterns, an excellent book is *Japanese Candlestick Charting* by Steve Nison. I personally don't use candlestick patterns for intraday trading, but I do like to see what the daily candlestick bars are doing to get a better feel of who is in control of the market—buyers or sellers.

3. I place a 200-period SMA (represented by the thick line in the chart examples) and a 500-period SMA (represented by the thin line in the chart examples) on the two-minute chart.

4. When the market is trading below both moving averages, I go long after the first two-minute bar closes inside the moving average channel.

5. When the market is trading inside the moving averages, I go long on a bounce off the bottom of the channel. I will wait for a two-minute bar to close on a bounce off the channel before placing a market order to go long.

6. I use a 50-cent stop. If the moving averages are trading wider than 50 cents, then when I am up 50 cents on the trade, I will move my stop to the moving average that triggered my entry. If the moving averages are trading narrower than 50 cents, then I will leave my original stop in place, and I won't trail it.

7. My target is the "other moving average."

8. I typically use this trade on KLAC, as does Hubert. However, it works with other volatile stocks as well.

## KLAC (KLA Tencor Corp), October 4, 2004

1. On October 4, 2004, KLAC broke down through the 200 SMA (see Fig. 12.1). After the first closing candlestick, I went short at the market and was filled at 43.83. I place a 50-cent stop at 44.33, and my target is the 500 SMA below. About 45 minutes later I am up 50 cents on the trade, so I move my stop down to the 200 SMA, which is trading at 43.91.

2. KLAC rallies and comes within 10 cents of my stop. It eventually rolls over and hits my target at 43.11 at point 2, and I am out of the trade for a gain of 72 cents. KLAC is liquid and will support a large number of shares on this trade. For 1,000 shares that is a profit of $720; for 10,000 shares that is a gain of $7,200. There will be a little slippage when going in and out of 10,000 shares at the market. When this hap-

pens I just take the average price, and I use that to determine where I will place my 50-cent stop. I will also trade KLAC single stock futures on this trade (KLAC1C). For those of you who aren't familiar with single stock futures, they are nice because the leverage is 5 to 1 without any margin interest costs. And these can be traded in an IRA through a trust account (meaning you can short in your IRA), and you can do these day trades with only a few thousand dollars in your account, instead of the $25,000 minimum you need to day trade stocks. One single stock futures (SSF) contract represents 100 shares of stock. With single stock futures, I will use limit orders instead of market orders because they are not as liquid as the underlying stock. However, the low volume that is currently present in SSFs is misleading. The liquidity is based more on the volume of the underlying stock. This is something I talk more about later in the "8/21 EMAs for Swings" chapter. My experience with single stock futures has been very positive, and I continue to add more of these contracts to my trading program.

## KLAC (KLA Tencor Corp), September 23, 2004

**1.** On September 23, 2004, KLAC pushes up through its 200 SMA (see Fig. 12.2). After the first two-minute bar closes above this level, I take a long at the market, and I'm filled at 40.76. I place a 50-cent stop at 40.26. My target is the 500

**FIGURE   12.1**

**F I G U R E  12.2**

KLAC - 2 min  NASDAQ

period moving average trading overhead. For this particular trade, the moving
averages are not 50 cents apart, so I won't be trailing my stop.

**2.** KLAC edges higher, and my target in the form of the 500 SMA is hit, and I'm out
at 41.07 for a gain of 31 cents.

## KLAC (KLA Tencor Corp), August 30, 2004

**1.** On August 30, 2004, KLAC rallies into the 200 SMA (see Fig. 12.3). When the
first bar closes back below this moving average, I go short at the market. I'm filled
at 38.24, and I place a 50-cent stop at 38.74. The moving averages are less than 50
cents apart, so I won't be trailing my stop on this trade.

**2.** KLAC goes pretty much straight down, and a little over 40 minutes later I am out
of my short at the 500 SMA. I'm filled at 37.82 for a gain of 42 cents.

## KLAC (KLA Tencor Corp), August 25, 2004

**1.** On August 25, 2004, KLAC comes down and tests the 200 SMA while trading
inside this moving average channel (see Fig. 12.4). Once the first two-minute bar

KLAC - 2 min  NASDAQ

closes above the 200 SMA after the test, I go long at the market. I'm filled at
37.10, and I place a 50-cent stop at 36.60. The moving averages in this case are
less than 50 cents apart, so I won't be trailing any stops on this trade.

2.  KLAC rallies to the 500 SMA, and I'm out at 37.58 for a gain of 48 cents. This is
    scalping at its finest, and although these aren't huge plays, some would argue that
    it beats flipping burgers for a living.

## KLAC (KLA Tencor Corp), August 23, 2004

1.  On August 23, KLAC sells off and breaks hard through the 200 SMA (see Fig.
    12.5). It closes pretty deep within the channel, but as soon as this first bar
    closes, I go short. I'm filled at 37.94. I place a 50-cent stop at 38.44. The 500
    SMA is not very far away, so I won't have the opportunity to trail my stop
    at all.

2.  It takes longer than I thought it would, but the 500 SMA is eventually hit, and I'm
    out at 37.61 for a gain of 33 cents.

KLAC - 2 min   NASDAQ

KLAC - 2 min   NASDAQ

## KLAC (KLA Tencor Corp), August 19, 2004

1. On August 19, 2004, KLAC slams through the 200 SMA (see Fig. 12.6). Once the first bar through closes below this level, I go short at the market. I'm filled at an average price of 37.44. I place a 50-cent stop at 37.94. The two moving averages are less than 50 cents apart, so there won't be any trailing on this trade.

2. The market chops around for a while, and KLAC doesn't so much fall to its 500 SMA as the 500 SMA rallies to the current price levels. Once this happens, I get out at the market. I'm filled at 37.15 for a gain of 29 cents. This is a good example of the "living, breathing, moving, horizontal channels" in action. There are no stationary straight lines on these setups. These babies move and ebb and flow with the market.

## KLAC (KLA Tencor Corp), August 17, 2004

1. On August 17, 2004, KLAC gaps down into the 500 SMA (see Fig. 12.7). Once I see a two-minute candlestick that closes back above the 500 SMA, (the third candlestick over from point 1), I go long at the market and am filled at 36.32. Once

**F I G U R E   12.6**

KLAC - 2 min  NASDAQ

**F I G U R E  12.7**

KLAC - 2 min  NASDAQ

again, the two moving averages are less than 50 cents apart, so I won't be trailing any stops.

2. KLAC pushes higher quickly, and eight minutes later I'm out at 36.76 for a gain of 44 cents.

## KLAC (KLA Tencor Corp), August 10, 2004

1. On August 10, 2004, KLAC sells off and hits the bottom of its 200 SMA (see Fig. 12.8). KLAC pushes through this level, and I'm poised to go long after the first two-minute bar closes back inside the channel. This takes place shortly thereafter, and I go long at the market. My fill is 38.53. Once again the moving averages are less than 50 cents apart, so I won't have to worry about trailing my stop.

2. KLAC grinds higher, and after a while the 500 SMA is touched. When this happens, I exit and take my profits at 38.80 for a gain of 27 cents. It is okay to place limit orders for targets, but because the two-minute charts move fast, the price of the moving average is going to fluctuate and change every couple of bars, so you have to keep an eye on it, or have the exits adjust automatically via a trading system.

**F I G U R E   12.8**

KLAC - 2 min   NASDAQ

## KLAC (KLA Tencor Corp), July 21, 2004

1. On July 21, 2004, KLAC drops back into its channel, through the 200 SMA, and I short once the first bar closes within the channel (see Fig. 12.9). I'm filled at 41.23, and I place a 50-cent stop. I do a quick check and see that the moving averages are less than 50 cents apart, and that of course means I won't be trailing any stops.

2. KLAC drifts down, and the 500 SMA is tagged. I cover at 40.81 and I'm out for a gain of 42 cents.

## KLAC (KLA Tencor Corp), July 12, 2004

1. On July 12, 2004, KLAC pushes back up into its channel via the 200 SMA (see Fig. 12.10). Once the first two-minute bar closes inside this channel, I go long, and I'm filled at 44.39. I place a 50-cent stop at 43.89. I duly note that the moving averages are greater than 50 cents apart. So, if I get to the point where I'm up 50 cents on this trade, I will move my stop up to the 200 SMA.

KLAC - 2 min  NASDAQ

KLAC - 2 min  NASDAQ

2. KLAC pushes higher, and once it trades through 44.89, I move up my stop to the 200 SMA, which is at 44.23. KLAC continues to rally straight up, and it runs right into the 500 SMA. When this happens, I close out my long at the market. I'm filled at 45.23 for a gain of 84 cents.

## KLAC (KLA Tencor Corp), July 1, 2004

1. On July 1, 2004, KLAC gaps down and hits its 200 SMA (see Fig. 12.11). Once it closes through this level, I go short, and I'm filled at 49.01. I immediately place a stop 50 cents away at 49.51. The moving averages are greater than 50 cents apart, so I will look to trail my stop down to the 200 SMA once I'm up 50 cents in the trade. KLAC ends up selling off quickly, and once it trades through 48.51, I move my stop down to 48.99, which is where the 200 SMA is trading at this time.

2. KLAC continues to sell off, and once it touches the 500 SMA, I start to cover, and I'm out at 48.44 for a gain of 57 cents.

## KLAC (KLA Tencor Corp), May 19, 2004

1. On May 19, 2004, KLAC sells off and enters its moving average channel (see Fig. 12.12). I go short when the first two-minute bar closes inside this channel. I'm filled

**F I G U R E   12.11**

**F I G U R E   12.12**

at 45.78, and I place a 50-cent stop at 46.28. Since the moving averages are wider than 50 cents apart, I will be looking to trail my stop once I'm up 50 cents. KLAC drifts down, and once price action falls through 45.28, I move my stop down to 45.89.

2.  KLAC continues to sell off, and once it hits the 500 SMA, I'm out at 44.94 for a gain of 84 cents.

## WHEN YOU'RE DANCING WITH THE MARKET, IT'S A GOOD IDEA TO LET IT LEAD

One of the things I like about this play is that it catches the ebbs and flows of the market nicely. All I have to do is sit back and "let the market lead." There really isn't any good time to try to force the market to do what you want it to do. This setup is a nice reminder of that, and all I have to do is sit back, relax, and follow my dance partner.

# CHAPTER 13

# THE 3:52 PLAY: CAPPING OFF
# THE DAY WITH A FINE CIGAR

## THIS IS WHERE THE OTHER PEOPLE START TO PANIC

The 3:52 play is a setup I discovered while working in a trading room observing over 100 other traders going through their daily gyrations with the market. It is commonly known among traders that 3:30 p.m. Eastern is a key reversal point in the markets. What was fascinating is that I would watch this room full of traders stare at the bounce (or sell off) that would start at 3:30, and then they would wait, wait, and wait some more. They would wait for confirmation, wait for an indicator-based buy or sell signal, wait for their mother to call and tell them it was okay to take the trade, or whatever. The point is they would *wait* to jump in on the move. Finally, they would succumb to the pressure to get in, and jump in on the move just as it was running out of steam. I would spend the rest of the session watching in fascination as they pointed, gyrated, and yelled at their computer screens as the markets drifted against them. Often they would wait until the last possible minute to get out of their S&P futures trades, which is 4:15 p.m. Eastern. They would wait in the hope that the markets would come back to them, and they spent this brief session praying that their position would work out. Sometimes it did, but often it did not because there were too many of them trapped and hoping for the same move. As the markets neared 4:15 p.m., they had no choice. They could not wait any longer, and they were forced to close out their positions. Like rats on a sinking ship, these traders would all head for the exits at once. If they were long, they would all be selling at once. If they were short, they would all be buying at once.

The interesting part of this is that the liquidity dries up after 4:00 p.m. Eastern. With the decreased liquidity that occurs from 4:00 p.m. to 4:15 p.m., these groups of traders can easily cause exaggerated movements in the markets in the final minutes before the closing bell. This causes the markets to move hard against them. I watched them do this day after day, assuming that one day they would catch on. They never did, and after a while I would just sit there and do the opposite of what they were doing, so while they were crying I was cashing in. This same setup continues to work today, and it is something I do nearly every trading day. Like a single malt scotch after a filet mignon, it's a great way to cap off a trading session.

## TRADING RULES FOR BUYS (SELLS ARE REVERSED)

This is a fade play. I let the 3:30 p.m. Eastern reversal happen, and then 22 minutes later, at 3:52, I take the opposite side of the move.

1. I use this setup for the E-mini S&Ps and the mini-sized Dow futures.
2. I set up a one-minute bar chart without any other indicators or interference.
3. At 3:30 p.m. Eastern I mark where the futures are trading. In the case of this example, the futures would have started rallying at 3:30 p.m. Eastern.
4. At 3:52 p.m. I take a short using a market order. I short at the opening of the 3:52 one-minute bar. This is assuming that the ES is at least 1 point away and that the YM is at least 10 points away from where it was trading at 3:30. On days when this does not occur, I don't take the trade.
5. My stop for the ES is 2 points, and my stop for the YM is 20 points. I do not trail stops for this play.
6. I hold onto the trade until 4:13 p.m. Eastern, at which point I close out at the market. Technically I could hold on until 4:15, but I don't want to get stuck in this trade overnight, which is why I give it two minutes of elbow room. If I discover my PC has locked up, that gives me enough time to call my broker and get out of my trade. (I use a broker who actually answers the phone and doesn't put me on hold.)
7. Even though the mini-sized Dow doesn't close until 5:00 p.m., I will still use 4:13 p.m. to mirror the E-mini S&P futures markets. By 4:15 I'm ready to take a break from trading for the day.

### E-mini S&P—December 2004 Contract, October 14, 2004

1. At 3:30 p.m. Eastern on October 14, 2004, the S&Ps start to rally, and since they are rallying off of 3:30, I will be looking to short this market at 3:52 (see Fig. 13.1). By watching a one-minute bar, I can see that the 3:51 p.m. bar closes at 1104.75. Then at 3:52 p.m. the bar opens at 1104.50, and I take the opposite side of this move. I short at the market, and I am filled at 1104.50. I place a two-point stop at 1106.50.

2. The traders who jumped on this 3:30 p.m. "pop" late are now starting to watch their trade go under water. The longer they hang on, the more nervous they get, and they start getting their stops hit, or just dumping their position using market orders. This pushes the market down even further. At 4:13 p.m., the one-minute bar opens at 1103.00. This is my time signal to get out, and I cover at the market for a gain of +1.50 E-mini S&P points. One of the things I like about this play is that there is a time limit. I know that when I get in, I will be getting out 21 minutes later. I also like the fact that I'm not looking for a big move. I'm mentally prepped to take a small scalp, and when this trade does move against me, it is typically for a very small loss, since my actual stop is rarely hit.

## E-mini S&P—December 2004 Contract, October 4, 2004

1. At 3.30 p.m. Eastern on October 4, 2004, the market sells off into the 3:52 p.m. timeframe (see Fig. 13.2). Since the market is selling off from this time reversal point, I am looking to take the opposite side of this move so I go long. All I am waiting for now is 3:52 p.m., which is my time trigger to get into the trade. At 3:52 p.m., I buy at 1136.00 and place a stop at 1134.00. Why do I wait for exactly 3:52 p.m. to fade this move? This is just the time I settled on after doing

**F I G U R E   13.1**

this on a trial-and-error basis for a long period of time. I cannot mathematically prove that getting in at 3:52 is better than getting in at 3:50. It's almost like asking whether people prefer blondes or brunettes. They may have a preference, but in the end all that matters is that they are able to get along with their choice and make a go of it.

2. The markets chops back and forth, and at 4:13 p.m., I am out at 1135.50 for –0.50. It is interesting to note that I am rarely stopped out on this play. Though I do take losses with this setup, they are typically very small.

## E-mini S&P—September 2004 Contract, July 27, 2004

1. From 3:30 p.m. Eastern on July 27, 2004, the market rallies into the 3:52 p.m. timeframe (see Fig. 13.3). At 3:51 the one-minute bar closes at 1094.75. I short at the open of the next bar, and I'm in at 1094.75. I place a two-point stop at 1096.75.

2. The market drifts down, and when the 4:13 p.m. bar starts, the S&Ps are being offered at 1093.25. I cover at the market and I'm out for +1.50.

**F I G U R E   13.2**

### FIGURE 13.3

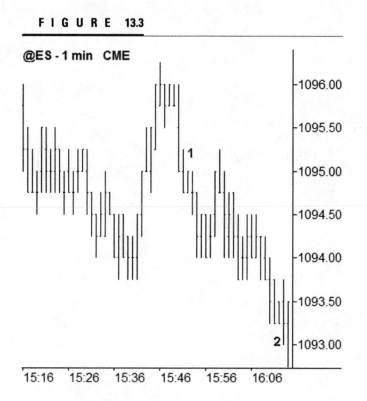

@ES - 1 min   CME

## E-mini S&P—September 2004 Contract, July 28, 2004

1. On July 28, 2004, the market rallies off of 3:30 p.m. Eastern and at 3:52 p.m. I short at 1096.75 (see Fig. 13.4). I place a two-point stop at 1098.75.
2. The market drifts down, gets as low as 1094.75, and then starts drifting back up. At 4:13 p.m. I cover at 1096.50 for a gain of +0.25.

## E-mini S&P—September 2004 Contract, July 29, 2004

1. On July 29, 2004, the market sells off from 3:30 p.m. Eastern into 3:52 p.m. (see Fig. 13.5). At 3:52 p.m., I buy in using a market order, and I'm filled at 1099.00. I place a stop at 1097.00.
2. The market starts moving higher after 4:00 p.m., and at 4:13 p.m. I sell using a market order. I'm out at 1100.50 for a gain +2.50.

## Mini-Sized Dow—September 2004 Contract, July 1, 2004

1. This trade also works well with the mini-sized Dow. I don't really have a preference for one market over the other for this play. Since the volume in the mini-sized

**F I G U R E   13.4**

**F I G U R E   13.5**

Dow is less than that of the E-mini S&Ps, the movements in this market can sometimes get a little more exaggerated from 4:00 p.m. to 4:15 p.m., which is a positive for this trade setup. On September 8, 2004, the mini-sized Dow sells off into 3:52 p.m., so I take a long and am filled at 10311 (see Fig. 13.6). I place a 20-point stop at 10291.

2. After 4:00 p.m. the markets start to rally on short covering, and at 4:13 p.m. I sell at 10322 for a gain of +21 points.

## Mini-Sized Dow—December 2004 Contract, September 13, 2004

1. On September 13, 2004, the mini-sized Dow sells off at 3:30 p.m. Eastern, so at 3:52 p.m. I go long using a market order, and I'm filled at 10309 (see Fig. 13.7). I place a stop at 10289. This is a good example because the market stabilized and started to drift higher at around 3:40 p.m. Shouldn't I then be shorting this rally into 3:52 p.m.? No! The key element to look for is the predominant move after 3:30 p.m. Remember our friends in the trading room? They see the move off 3:30 p.m., and then they wait, wait, wait to get in. So in this example they are shorting

**F I G U R E   13.6**

@YM - 1 min   CBOT

**F I G U R E   13.7**

@YM - 1 min   CBOT

the dead lows of the move, and they will spend the rest of the session covering their shorts for a loss. My basic rule of thumb on this trade is as follows: If it is not crystal clear, then I just don't take the trade. For example, if the market is dead quiet into the final hour of trading and there isn't any reaction at 3:30 p.m., then I don't have a trade to take. This setup is either very obvious, or there isn't a setup. There is usually a clear setup four days out of five.

2. The short covering continues right into the close, and at 4:13 p.m. I am out at 10321 for a +12 point gain. Note, this trade could also have been done in the September 2004 contract, which was still active though set to expire on Friday, September 17. Remember, during rollover week, the next front month becomes the most active contract the Thursday of the week before expiration. Expiration during this time was setup for Friday, September 17, so the December contract became the official front month on Thursday, September 9. During rollover week both contracts will trade actively, but volume starts pouring into the next contract out, and a trader will want to begin trading that next contract on that Thursday of the week before expiration.

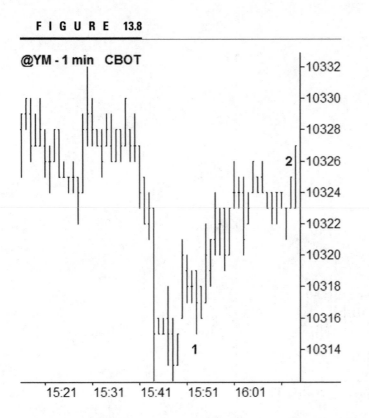

**F I G U R E   13.8**

Mini-Sized Dow—December 2004 Contract, September 14, 2004

1. On September 14, 2004, the market starts to sell off near the 3:30 p.m. Eastern timeframe (see Fig. 13.8). Since it is selling off, I'm waiting for my time entry to go long. My time entry at 3:52 p.m. appears, and I go long at the market. I'm filled at 10318, and I place my 20-point stop at 10298.

2. At 4:13 p.m. I cover at 10324 for a gain of +6 points. This brings to light the vast differences between scalping and swing trading. A trade like this won't pay the mortgage, but it does allow me to pick up an extra shot of espresso the next time I'm at Starbucks. Of course, the idea here is that scalp trades are used to generate monthly income, and swing trades are used to create wealth.

## Mini-Sized Dow—December 2004 Contract, September 24, 2004

1. On September 24, 2004, the mini-sized Dow starts selling off at 3:30 p.m. Eastern (see Fig. 13.9). I wait until 3:52 p.m., at which point I fire off a market order to buy. I'm filled at 10037, and I place a stop at 10017.

**F I G U R E   13.9**

2. The market chops higher, and at 4:13 p.m. I close out my long at 10044, a gain of +7 points.

## Mini-Sized Dow—December 2004 Contract, September 27, 2004

1. On September 27, 2004, the markets start selling off at 3:30 p.m. Eastern (see Fig. 13.10). I sit back, imagining all the traders who are now chasing the market, trying to get short. At 3:52 p.m. I place a market order to go long, and I'm filled at 9988. The market continues to sell off, coming close to my 20-point stop at 9968.

2. I can now watch as the same traders who chased the market short start to take some heat and start to cover. The market rallies hard, but the main part of this rally just gets me back to even. At 4:13 p.m. I offer my contracts out for sale, and I'm filled at 9990 for +2 points. Well, I won't even be able to do much at Starbucks with this trade, but I of course appreciate that I can still wear flip flops to the office.

## Mini-Sized Dow—December 2004 Contract, October 6, 2004

1. On October 6, 2004, the market starts to sell off at 3:30 p.m. Eastern, stabilizes about 10 minutes later, and starts to edge higher (see Fig. 13.11). Because the ini-

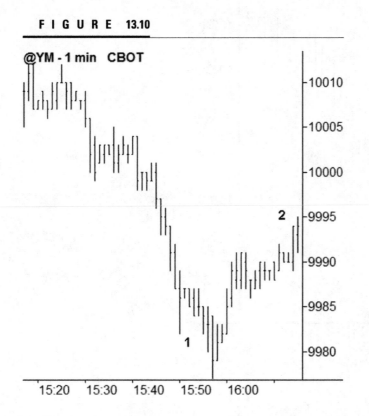

**F I G U R E   13.10**

tial move off of 3:30 p.m. was a down move, I am looking to do the opposite and go long. At 3:52 p.m. I go long with a market order, and I'm filled at 10220. I place a 20-point stop at 10200.

2. All the traders who chased that 3:30 p.m. short start getting smacked around. Their plight turns into my profit, and at 4:13 p.m. I offer out my contracts. I'm filled at 10239 for a gain of 19 points. Today I can buy everyone in the office Starbucks with my last trade. No joke. When we walk into Starbucks on these days, the Starbucks employees whisper, "Here comes the ring leader." Where else can five people walk into a coffee shop and get a round of flavored water for $20? On principle I had to buy stock in the company. This way I don't feel like I'm getting ripped a new one; I'm just helping to increase the value of my investment. (What's the phrase? Denial ain't just a river in Egypt.)

## Mini-Sized Dow—December 2004 Contract, October 8, 2004

1. On October 8, 2004, the market rallies from 3:30 p.m. Eastern right into 3:52 p.m., at which point I go short at the market, and I'm filled at 10049 (see Fig. 13.12). I place a stop at 10069. We come within eight points of my stop and then start to reverse.

2. At 4:13 p.m. I cover my short, and I'm filled at 10037 for a gain of +12 points.

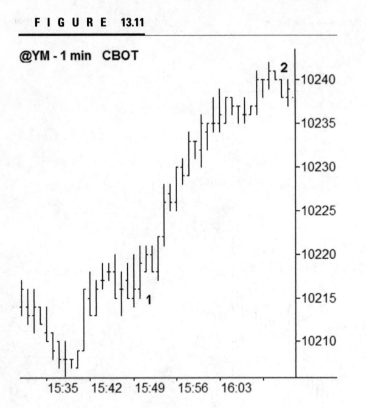

@YM - 1 min  CBOT

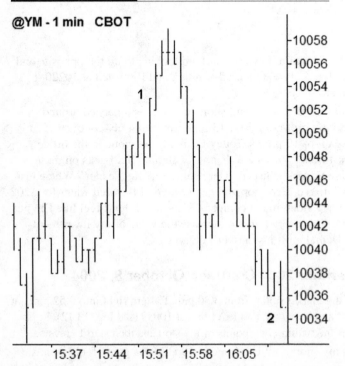

@YM - 1 min  CBOT

### Mini-Sized Dow—December 2004 Contract, October 13, 2004

1. On October 13, 2004, the market rallies nicely off of 3:30 p.m. Eastern, and as we hit 3:52 p.m. I short faster than a Boston Red Sox fan drinking a beer after their team won game 7 against the Yankees after being down 3–0 (see Fig. 13.13). (I had to put that in on October 18, I was at game 4, six seats behind home plate. The game lasted 14 innings and was the most memorable sports experience of my life.) I'm filled at 9994, and I place a stop at 10014.

2. The market drifts down immediately, and at 4:13 p.m. I cover at 9984 for a gain of +10 points.

## SUMMING UP THE 3:52 PLAY

I like this trade because it is simple and effective, and it goes clearly against the masses who chase this move off of the 3:30 p.m. reversal timeframe. Like it or not, futures trading is a zero sum game. For someone to win, someone else has to lose. This trade clearly takes advantage of traders' emotions and cleanly separates the winners from the losers.

F I G U R E   **13.13**

# BOX PLAYS—ON DAYS WHEN THE STOCK MARKET IS DEAD IN THE WATER, LOOK TO THE CURRENCIES

## MEASURING THE LENGTH OF THE MOVE BEFORE IT OCCURS

The one thing I can say for certain about the markets is that they will never move straight up or straight down forever. A market can definitely rip higher for a long time, but at some point it will have to rest and consolidate, and sometimes it will even come back down to earth and reverse all those spectacular gains. Just as runners can sprint for only a limited amount of time before their body gives out, a market can move only so far before it needs to pause, take a rest, and build up its energy reserves for the next major move.

Box plays are used to discover situations in which a market is taking a break before getting ready for its next major thrust, whether it is the next spurt higher or the next spurt lower. My favorite markets in which to use this play are the forex currency markets. Although these plays also work well on the currency futures, especially the euro (EC), I've found the forex markets tend to set up "cleaner" for this play, with fewer stray ticks and more liquidity in the various currency pairs.

The most popular currency to trade is the Euro. This is not to be confused with the Eurodollar contract that trades on the CME, symbol ED. Eurodollars are U.S. dollars on deposit in commercial banks outside of the United States. Eurodollars are an interest rate products that portfolio managers can use to hedge short term interest rate risk with all kinds of complicated strategies. This is the most liquid contract in the world but it doesn't move, and I don't trade it. To clarify, I'm talking about the euro/dollar currency cross, which is the actual currency I get in my hands when I go to Europe and exchange my U.S. dollars for Euros. On the CME, this is called Euro FX, symbol EC. In the forex markets, it is called the euro dollar cross, symbol EURUSD.

To review, on the CME and in the forex markets, the euro moves in increments of 1/100 of a cent. On the CME, this move is called a *tick*, and is worth $12.50 per contract, making a full one-cent move worth $1,250 per contract. In the forex markets, this move is called a *pip* (price interest point) and is worth $10, making a full one-cent move worth $1,000.00 per contract. There is also a mini-forex contract available in which each pip is worth $1, and a full one-cent move here would be worth $100. It is important to keep in mind, however, that there are many other trading opportunities out there in the currency world besides the euro. Often times the other currency pairs move and trend better for the simple fact that there are not a lot of retail traders jumping in and out of these other markets. Trades in the Euro make up only about 10 percent of my currency trading.

There are arguments on both sides concerning which market is better for currencies—futures or the cash forex markets. With the futures, the spreads are a little tighter, and the commission is the same as trading regular futures contracts, but there are no guaranteed fills, and slippage can be a real issue. With forex, the spreads are a little wider, fills are guaranteed in all but extreme market conditions, and there aren't any commissions to pay. This works out as follows: If a trader buys one contract on the CME, they will pay roughly $8 in commission plus the $12.50 spread for a total outlay of $20.50. In forex a trader will pay a 3 pip spread at $30 and no commission. The difference between the two in this case is $9.50. However, I've found that 1-2 tick slippage in the futures markets is quite common. Add 1 tick slippage and that $20.50 is now $33, three dollars more than the forex trade. In the end, the costs are about equal. I am a redundancy freak, so I trade both. If for some reason I have a problem with the futures contract, then I can hedge my position in the forex market. In general, however, I like to keep my stock index futures trades separate from my currency trades. By having separate accounts, I can easily measure my performance in trading these various markets. Therefore, most of my currency trades are in the forex markets, in a separate account from my stock index futures trades. In addition, the biggest argument in favor of the forex markets is the fact that there is much better liquidity in the other currency pairs, such as the EURJPY, GBPJPY, and so on. All of these currencies trade very technically, and the more charts that a trader has available to watch, the more opportunities that will set up. For an individual who has never traded currencies in the forex markets and is interested in doing so, the best idea is to open up a demo or mini-forex account to get the proverbial feet wet. For more information on how to do this and set up an account, as well as more information and other plays specifically designed for the forex markets, www.razorforex.com is a good resource.

Okay, back to the box play. I'm looking for a period of horizontal consolidation with at least two tests of the highs and two tests of the lows. Once I get these two tests, then I'm looking to buy a breakout of the box, or sell a breakdown of the box. My target on these trades is the width of the box. These plays can be done on all time frames. An individual who is primarily a day trader can execute this setup utilizing 1-, 2-, 3-, 5- and even 15-minutes charts. An individual who also likes to swing trade can look for these setups on the 60-minute, 120-

minute, 240-minute, and daily charts. I trade these as both swing and intraday plays, with each timeframe independent of the other timeframes. This means I could have a 60-minute box play going on with one set of parameters, and a 5-minute box play going on with a totally different set of parameters. Also, since the forex markets actively trade 24 hours, these box plays can be set up at any time. It is important to remember that there are multiple major openings each day. Tokyo, London, Australia, New York—and other markets—all open around 8:00 a.m. in their local time. There isn't a bell or anything that rings. Traders waltz into their offices, and when they get to their desks, they start placing orders for their clients. Because of this, these consolidation patterns tend to break quickly, and once they do, they tend to trend really well.

I like to try to get some sleep each night, but on those nights when I get shafted by the wait staff (i.e., I order decaf coffee after dinner but they give me caffeinated, so I end up lying in bed staring at the ceiling), I can at least get up and check if a box play is forming overnight. Although I will look for box plays throughout the trading day, I also like to scan through the charts before I go to bed. If there are any box plays setting up, I will place my orders, hit the sack, and see how my trades worked out in the morning. This works out great—my friends joke with me because I can't sleep very well unless I have a position on.

## TRADING RULES FOR BUYS (SELLS ARE REVERSED)

Box plays are momentum plays. I will buy a breakout and short a breakdown.

1. I like to set up a simple bar chart on the timeframe I want to play. I will search through various timeframes to see where box plays are currently setting up. For this example I use a 15-minute chart.

2. As the market action progresses, I take a horizontal line and start marking highs and lows. I usually have to adjust this horizontal line a few times as the market action develops. Once I get two tests of one of the lines, I have a potential box play developing.

3. At this point I am watching to see if I get another test on the opposite side of the box. Let's assume in this example that I do, and now I have two tests of the highs and two tests of the lows. The width of the box is 20 ticks. Now, a trader isn't going to know that a box is in place until the prices hold the fourth test and move back into the center of the box. Once prices have moved back up into the box by about 25 percent, my box is complete. For example, if the width of the box is 20 ticks, then I would want to see prices move back into the box by at least 5 pips after the fourth price test.

4. Now that I have my box, I place two orders. I place a buy stop order one tick above the high end of the box. I place a sell stop order one tick below the low of the box. Whichever way the market breaks, I am sitting there with my order waiting to get filled.

5. My buy stop is hit. For my stop, I just leave my sell stop in place, as this now becomes my stop loss order on this trade. This represents a risk-to-reward ratio of a little over 1:1.

6. I stay in my play until my stop or my target is hit. I do not trail stops.

## Euro FX—December 2004 Contract, October 5, 2004

1. This is a 15-minute chart of the euro currency futures contract that trades on the CME (see Fig. 14.1). On October 5, 2004, there is a high point marked at 1.2319. I draw a horizontal line over this level to see if this will hold and become the top of a new box.

2. A few hours later the markets make a low and bounce, and this is where I draw the horizontal line for the bottom of the channel. Now that I have my first highs and lows, I need secondary tests of both these levels in order to have a box.

3. About five hours later a test of the upper end of the range occurs.

4. And about two hours after that another downward test occurs. I now have a box, and I can set up my orders. I place a buy stop order one tick above the high of the box. The high of the box is 1.2319, so I place my order at 1.2320. The lower end of the box is at 1.2306, so I place a sell stop order at 1.2305. It is important to note that each box does not set up in a "picture perfect" way. In this chart, there is a wayward tick at point 4 that pushes through the horizontal line. I'm more concerned about the two levels that were tested, which is why I keep the line of the first test at point 2. The basic rule of thumb for boxes is this: If you have to sit back and wonder if there is really a box on the chart, then there isn't a box on the chart. Once boxes form, they are very obvious. It is not critical if you include the wayward ticks in your box if they are only a few ticks away. This is a trade in which a few ticks usually won't make or break the trade.

5. At point 5 my sell stop is hit, and I'm now short at 1.2305. My target is the width of the box. Since the width of the box is 13 ticks, I subtract .0013 from 1.2305, and I get 1.2292. I place a limit buy at this level to cover my position. I leave my original buy stop in at 1.2320 as this will be my stop. Note that even though I am getting in the trade a little "outside the box," I still use the exact width of the box as my target.

6. My target is hit at 1.2292, and I'm out for a gain of 13 ticks, or a gain of $162.50 per contract.

## Euro FX—December 2004 Contract, September 27, 2004

1. This is an example of another box play on the CME euro currency futures contract, though this is on a 60-minute chart (see Fig. 14.2). This box takes a period of two days to develop, over September 27 and 28, 2004. At point 1 a high is established at 1.2305, and I draw a horizontal line. Two bars later the market pushes higher to 1.2310, and I move my horizontal line up to this level (see Fig. 14.3).

2. The market sells off for six hours and bottoms out. I draw a line at this point, 1.2276, and I have a potential bottom of my box. I now need another test of the highs and test of the lows.

3. The euro rallies for four hours and tests the upper end of the box. It makes a high of 1.2305 before turning back and heading lower.

@EC - 15 min  CME

1
1.2319
BUY STOP
3
13 Ticks
1.2306
2
4
5
SELL STOP
6

16:45  19:30  21:15  10/06  2:30  4:15  6:00

1.2325
1.2320
1.2315
1.2310
1.2305
1.2300
1.2295
1.2290
1.2285
1.2280
1.2275
1.2274
1.2270
1.2265

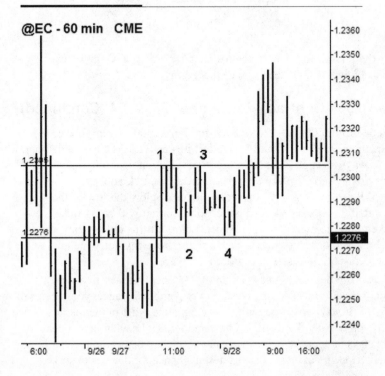

@EC - 60 min  CME

1.2305
1
3
1.2276
2
4

6:00  9/26  9/27  11:00  9/28  9:00  16:00

1.2360
1.2350
1.2340
1.2330
1.2320
1.2310
1.2300
1.2290
1.2280
1.2276
1.2270
1.2260
1.2250
1.2240

**F I G U R E   14.3**

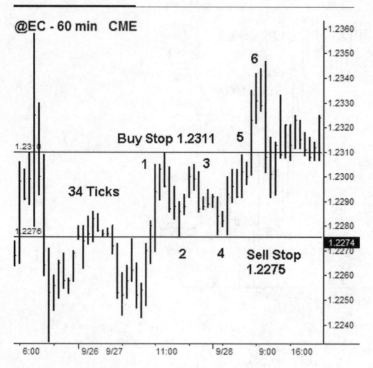

4. Five hours later there is another test of the lows, at 1.2276, and we now have a box. Let's look at Figure 14.3 to see where I placed my orders.

## Euro FX—December 2004 Contract, September 27, 2004 (Continued)

1. As prices continued to fluctuate, I have moved my horizontal line up to 1.2310, which is the new top of the box. Could I have left this at 1.2305? Yes. Remember, when it comes to wayward ticks that are a few ticks away, it generally does not have any impact on the trade. I place a buy stop order one tick above this level at 1.2311 at point 5. I also place a sell stop order one tick below the low of the box, at 1.2275. I note that this box is 34 ticks wide, so my target will be 34 ticks, whether I'm taken into the market long or short. Later, it turns out my buy stop is hit. I place a limit sell order for my target 34 ticks above my entry, which is 1.2345. My stop is my original sell stop order at 1.2275.

2. My target is hit, and I'm out for 34 ticks, a gain of $425 per contract. If you aren't using OCO (order cancels order) orders, be sure to remember to cancel your open sell stop order at 1.2275. If you don't, you will be leaving a live order in the market, and if this level is hit, you will get filled with an unwanted trade. Leaving in an open order in the markets is like leaving your food out overnight when camping near bears. Sure, nothing may happen, but there is also a decent chance for disaster to strike.

## Forex Markets—EURUSD, October 15, 2004

1. This is a 15-minute chart of the euro currency on the forex market (see Fig. 14.4). The reason it says "EURUSD" is that this is the indication that this is the Euro as it is trading in relation to the U.S. dollar, as opposed to the euro as it is trading against the pound, yen, or some other currency. By now this drill should be familiar. We get two tests of the highs and two tests of the lows, and we get our box via the levels marked 1, 2, 3 and 4 in Figure 14.4. I adjust my lines so that the high of the box and the low of the box are represented, and I place my orders. I have a buy stop in at 1.2402 and a sell stop at 1.2375.

2. This box stays in place for a long time. It's a relatively tight box at 24 pips. Typically, the longer the box is in place, the more energy it is building up, and the more forceful the move will be when it eventually breaks.

3. At 7:30 a.m. Eastern it breaks the box and hits the buy stop labeled point 5. I'm filled, and the target hits shortly thereafter, for a gain of 24 pips, or $240 per contract. This particular move keeps right on going. Some traders I work with will take half their position off once the initial target is hit, and then trail the other half. This all comes back to formulating a business plan that best fits a trader's personality—something I talk about in great detail at the end of the book.

## F I G U R E   14.4

For me, the box play is a high-probability play in and of itself, and I stick with the original stops I have laid out in this chapter. However, I will scale out of multiple-lot positions as they are going my way, and I'll show an example of that at the end of this chapter.

## Forex Markets—EURUSD, May through June, 2004

1. This is a daily chart of the euro on the forex markets (see Fig. 14.5). This is an example of a swing trade and a bigger example of the "power of the box." On May 20 and May 21, 2004, we form the lows at 1.1620.

2. On May 27 the market loses steam from its vault higher and sells off, forming the highs of the box 312 pips later (a little over 3 cents).

3. On June 4 and June 5 the market retests the lows of the box.

4. And on June 16 there is a retest of the highs of the box. Once this happens, I place my orders. I use a buy stop at 1.1933 and a sell stop at 1.1619.

**F I G U R E 14.5**

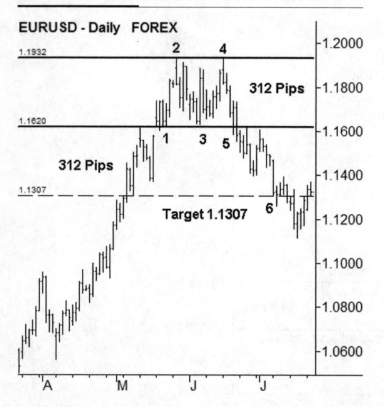

5. My sell stop is hit at 1.1619 at point 5. Since the width of the box is 312 pips, I calculate my target accordingly, and I place a buy limit order at 1.1307. My stop is my original buy stop order at 1.1933.

6. The market moves down nicely and then shoots back higher. Anyone using a trailing stop for this trade would have been stopped out for a small gain. The reason I keep my stop wider, and the reason I do not trail it, is that I know this is a high-probability play, and I want to give this setup "room to move" in order to give it a chance to work out. My target is hit nearly two weeks later for a gain of 312 pips, just over three large in trader speak, or $3,120 per contract. Next.

## Forex Markets—EURUSD, August 3, 2004

1. On August 3, 2004, the euro forms a box on the 15-minute charts (see Fig. 14.6). The first high is marked here at point 1.

2. A few hours later we get a potential low for the box, and I draw a horizontal line at the lows here.

**F I G U R E   14.6**

3. The market bounces, and we get a retest of the highs.

4. Then the euro sells off nicely, and we get a retest of the lows. Since this low pushed a little lower than the low at point 2, I go ahead and move my horizontal line down to reflect this low. Once I have these lines set up, I place my orders. I use a buy stop at 1.2062 (one pip above the highs) and a sell stop at 1.2042 (one pip below the lows).

5. My sell stop is hit at 1.2042. Since the width of the box is 18 pips, I calculate my target, and I place a limit buy order at 1.2024. My stop is my original buy stop order at 1.2062.

6. My target is hit, and I'm out for a gain of 18 pips, or $180 per contract. I don't have to remember to cancel my open buy stop because my execution software does it for me automatically.

## Forex Markets—EURUSD, August 19, 2004

1. On this 15-minute chart of the EURUSD we get a first test of the highs at 1.2347 (see Fig. 14.7). Once the market sells off from this level, I draw a horizontal line across the high.

**F I G U R E  14.7**

2. The market sells off and pushes as low as 1.2323. I start off drawing a line at this level. Later I move this line back up to 1.2331 because the rest of the price support tests are much closer to this level than the "wayward tick."

3. Here we get another test near the highs.

4. And we get another test near the lows. Once the four price tests are complete, I place a buy stop order at 1.2348 and a sell stop order at 1.2330. Although this box isn't perfect, there is no doubt that we have a nice horizontal channel in place.

5. My buy stop order is hit. Since the width of the box is 16 pips, I place a sell limit order for my target at 1.2364. My sell stop remains in place as my stop on this play.

6. My target is hit, and I'm out for 16 pips, a gain of $160 per contract. As you can see, I could have also used the low of the "wayward tick" in my calculations, and this would have been a more profitable trade. The bottom line is that when it comes down to a few ticks, it is not a big deal where you place your horizontal line, as long as it is crystal clear that a box is in place. This applies to nearly all setups. If you have a setup, and you miss the trade because you were trying to get the perfect entry, then you are the chump that just got played by the market. Good setups take time to develop and shouldn't be squandered away. Generally, traders who miss their "perfect entry" usually end up chasing the markets as prices run away from them. Afraid of missing the move, they frantically jump on board. Unfortunately this action shifts them into the group of traders who just bought the top or sold the bottom. What was a great setup suddenly turns into a losing trade. As with most of the scenarios in this book, I'm speaking directly from the painful and frustrating experiences all newer traders have. This particular scenario is where the following often quoted trader saying comes into play: *Don't be a dick for a tick*. I keep this somewhat crude phrase handy so that when I see a setup, I just get into the trade and try not to finesse my entry. Entries are a dime a dozen. It's the exits that make you money.

## Forex Markets—AUDUSD, May 30, 2005

1. On this 120-minute chart of AUDUSD we get a first test of the highs at 0.7638 (see Fig. 14.8). Once the market sells off from this level, I draw a horizontal line across the high.

2. The market sells off and pushes as low as 0.7584. I start off drawing a line at this level. The market bounces and retests this level again before moving higher.

3. At point 3 we get another test of the highs, pushing up a little bit above the previous highs.

4. Once this high is tested, the markets stair-step their way back to the lows at point #4. After the four price tests are complete, and prices rally about 25 percent back into the box (the width of the box is 54 pips, so 25 percent of this is about 14 pips), I place a buy stop order at 0.7639 and a sell stop order at 0.7583. Prices rally almost all the way to the top of the channel before rolling over and heading lower. Finally, on May 30, 2005, my sell stop is hit. It is important to remember

**F I G U R E   14.8**

that I had to wait patiently for this setup to execute. After I placed my buy and sell stops, I had to wait 44 hours before one of them was hit.

5.  After my sell stop is hit, my original buy stop becomes my stop loss on this trade. My target is the width of the box, which is 54 pips away at 0.7530. The markets move quickly down to this level but don't quite make it. Then they bounce all the way back to my entry, pause, and then reverse back lower, plunging violently into my buy limit order. I'm out for 54 pips, a gain of $540 per lot being traded. I want to emphasize again how important it is to be patient in trading and waiting for the right setup. This trade took 76 hours to setup. Then, once I placed my orders, it took another 44 hours for one of them to be hit. And after I was filled, it took another 34 hours for my target to get hit. This one trade spanned 154 hours. In trading, patience is a virtue, while impatience triggers devastation.

## Forex Markets—EURGBP, April 12, 2005

1.  On this 120-minute chart of EURGBP we get a first test of the highs at 0.6867 (see Fig. 14.9). Once the market sells off from this level, I draw a horizontal line across the high.

2.  The market sells off and prints a low of 0.6848 before bouncing higher. I draw another line beneath this level.

FIGURE 14.9

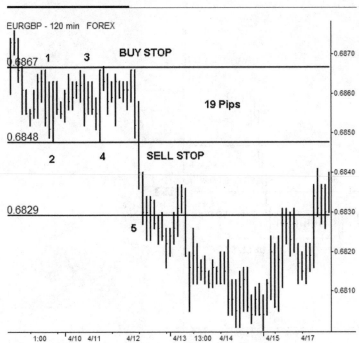

3. Prices firm and rally back up to the highs. Once this level tests and prices roll over, I wait to see if a retest of the lows will hold.

4. And we get another test near the lows. Once the four price tests are complete, I wait to see if the markets can rally at least 25 percent back into the box. Since the width of the box is 19 pips, 25 percent would be about 5 pips. Once this happens I place a buy stop order at 0.6868 and a sell stop order at 0.6847. This box is pretty clean.

5. Prices come back up to retest the highs, sell off to the middle of the box, come back up yet again to test the highs, and then finally rollover and go through the lows, filling my sell stop order. My buys stop order stays in place as my stop. EURGBP sells off quickly and my target is hit on the second bar at point 5. (Of course, quickly is a relative term as these are 120-minute bars). This currency pair is worth around $18 a pip, so the 19 pip target yields a gain of $342 per lot.

## Forex Markets—USDCHF, June 10, 2005

1. On this 60-minute chart of USDCHF, there is an initial test of the highs at 1.2577 (see Fig. 14.10). Prices quickly fall from this level and I draw a horizontal line across the high.

2. USDCHF sells off to 1.2519 at point 2. Once prices start to rally off this level I place a horizontal line across the lows.

FIGURE  14.10

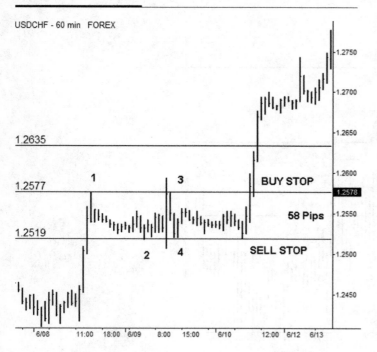

USDCHF - 60 min  FOREX

3. Prices shoot up and retest the highs at point 3.

4. This is quickly followed by another test of the lows at point 4. Once prices rally about 25 percent back up into the box, I place my orders, with a buy stop at 1.2578 and a sell stop at 1.2518. Twenty hours later, after retesting the lows yet again, prices firm and bust out through the highs, triggering my buy stop order. My sell stop remains in place as my stop loss on the trade. Prices plow forward and it doesn't take long for my target to get hit. The gain is good for 58 pips, or roughly $464 per lot.

## Forex Markets—EURJPY, April 7, 2005

1. On this 60-minute chart of EURJPY we get a first test of the highs at 140.03 (see Fig. 14.11). Once the market sells off from this level, I draw a horizontal line across the high.

2. The market sells off to point 2 at 139.66 and bounces. I draw a line underneath this level.

3. We rally quickly back up to the highs for the third test.

4. Once prices test the highs, they quickly roll over and test the lows and we now have the fourth test of the box in place. Once prices rally back 25 percent into the box, I place my orders, a buy stop at 140.04 and a sell stop at 139.65.

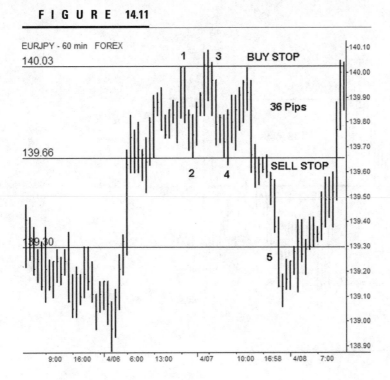

**FIGURE   14.11**

5. Prices rally to just beneath my buy stop, and then roll over and trigger my sell stop. My buy stop stays in place as my stop loss order. Prices consolidate near the lows for about 5 hours before breaking lower and hitting my target at 139.30 for a gain of 36 pips, or about $288 per lot.

## Forex Markets—GBPJPY, May 16, 2005

1. On this 240-minute chart of GBPJPY, we get a first test of the lows at point 1 at 197.86 (see Fig. 14.12). Once the market rallies off of this level, I draw a horizontal line across the lows.

2. The market rallies and stays in the upper part of its range for a long time. We test the highs three times before selling off to test the lows again. Even though we test the highs three times, this only counts as test 2 of the box. For this upper part of the range to become an official part of the box, it has to be offset with another corresponding test of the lows. (For example, three tests of the highs and one test of the lows does not make a box). I keep my line across the highs at 199.24 and wait to see if we will get another test of the lows.

3. At point 3 the market finally sells off and retest the lows.

4. It doesn't take long for the market to rally back up and test the highs of the box at point 4, and once prices fall back to within 25 percent of the boxes range, I set up my buy stop order at 199.25 and my sell stop order at 197.85.

F I G U R E   14.12

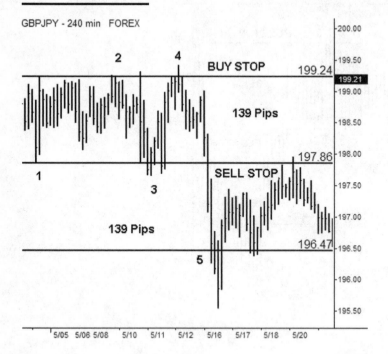

GBPJPY - 240 min  FOREX

5. Prices continue lower and hit my sell stop order. My buy stop order stays in place as it is now my stop loss. Prices proceed quickly and without pause down to my target, and I'm out for a gain of 139 pips or about $1,112 per contract.

## Forex Markets—EURJPY, August 4, 2005

1. This play was particularly fun as it occurred while I was finishing the rewrites on this chapter, and I was able to capture this live on my execution platform. On this 15-minute chart of EURJPY we get a first test of the highs at 1.3784 (see Fig. 14.13). Once the market sells off from this level, I draw a horizontal line across the high.

2. The market sells off and pushes as low as 137.63. Once prices rally off of this level, I draw a horizontal line across the lows.

3. Here we get another test near the highs at point 3.

4. The markets drift back down and retest the lows. Once prices rally back about 25 percent into the box, I place a buy stop order at 137.85 and a sell stop order at 137.62.

5. The market rallies right off the lows to and through the highs. My buy stop order is triggered, and shortly thereafter my target is hit for a gain of 21 pips, or $168 per contract.

**F I G U R E   14.13**

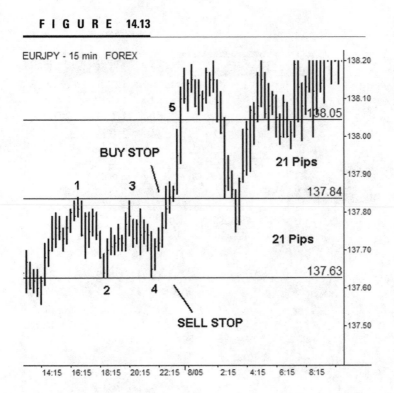

## Ringing the Cash Register—
## Scaling Out of a Position as It Goes Your Way

My style within a strategy is to get into the trade all at once and then scale out as the trade goes my way. My goal is to still have one third to one half of my position left if and when the strategy hits my target. This is one big advantage in trading multiple lots. With one lot, I would just stay in the trade from start to finish. With multiple lots, a trader can start peeling off contracts so that if the trade does reverse and gets stopped out, the overall loss will be offset by any gains already booked, thus increasing a traders risk-to-reward ratio. On this particular play, my buy stop order was for 75 lots. Once the markets triggered my buy stop, I scaled out in thirds all the way up to my target (see Fig. 14.14). This snapshot of my execution platform shows that I sold 25 lots at 137.93, another 25 lots at 138.05, and the final 25 lots at 138.07, for a total gain on the play of $14,957.62. Because I literally executed this trade while scrambling to make the deadline for this chapter, it put into perspective how much writing a book really is a labor of love, albeit painful. This is my first book, but I'm guessing that my year of toil in trying to fill hundreds of blank pages with semi-useful material will probably net me about the same amount as this two hour trade. (I'm sure there is a lesson in there somewhere.)

*If you wish to drown, do not torture yourself with shallow water.*

BULGARIAN PROVERB

**F I G U R E    14.14**

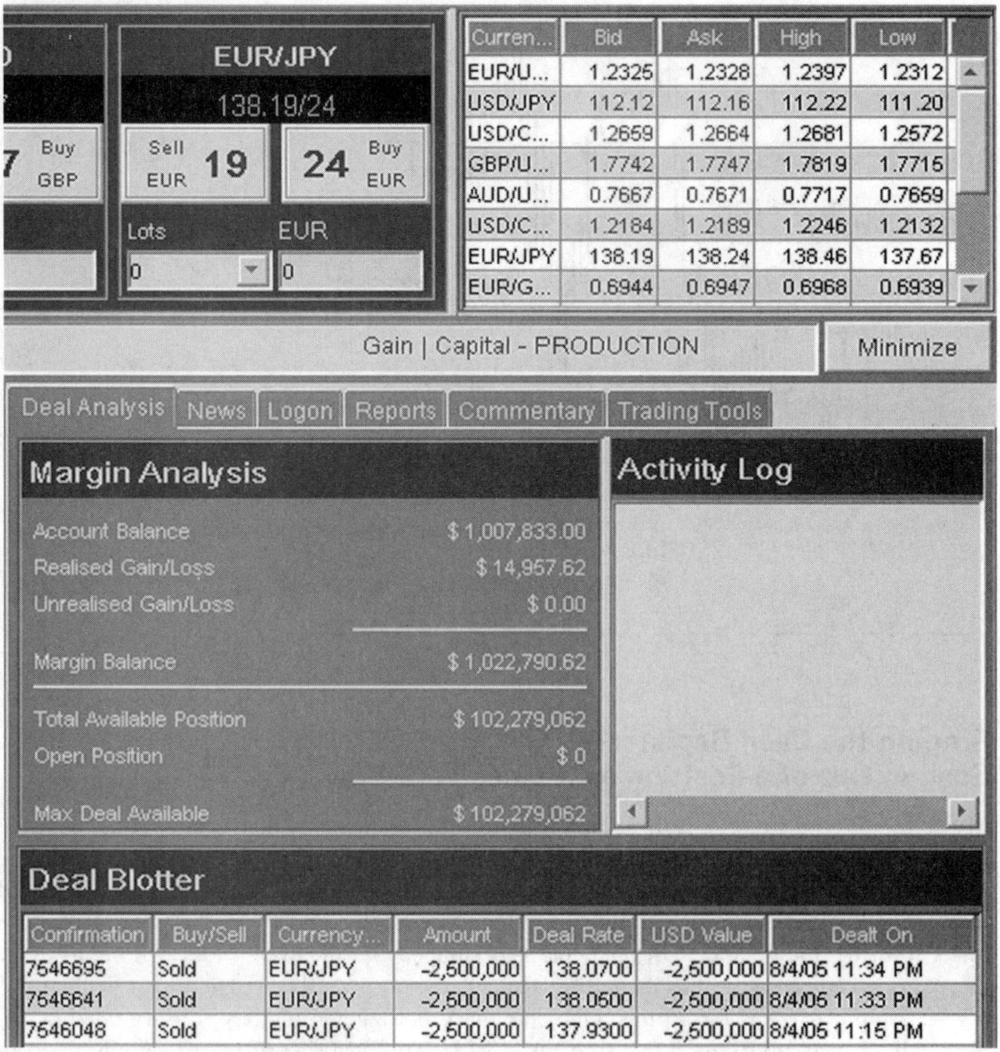

| Curren... | Bid | Ask | High | Low |
|-----------|------|------|------|------|
| EUR/U... | 1.2325 | 1.2328 | 1.2397 | 1.2312 |
| USD/JPY | 112.12 | 112.16 | 112.22 | 111.20 |
| USD/C... | 1.2659 | 1.2664 | 1.2681 | 1.2572 |
| GBP/U... | 1.7742 | 1.7747 | 1.7819 | 1.7715 |
| AUD/U... | 0.7667 | 0.7671 | 0.7717 | 0.7659 |
| USD/C... | 1.2184 | 1.2189 | 1.2246 | 1.2132 |
| EUR/JPY | 138.19 | 138.24 | 138.46 | 137.67 |
| EUR/G... | 0.6944 | 0.6947 | 0.6968 | 0.6939 |

**EUR/JPY**

138.19/24

Sell EUR **19**    **24** Buy EUR

Buy GBP

Lots  0    EUR  0

Gain | Capital - PRODUCTION          Minimize

Deal Analysis | News | Logon | Reports | Commentary | Trading Tools

**Margin Analysis**

| | |
|---|---|
| Account Balance | $ 1,007,833.00 |
| Realised Gain/Loss | $ 14,957.62 |
| Unrealised Gain/Loss | $ 0.00 |
| Margin Balance | $ 1,022,790.62 |
| Total Available Position | $ 102,279,062 |
| Open Position | $ 0 |
| Max Deal Available | $ 102,279,062 |

**Activity Log**

**Deal Blotter**

| Confirmation | Buy/Sell | Currency... | Amount | Deal Rate | USD Value | Dealt On |
|--------------|----------|-------------|--------|-----------|-----------|----------|
| 7546695 | Sold | EUR/JPY | -2,500,000 | 138.0700 | -2,500,000 | 8/4/05 11:34 PM |
| 7546641 | Sold | EUR/JPY | -2,500,000 | 138.0500 | -2,500,000 | 8/4/05 11:33 PM |
| 7546048 | Sold | EUR/JPY | -2,500,000 | 137.9300 | -2,500,000 | 8/4/05 11:15 PM |

## SUMMING UP THE CURRENCY BOX PLAY

I always enjoy the act of giving presents and opening them over the holidays. I find that I enjoy that feeling almost as much as discovering a new "box" to open up in the currency markets. With this play, Christmas seems to happen a few times each week instead of just once a year.

In parting, I can't emphasize enough how important it is for traders to find a market that fits their own personality if they hope to be successful. If you find that you are happy only if you are buying breakouts and selling breakdowns, then the currencies are probably your market of choice. Currencies break and trend well, while the E-mini S&Ps tend to suck in traders with false breakouts and breakdowns. In other words, if you are buying breakouts in the S&Ps and getting killed, then give the currencies a try.

# CHAPTER 15

# HOLP AND LOHP— CATCHING TREND REVERSALS WITHOUT GETTING SMASHED

## BUYING A MARKET JUST BECAUSE IT IS CHEAP OR SHORTING A MARKET JUST BECAUSE IT IS EXPENSIVE IS DANGEROUS—UNLESS IT'S DONE LIKE THIS

When it comes to the financial markets, the bottom line is that current action is going to be determined by one thing and one thing only: the price that people are willing to pay right now. A stochastic can be overbought, a MACD (Moving Average Convergence Divergence) can be rolling over as a potential short, and moving averages can be violated to the extreme. Whatever the case, it doesn't mean price action is going to reverse. There is a high probability to be sure, but that doesn't mean it's going to happen. On the contrary, prices can still keep trending higher or lower in these cases of extreme overbought or oversold readings for a long, long time. In 1999, overbought stayed overbought for months and months. In 2000 and 2001, oversold stayed oversold almost continuously. Everyone who screamed, "It's a bargain" on the way down learned many times over the meaning of pain.

I hear stories nearly every day from people who bought a stock "because it looked cheap" only to have it continue to crater on a daily basis. Some of these stocks like EXDS (Exodus Communications, Inc.) and WCOM (WorldCom, Inc.) got real cheap, real fast. Eventually the people who bought these stocks on the way down either got frustrated and couldn't take the pain anymore so they sold, or, in many instances, they got out using one of the best tried-and-true sell signals on the planet—the company declared bankruptcy, and the stock went to zero. The opposite is also true in that I've heard plenty of war stories about traders shorting a stock "because it looked too high." They were soon experiencing shell shock as the stock continued to race higher and destroy their account.

Speaking of shorting, I always find it amusing that brokers talk about how dangerous shorting a stock is, because the potential losses are "infinite." Well, I have yet to see a stock rise to infinity, but I've seen plenty of stocks go to zero. Never mind the fact that brokers and trading firms make a huge living shorting stock to the public.

In trading, it is never a good idea to try to catch a falling knife (buy a steep sell off) or step in front of a freight train (short a frantic rally) just because prices "look too low" or "look too high." How, then, does a trader catch a reversal without risking life and limb?

That is where this setup comes into play. This method for catching market tops and bottoms is based on the one solitary thing that matters most in trading: price.

## TRADING RULES FOR SELLS (BUYS ARE REVERSED)

This is a reversal play. I will short tops and buy bottoms only upon confirmation of this setup. I generally use this for swing plays, but it is valid on all timeframes including smaller time frames for intraday plays. HOLP and LOHP are acronyms for "high of the low period" and "low of the high period." We refer to them as "HOPE" and "LOPE."

1.  Identify a trending market, or individual stock, that is ideally making new 20-day (or period) highs. This is a rule of thumb and markets that are only making 17- or 18-day (or period) highs are also fine. The point is that you want to see a definitive trend and be ready to step in when that trend reverses.

2.  Identify the high bar in the uptrend. This is typically the current bar, but it could be a few bars back. By "high bar" I mean the bar with the highest intraday price prints in the entire move higher.

3.  Once I identify the high bar, I will then go short once price action closes below the low of this high bar. (Say that really fast three times.)

4.  The initial stop is the high of the high bar. If I am still in the trade on the third day, or period, I will start to use a two-bar trailing stop. I will exit this trade when the current bar closes above the price level represented by the two-bar trailing stop.

5.  Due to retracement price patterns while in a play, the two-bar trailing stop will have to at times be held on the current "stop bar" until the trend resumes. Once the trend resumes, the two-bar trailing stop can also be resumed. This doesn't happen very often, and I realize it makes no sense while reading this text. Don't worry, it is not subject to interpretation, and it will become clear when you see a specific example. I will focus specifically on this in Fig 15.13.

    This setup works in all markets, in all timeframes. I usually use this play on individual stocks and their corresponding stock options, stock index futures, and the forex currencies on the 60-minute and daily charts.

## E-mini S&P—December 2004 Contract, October 7, 2004

1. Figure 15.1 is an example of the entry method. This particular chart is a daily representation of the E-mini S&P futures. Once I've gone over this entry method, we will jump into the exit strategy. It is important to understand how to enter this trade. The white bar labeled point 1 represents the "high bar" in the uptrend. The low of this high bar is 1133.50. This high represents the highest prices seen in at least 20 days. In fact, the last time the S&Ps were at this price level was back on July 1, 2004.

2. Since the black bar labeled point 2 broke the low of the high day, we enter this position at the close of this day. My entry is 1131.50. This trade does not have an exit at the time this snapshot was taken because an exit signal has not fired off. I usually get a few questions here when I discuss this trade. The first is, "Can I enter the trade intraday as soon as it breaks the low of the high day instead of waiting for the close?" My answer to this is that you can, but I really want to see a close to show that the market means business. Often I would take this trade intraday, only to have it close back up above the low of the high day, which invalidates the trade. By waiting for the close, you are getting extra insurance that this reversal is valid. The other question I get usually has to do with entry points and in knowing which bar is actually going to be the high bar. Of course, you don't know which

**F I G U R E   15.1**

@ES - Daily  CME

**F I G U R E   15.2**

@ES - Daily   CME

2 Bar trailing stop is
at 10-07-04

1132.25

3

2

1

Oct

1150.00

1140.00

1130.00

1120.00

1110.00

1108.25

1100.00

bar is going to be the high bar that kicks off the reversal until the price break actually occurs. Is it going to be this bar? Or are we going to get another, higher bar first? All you can do is continue to watch the new bars develop. When I identify a high bar, I keep an eye to see if price action closes below the low of that high bar. If the next bar goes even higher, then this new, higher bar becomes the high bar. In essence, I'm trailing an imaginary sell stop order. As prices advance higher, so will my entry until we finally get a break of the low of the high bar. Although this is a simple concept, I have found that it takes a few examples for people new to this setup to get the hang of it. That said, let's look at some more examples.

## E-mini S&P—December 2004 Contract, October 7, 2004

1. This daily chart of the E-mini S&Ps (Fig. 15.2) is the same as Figure 15.1. However, this chart focuses on the initial reversal trade off the lows. The bar labeled point 1 takes place at the end of the September, marking the lows of this particular move, which aren't quite 20-day lows, but they are 18-day lows, which is fine. I want to buy a close above the high of the low day. The high on this day registered at 1112.50.

2. The next day we close above this bar, and I enter this trade right after the 4:00 p.m. Eastern close of the regular cash session. I am filled at 1115.25. My initial stop is the lows of bar 1 just above 1100.00.

3. I'm in this trade for seven days. In the bar labeled 3 the S&Ps close below the low of the previous two bars. Once this happens, I exit right after 4:00 p.m. and get out at 1132.25 for a gain of +17.00 points, or $850 per contract. Note that the exit of this long also coincides with the initialization of the new short position in Figure 15.1. This doesn't always happen, but it does once in a while.

## Mini-Sized Dow—September 2004 Contract, August 6, 2004

1. On August 6, 2004, the mini-sized Dow establishes a new low within its current trend, and then starts to rally (see Fig. 15.3). This bar marks the low day, so I'm looking to buy a break of the high of this low day.

2. It takes seven trading days to close above the high of the low day. When this finally happens on August 17, I get in after the close, and my entry is 9974. My

**F I G U R E   15.3**

initial stop is the low of the bar that triggered off this trade, near 9770. Once I'm in the trade for two days, I start using a two-bar trailing stop.

3. On August 26, this bar closes below the close of the two-bar trailing stop. I'm out at 10121 for a gain of +147 points, or $735 per contract.

## Mini-Sized Dow—September 2004 Contract, June 23, 2004

1. On June 23, 2004, the mini-sized Dow futures put in a nice high bar (see Fig. 15.4). The low of this high day is 10343.

2. On June 28, the YM closes below the low of the high day at point #2. I enter this position short at the close of this day at 10329. I start off with a stop at the highs of the high day, and once I'm in the trade for two days, I start to use a two-bar trailing stop. Remember, I'm looking for a *close* above these levels as a signal to exit the trade.

3. On July 27, I exit at the close of bar 3 at 10061 for a gain of +268 points, or $1,340 per contract.

**F I G U R E   15.4**

## E-mini Nasdaq—September 2004 Contract, August 13, 2004

1. On August 13, 2004, the high of the low day on the E-mini NASDAQ is 1317.50 (see Fig. 15.5).
2. On August 16, since the bar labeled 2 broke the high of the low day, I enter this position at the close of this day at 1322.00.
3. On August 30, I exit at the close of bar 3 at 1367.00 for a gain of +45 points, or $900 per contract.

## E-mini Nasdaq—September 2004 Contract, June 30, 2004

1. On June 30, 2004, the low of the high day is 1506.00 on the daily NQ chart (see Fig. 15.6).
2. On July 1, since the bar labeled 2 broke the low of the high day, we enter this position at the close of this day at 1494.00.
3. As the NQ sells off, we start using the two-bar trailing stop. On July 29, prices close above our trailing stop, and we exit at the close of the bar labeled point 3 at 1401.50 for a gain of +92.50 points, or $1850 per contract.

**F I G U R E   15.5**

## F I G U R E  15.6

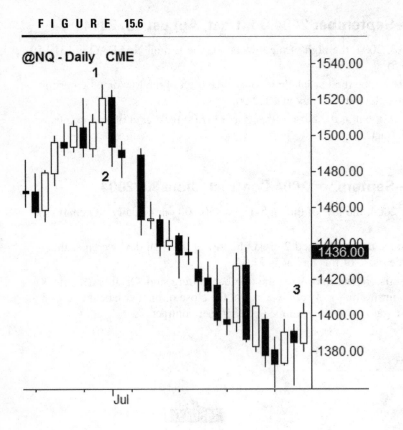

### 30-Year Bond—September 2004 Contract, July 28, 2004

1. On July 28, 2004, the high of the low day is 106 26/32 for the 30-year bonds, which can be seen on the bar labeled point 1 (see Fig. 15.7).

2. On July 29, since the bar labeled 2 broke the high of the low day, we enter this position at the close of this day at 106 31/32.

3. We start trailing our stop, and on August 23, we exit at the close of the bar labeled point 3 at 110 16/32.

### Forex Markets—EURUSD, December 31, 2004

1. On December 31, 2004, the EURUSD breaks and closes below the low of the high day (see Fig. 15.8). The entry on the short side is 1.3553.

2. The market continues to drop lower for five days in a row before bottoming out. On January 12, the stop is triggered, and we are out at 1.3254 for a gain of 299 pips, or $2,999 per lot.

**F I G U R E   15.7**

@US - Daily   CBOT

3. On February 4, the EURUSD makes new nearly 20-day lows and is now a candidate for this setup. The entry signal fires off on February 9 with a close above the high of the low day. The entry is taken at 1.2803.

4. The markets work higher until the 2-bar trailing stop is hit on March 1 at 1.3186, for a gain of +386 pips, or $3,860 per lot being traded.

## GOOG (Google Inc)—September 2, 2004

1. On September 2, 2004, the high of the low day is 102.37 on the bar labeled point 1 on GOOG (see Fig. 15.9). The low here isn't a 20-day low, but GOOG had just gone public on August 19, 2004, 11 days prior.

2. On September 10, since the bar labeled 2 broke the high of the low day, we enter this position at the close of this day at 105.33.

**F I G U R E   15.8**

**F I G U R E   15.9**

3. We start trailing the stop, and on October 12, we exit at the close of bar 3 at 136.55, for a gain of just over 30 points.

## TZOO (Travelzoo Inc)—August 30, 2004

1. On August 30, 2004, the high of the low day is 42.37 on the bar labeled 1 on TZOO (see Fig. 15.10).
2. On August 31, since the bar labeled 2 broke the high of the low day, we enter this position at the close of this day at 45.00.
3. On September 28, we exit at the close of bar 3 at 56.42. This is one of those trades where, in hindsight, it would have been "genius" to exit at the intraday break of the two-bar trailing stop. That exit was around $70. However, I have done this play both ways, and I've found that the intraday stop will frequently get a trader out of a position that still has a lot of room to move. Regardless, we still netted nearly 12 points on this trade.

## EXM (Excel Maritime Carriers Ltd)—September 2, 2004

1. On September 2, 2004, the high of the low day is 23.50 at bar labeled 1 on EXM (see Fig. 15.11).

**F I G U R E   15.10**

**F I G U R E   15.11**

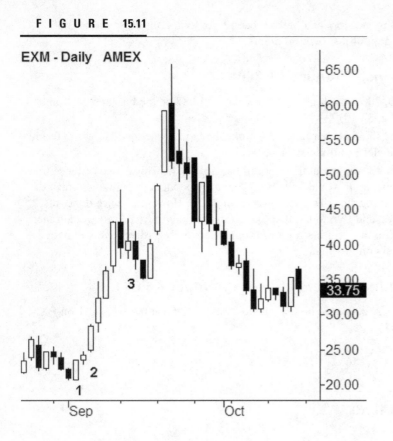

EXM - Daily   AMEX

2. On September 3, since the bar labeled 2 broke the high of the low day, we enter this position at the close of this day at 24.21.

3. On September 15, our trailing stop is hit and we exit at the close of bar 3 at 38.00 for a gain of nearly 14 points. On this play we got stopped out just before the stock rocketed higher another 30 points in just three trading days. This goes back to being a "genius in hindsight."

## Forex Markets—EURGBP, June 16, 2005

1. I like this particular example because it demonstrates how important it is for a trader to stick to their setups. On June 16, the EURGBP made new lows, and the next day prices reversed and closed above the high of this low day, firing off a long signal (see Fig. 15.12).

2. I went long, and a group of other traders I work with also went long. Our entry was 0.6709.

3. EURGBP rolled over and closed below our two-bar trailing stop. Our exit was 0.6632, at point 3 on June 23, for a loss of 77 pips. This bar also marked a fresh low, and became the new signal bar in this setup.

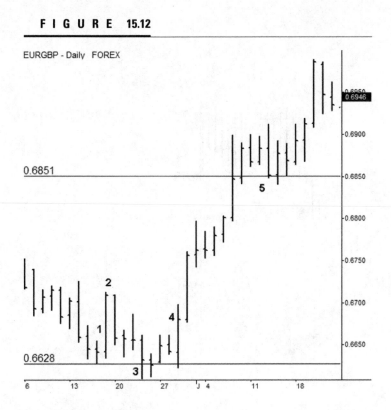

**F I G U R E   15.12**

4. On June 29, at point 4, we get another close above the high of the low day, and I
   take the entry at 0.6680. Other forex traders I work with passed on this setup, having felt the sting of the first loss.

5. EURGBP rallies nicely, and the two-bar trailing stop gets hit on July 13 at point 5,
   at 0.6851, for a gain of 171 pips. The point of this example is to show the importance of not filtering out a particular setup because of how you feel about it. If the
   previous setup was a loss, many newer traders will hold off on taking the next
   setup because of their feelings associated with the last time they took the play. In
   reality, our feelings have nothing to do with how the next trade will work out. We
   never really know what the market is going to do next, but we can plod along, follow our setups, and try to make a living.

## Forex Markets—GBPUSD, August 29, 2003

1. In this example I will also focus on rule 5, which talked about holding a stop in
   place until the trend resumes (see Fig. 15.13). As I said, this doesn't happen very
   much, but it does happen once in a while, and it will make sense once I show it to
   you. This is a weekly chart of GBPUSD. I like to use the weekly chart to catch

**F I G U R E  15.13**

GBPUSD - Weekly  FOREX

macro trend reversals, as these can result in big plays. The stops are also wider, so it is important to position size correctly on this larger timeframe. In this weekly chart, a new low bar is created during the week of August 29, 2003, with a low of 1.5620. The very next week, prices dip below this level to 1.5612, creating a new low bar. Because this is a weekly bar, the only time action is taken is at the end of the week. These plays require a lot of patience.

**2.** There is a close above the high of the low week ending September 12, at point 2. The entry is 1.6037.

**3.** GBPUSD rallies strongly the following week and then edges up for the next several weeks. During the week of November 9, labeled at point 3, prices fall below the two-bar trailing stop intraweek, but rally and close above the lows by 30 pips. At this point, if we move the two-bar trailing stop up to the next bar, we would be stopped out because prices are already trading below that new stop. This is what I talked about in rule 5. Because of this, I just leave my closing stop in place, which is designated by the longer line reaching out from point 3. I will just leave my stop here until I am stopped out or until prices make new trend highs.

**4.** At point 4 prices make new trend highs, and I go ahead and resume my two-bar trailing stop.

**5.** GBPUSD rallies strongly until my two-bar trailing stop is hit during the week ending on March 5, 2004, about six months after the entry, for a gain of 2,424 pips, or $24,240 per contract. This is the type of trade that makes the forex markets interesting, because a trader could take a $50,000 account in this example and make a million dollars on the trade. Needless to say, there is also the obvious risk of losing the entire $50,000. It wouldn't be fun if it was easy.

## SUMMING UP THE HOLP AND LOHP PLAYS

There are two ways to try to catch tops and bottoms: the wrong way, and the only way. Shorting a stock or a market just because it is too high is the trader's rendition of committing suicide. Just as a dog will generally let you know when it's about to attack, a market will let you know that it is about to reverse. All you have to do is pay attention and be alert to the appropriate entry signal.

CHAPTER

# PROPULSION PLAYS—SWING PLAYS USING STOCKS, SINGLE STOCK FUTURES, AND STOCK OPTIONS

## SETTING UP FOR THE BIGGER MOVES IN INDIVIDUAL STOCKS

To me, some of the greatest risk-takers on Wall Street are long-term investors. They will stubbornly hold onto a stock they bought three years ago because they have a "long-term view." It doesn't matter that the company is beating off creditors with a lead pipe. It doesn't matter that the stock is down over 80 percent from the entry price. It doesn't even matter if the CFO was recently seen sharing an $8 \times 8$ cell with Martha Stewart. What matters is that, come hell or high water, they have blind faith that by stepping back and taking the long-term view, all will be well in the end. All's well that ends well, right? Of course. Unfortunately, this ain't Shakespeare's play; this is Wall Street.

This came to light in glaring, full color for me in early 2000. First, there was the Super Bowl. I don't even remember who played in that game, but I do remember the 18 commercials that played advertising various dot-com companies that were blowing their whole annual marketing wad on this one 30-second spot. I also remember that this was the time the first ever "day trading expo" took place in southern California. Finally, I remember my refrigerator breaking down. It wasn't the actual breaking down that was significant, but the man I called out of the

Yellow Pages who came to fix it for me was. The job took him exactly 84 minutes. The first 12 minutes were spent fixing the refrigerator. The rest of the time he spent preaching to me about his favorites stocks in the NASDAQ and why Cisco was worth $500 a share. I tried to stop him halfway through his lecture to let him know that a fleck of saliva was hanging off his chin, but he wouldn't let up. As he preached the gospel of the Internet, I realized that there was so much excitement in this current market that it really didn't matter how far down it went when the crash finally came—people were now believers, and they would hold on until they got their margin call. By the time he left, I started looking at my charts for any breaks of the low of the high day. There weren't any that day, but a month later there were plenty.

I do focus some of my efforts on finding newer companies that have the potential to make a big splash with a new product, such as a RIMM (Research in Motion Ltd) or a TASR (Taser International Inc). There are many long-term trend-following opportunities in the markets, on both the long and the short side. However, finding the next Microsoft is not my trading niche. If I do find it, great, but in the meantime, I'm going to keep looking for setups. Therefore, most of my "long-term" efforts in the stock market are involved in swing trading, and one of my favorite setups is what I call propulsion plays. This is a systematic approach to getting positioned in stocks over a few days to a few weeks. Seventy percent of the time individual stocks spend their days backing and filling in a tight range, building up steam for their next major move. This approach looks for stocks that are done with their "resting period" and are getting ready to spurt higher (or lower) once again.

The idea is to already be in the stock when it makes a push higher (for longs) or lower (for shorts), instead of trying to chase it intraday. The reason I like to do this is that there are many times in the market when very few intraday trading opportunities in the stock indexes set up. Some of the sectors are up, some are down, resulting in a very choppy and quiet overall market. However, during these times, there are always going to be individual stocks that are making a move. By being positioned in these stocks over the course of a few days to a few weeks, I don't feel forced to get into intraday trades in the stock index futures when nothing is really setting up. This is because I already have positions on that are set up to take advantage of their next "mini-move."

For this setup, I'm focusing mostly on individual stocks. However, on individual stocks that also trade single stock futures (SSFs) and stock options, I will consider plays in those instruments as well. Because SSFs are so new and because most people play options incorrectly, I'm going to spend a little time reviewing how they work and how I use them. Let's review.

## THE TRADER'S GUIDE TO SINGLE STOCK FUTURES

Single stock futures (SSFs) are futures contracts on individual stocks. There are currently around 130 well-known stocks such as IBM, QCOM, EBAY, GOOG, RIMM, and MSFT that have futures on them. This is a recent development since it was only in late 2000 that Congress passed legislation lifting the ban on these products, which were already trading in Europe and other countries. There are also futures contracts available on many exchange traded funds (ETFs). To get a complete listing of all these futures contracts, a trader can visit www.onechicago.com.

One Chicago is an electronic exchange that is a joint venture of the Chicago Board Options Exchange (CBOE), Chicago Mercantile Exchange Inc. (CME), and the Chicago Board of Trade (CBOT). Now, how do they work and how does a trader use them?

Many brokers have been slow to adapt to these new trading instruments, but they are starting to catch on. Because these are futures contracts, traders need to have a futures account in order to trade them. On top of that, they also need to be trading with a broker that is set up to trade them, as not every broker is equipped to handle these trading instruments. Once that is completed, these are traded just like a normal futures contract, and they are available through eCBOT and Globex, just like the mini-stock index futures.

Whereas mini-stock index futures contracts like the YM and ES trade quarterly, the SSFs trade monthly. Traders who aren't familiar with the letter codes for the various months should write this down and tape it to their wall as a reference guide. These are applicable to all futures contracts:

F  =  January

G  =  February

H  =  March

J  =  April

K  =  May

M  =  June

N  =  July

Q  =  August

U  =  September

V  =  October

X  =  November

Z  =  December

To get a quote on an EBAY (eBay Inc) single stock futures contract in TradeStation, a trader would type in EBAY (underlying stock symbol) 1C (One Chicago) V (Month Code) 05 (Year). So the final quote for the EBAY October 2005 SSFs would look like this: EBAY1CV05.

There are a few nice features regarding SSFs that I find attractive. First, the "$25,000 day trading rule" does not apply. Active traders who have a $50,000 account and who tie up $26,000 of that in options trades will suddenly find themselves out of luck. They will not be able to execute any new stock or options trades because the broker won't count the option value toward the traders' equity. This situation would draw their "countable" account balance below $25,000, and traders would be locked out of initiating any new trades. An annoying feature to be sure. SSFs provide the leverage of "just in the money" options without the restrictions constraining "pattern day traders" and their account size. Here are a few additional key points:

- On stock accounts, a trader can get a 2:1 overnight margin, and the interest charged is the same amount a person would pay for a mediocre deal on a credit card. For SSFs, the equivalent of a 5:1 margin is available, and there are no interest fees.

- 5:1 leverage equates to having to put up 20 percent of the purchase price of the underlying stock. A trader who buys $10,000 worth of IBM (100 shares at $100) by using one IBM SSF contract would have to put up only $2,000. A trader who buys 10 contracts IBM1C at $95 ($95,000 worth of IBM) would put up $19,000, and so on.

- When shorting stocks, a trader has to wait for an uptick in order to get filled. There isn't any uptick rule for short selling an SSF contract. This is becoming less important as more and more actual stocks are becoming shortable on downticks.

- One SSF contract equals 100 shares of stock.

- A one-point move equals $100 per contract.

- These are monthly contracts that expire the third Friday of each month, just like options. If traders own a February contract on the day it is expiring, they will need to sell the February contract and buy the March contract. This is also known as "rolling over" into the next month. If traders hold onto the contract through expiration, they will have the stock "delivered" into their account. Don't worry about forgetting, because brokers don't want to deal with this, and they will call and pester you to close out your position days before expiration.

The biggest question I get about SSFs has to do with their volume. For many of these contracts, there is not a lot of volume traded at this time, and this is an obvious concern for traders. However, it is important to note that the "real volume" of an SSF contract is in the underlying stock itself. The LMMs (lead market markers) and MMs (market markers) for SSF products make their living buying and selling SSF contracts and immediately hedging or arbitraging that position with the underlying cash stock. Because of this, they will fill any order that is in line with the underlying volume of the stock. Since most of these stocks trade millions of shares, getting a fill is not an issue. There have been days when I've been the only one trading the SSF, and yet I have no problem getting in and out of the position. On those days, which rarely happen anymore because volume is steadily growing, it's fun knowing I'm the only person in the entire world who made money on that trade.

The other question I get from traders involves the spreads. If there aren't any orders coming in, then the LMMs and MMs keep the spreads wide. This is so that they don't end up trading against each other. However, once a real order comes in, they will close the bid and ask to be in line with the underlying stock and snap it up. Because of this, I never use market orders when getting into an SSF trade. I just look to see where the underlying stock is trading and place a limit order based on the underlying price of the stock.

The other thing to remember about SSFs is that their charts are pretty much worthless at this time. The volume is sporadic, so the charts aren't very clean. The best way is to chart the underlying cash stock and then base all decisions to get in and out of the SSFs on the underlying stock. What I will do is set up the chart of an underlying cash stock and then put the quotes for both the cash stock and the SSF contract below it so I can see where the current bid ask is located. However, because most of my trades in the SSFs are swing trades, I don't even watch the charts intraday. I just set up my limit orders the night before based on the cash chart and then wait until the end of the day to see if I'm filled.

We'll look at a couple of sample plays on EBAY and QCOM in a moment. First I want to discuss options quickly.

# THE ONLY WAY TO PLAY INDIVIDUAL STOCK OPTIONS

I'm writing this section based on the premise that the reader knows at least a little about what options are and how they work. If not, that's okay. There are plenty of Web sites out there that explain them in detail, and I would recommend reading more about what options are and how they work if you plan on using them. I'm just going to give a quick rundown and share how I incorporate them into my trading plan.

There are many complicated option strategies available, and many people spend hundreds of hours looking for the perfect strategies to generate "guaranteed income." Most of these strategies work great when the markets are range-bound—which they are most of the time. Then along comes the inevitable big rally or watershed decline and all these people get hosed. For a period of years in the mid-1990s, a lot of traders and funds made a nice living selling naked puts. These are put options whose writers do not have a short position in the stock on which he or she has written the put. The goal here is that the options expire worthless, and the put writers collect the premium. Many books started popping up on the shelves about "taxi-driver millionaires" who discovered this "amazing get rich quick" trading strategy. Then along came October 27, 1997.

The markets had been drifting down through October, and many of the taxi drivers, as well as several large funds with a few hundred million in assets, were busy selling naked puts. The brokers who worked with the funds started getting nervous because the positions had gone against the funds to the point where it wouldn't take much of a further decline to start forcing margin calls. The brokers, who didn't quite understand the strategy being used by the funds, started to place discreet calls to other traders asking what would happen "if the Dow dropped a couple of hundred points" over the next week or so. The answer was easy—these funds would be forced to dump their positions because of margin calls, and this would create tremendous downward selling pressure in the overall markets. The S&P 500 floor traders at the CME got wind of this and started prepping for the slaughter.

On October 16, 1997, the Dow broke through its most recent uptrend line as seen on point 1 in Fig. 16.1. The Dow then rallied and closed at 8034.65 on October 22, just below its broken trendline, at point 2. This is a common occurrence in all markets—once a trendline is broken, the markets will come up and test it last time before rolling over. I call it, "kissing the trendline goodbye." On October 24, at point 3, the Dow closed at 7715.41, down 319.24 points. This started the round of forced margin calls after the close, which was on a Friday. The margin call selling would take place on Monday. The Dow opened Monday at 7633.14, down 82.27. Then the forced selling via the margin calls began— and the S&P pit traders, who knew what was happening, simply stepped back and walked away from the bids. With no support in the markets, the Dow dropped quickly and closed at 7161.39, down 554.02 points on the day as seen at point 4. By the time the closing bell rang on Monday, everyone who was selling naked puts for a living had lost a substantial amount of money. The funds that were involved not only lost all the money under their management; they ended up owing money to the brokers. Well, more correctly, the people who had invested in the fund lost all their money, and ended up owing more than they had put into the fund. Many metaphors

**F I G U R E  16.1**

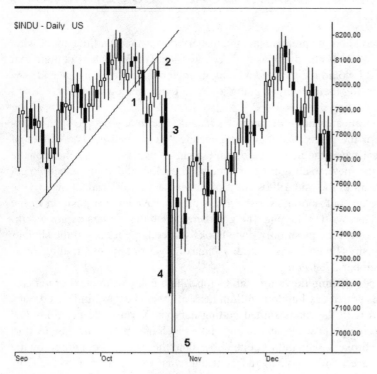

$INDU - Daily  US

come to mind here, but I will pass as most of them are quite graphic in nature. Once all these people were cleaned out, the markets were set to rally. The very next day the markets pushed down to new lows, touching 6927 at point 5, shedding just over 1,000 points in three trading days, before putting in a hard bottom. The Dow then closed at 7498.32, up 336.93 points on the day, and went on to rally steadily from there. Once all of the naked put sellers were cleaned out, there was nothing to do but resume the uptrend.

Okay, so how do I use options? The only way I use options is as a means for owning a stock at a cheaper price. Because of the premium and time decay, I am very specific about the options I buy. For example, I won't buy out of the money options, as they are all premium and a sucker's game. Therefore, I want to look at options that are trading in the money ("in the money" means when the option's strike price is below the current market price for call options, and when the strike price is above the current market price for put options) if not more, in order to buy an option where the premium constitutes less than 30 percent of the overall purchase price. As I'm writing this in early 2005, the premium of options is generally low, so I can usually buy options just one strike in the money to meet this criterion. In 1999 and 2000 option premiums were at extremes, and I often had to go 5–10 strikes in the money to buy options that met my criteria. I remember when QCOM was at $250 before its infamous "run to a thousand" at the end of 1999. At the money call options were $45. In order to buy calls that were only 30 percent premium, I had to go nearly 15 strikes in the money.

The option table represented in Figure 16.2 shows different strike prices and expiration months for GOOG. At the time this was created, in early November 2004, GOOG was trading at $191.67. If I am interested in buying a call on this stock, I'll start looking at the near month contracts that are in the money. Because GOOG is a higher-priced, volatile stock, the option premiums are going to be high—the higher the volatility, the higher the premium. In this case, I look at the November 180 calls, which are two strikes in the money. The premium on these is still excessive, and I need to go down one more strike price, to the November 175 calls, to meet my criterion of the premium being less than 30 percent of the overall purchase price. The amateur option trader in this case is going to buy the November 220 calls because they are so "cheap" at $2.55. Never mind that they will expire as worthless. For puts, I first look at the November 200 puts, but they are too expensive. I look at the 210s, and they are close but the 220s are better with respect to the amount of premium I want to pay. Remember, all I'm trying to do is buy (or short) the actual stock at a cheaper price. This means I don't want a lot of premium. Looking at the next month out in December, these same strike prices jump up excessively in price, so I want to stay with the near month contracts and wait until expiration to roll over into December if I have to. I'll explain more about how to figure out premium shortly.

In contrast to GOOG, IBM is a more stable stock, and the premiums here aren't that high. With the stock trading at $91.20, I first look at the November 90 calls, but they have

**F I G U R E   16.2**

Options1

GOOG          OK

GOOGLE INC 191.67    CALLS    Bid: 118.39  BSize: 1    Vol: 13.9M    Nov03 18:40    Today's Date: 11/3/2004    PUTS
Ask: 264.69  ASize: 1    Volatility: 64.96

| OpInt | Vol | Bid | Ask | Change | Last | ymbol(shor | Symbol | ymbol(shor | Last | Change | Ask | Bid | Vol | OpInt |
|---|---|---|---|---|---|---|---|---|---|---|---|---|---|---|
| 4.17K | 106 | 37.70 | 38.00 | -5.20 | 36.90 | GOO KZ | NOV04 155.00 | GOO WZ | 0.95 | +0.10 | 1.05 | 0.90 | 1.85K | 8.97K |
| 4.48K | 569 | 33.20 | 33.40 | -2.70 | 33.10 | GOO KY | NOV04 160.00 | GOO WY | 1.35 | -0.10 | 1.50 | 1.30 | 936 | 7.00K |
| 3.90K | 108 | 28.80 | 29.10 | -3.10 | 28.50 | GOO KX | NOV04 165.00 | GOO WX | 2.15 | +0.15 | 2.10 | 2.00 | 1.25K | 6.64K |
| 4.94K | 206 | 24.60 | 25.00 | -3.40 | 24.40 | GOO KW | NOV04 170.00 | GOO WW | 2.95 | +0.25 | 3.00 | 2.80 | 2.33K | 6.60K |
| 3.77K | 447 | 20.80 | 21.20 | -2.70 | 20.50 | GOU KO | NOV04 175.00 | GOU WO | 4.20 | +0.40 | 4.10 | 4.00 | 1.44K | 8.16K |
| 7.35K | 1.63K | 17.40 | 17.70 | -2.60 | 17.40 | GOU KP | NOV04 180.00 | GOU WP | 5.80 | +0.70 | 5.80 | 5.50 | 2.47K | 8.09K |
| 6.26K | 1.73K | 14.30 | 14.60 | -1.70 | 14.60 | GOU KQ | NOV04 185.00 | GOU WQ | 7.60 | +0.40 | 7.50 | 7.40 | 1.86K | 4.22K |
| 5.53K | 2.54K | 11.50 | 11.80 | -2.20 | 11.50 | GOU KR | NOV04 190.00 | GOU WR | 10.00 | +1.00 | 9.90 | 9.60 | 2.10K | 5.10K |
| 4.27K | 3.43K | 9.30 | 9.30 | -2.00 | 9.10 | GOU KS | NOV04 195.00 | GOU WS | 12.60 | +1.10 | 12.30 | 12.20 | 1.46K | 1.85K |
| 9.55K | 5.52K | 7.10 | 7.30 | -1.80 | 7.20 | GOU KT | NOV04 200.00 | GOU WT | 15.80 | +1.70 | 15.60 | 15.20 | 1.38K | 3.52K |
| 8.48K | 4.37K | 4.30 | 4.30 | -1.50 | 4.30 | GOU KB | NOV04 210.00 | GOU WB | 22.10 | +0.60 | 22.70 | 22.30 | 279 | 253 |
| 7.00K | 3.08K | 2.50 | 2.55 | -0.85 | 2.55 | GOU KD | NOV04 220.00 | GOU WD | 31.00 | +1.60 | 30.80 | 30.50 | 102 | 197 |
| 4.38K | 2.58K | 1.40 | 1.55 | -0.65 | 1.45 | GOU KF | NOV04 230.00 | GOU WF | 39.90 | +2.50 | 39.70 | 39.30 | 17 | 90 |
| 3.78K |  | 41.10 | 41.50 | +1.60 | 44.90 | GOO LZ | DEC04 155.00 | GOO XZ | 4.50 | -0.10 | 4.60 | 4.30 | 118 | 2.75K |
| 1.69K | 20 | 37.30 | 37.70 | -1.80 | 40.40 | GOO LY | DEC04 160.00 | GOO XY | 5.50 | +0.20 | 5.70 | 5.40 | 390 | 2.51K |
| 1.21K | 1 | 33.50 | 33.90 | +2.70 | 39.50 | GOO LX | DEC04 165.00 | GOO XX | 6.90 | +0.10 | 7.00 | 6.70 | 130 | 5.53K |
| 4.49K | 103 | 30.10 | 30.50 | -2.40 | 30.50 | GOO LW | DEC04 170.00 | GOO XW | 8.50 | 0.00 | 8.60 | 8.30 | 617 | 2.36K |
| 966 | 162 | 26.70 | 27.10 | -3.00 | 26.80 | GOU LO | DEC04 175.00 | GOU XO | 10.40 | +0.60 | 10.20 | 9.90 | 132 | 1.57K |
| 2.79K | 173 | 23.80 | 24.20 | -1.90 | 23.80 | GOU LP | DEC04 180.00 | GOU XP | 12.00 | +0.70 | 12.20 | 11.90 | 308 | 2.46K |
| 5.59K | 132 | 21.00 | 21.40 | -2.70 | 20.80 | GOU LO | DEC04 185.00 | GOU XO | 14.30 | +0.30 | 14.40 | 14.10 | 339 | 1.55K |
| 2.44K | 420 | 18.50 | 18.90 | -2.60 | 18.30 | GOU LR | DEC04 190.00 | GOU XR | 17.20 | +1.20 | 17.00 | 16.60 | 483 | 1.62K |
| 1.85K | 481 | 16.20 | 16.60 | -2.50 | 15.80 | GOU LS | DEC04 195.00 | GOU XS | 19.80 | +0.80 | 19.70 | 19.30 | 132 | 974 |
| 4.34K | 1.80K | 14.40 | 14.50 | -2.20 | 14.10 | GOU LT | DEC04 200.00 | GOU XT | 22.70 | +1.30 | 22.60 | 22.20 | 194 | 797 |
| 5.20K | 600 | 10.70 | 11.00 | -1.90 | 10.50 | GOU LB | DEC04 210.00 | GOU XB | 28.90 | +3.00 | 29.20 | 28.80 | 161 | 336 |
| 3.31K | 454 | 8.00 | 8.30 | -1.70 | 7.80 | GOU LD | DEC04 220.00 | GOU XD | 36.10 | +2.50 | 36.40 | 36.00 | 67 | 223 |
| 929 | 751 | 5.90 | 6.20 | -1.30 | 6.00 | GOU LF | DEC04 230.00 | GOU XF | 41.90 | +0.10 | 44.30 | 43.90 | 70 | 201 |
| 492 | 20 | 49.90 | 50.40 | -1.10 | 52.80 | GOO CZ | MAR05 155.00 | GOO OZ | 11.50 | -1.30 | 13.30 | 12.90 | 44 | 3.04K |
| 1.22K | 13 | 46.60 | 47.10 | -0.70 | 49.40 | GOO CY | MAR05 160.00 | GOO OY | 14.00 | -0.90 | 14.80 | 14.40 | 34 | 674 |
| 705 | 23 | 43.40 | 43.90 | -2.60 | 45.70 | GOO CX | MAR05 165.00 | GOO OX | 15.60 | -1.10 | 16.70 | 16.20 | 67 | 1.70K |

too much premium (see Fig. 16.2). The 85s fit the bill nicely. On the put side, the first strike in the money, the 95s, work fine. Note that I could even go out to the next month, the December 95s, and pay only a little extra in premium. I like to focus on the near month contract in order to reduce premium. However, if the option is set to expire in less than two weeks, then I will go ahead and buy the next month out, though I may have to go even deeper in the money. Following are a few more notes of interest on options contracts:

- One option contract equals 100 shares of stock.
- Buy 10 GOOG Nov 190 calls at $12, and that will cost $12,000.
- To buy an equivalent 1,000 shares of the stock at $190 would cost $190,000.
- If GOOG rallies by 10 points, these options will move about 6 points. This depends on how far in the money they are. The further they are in the money, the more they will move "dollar for dollar" with the underlying stock.
- Sell the 10 GOOG calls at $18 ($18,000) and pocket $6,000.
- Maximum loss on this trade is the option's cost, $12,000.

By contrast to this last bullet point, if a trader bought 1,000 shares of GOOG at $190 and it gapped down 30 points on an earnings report, the trader would be out $30,000. Options do limit risk if they are purchased correctly. Now that we've reviewed SSFs and stock options, let's get down to the play itself.

**FIGURE 16.3**

Options1

IBM OK

INTERNATIONAL BUSINESS MACH: Bid: 90.65 BSize: 4 Vol: 6.55M Nov03
91.20 c Ask: 91.07 ASize: 2 Volatility: 15.78 20:09 Puts

| OpInt | Vol | Bid | Ask | Change | Last | ymbol(shor | Symbol | ymbol(shor | Last | Change | Ask | Bid | Vol | OpInt |
|---|---|---|---|---|---|---|---|---|---|---|---|---|---|---|
| 320 | | 16.10 | 16.30 | +0.10 | 15.40 | IBM KO | NOV04 75.00 | IBM WO | 0.05 | 0.00 | 0.05 | 0.00 | | 3.32K |
| 2.06K | 107 | 11.10 | 11.30 | +0.70 | 11.10 | IBM KP | NOV04 80.00 | IBM WP | 0.05 | 0.00 | 0.05 | 0.00 | 5 | 18.5K |
| 12.9K | 906 | 6.10 | 6.40 | +1.00 | 6.40 | IBM KQ | NOV04 85.00 | IBM WQ | 0.10 | -0.15 | 0.10 | 0.05 | 98 | 18.1K |
| 29.5K | 9.45K | 1.80 | 1.90 | +0.30 | 1.85 | IBM KR | NOV04 90.00 | IBM WR | 0.80 | -0.50 | 0.80 | 0.75 | 1.29K | 6.13K |
| 7.33K | 993 | 0.10 | 0.20 | +0.02 | 0.17 | IBM KS | NOV04 95.00 | IBM WS | 4.00 | -1.00 | 4.10 | 4.00 | 352 | 660 |
| 261 | | 0.00 | 0.05 | 0.00 | 0.05 | IBM KT | NOV04 100.00 | IBM WT | 8.80 | -0.80 | 9.10 | 8.80 | 12 | 245 |
| | | 0.00 | 0.05 | 0.00 | 0.00 | IBM KA | NOV04 105.00 | IBM WA | 13.40 | -1.00 | 14.10 | 13.80 | 35 | 120 |
| 81 | 10 | 16.10 | 16.40 | +0.80 | 16.20 | IBM LO | DEC04 75.00 | IBM XO | 0.10 | 0.00 | 0.10 | 0.00 | | 517 |
| 960 | 14 | 11.20 | 11.40 | +0.80 | 11.40 | IBM LP | DEC04 80.00 | IBM XP | 0.10 | -0.05 | 0.15 | 0.05 | 125 | 2.75K |
| 5.15K | 210 | 6.50 | 6.70 | +0.60 | 6.60 | IBM LQ | DEC04 85.00 | IBM XQ | 0.40 | -0.20 | 0.40 | 0.35 | 192 | 4.55K |
| 6.86K | 1.53K | 2.60 | 2.75 | +0.50 | 2.75 | IBM LR | DEC04 90.00 | IBM XR | 1.45 | -0.55 | 1.55 | 1.40 | 271 | 1.67K |
| 7.91K | 2.55K | 0.60 | 0.70 | +0.06 | 0.61 | IBM LS | DEC04 95.00 | IBM XS | 4.20 | -1.10 | 4.50 | 4.30 | 39 | 304 |
| 1.21K | 10 | 0.05 | 0.15 | +0.10 | 0.20 | IBM LT | DEC04 100.00 | IBM XT | 9.60 | +0.40 | 9.10 | 8.90 | | 54 |
| 4 | | 0.00 | 0.05 | 0.00 | 0.05 | IBM LA | DEC04 105.00 | IBM XA | 14.80 | +0.10 | 14.10 | 13.80 | | 50 |
| 296 | 42 | 16.40 | 16.60 | +0.60 | 16.70 | IBM AO | JAN05 75.00 | IBM MO | 0.20 | 0.00 | 0.20 | 0.10 | | 5.17K |
| 13.2K | 80 | 11.60 | 11.80 | +0.90 | 12.30 | IBM AP | JAN05 80.00 | IBM MP | 0.30 | -0.10 | 0.35 | 0.30 | 179 | 25.6K |
| 13.2K | 1.60K | 7.00 | 7.20 | +0.20 | 7.20 | IBM AQ | JAN05 85.00 | IBM MQ | 0.80 | -0.25 | 0.80 | 0.70 | 367 | 22.8K |
| 39.7K | 732 | 3.30 | 3.50 | +0.30 | 3.40 | IBM AR | JAN05 90.00 | IBM MR | 2.00 | -0.55 | 2.10 | 1.95 | 4.50K | 27.6K |
| 26.6K | 1.51K | 1.15 | 1.25 | +0.10 | 1.20 | IBM AS | JAN05 95.00 | IBM MS | 4.90 | -0.40 | 4.90 | 4.70 | 127 | 10.9K |
| 36.1K | 383 | 0.30 | 0.40 | +0.05 | 0.35 | IBM AT | JAN05 100.00 | IBM MT | 9.10 | -0.70 | 9.20 | 8.90 | 2 | 9.12K |
| 4.06K | 338 | 0.05 | 0.15 | -0.02 | 0.13 | IBM AA | JAN05 105.00 | IBM MA | 13.90 | +0.50 | 14.10 | 13.80 | 19 | 1.04K |
| 93 | | 16.90 | 17.20 | +0.47 | 16.90 | IBM DO | APR05 75.00 | IBM PO | 0.50 | -0.05 | 0.55 | 0.45 | 80 | 2.88K |
| 430 | 23 | 12.40 | 12.60 | +0.40 | 12.40 | IBM DP | APR05 80.00 | IBM PP | 0.85 | -0.15 | 0.90 | 0.85 | 230 | 4.87K |
| 2.30K | 18 | 8.20 | 8.40 | +0.20 | 8.50 | IBM DQ | APR05 85.00 | IBM PQ | 1.60 | -0.30 | 1.70 | 1.60 | 215 | 5.59K |
| 19.0K | 380 | 4.70 | 4.90 | +0.40 | 4.70 | IBM DR | APR05 90.00 | IBM PR | 3.10 | -0.41 | 3.20 | 3.00 | 410 | 12.2K |
| 5.79K | 400 | 2.25 | 2.30 | +0.30 | 2.40 | IBM DS | APR05 95.00 | IBM PS | 5.30 | -0.70 | 5.80 | 5.60 | 313 | 1.72K |
| 3.11K | 1.47K | 0.95 | 1.00 | +0.10 | 1.00 | IBM DT | APR05 100.00 | IBM PT | 8.90 | -1.30 | 9.50 | 9.30 | 80 | 1.44K |
| 742 | | 0.30 | 0.40 | +0.05 | 0.40 | IBM DA | APR05 105.00 | IBM PA | 13.40 | -1.40 | 14.10 | 13.90 | 81 | 614 |

# TRADING RULES FOR BUY FADES (SELLS ARE REVERSED)

This is a fade play that focuses on swing positions that last a few days to a few weeks. I am looking to sell strength and buy weakness.

1. For these plays I am utilizing a daily chart. Because these plays are meant to last a few days to a few weeks, I'm not interested in what is happening on a 5- or 15-minute chart. I want to be able to step back and look at a slightly bigger picture without all the noise found in intraday charts.

2. The only indicators I place on the daily chart are an 8 and 21 period exponential moving average (EMA).

3. For longs, I want to see the 8-period EMA trading above the 21-period EMA. Once this upward cross happens, then I can start looking for a setup to occur.

4. The specific setup I'm looking for, once the 8 EMA has crossed above the 21 EMA, is a pullback to the 8-period EMA.

5. The initial stop is the 21-period EMA or 4 percent of the stock price, whichever is greater. Typically the initial stop turns out to be this 4 percent level. Note this 4 percent level is based on the price of the stock, not my equity level. That is, I'm not risking 4 percent of my equity on one trade; I'm risking 4 percent in the price of the stock. I could have 10 stocks going at one time.

6. Once I'm up 4 percent on the position (I call this my *watermark level*), I will then move up my stop to the 21-period EMA. I will then use this 21 EMA as a trailing stop until my target or trailing stop is hit.

7. My target is an 8 percent move in the price of the stock from my entry price. Although I focus mostly on stocks when using this play, it can also be used on the stock index futures. However, the percentages will be different. On a daily chart, instead of an 8 percent target, I just use a 1 percent target and a 0.5 percent stop to start. If the mini-sized Dow is at 10604, then my target is 106 points, and my initial stop is 53 points, or the 21 EMA, whichever is greater. On a 60-minute chart I cut this in half, using a target of 1/2 of 1 percent and a stop of ¼ of 1 percent, or the 21 EMA, whichever is greater. To get these, I just multiply the price of the index by .005 for the target and by .0025 for the stop. A sample play of this nature is discussed in Chapter 18.

8. The easiest way to figure out all these levels is to quickly set up an Excel spreadsheet with the formulas already in place (see Figure 16.3).

9. One way to increase the odds of success slightly on long setups is to trade only stocks where the 8-period EMA is higher than the 21 EMA on the weekly charts. This condition can last on a weekly chart for months and even years. If this setup exists on the weekly charts, then it's just a matter of waiting for an entry on the daily chart as per this setup. This process is discussed in more detail in Chapter 18.

Figure 16.4 is a snapshot of the exact Excel spreadsheet I use to calculate my key stop and target levels. All I do is enter my entry price in the highlighted box. If I'm long on the stock, then I use the "long" box and vice versa. Once the price is in, the Excel spreadsheet calculates all the levels for me automatically. The formulas are very simple. For example, the target is calculated by taking the entry price and multiplying it by .08 (8%). The initial stop is calculated by taking the entry price and multiplying it by .04 (4%) and subtracting it from the entry. The 4 percent watermark level is calculated by taking the entry price, multiplying it by .04 (4%), and adding it to the entry price. I use to do all this manually, and it is a real buzz killer.

## EBAY (eBay, Inc.)—August 19, 2004

1. On August 10, 2004, EBAY crosses above its 8 EMA (see Fig. 16.5). However, since the 8 EMA is still trading below the 21 EMA, I am not interested in setting up a buy order just yet. I need to wait for the 8 EMA to cross up through the 21 EMA before I set up my first buy order. Note: On all these charts, the 8 EMA is the skinny moving average line, and the 21 EMA is the thicker moving average line.

2. On August 19, the 8 EMA crosses up above the 21 EMA. I'm now ready to start bidding for a long, and my entry point will be a pullback to the 8 EMA. The next day I am filled at 79.28 when the market pulls back to the 8 EMA. Now that I'm in the trade, I need to check where to place my stop. The 21 EMA is at 79.08, which is not very far below my entry level. A 4 percent stop would be placed at 76.11. Since the 4 percent stop is greater, this is the stop I will use to start out with. My target is 8 percent up from my entry, which is 85.62. Remember, once I'm up 4 percent in the position, I will then move my stop up to the 21-period EMA. The initial stop and target for this play is highlighted on the chart with the horizontal lines.

3. On August 25 EBAY pushes higher and hits my target, and I'm out for just over $6 per share ($6.34). Now that I'm out, its time to start looking for the next pullback

**F I G U R E   16.4**

| | | | Points | Price |
|---|---|---|---|---|
| | **LONG** | | | |
| Enter Price | | $ 88.45 | | |
| | | | Points | Price |
| | | Target | 7.08 | 95.53 |
| | | Initial Stop | 3.54 | 84.91 |
| | | Up 4% | 3.54 | 91.99 |
| | **SHORT** | | | |
| Enter Price | | $ 25.10 | | |
| | | | Points | Price |
| | | Target | 2.01 | 23.09 |
| | | Initial Stop | 1.00 | 26.10 |
| | | Up 4% | 1.00 | 24.10 |

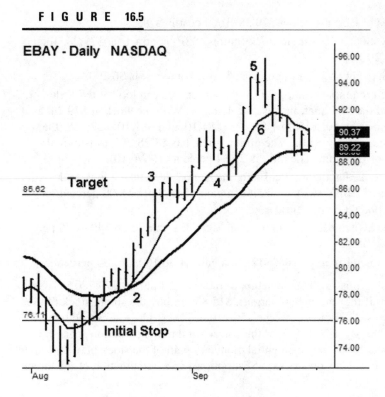

F I G U R E   16.5

EBAY - Daily  NASDAQ

to the 8-period EMA. A trader could have also followed this same play using single stock futures or in the money call options. I will review those possibilities for this play in a moment.

4. On September 9, 10 trading days later, EBAY pulls back to its 8-period EMA, and I am filled at 87.95. I do a quick calculation and see that my target is going to be 95.78 and my stop is 84.43. I set my parameters and let my orders babysit my position.

5. Four trading days later my target is hit, and I'm out of the trade.

6. On September 17 the market pulls back to the 8 EMA once again. I take the trade, and I get in at 91.74 and set my parameters. This would be a stop of 88.07 and a target of 99.08. At the time I did this chart, I was still in the trade, so it is "active."

I'd like to take a moment and examine the first EBAY play detailed in Figure 16.5 more closely. This play could also have been executed using single stock futures or in the money call options. It is useful to compare these trades to the actual stock trade to get an idea how this setup could have been followed on these various trading instruments. This will also give a trader an idea of the risk-to-reward parameters for each scenario. Although it's the exact same play across all three instruments, the amount risked verses the amount gained is different for all three scenarios. Let's take a look:

- Buy 1,000 shares of EBAY stock at $79.28. Total cost is $79,280.
- Buy 10 EBAY1C September single stock futures (SSF) contracts at $79.28. Total cost is $15,856 (20% of $79,280).
- Buy 10 EBAY September 75 call options at $6.10. Total cost is $6,100.
- To figure out the premium on an options contract, people can look at the Delta, or, if they aren't familiar with that, just use a calculator: With the stock at $79.28, a $75 call option costs $6.10. $75.00 + $6.10 = $81.10, and $81.10 − $79.28 (the actual price of the stock) = $1.82. The option, then, has $4.28 of intrinsic (real) value and $1.82 of premium. The ratio is 29.84 percent (1.82/6.10).
- Now that we've looked at the total costs for each entry, let's take a look at the exits: Sell 1,000 shares of EBAY stock at $85.62, a gain of $6,340 or 8.00 percent (or 16.00 percent if bought on margin).
- Sell 10 EBAY1C September SSF contracts at $85.62, a gain of $6,340 or 40 percent.
- Sell 10 EBAY September 75 calls at $12.20, a gain of $6,100, or 100 percent.

As you can see, using this exact same setup, a trader could put up $79,280 in cash to buy the stock (or $39,640 if they are using margin), $15,856 to buy the single stock futures, or $6,100 to buy the options. The dollar outcome of the trade is very close across all three scenarios—a little over $6,000. By using SSFs or the correct in the money option strike prices, a trader can risk less capital for the same potential monetary gain of the stock play. It is up to the trader if they want to just focus on stocks, SSFs, options, or a combination of the three.

## QCOM (Qualcomm, Inc.)—August 19, 2004

1. The 8 EMA pushes above the 21 EMA, and I place my bid (see Fig. 16.6). Two days later, on August 20, 2004, I am filled at 35.47. I place a stop at 34.05 and a target at 38.31. By the time trading is done this day, the stock is already up by 4 percent from my entry, so I move my stop up to the 21 EMA, which is 35.34.
2. On Monday, August 23, QCOM continues to push higher, and my target is hit. I immediately set up a bid to buy the next pullback to the 8 EMA.
3. On August 30 my trailing bid is hit, and I'm in at 37.51. I place a stop at 36.01 and a target at 40.51.
4. About two weeks later, on September 13, my target is hit. Note that when the stock is up by 4 percent from my entry on September 7, I raise my stop to the 21 EMA at 37.42, and I trail this stop until my target is hit.

As I did with EBAY, let's take a look at executing this same QCOM play across all three trading instruments. Here is how the entries would break down:

- Buy 1,000 shares of QCOM at $37.51. Total cost is $37,510.
- Buy 10 QCOM1C September SSF contracts at $37.51. Total cost is $7,502 (20 percent of $37,510).

F I G U R E   16.6

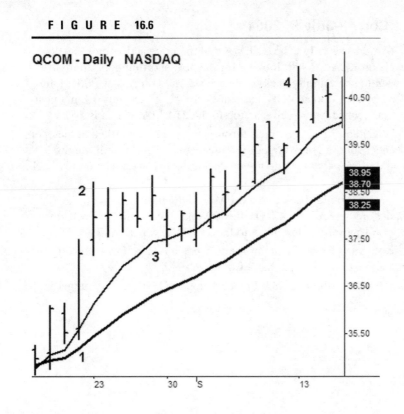

QCOM - Daily  NASDAQ

- Buy 10 QCOM September 35 calls at $3.10. Total cost is $3,100.

To figure out the premium on the QCOM options, just take $35.00 + $3.10 = 38.10. There is $2.51 of real value ($37.51 – $35.00) and 0.59 cents of premium (3.10 – 2.51 = 0.59). The ratio is 19.03 percent (0.59/3.10).

We've looked at the total costs for each entry, so now let's take a look at the exits:

- Sell 1,000 shares of QCOM at $40.51, a gain of $3,000 or 8 percent, or 16 percent if using margin.
- Sell 10 QCOM1C September SSF contracts at $40.51, a gain of $3,000 or 40 percent.
- Sell 10 QCOM September 35 calls at $5.90, a gain of $2,800, or 90.32 percent.

Once again, using this exact same setup, a trader could put up $37,510 in cash to buy the stock (or $18,755 if they are using margin), $7,502 to buy the single stock futures, or $3,100 to buy the options. The dollar outcome of the trade is very close across all three scenarios—about $3,000. Now that you have the idea, I'm just going to focus on the actual stock plays for the rest of this chapter. Of course, not all stocks have options and single stock futures available on them, so some of these plays can only be executed on the actual stock.

## KLAC (KLA Tencor Corp)—July 9, 2004

1. When the 8 EMA crosses below the 21 EMA and the price action moves below both these levels on KLAC, I start looking for the next shorting opportunity (see Fig. 16.7). I want to short a rally back to the 8 EMA, and on July 9, 2004, I am filled at 46.19. I place a stop at 48.04 and a target of 42.49. On July 13, my position is up by 4 percent so I move up my stop to the 21 EMA, which is 46.84.

2. On July 14 KLAC gaps down and opens through my target. I'm filled at the open at 41.61, 88 cents better than my target for a nice gain. KLAC is still trading below its 8 and 21 EMAs, so I set up my next short, which would be a rally back to its 8 EMA.

3. On July 20 the market rallies back to the 8 EMA, and I'm filled at 41.81. My stop is 43.48, and my target is 38.47. On July 22, the stock is up by 4 percent from my entry, so I move my stop down to the 21 EMA, which is 42.84.

4. On July 26, my target is hit, and I'm out for an 8 percent gain. I start looking to short again at the next rally back to the 8 EMA.

5. On July 29 I'm back in short at 39.33. I place a stop at 40.90, and my target is 36.18.

F I G U R E   16.7

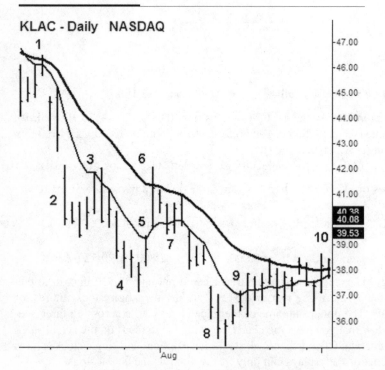

KLAC - Daily  NASDAQ

6. The next day KLAC gaps up on positive news and rallies to my stop. I'm out for a 4 percent loss. I note that the 8 EMA has not crossed above the 21 EMA. I sit back and wait, because if KLAC trades and closes back below its 8 EMA, I will set up an order to short the next rally back to its 8 EMA.

7. A few days later on August 3 KLAC closes below its 8 EMA. I set up an order to short a rally back to its 8 EMA, and on August 4 I am filled at 39.93. I place a stop at 41.53 and a target at 36.74. The stock pushes higher, and on August 5 it comes within spitting distance of my stop, but doesn't make it and closes well off its highs.

8. On August 10 I have a 4 percent gain registered, so I move my stop down to the 21 EMA, which is 40.29. On August 11 KLAC gaps lower and pushes lower all day, hitting my target.

9. KLAC is still trending lower according to the 8 and 21 EMAs, so I set up another order to short a rally to the 8 EMA. On August 17 KLAC rallies, and I am filled at 37.15. I place a target at 34.18 and a stop at 38.64.

10. The market chops back and forth for a while, and on September 1 I am stopped out for a 4 percent loss.

## QLGC (QLogic Corp)—June 14, 2004

1. On June 14, 2004, the 8 EMA on QLGC crosses below the 21 EMA, setting up a situation in which I could start taking new plays (see Fig. 16.8). I place an order the next day to short a rally back up to the 8 EMA, and I'm filled at 28.14. I place a stop at 29.27 and a target at 25.89.

2. On June 16 QLGC dry heaves and pukes for a nice down day. It gets close to my target, but not quite. Since I'm up over 4 percent on the play, I move down my stop to the 21 EMA, which is 28.22. The very next day my target is hit at 25.89. I'm now flat on QLGC, and I begin looking at new entries. A new entry, of course, would mean a rally back to the 8 EMA.

3. I place my order and am filled on June 22 at 26.68. I place a target at 24.55 and a stop at 27.75.

4. QLGC continues to rally, and on June 25 I'm stopped out for a 4 percent loss.

5. The day after I'm stopped, QLGC moves back below its 8 EMA and closes below it. This is the trigger I'm looking for before I set up my next trade. I need to see a close back below the 8 EMA in order to start setting up orders for a new short position. The next day I set up an order to short a rally back to the 8 EMA, and I'm filled on June 28 at 26.86. My stop is 27.93, and my target is 24.71. QLGC starts moving my way, and on July 1 I am up by more than 4 percent on this position. At this point I move up my stop and start using the 21 EMA as a trailing stop, starting with 27.12.

6. QLGC continues to bleed like a stuck pig, and on July 6 I am out at my target. I set up an order to short a rally back to the 8 EMA.

7. On July 9 my order is hit, and I'm short at 25.85. I place a stop at 26.88 and a target at 23.78. On July 14 QLGC comes close to my target, but "close" only works when you are throwing a grenade. My target isn't hit, but I do move my stop down to the 21 EMA, which is 26.03.

8. The next day QLGC moves higher, and I'm stopped out for a loss of –18 cents. One question I usually get in a situation like this is, "Hey, since the stock was so close to your target, why didn't you just take the profit?" The main reason I don't is that by bringing that "human judgment" into the equation, you do two things: First, instead of this being a relaxed system to trade, it now becomes an intense system because you have to watch the moves closely on an intraday basis in order to decide when to get out. Second, I've found that most traders, when they are in a trade, lose all objectivity. By actively managing this trade, many people will close it out as soon as it starts to go against them, or they'll start taking profits too soon. In this respect, you might as well be day trading without a plan, which is the most common reason traders lose money. Choose your setup, choose your parameters, and stick to them! How else can you measure the effectiveness of a system unless you stick with the parameters?

9. On July 16 QLGC closes back below its 8 EMA, so I set up another order to short. I'm filled on July 20 at 25.10. My stop is 26.10, and my target is 23.09.

10. QLGC bleeds lower, and my target is filled on July 28. Remember, once I am up by 4 percent in the position, I start using the 21 EMA as a trailing stop.

11. On July 29 QLGC bounces back up to its 8 EMA, and I'm filled on a short at 24.09. My target is 22.16, and my stop 25.05. On August 5 I am up by 4 percent in the position, so I move my stop down to the 21 EMA, which is 24.23.

12. On August 12 my target is hit, and I'm out for an 8 percent gain.

## CEPH (Cephalon, Inc.)—May 3, 2004

1. On May 3, 2004, the 8 EMA on CEPH crosses below the 21 EMA (see Fig. 16.9). I set up an order to short the next rally back up to the 8 EMA. On May 5 my entry is hit at 57.42. My target is 52.83, and my stop is 59.72.

2. On May 7, in addition to celebrating my birthday (after you turn 21, what's the point?), CEPH moves up by over 4 percent so I adjust my stop to the 21 EMA, which is 57.30. This now becomes a trailing stop that I update at the end of each trading day.

3. On May 19 my target is hit. This is a pretty typical swing trade, where I'm in the position for a little over two weeks, and my daily management of the trade is at the absolute minimum so I can focus on other things. A pure day trader who was flipping in and out of CEPH during this time could have easily done 30 trades and had nothing to show for it except a pile of commission costs.

## SBUX (Starbucks Corp)—May 24, 2004

1. As long as there are day traders, Starbucks will be able to charge as much as it wants for a cup of coffee. There is no bid and ask when it comes to a Grande

FIGURE 16.8

QLGC - Daily NASDAQ

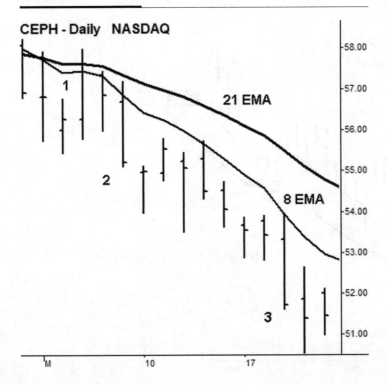

FIGURE 16.9

CEPH - Daily NASDAQ

315

Latte. Traders will take that one "at the market." On May 24, 2004, SBUX has its 8 EMA cross up above its 21 EMA (see Fig. 16.10). This is my signal to set up a bid to buy the next pullback to the 8 EMA. On May 25 my order is hit, and I'm filled at 38.64. I place a stop at 37.09, and my target is 41.73.

2. On May 27 SBUX moves up by 4 percent from my entry, so I move my stop up, using a trailing 21 EMA. My stop on this day is moved up to 38.71. The stock continues to push higher, and on June 3 my target is hit. I start to set up my next bid on a pullback to the 8 EMA.

3. On June 14 SBUX pulls back, and I am filled at 41.96. My stop is 40.28, and my target is 45.32. The stock grinds higher from this point, and on June 18 it hits my 4 percent watermark. I tighten my stop, using the 21 EMA as my guideline. My new stop is 41.51. On June 25 and June 30 the stock pulls back very close to the 21 EMA, and obviously very close to my stop. However, it doesn't hit, and I'm still in the trade.

4. On July 2 SBUX firms, and my target is hit for a gain of +$3.36 or 8 percent.

## GS (The Goldman Sachs Group, Inc.)—August 24, 2004

1. On August 24, 2004, the 8 EMA on GS crosses up above the 21 EMA (see Fig. 16.10). I start setting up bids to buy the next pullback to the 8 EMA. On August 25 I am filled at 87.75. I place a stop at 84.24, and my target is 94.77.

**F I G U R E   16.10**

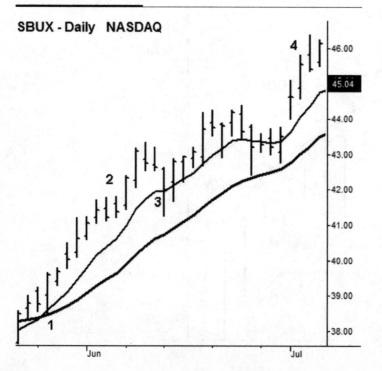

SBUX - Daily  NASDAQ

2. On September 7 this position is up by 4 percent from my entry, and I adjust my stop to reflect the current position of the 21 EMA, in this case 89.06.

3. I update and change my stop at the end of each day, reflecting the movement in the 21 EMA. GS pulls back and hits its 21 EMA nine trading days after I start using the trailing stop. I am out at 91.05 for a gain of +3.30 or +3.76 percent. This is another good example of a low-maintenance trade that lasts the better part of a month. This is a very manageable type of trade for people who work full time. I should know, because these are the main types of trades I did when I was doing my stint in the corporate world.

## PSFT (PeopleSoft, Inc.)—August 27, 2004

1. I like this example because this does tend to happen more often than you would think. This setup keeps you in the direction of the most recent order flow. Typically when stocks come out with really good news or really bad news, there are always people "in the know" who get positioned for these moves before the news is released. This pushes the stock higher (for good news) or lower (for bad news) before the story hits the wire since these insiders load up or dump shares. When the news hits, they get out—and often I can too because I'm following these setups.

**F I G U R E   16.11**

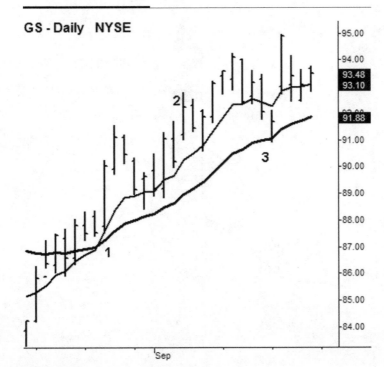

GS - Daily  NYSE

With PSFT, the 8 EMA crosses the 21 EMA on August 25, 2004 (see Fig. 16.12). I set up an order to buy the first pullback to the 21 EMA. On August 27 PSFT pulls back, and I am filled at 17.11. My stop is 16.43, and my target is 18.47. On September 1 I'm up by 4 percent, so I start to trail my stop using the 21 EMA.

2. On September 3 my target is hit, and I set up an order to buy the first pullback to the 8 EMA.

3. The pullback actually occurs on this very same day, and I'm filled at 17.62. I place a stop at 16.92, and my target is 19.03.

4. The stock doesn't do a whole lot for the next three trading days, but on the fourth day it gaps higher on the ORCL (Oracle Corp) takeover news and opens at 19.97, 94 cents above my target. I'm out for a +13.34 percent gain. Although I had no clue that this would be announced, I did know that the order flow on the stock was positive based on this particular setup, so the odds were in my favor that the path of least resistance would be higher.

## TZOO (Travelzoo, Inc.)—August 13, 2004

1. TZOO was one of the hyped stocks of 2004, and using this setup, I was able to catch a few of the moves. On August 13, 2004, the 8 EMA crosses up and through the 21 EMA (see Fig. 16.13). Once this happens I set up an order to buy

**FIGURE   16.12**

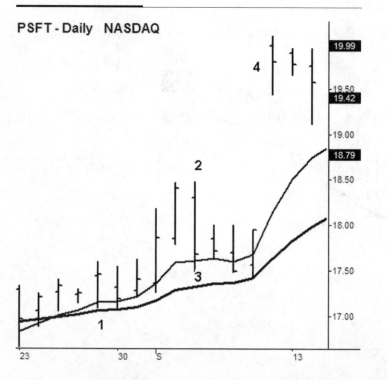

PSFT - Daily  NASDAQ

the next pullback to the 8 EMA. A few days later, on August 18, I am filled at 30.29. I place a stop at 29.08 and a target at 32.71.

2. TZOO ramps higher soon after I enter the stock, and my target is hit later that same day. Once I am out, I place another order to buy a pullback to the 8 EMA.

3. On August 24 the pullback occurs, and I am filled at 37.03. I set my target at 39.99 and my stop at 35.55.

4. Similar to my last trade, TZOO ramps up, and my target is hit the very same day. Like a robot, I set up an order to buy the next pullback to the 8 EMA.

5. On August 30 I had a bid set at 40.81. The stock gapped below this level and opened at 39.24, where I was filled. This is a good example of what I do in this type of situation, because I place my orders before the market opens and don't wait and try to "finesse my entry" after the market opens. When you have a limit order in place, and the stock opens below that level, then your order becomes a market order because it is "at this price or better." However, I will update my stop and target based on my actual entry price. In this case, my entry price was 39.24, so I use a stop that is 4 percent lower than this price, which is 37.67, and a target that is 8 percent higher than this price, which is 42.38.

F I G U R E   16.13

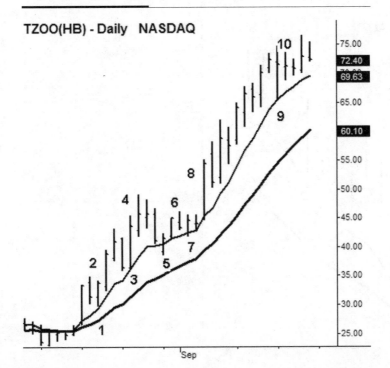

6. On August 31, the very next trading day, my target is hit. I know what I'm going to do now—I'm going to bid for the next pullback to the 8 EMA. It's like kissing your spouse goodbye when you leave for work in the morning; after a while its automatic and you don't have to think about it.

7. On September 2 I'm filled at 42.36, and I set my stop at 40.67, and my target at 45.75.

8. A few days later my target is hit. Time to buy the next pullback.

9. The market pulls back many times but never quite to the 8 EMA until September 20, where I'm filled at 66.34. I place a stop at 63.69, and my target is 71.65.

10. My target is hit the very same day.

## SNDK (Sandisk Corp)—August 31, 2004

1. On August 31, 2004, I buy a pullback to the 8 EMA on SNDK, and I'm filled at 23.30 (see Fig. 16.14). I place a stop at 22.37 and a target of 25.16. On September 8 SNDK gets close to my stop and closes near the lows. After I see this, I assume I'm going to get stopped out the next day, but the important thing is that I do not alter my parameters. It doesn't matter what I think, as long as I don't touch the parameters!

**F I G U R E   16.14**

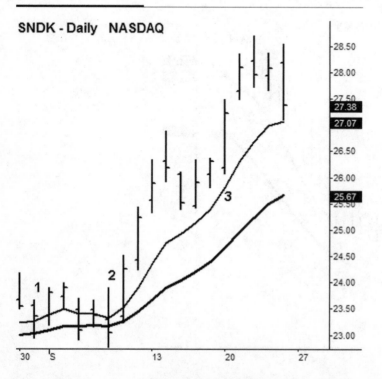

2. Two days later the stock has reversed, and I'm out at my target on September 10. It's time to set up my next bid to buy SNDK on a pullback to the 8 EMA.

3. I trail up my bid and it's almost hit on September 20 and again on September 24, but close enough doesn't cut it. I don't get filled again on this play during this time frame.

## SUMMING UP THE PROPULSION PLAYS

There are two main things that I like about the propulsion play. First, I don't have to watch the markets all day in order to get my entry. I can set up the orders the night before and then check at the end of the day to see which of my orders got filled. Second, I like that these plays have specific targets. I've tried this method by just using trailing stops, but the results were not as good. Sure, once in a while I would catch a stock that would have a parabolic move, but more often than not a perfectly nice profit would roll back over into a breakeven trade. Through trial and error, I have found that by setting a firm 8 percent target using a GTC (good till cancel) order, my profitability improved. Remember, you don't want to become one of the many brokerage clients that the staff pokes fun at. They call GTC orders "good till close," because any time the stock gets close to the client's target, the client calls up and cancels the order "because it looks like it will go even higher." Of course, most of these stocks end up heading back lower and getting sold for a loss. Establish the parameters, then treat your parameters like good employees and let them do their job.

# 17
## C H A P T E R

# MARKET PROFILE—
# REMOVING THE MYSTERY

## FOLLOWING IN THE FOOTSTEPS OF ELEPHANTS

Market Profile is a mystery to most traders, and I want to spend a little time talking about it and at least introduce it to traders who have never used it, since it is becoming increasingly more important to understand how to use this technique. I want to emphasize that this is an introduction—there are entire books written on Market Profile, and unfortunately, none of them is easy to read.

One of my trading partners, Alex (alleyb—his name in our trading room), uses Market Profile extensively, and he was kind enough to research the examples for this chapter. Again, this is intended to be an introduction into this methodology, so if you are already familiar with Market Profile, there shouldn't be any new information for you here. For the uninitiated, the goal of this chapter is to just introduce you to this technique and give you a basic understanding of how it works.

I must point out that I do not use a specific strategy for trading Market Profile. Rather, I use it to get a bias on the markets. If Market Profile is telling me that the sell side is more attractive than the buy side, then I will focus on short setups and generally ignore buy setups, and vice versa. By setups, I mean the setups I've already discussed in this book. Also, I personally do not do my own Market Profile analysis on the markets. It is not my area of expertise, and I would rather just look at what other experts are doing in this area and view their research. I keep an updated resource list on this at www.tradethemarkets.com. With Market Profile, people can't hide what they are doing, which is the beauty of this analysis technique, and this will become incredibly more important as the financial markets come kicking and screaming into the electronic age. Let's take a look.

Market Profile or *MP*, as I refer to it here,was originated by Pete Steidlmayer in 1982 and was licensed to the Chicago Board of Trade in 1984. In its simplest form, MP is one of the most accurate methods for analyzing market data available, and it is becoming even more important as markets make the switch from open outcry to all electronic. MP organizes data and puts them into a picture type of view that represents time, price, and volume. The picture is shown on a vertical axis in the shape of a bell curve. The price component of this picture is displayed on a vertical axis. This part is easy enough to understand. Now it gets a little more interesting.

The time portion of this visual is displayed utilizing letters of the alphabet. These letters represent the time or time brackets, and they are displayed on a horizontal axis. Finally, the third part of this picture, volume, is shown in the form of a histogram and takes different shapes depending on the provider of the data.

MP shows in real time the development of pricing patterns, which is sometimes referred to as *price discovery*. It shows the market organizing data into a unique format in which it is possible to view whether a price is being accepted or rejected over time and through volume. It is possible with constant analysis to establish whether the majority of market participants are long or short and if they are trying to add to or liquidate their positions.

It also provides an opportunity for establishing the reference points of the market. Examples of this include establishing areas of fair or unfair value. Because these data are organized as a picture, high-volume prices and low-volume prices, both of which act as support or resistance, stand out clearly. In addition, the data can establish possible price projections by knowing how the various participants are positioning themselves.

Any market exists to facilitate trade. In simplistic terms this means that the markets travel up and down to establish points of reference at which the majority of buyers and sellers are satisfied in an attempt to establish value. Value is not necessarily viewed by different timeframe participants in the same way. What may be fair to one is unfair to another. MP attempts to create balance and moves through varying degrees of imbalance or trend or vertical moves followed by renewed periods of balance or consolidation or horizontal moves. This is how the bell curve is created and takes shape, and from this the long-term MP can be used to establish short-term moves.

## SPECIFIC EXAMPLES OF MARKET PROFILE IN ACTION

Let's look at a few examples of Market Profile.

- Figure 17.1 depicts a daily MP time price opportunity (TPO) together with the open, opening range, 50 percent of each day, close, and value range.
- The contract shown is the CME big S&P 500 December futures contract, covering September 16 through September 23, 2004. This contract is also referred to as the

*Spoos* (pronounced *spooze*), with the quantity traded often referred to as *cars* and points made or lost on a play often referred to as *handles*. September 21 was the U.S. Federal Reserve or Fed interest rate announcement day. On September 22 the Spoos opened on a gap and underneath the bottom of several of the previous days distribution giving a low risk sell opportunity. This sell opportunity was taken at the opening at 1122 and covered on the close for a profit of 8 points.

- An additional sell was generated on September 23 on the higher open and at the base of value of the previous day. If the market had wanted to go up, the stop would have been just above the top of value on September 22.

## S&P Futures, December 2004 Contract, September 13, 2004

- Figure 17.2 depicts the weekly MP on the big S&Ps again with TPO and value range for the weeks shown.

## F I G U R E   17.1

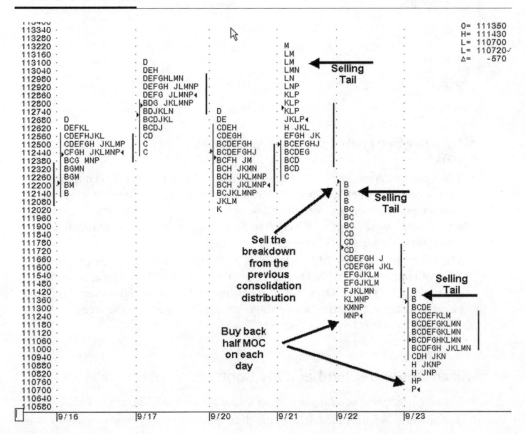

**F I G U R E  17.2**

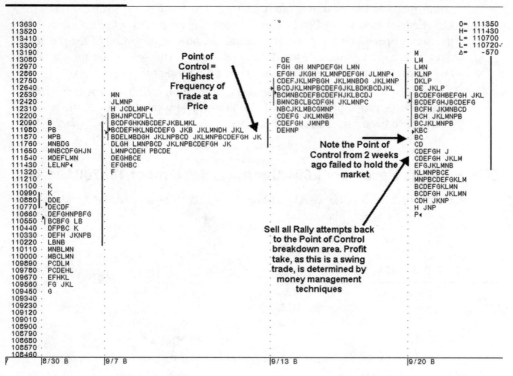

- The time covered is the last week of August and the first three weeks of September 2004.
- The week of September 13 clearly shows that value was being driven higher versus the previous week's value range, and as long as the close remained greater than the point of control from the week of September 7 at 1118.70, then the best trading ideas were longs or to stay flat. Short wasn't an option—unless prices broke down through 1118.70.
- The week of September 20 clearly showed the rejection of the previous week's point of control at 1127.50. The markets rolled over from here and accelerated down through 1118.70. Once this happens, the trader can set up a short. To find a target, a trader then starts to look for the bottom of value from the week of August 30, which is listed at 1102.20.

## Mini-Sized Dow—September 2004 Contract, September 2, 2004

- Figure 17.3 depicts several versions of single prints where there was a single TPO.
- The contract shown is the CBOT mini-sized Dow December futures contract.

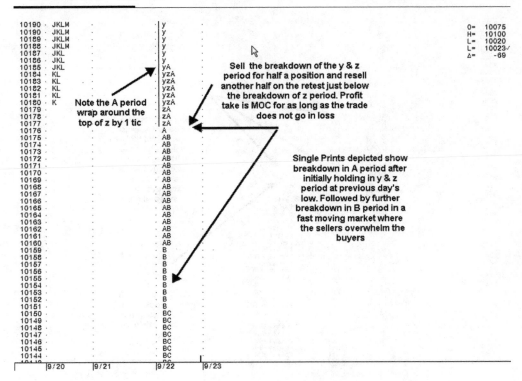

**F I G U R E   17.3**

- The first example is the A wrapped around the top of z at 10185.
- The second example is the single A, which is a breakdown point at 10176.
- The third example is several again at a breakdown point from 10159 through 10151.
- The first example denotes that there is in fact a seller in control, the second example is obvious as a breakdown level, and the third example depicts a market trending, hoping to find a buyer. Instead it is being rejected by the buyers and shows that sellers are in control.

## Euro FX—December 2004 Contract, September 22, 2004

- Figure 17.4 depicts the top part of an MP distribution pattern across three days.
- The contract shown is the CME Euro FX December futures contract, also referred to as the euro.
- The N period print at 1.2341 on September 22 gives a powerful sell signal where the previous day's high at 1.2340 was exceeded by one tick. This move was followed quickly by a rejection of this level.

**FIGURE 17.4**

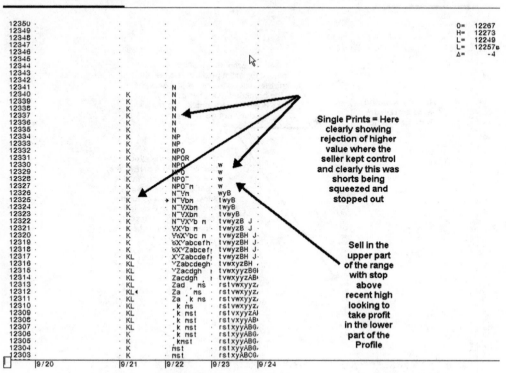

- The September 21 close to the end of day shows a late running profile in K period, which together with the N period single print and the September 23 retest and rejection at 1.2330 show a seller in control. On a daily chart this can lead to a multiday move—in this case lower and a stop close order a few ticks above the high can be used initially for risk management.

## E-mini Nasdaq—December 2004 Contract, September 8, 2004

- Figure 17.5 depicts a daily MP TPO together with the open, opening range, 50 percent of the day, close, and value range.
- The contract shown is the CME E-mini Nasdaq December futures contract.
- A neutral day is a rotational day in which the market rotates on either side of the opening range, showing that the market is distributing with buyers at the low end and sellers at the top end of the day's range. September 8 and 9 are both neutral days.
- On September 8 we see how the D and E time periods are above the B. Additionally, note how the letters M and P are below the B. The B time period is the opening range in this instance.

**FIGURE 17.5**

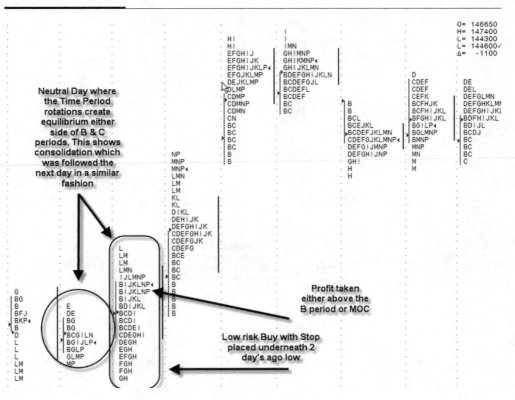

- The second example shows C, D, E, F, G, and H all below B and J, L, M, N, and P above B. The next chart continues with this example.

## E-mini Nasdaq—December 2004 Contract, September 8, 2004

- Figure 17.6 of the NQ covers the time period of September 8 through 17 and shows the move from neutral days followed by trend and then consolidation that returns back to neutral again.
- Neutral days can be the hardest to detect if they are looked at only by themselves without relation to previous days' activity. Without these additional data as a reference, what appears to be a directional move can just as easily turn around and go the other way. These days are classic for getting people to buy high and sell low.

## Emini Russell—December 2004 Contract, September 10, 2004

- Figure 17.7 depicts a daily MP TPO together with the open, opening range, 50 percent of the day, close, and value range.

**FIGURE   17.6**

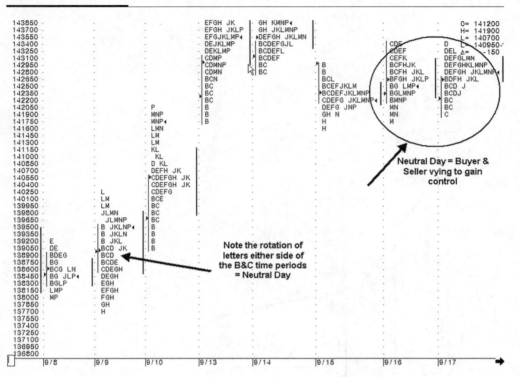

- The contract shown is the CME E-mini Russell 2000 December futures contract.
- In the first example, the Russell developed a buying tail in the B period of September 10 going right into the middle of the previous day's range. Note the lack of trade on September 9 in the middle of the MP creating a form of gap. This occurred after the initial early sell created a buying opportunity which became more evident in the C period. Profits could have been taken either at the developing point of control/high volume or MOC.
- The second example shows again on September 13 the buyer driving the market higher after having opened on a gap up and with a range extension for the first two hours through the E time period. Note that late in the day profit takers were afforded a second chance to buy this time in the N period, which traded right down to the bottom of the C period before bouncing back to midrange of the day.

## SUMMING UP MARKET PROFILE

MP can be used in all markets. It is based on the statistical analysis of time, price, and volume, and, therefore, it has stood and will continue to stand the test of time. With the advent of mar-

**F I G U R E   17.7**

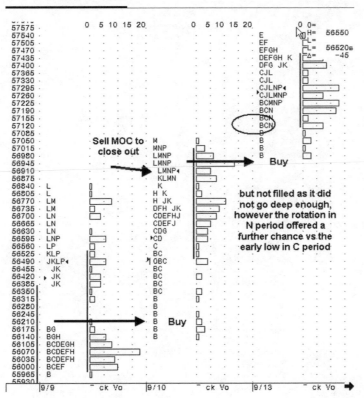

kets moving to electronic platforms, MP has suddenly taken on more meaning. Why is this? Everyone is currently trying to adjust to the change of not being able to hear from the floor brokers what the various market participants are up to. What are the locals doing? What about the commercials? Funds? The general public? As more and more markets go electronic, the footprints and actions of these groups are easier to hide, and one of the biggest advantages traders have is lost. However, by using MP, these footprints and actions are picked right back up again, giving the advantage back to the trader who learns how to use this analysis technique.

I must emphasize that this chapter on market profile is just that—a chapter on market profile. People are starting to take a renewed interest in MP, and I wanted to provide a brief introduction for those who don't know anything about it. The setups I've already discussed in this book are used independently of any MP analysis. MP is just a tool and for anyone who is familiar with this analysis technique, it can be used in conjunction with the setups already discussed. For example; if MP is pointing higher, then a trader can know nothing about MP and still take the 5-minute squeeze as it fires off long. The point of this is that everything out there—whether it is Fibonacci numbers, Bollinger Bands, Eliot Waves, Market Profile, or whatever—is just a tool. It is up to the trader to find a couple of good tools that will help them with their overall trading plan, and then establish specific setups and specific money-management parameters for their plays.

# PART THREE

## Heading Back into the Real World of Trading

C H A P T E R

# THE PREMARKET CHECKLIST—CREATING A GAME PLAN FOR THE NEXT TRADING DAY

*In a calm sea every man is a pilot.*

SPANISH PROVERB

## LIKE RUNNING A CREDIT CHECK, TO UNDERSTAND WHAT THE MARKET IS GOING TO DO IN THE FUTURE, IT HELPS TO UNDERSTAND ITS PAST

Although I base much of my daily trading decisions on specific setups, I also like to analyze how the market has recently been behaving. My goal in doing this is to be constantly aware of the path of least resistance, since I want to set up the bulk of my trades directly along that path. To that end, I have developed a quick daily checklist, and, on Sundays, a more detailed and thorough checklist. The purpose of this is to mentally prepare myself for the trading day ahead. There will be times when my analysis is totally off, but I've found that the act of mentally reviewing potential scenarios before the opening bell prepares me for just about anything. The market can be easy to trade when the going is smooth, but there are plenty of times when the market will throw a curve ball. In these situations, it's the prepared traders who consistently come out on top.

The first thing I do in this regard is to look at the markets I'm trading from a top-down approach, starting with the monthly charts and working my way down to the 60-minute charts. In this example I analyze the S&P 500, but I do this with every market that I'm following. In doing this analysis, all the charts I'm looking at have the following indicators placed on them:

1. The 8-, 21-, and 200-period exponential moving averages (EMA). In the charts shown in the pages that follow, the 8-period EMA is the thinnest line, while the 200-period EMA is the thickest line. I will also look at the 50 and 100 EMAs, but they aren't as important to me.

2. A slow stochastic with the default TradeStation settings of 14, 3, 3.

3. A MACD with the default TradeStation settings of 12, 26, 9.

4. A TTM squeeze indicator—this is the same indicator discussed in Chapter 10.

## MONTHLY CHART ANALYSIS

I always like to start off with the monthly charts. Even though I'm going to be doing most of my trading in the futures market, for the stock indexes I will look at the cash index for monthly charts. This is because there is much more history here to view, as the cash index has been around a lot longer than the stock index futures contracts.

The first thing I look at is the stochastic and MACD readings. These represent "pressures" on the market. Is the pressure more to the upside (buying pressure) or downside (selling pressure)? In general, I want to establish positions that are on the same side as the current dominant pressures in the market I am trading. My rule of thumb for this is as follows:

*The stochastic is the heads-up, and the MACD is the confirmation.*

This brings me to why I place little value on whether a stochastic is overbought or oversold. According to the stochastics in Figure 18.1, the S&P was overbought starting in the middle of 1995, and it stayed overbought until the middle of 1998—three long years. During that time this "overbought" market rallied by over 100 percent. To me, an overbought stochastic is actually a bullish sign—if the MACD is also in a buy. This brings me to my next guideline:

*What I'm looking for is MACD crossovers.*

The stochastics are valuable in that they will turn first, and therefore they can give me a heads-up that a MACD cross might occur. That said, I don't act on it unless and until a MACD crossover actually does occur.

**F I G U R E** **18.1**

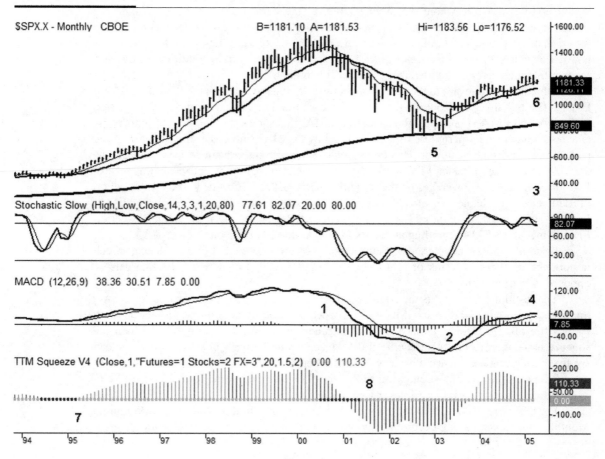

At point 1 the monthly MACD crossed over into a sell signal in May 2000, about two months after the stochastics crossed into a sell. Once this happened, the path of least resistance on the monthly S&P chart officially switched from higher to lower. This means that, for longer-term swing and position trades, I would start spending more time focusing on short setups and generally ignore long setups. I would do this until the monthly MACD went back into a crossover buy, and that happened at point 2, nearly three years later. Once this occurred, I started focusing more on long swing-trading setups and generally ignored most short trading setups. Remember, I'm talking about swing and position trades here, not day trades.

The snapshot of this chart was taken on April 5, 2005. At point 3, I can see that the stochastics are trying to roll over into a sell. What does this mean to me? It means that, potentially, the MACD *could* roll over into a sell. However, at point 4 we can see that the MACD is still in a buy. For me, this means that, for longer-term swing and position plays, I will still continue to focus on the long side *until the monthly MACD rolls over into a sell.*

The next thing I like to look at is the key moving averages. First I will look at the 200-period EMA just to see where that is in relation to the current market prices. This is the strongest moving average and represents serious support or resistance—it was enough to stop the crash of 2000, as seen at point 5. In this current snapshot of the S&P, the 200-period EMA is way down at 849.60 and isn't much of a factor in the current market conditions. However, the fact that the market is trading above this level is bullish.

What is more relevant to the short term is the relationship between the 8- and 21-period EMAs. The first thing I'm looking for is to see which moving average is on top of the other. If the 8-period EMA is on top of the 21-period EMA, this shows that the path of least resistance is higher. If the 8-period EMA is trading below the 21-period EMA, this shows that the path of least resistance is lower. This crossover is a confirming indicator for the MACD, as the MACD will fire off faster. I like to use these moving averages in my entries. In this regard, I will use these moving averages on the monthly charts just as I described how I use them on the daily charts in Chapter 16, where I will buy pullbacks or short rallies to the 8-period EMA. In this current chart, at point 6, I can see that the S&Ps are trading right at their 8-period EMA. Since the 8 EMA is trading above its 21 EMA, this is a buy zone.

I also like to look at where the 50 and 100 EMAs are located, but I don't place as much importance on them in terms of establishing a trade. I will use these more as targets as opposed to entry points.

The last thing I look at is the squeeze. Most of the time the squeeze is not doing anything, so I just glance at it to see if it is in the process of setting up a move. However, when it does fire off, as it did at point 8, this takes precedence over everything else. When the squeeze is on, then I'm in this trade until the squeeze is no longer valid. At point 7 you can see that a long squeeze occurred in early 1995. This signal fired off at the beginning stages of one of the strongest and most enduring rallies the S&P has ever seen. To that end, I like to know when a squeeze is in play. I never fight the squeeze.

For this current chart, there isn't a squeeze play that has fired off or is even developing. Monthly squeezes are a rare occurrence, with only two of them in the last 10 years.

## WEEKLY CHART ANALYSIS

Once I am done with the monthly chart, I take a quick glance at the weekly chart (see Fig. 18.2). Note that here I have switched back to the ES futures contract, because with the weekly ES chart, there is enough data to get accurate information going back a few years. All the same guidelines apply. What I'm most interested in here is what is happening as of today, April 5, 2005.

We can see at this point that the weekly chart has been in a MACD sell for about a month, and during this time the S&P has fallen by about 60 points. The stochastics at point 3 have taken it on the chin and are oversold. Remember, however, that I couldn't care less about that. What I'm interested in is the weekly MACD at point 2. Is it turning higher? No, it is still in a sell. In addition, the squeeze at point 3 has three black dots. This is not a signal, but it is a heads-up that a squeeze is in progress, and I want to pay attention to which direction this eventually fires off. Finally, I look at the moving averages at point 4, and I can see that the 8 EMA has crossed below the 21 EMA, a bearish development. We are right at the 21 EMA.

**F I G U R E   18.2**

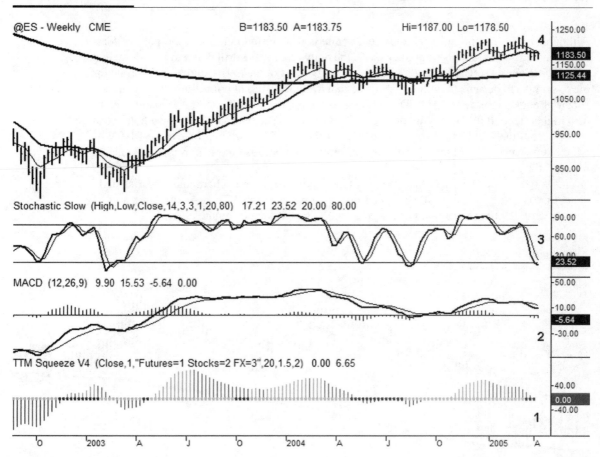

What to do here? This is what I call a *mixed market*. The monthly chart is bullish, and the weekly chart is bearish. In this situation, the sell signals on the weekly chart will create buying opportunities on the monthly chart. This is an important distinction to understand. Just because the weekly chart is in a sell doesn't mean that the world is coming to an end. Yes, it absolutely creates shorting opportunities, but the monthly charts are still in a buy, and this means that the longer-term path of least resistance is higher. I want to point this out because typically this type of situation creates many bears and many negative attitudes, because a weekly sell signal can generate a devastating beating to bulls. But, in the bigger scope of things, I'm looking for the weekly chart to turn higher and move back in line with the monthly chart. The best trading opportunities occur when the weekly charts line back up with the monthly charts.

For setups, the weekly chart is still in a sell, meaning that short setups are appropriate. However, before I would set anything up, I would want to first look at the daily charts to see if the pressures on this timeframe are lower or higher.

## DAILY CHART ANALYSIS

Although I will use the monthly and weekly charts to help me determine the path of least resistance for swing and position trades, it is the daily chart that I drill down to in order to get my specific entry levels. Figure 18.3 shows the daily chart of the S&Ps, and now it is time for me to set up a trade. The first thing I notice is that the stochastics at point 1 are turning higher. I then of course look to the MACD at point 2 to see what it is doing, and it is also trying to turn higher, though it hasn't quite done it yet. At point 3 I see that the S&Ps have held a test of support at the 200 EMA. However, at point 4 the 8 EMA is trading below the 21 EMA, which is negative. The squeeze also doesn't help me out because there aren't any signals on it at this time.

Okay, so now I have a bullish monthly chart, a bearish weekly chart, and a bearish daily chart that is trying to turn bullish. Can I do anything with this? There really isn't a clear answer here. It's time to keep on drilling down. Let's visit the 60-minute chart.

**F I G U R E   18.3**

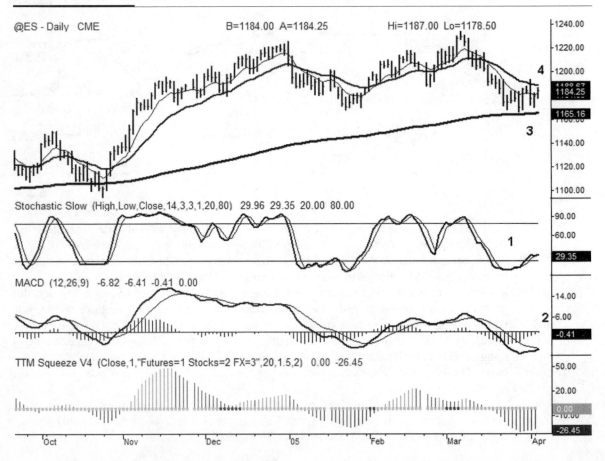

## 60-MINUTE CHART ANALYSIS

The 60-minute chart reveals a bullish stochastic at point 1, and when I check the MACD at point 2, I can see that the MACD is also pointing higher, which is bullish (see Fig. 18.4). In looking at the moving averages at point 3, I can see that the 8 EMA is trading above the 21 EMA, which is bullish, but the market is below its 200 EMA, which is bearish. Is there a trade here? Take a moment before reading on and figure out what you would do in this situation. I want you to take a trade based on what we've just talked about. Would you go long or short? What's your entry level? What's your stop? What's your target? Spend a few minutes on this before moving on to the next paragraph.

Today is Tuesday, April 5, 2005. Here is what I'm going to set up for tomorrow, Wednesday, April 6, 2005. I'm going to set up a buy order at 1183.50, right above the 8-period EMA. Since this is a 60-minute chart, I'm going to use a target of ½ of 1 percent,

**F I G U R E   18.4**

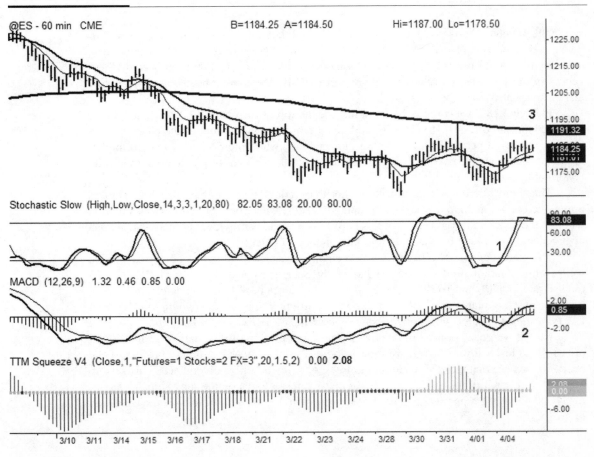

which is 5.9175. I will round this up to 6.00, which would make the target 1189.50. This is right below the 200 EMA, which is a good place for a target. If the 200 EMA had been below my target, then I would not take the trade. My stop will be 2.95875 (¼ of 1 percent), which I will round up to 3.00. This makes my stop 1180.50. This is just below the 21 EMA. If we get up ¼ of 1 percent in the play (three points to 1186.50), I will move my stop up to the 21 EMA and trail it from there. If this looks familiar, this is the propulsion play described in Chapter 16.

For my swing plays, I want to play them in the direction of the path of least resistance according to the MACD. The monthly charts are higher, and the daily chart is about to turn higher. Two of the three timeframes are pointing higher. Then when I drill down to the 60-minute chart, I see one of the setups that I utilize staring me right in the face. So I set it up. Simple as that.

However, before we get too excited about a potential play, let's double-check the path of least resistance by looking at two more charts.

## DAILY RSI CHART ANALYSIS

While the previous charts give me an idea of the overall buying or selling pressure, as well as give me an indication of key levels I need to be watching out for during the next trading day, there is still a piece missing. What I want to see next is if there are any bullish or bearish divergences in the seven-period relative strength index (RSI). These are a heads-up to a pending market reversal.

In Figure 18.5 we can see that at point 1 at the top of the chart, the S&P made a nice rally into the end of 2004. However, if we look at point 1 at the bottom of the chart, we can see that the seven-period RSI was making lower lows, while the S&P was making higher highs. This is a massive bearish divergence and essentially is a heads-up that the current rally is not going to last.

That's great, but how does a person enter that trade? That is a great question. Think a minute before going on to the next paragraph and decide what you would do in this situation with the tools you've learned so far in this book. The market is rallying, but there is a bearish divergence. I'm looking for the market to fall—how do I enter?

There are a couple of different ways to enter. Plays described in this book that worked well in this situation are discussed in Chapters 8 (Scalper Buys and Sells), 11 (Bricks), 15 (HOLP and LOHP), and 16 (Propulsion Plays). This comes back to the fundamental basis of my whole trading plan—*even if I feel 100 percent sure that the market is going to roll over, I will not establish a short position until one of my setups generates a short signal.*

Now if we got to point 2 in the upper right-hand portion of the chart, we can see that prices made lower lows. Then if we look to point 2 in the lower right-hand portion of the chart, we can see that the RSI made higher lows, creating a bullish divergence. This sets up a potential reversal in the markets, meaning that I want to focus on the long side. This confirms that the play we just set up in the last section with the 60-minute charts is the right way to go.

**F I G U R E   18.5**

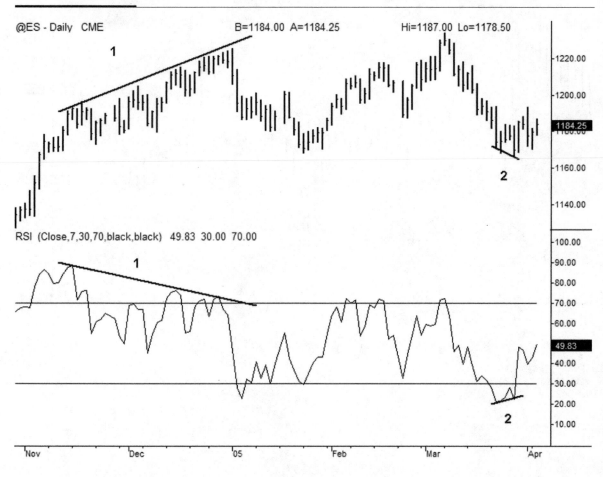

## 60-MINUTE RSI CHART ANALYSIS

On this 60-minute chart (see Fig. 18.6) there are two bullish divergences in place within the current market action. I've marked one of them—can you find the other one?

The one I've marked shows the RSI making higher highs, yet prices have not made higher highs. This is bullish. The RSI is essentially leading the market higher. The second divergence takes place when the ES made lower lows on April 1, yet the RSI made higher lows. This is a bullish divergence and also positive. After looking at both these RSI charts, we can clearly see that the long side is the path of least resistance in the short term.

What if I'm wrong? What if news about oil hits tomorrow, driving it higher by $5 a barrel and that kills the stock market? Then I'm stopped out. Next trade. This is about putting the odds in your favor, not guarantees.

**F I G U R E   18.6**

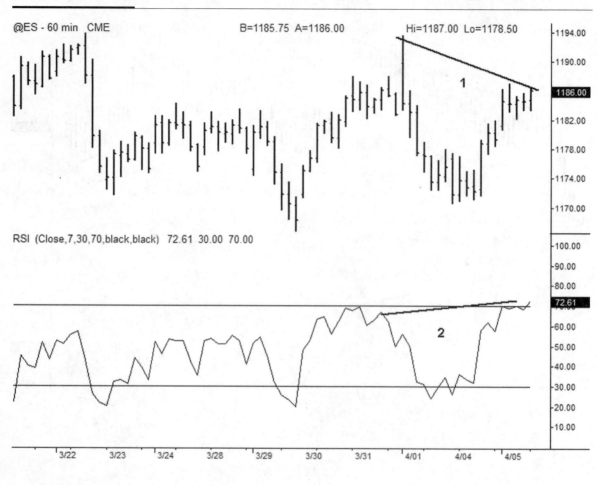

## INDEX RADAR SCREEN ALERT

Looking at one index in a couple of different timeframes can be a handful to track. But what happens if you are looking at all these different charts and timeframes for three to four different indexes, a couple of sectors, and a handful of stocks? It can get confusing. However, knowing what's going on across multiple trading instruments and multiple timeframes gives a trader a much better feel for the overall markets. To that end, I've put together the following table to help me keep it all straight (see Fig. 18.7).

This table gives me the opportunity to write in my chart interpretations in an easy-to-read, take-it-all-in-at-a-glance worksheet. With the key indexes that I'm viewing on the far left, I can then go through the stochastics, MACD, RSI, and squeeze on all the different indexes in all the different timeframes. For stochastics and MACD, I have M, W, and D as

| Index | Close | Change | STOCH | | | MACD | | | RSI (7) | | | Squeeze | | |
|---|---|---|---|---|---|---|---|---|---|---|---|---|---|---|
| | | | M | W | D | M | W | D | W | D | S | W | D | S |
| DOW | 10421.14 | +16.84 | S | S | B | B | S | B | S | B | B | N | N | N |
| S&P 500 | 1176.12 | +3.20 | S | S | B | B | S | B | S | B | B | R | N | N |
| OEX 100 | 559.49 | +2.00 | S | S | B | B | S | B | S | B | B | R | N | R |
| NDX 100 | 1476.72 | +7.37 | S | S | B | B | S | B | S | S | B | N | S | R |
| Naz Comp | 1991.07 | +6.26 | S | S | B | B | S | B | S | S | B | N | N | R |
| Rus 2000 | 613.76 | +2.21 | B | S | B | B | S | B | S | S | B | N | N | S |

headings for *monthly chart*, *weekly chart*, and *daily chart*. For the RSI and squeeze I have W, D, and S as headings for *weekly chart*, *daily chart*, and *sixty-minute chart*. I can then go through and see at a glance that the monthly and daily MACDs are in buys across the board, and the 60-minute RSIs are also in buys (as they are showing bullish divergences) as well as some of the daily RSIs. For the squeezes, I have N, R, S, and B representing *neutral*, *red dot*, *sell*, and *buy*. Neutral just means that there currently isn't a signal in place, nor is a squeeze even in a heads-up. The red dot (which is the black dot in this book because of the black and white charts) means that a squeeze play is setting up, but hasn't yet fired. Whenever I see a market that is in R mode, I start paying close attention because I want to see when it fires off. Finally, after it does fire off, if it's a long squeeze, that is a B for buy, and if it is a short squeeze, that is an S for sell.

It may seem like a lot of work, but it doesn't take long to do. The monthly and weekly charts do not change very often—most of the attention is spent on the daily and 60-minute charts. I update this table each evening after the stock markets are closed, and post the results in my daily newsletters. One of the reasons I started sending out newsletters in 1999 was that it forced me to keep these tables updated each and every day, no matter what else was going on in my life.

By having everything in place, I can see when one index is breaking down before all the others, like the NASDAQ did in early 2005. When one index starts to buck an overall trend, that is a heads-up that the rest are setting up to roll over as well.

## SECTORS AND KEY STOCKS RADAR SCREEN ALERT

This radar screen alert is the same as for the indexes, except that this will have key sectors and key stocks that I'm watching (see Fig. 18.8). It is set up just the same and works just the same. When markets turn, you can see it first in the key sectors and stocks that make up the index. Also, if I'm looking for trading ideas and I can see that the semiconductors, for example, have just fired off a short squeeze, it is fairly easy to figure out where I should go looking for short plays.

Both these radar screens are included in the daily newsletter I write. Traders who want to do these themselves will benefit from the exercise. Traders who simply don't have time or like to have a second opinion can get these daily readings from my own research.

**F I G U R E   18.8**

| Sector | Close | Change | STOCH | | | MACD | | | RSI (7) | | | Squeeze | | |
|---|---|---|---|---|---|---|---|---|---|---|---|---|---|---|
| | | | M | W | D | M | W | D | W | D | S | W | D | S |
| Banks | 95.91 | +0.07 | S | S | B | B | S | B | S | B | S | N | N | N |
| Brokers | 145.17 | -1.05 | B | S | B | S | S | B | B | B | S | N | N | N |
| Semis | 409.42 | -1.80 | S | S | B | S | S | B | B | S | B | N | N | R |
| PC Tech | 674.78 | +2.02 | B | S | B | B | S | B | B | S | S | N | N | N |
| Retail | 428.64 | +4.82 | B | S | B | B | S | B | B | B | B | N | N | R |
| IBM | 90.32 | -0.12 | B | S | B | B | S | B | B | B | B | R | N | N |
| GE | 35.29 | -0.18 | B | S | B | B | S | B | S | B | B | R | R | R |
| MER | 56.29 | +0.34 | B | S | B | S | S | B | B | B | S | N | N | R |

# THE KEY TO READING DAILY VOLUME

I like to watch the daily volume in the cash indexes to see how much activity there is going on behind the moves. Each day I take the volume and key it into an Excel spreadsheet like the one shown in Figure 18.9.

What I'm looking for is the strength or lack of strength behind the move. If the markets push higher, I've got to see two things in order to validate the move: First, the volume has to be greater than it was the day before. Second, the volume has to be greater than the 50-day average volume. The bigger the difference in these numbers, the better the odds that the move is the real deal and the start of something big. Conversely, if the markets have a big day to the upside and the volume is lighter than that of the previous day and lighter than the 50-day average volume, then the more trouble I have believing in the move. The lower the actual volume in relation to these other numbers, the greater the chance that the move was a mere probe and is going to reverse violently at the drop of a hat.

Think of it this way—a car going uphill on a full tank of gas has a much better shot at making it than a car that is running on fumes. High-volume days show the markets riding on a full tank of gas, while low-volume days show the markets riding on fumes.

# THE KEY PRICE LEVELS TO KNOW EACH AND EVERY TRADING DAY

There is a specific set of numbers that I want to be aware of every day, because these are critical in helping me to establish trades and staying on the right side of the market (see Fig. 18.10).

I like to follow most of these price levels in the S&P futures, just because it is the biggest and broadest index and tells me a lot about what is going on in the market. However, I also like to do the same in the Dow, NASDAQ, and Russell futures. For the sake of this example, we focus mostly on the S&Ps, but bring in the other indexes for part of it as well.

The first thing I want to look at is today's close in relation to the prior three-day highs and lows. Did today's price eclipse either of these levels or was it contained within these lev-

**F I G U R E  18.9**

| Volume | NYSE Market Reading | | | Nasdaq Market Reading | | |
|---|---|---|---|---|---|---|
| | NYSE | Day Before | Percent | Nasdaq | Day Before | Percent |
| UP | 1,223,832,000 | 944,072,000 | 29.63% | 1,405,734,000 | 1,147,448,000 | 22.51% |
| DOWN | 252,459,000 | 494,847,000 | -48.98% | 238,069,000 | 808,448,000 | -70.55% |
| Unchanged | 12,077,000 | 33,701,000 | -64.16% | 20,243,000 | 26,933,000 | -24.84% |
| Total | 1,488,368,000 | 1,472,620,000 | 1.07% | 1,664,046,000 | 1,982,829,000 | -16.08% |
| 50 Day Avg* | 1,502,598,000 | 1,502,598,000 | -0.95% | 2,010,802,050 | 2,023,950,200 | -17.24% |

**F I G U R E  18.10**

| S&P Futures Prior Three Days Highs/Lows + Monthly & Weekly Levels | |
|---|---|
| TODAY'S CLOSE | 1050.50 |
| Prior 3 Days HIGH | 1058.75 |
| Prior 3 Days LOW | 1043.25 |
| Break and hold these levels today? | Broke highs intraday, failed |
| Close: Upper/Middle/Lower 3rd Today? | Lower |
| Prior Week High/Low + Current Level? | 1064.50/1043.25 Mid: Neutral |
| Prior Month High/Low + Current Level? | 1055.75/995.00 Mid: Neutral |
| Low of High Week (week ending 10/17) | 1043.25   Above: Bullish |
| Low of High Month (mo ending 10/31) | 995.00  Above: Bullish |
| Number of days in current trend | 1 day down |
| Key Gaps on the S&P Futures:<br>9:30 a.m. – 4:15 p.m. Eastern | 1049.50 on 11/3<br>1030.75 on 10/28<br>994.00 on 9/30 |
| Key Gaps on the DOW Futures:<br>9:30 a.m. – 4:15 p.m. Eastern | No Gap on 11/3<br>9587 on 10/28<br>9258 on 9/30 |
| Key Gaps on the Nasdaq Futures:<br>9:30 a.m. – 4:15 p.m. Eastern | 1418.00 on 11/3<br>1377.50 on 10/28<br>1338.50 on 10/2<br>No Gap on 9/30 |

els? If it eclipsed either of these levels, then we have a trending market. If it stayed contained in these levels, then we have a trading range. It is very important to always understand what type of market environment you're currently in, and this is one of the easiest and most accurate ways to tell. If today is Thursday and the close is 1050.50, then you just look at a daily chart and review the highs and lows for Wednesday, Tuesday, and Monday. Did Thursday's close make it past these levels, or was it contained within these levels?

I also like to note where the close was in relation to the day's range. Did the market close at the top or its range? If so, there is a good chance for upward continuation tomorrow. Did it close near the bottom of its range? Or did it close in the middle—indicating massive indecision.

Next I want to see where the highs and lows are located for the prior day, prior week, and prior month. These are all important support and resistance levels, and I want to know where they are sitting in relation to current market prices. I like to note if we are trading above any of these levels, which is bullish, or below any of these levels, which is bearish. If we are stuck in the middle, then I call that neutral.

After this I'm looking at HOLP and LOHP levels (as discussed in Chapter 15). Any moves above or below these key levels are a major opportunity. I also like to note whether we are trading above or below these key levels, because that is also bullish or bearish.

The next number I want to know is the number of days in the current trend. The reason for this is that many trends reverse after three days, so I want to be aware if we are in the third day of a trend. Also, after six to seven consecutive days markets just lose their gas and fail to move any further. I want to know about this so I'm not the last one jumping on the bandwagon.

Finally, I want to know where all the open gaps are sitting. Remember in Chapter 6 when we talk about open gaps filling within 5–10 trading days? It's important to know where those gaps are located.

## PIVOT NUMBERS, OF COURSE

We have talk extensively about pivots in Chapter 7, so I'm not going to explain again why I look at them. However, I do like to have them handy so I can look at them before the trading day. By placing them in this easy-to-use Excel spreadsheet (see Fig. 18.11), I can quickly glance at these levels and see if any of them line up with the key price levels we just talked about. Is the daily pivot also lined up with an open gap? That is important because that level will be particularly strong on that trading day.

In addition to the daily pivots, I'm looking for confluence among the weekly and monthly pivots with my list of key numbers (see Fig. 18.12).

## KEY SENTIMENT READINGS

We talk about the put-call ratios in Chapter 5. I like to record where it closes on the day, as well as note where the 10-day moving average of the put-call ratio is trading. While the daily number is good for gauging market direction on that particular trading day, the 10-day moving average pinpoints major market turns. The following chart (Fig. 18.13) from Decision Point shows the key turning points in the markets based on the reading of the 10-day moving average on the put-call ratio. This is data that you can get from TradeStation, but I just subscribe to www.decisionpoint.com and get it there. It's $20 a month and provides nearly every key historical technical study on the planet, and it's where I spend a lot of quality time each weekend.

FIGURE  18.11

| Daily Pivots & Midpoints | | | |
|---|---|---|---|
| | S&P Futures | DOW Futures | Nasdaq Futures | |
| High | 1125.00 | 10315 | 1435.50 | High |
| Low | 1109.50 | 10153 | 1408.50 | Low |
| Close | 1122.50 | 10278 | 1431.50 | Close |
| R3 | 1144.00 | 10506.33 | 1468.83 | R3 |
| Mid | 1139.25 | 10458.50 | 1460.50 | Mid |
| R2 | 1134.50 | 10410.67 | 1452.17 | R2 |
| Mid | 1131.50 | 10377.50 | 1447.00 | Mid |
| R1 | 1128.50 | 10344.33 | 1441.83 | R1 |
| Mid | 1123.75 | 10296.50 | 1433.50 | Mid |
| Pivot | 1119.00 | 10248.67 | 1425.17 | Pivot |
| Mid | 1116.00 | 10215.50 | 1420.00 | Mid |
| S1 | 1113.00 | 10182.33 | 1414.83 | S1 |
| Mid | 1108.25 | 10134.50 | 1406.50 | Mid |
| S2 | 1103.50 | 10086.67 | 1398.17 | S2 |
| Mid | 1100.50 | 10053.50 | 1393.00 | Mid |
| S3 | 1097.50 | 10020.33 | 1387.83 | S3 |

Figure 18.14 shows that whenever the put-call ratio gets near 1.00, this excessive bear-ishness in the form of put buying puts a bottom into the market. All these shorts then spend the next several weeks frantically covering their positions. The opposite is also true. When the crowd gets frothy and overly bullish, driving the PC ratio to 0.70, the market is overloaded with bulls and either halts its advance or rolls over.

I also like to look at AAII investor sentiment, because this is a good gauge of how traders are feeling about the current market. This is also a contrarian indicator. When there are too many bears, look for the markets to bottom out and reverse. When there are too many bulls, look for markets to take a breather or roll over.

Figure 18.15 is a chart is from April 5, 2005, the day I'm writing this. You can see that we are at excessive bearish levels. This tells me that the market is looking to bottom out and starting to beat up on all the shorts.

The other item I have listed in Figure 18.13 is the daily arms index reading, which is shown in Figure 18.15. This is the indicator we discuss in Chapter 5, and I'm looking for read-ings of over 2.0 or under 0.50 as key action signals.

F I G U R E   18.12

| Weekly Pivots | | | |
|---|---|---|---|
| | S&P Futures | DOW Futures | Nasdaq Futures | |
| High | 1159.00 | 10634 | 1485.00 | High |
| Low | 1101.00 | 10070 | 1398.00 | Low |
| Close | 1118.00 | 10205 | 1431.50 | Close |
| R3 | 1209.00 | 11100.00 | 1565.33 | R3 |
| R2 | 1184.00 | 10867.00 | 1525.17 | R2 |
| R1 | 1151.00 | 10536.00 | 1478.33 | R1 |
| Pivot | 1126.00 | 10303.00 | 1438.17 | Pivot |
| S1 | 1093.00 | 9972.00 | 1391.33 | S1 |
| S2 | 1068.00 | 9739.00 | 1351.17 | S2 |
| S3 | 1035.00 | 9408.00 | 1304.33 | S3 |

| Monthly Pivots | | | |
|---|---|---|---|
| | S&P Futures | DOW Futures | Nasdaq Futures | |
| High | 1158.75 | 10750 | 1525.50 | High |
| Low | 1122.00 | 10417 | 1452.00 | Low |
| Close | 1144.50 | 10582 | 1471.50 | Close |
| R3 | 1198.25 | 11082.00 | 1587.50 | R3 |
| R2 | 1178.50 | 10916.00 | 1556.50 | R2 |
| R1 | 1161.50 | 10749.00 | 1514.00 | R1 |
| Pivot | 1141.75 | 10583.00 | 1483.00 | Pivot |
| S1 | 1124.75 | 10416.00 | 1440.50 | S1 |
| S2 | 1105.00 | 10250.00 | 1409.50 | S2 |
| S3 | 1088.00 | 10083.00 | 1367.00 | S3 |

F I G U R E   18.13

| Key Sentiment Readings | Reading | Rating |
|---|---|---|
| Today's Put/Call Close | 0.78 | Neutral |
| 10 Day MA of CBOE Put/Call Ratio | 0.74 | Neutral |
| 10 Day MA of OEX Put/Call Ratio | 0.97 | Neutral |
| Investors Intelligence Advisor Sentiment | Bulls 56.30% | Bears 21.40% |
| AAII Investor Sentiment | Bulls 58.00% | Bears 17.00% |
| Daily Arms Index | 1.20 | Neutral |

F I G U R E   18.14

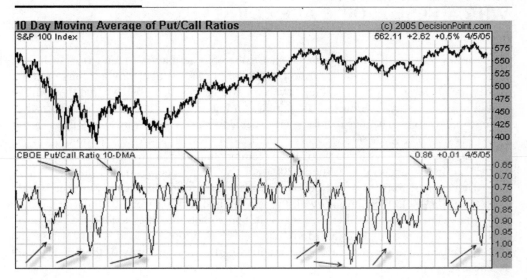

F I G U R E   18.15

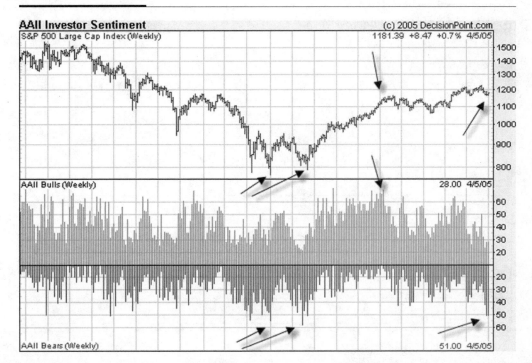

# IT'S A GOOD IDEA TO KNOW
# WHAT THESE PEOPLE ARE DOING

The last key number in this series is the NYSE member net buy/sell numbers, which I get from www.decisionpoint.com. This shows whether NYSE members are net long or short. If they are net long, it is because they have very strong reasons to believe that they will be able to distribute their holdings to the public at a higher price. If they are net short, they have strong reasons to believe that they will be able to buy back their inventory at a cheaper price. These people make a lot of money, and I like to follow what they are doing.

Figure 18.16 shows a couple of huge readings that came into play over the past few years. The first was during the March 2003 bottom. These people loaded the boat with a record amount of longs. Lo and behold the markets moved significantly higher shortly thereafter. They sold their inventory all the way up and then reloaded the boat in October 2003 just before the next leg higher. Finally, in September 2004 they loaded the boat again with a record number of long positions. The markets chopped around for six weeks and then rocketed into 2005. If these people are loading the boat one way or the other, I want to know about it.

**F I G U R E   18.16**

## MISCELLANEOUS ITEMS

The final things I want to know about are any key economic and earnings reports that are coming out on the day. I'm not concerned with every company that is reporting, but I want to know if a big one like MSFT or IBM is coming out with numbers after the close. I also want to know when key economic reports are going to be hitting the tape. There are two main reasons for this. First, if traders are waiting for a key earnings or an economic report, they will generally stand aside to see how the market reacts. This means that the markets are going to be choppy, and I don't want to be trying to catch trends intraday if the markets are going to be choppy. On these days I will focus on fading pivots levels and fading extreme tick readings—these are the best plays I've found to follow on days where the trading is light and choppy. The second thing I'm looking for isn't the actual number itself, *but how the markets react to it*. The number, whether it is earnings or economic, has no importance. What is important is if the market sells off on the news, rallies on the news, or ignores the news.

The market is efficient at pricing in information before it ever comes out. In addition, large firms have access to the same research as the government, and they hire an army of economists to figure out what the numbers are going to be before they are announced. These reports mean little in the grand scheme of things because they get priced in well before the actual number is released.

The moral of the story? Find a couple of setups and stick to them and don't get sucked into the "waiting for the next report" game. Just because it's hyped on CNBC doesn't mean it's a good idea to place a lot of importance on it.

## WHAT DOES YOUR MOTHER THINK?

My final piece of research has to do with random comments I hear from people who are not in the industry. A classic example is a recent conversation I had with my mother, who mentioned that she had read about eBay in *Business Week*. Was it a good time to buy? Normally in situations like this I just run out and look for a short setup on the stock, but, because it was my mother, I told her I would hold off on buying it for now. Then I shorted it. A few weeks later it got killed on earnings.

Anything that is just now hitting the ears of the nontrading public is a major signal. This typically means that the people who are usually the last to know are thinking about finally getting in. I can't think of a better topping signal in my arsenal of trading tools.

As I'm writing this, there is this same flurry of activity going on in real estate. More and more random people are talking about things like buying parcels of land sight unseen from out of the back of magazines because "real estate is doing so well." It's almost at the same ferocity as when Beanie Babies topped out and crashed back to earth. Pretty soon we are going to start seeing major magazine covers talking about how everyone is making money in real estate. Shortly thereafter, prices will start to soften. And no, it's not different this time.

## SUMMING UP THE PREMARKET CHECKLIST

I've got a quote on my wall that says, "Fortune favors the prepared mind." There is a big difference between getting lucky on one trade and being able to consistently make money in the markets. There is also a delicate balance between being prepared and overanalyzing, but the basic set of tools and numbers discussed in this chapter will give traders a huge leg up without drowning them in barrels of information.

All this data is available to every trader. It's a good practice to take the time to go through and line up this information each day. If you don't have the time or would like supplemental information, this is the same routine I go through each evening. I post the same daily checklist I've reviewed in this chapter in a newsletter that comes out 5 evenings per week (each night the stock market is open). In addition to this information, I also post the swing trades I'm setting up the next trading day, with the exact entry, exit, target, and stop loss levels. There is one newsletter that focuses on the stock indexes, and has plays in the stocks, options and futures markets. There is also a second newsletter that focuses on the forex markets.

In addition to these key levels, I also include a nightly video embedded into the newsletter that records my computer screen. With this technology, I'm able to flip through ny charts and make comments, discussing the way the vaious markets are setting up and talking about what I think is going to happen—and the orders I am placing—for the next trading day. This technology is great as it allows a person to look over my shoulder as I'm doing my research each night. I don't rehearse—it's all recorded live so you get my first impressions as well as the coughs and telephone interruptions. A trader can just click on the video link, turn up the speakers on their computer, and watch and listen.

For information on the newsletters, you can visit the following websites.

- www.tradethemarkets.com
- www.knowthemarkets.com
- www.johnfcarter.com
- www.masteringthetrade.com

It's probable that all of these websites will be tied in together by the time this book comes out. As I'm writing this, we are in talks with forex brokers who are interested in picking up the forex newletter subscription costs for clients who trade through them. As this is "in the works" and not yet finalized, we thus have multiple websites "prepared." Information is also available toll free at 888-898-8118 within the United States and +1 512-266-8659 for callers outside of the United States.

# CHAPTER 19

## THE TRADER'S
## BUSINESS PLAN

*No one ever won a war by dying for his country. He won it by making the other poor dumb bastard die for his country.*

—GENERAL GEORGE S. PATTON

### WHO GETS TO THE WORLD SERIES—THE TEAM WITH A PLAN OR THE TEAM THAT DECIDES TO WING IT?

A two-foot-long Arrowana is a voracious predator fish. A single-minded creature, it has one basic rule of thumb that it follows each and every day: If it thinks something will fit into its mouth, it will eat it. When traders visit my office to watch me trade, they are often surprised to learn that their first assignment is to feed Martha, my two-foot-long pet Arrowana. They have to take the net, dip it into the feeder tank filled with goldfish, and choose a victim. Martha is used to this routine by now and begins to shimmer with excitement and anticipation. The goldfish is released. The water boils and churns as the predator lunges, and a few seconds later all that remains of Nemo is a few scales and a bit of fin. Steve Patrow, a visiting trader, summed it up succinctly when he said, "That just seems really cruel."

"Yep," I replied. "Almost as cruel as sending a trader out into the markets without a fully developed trading plan." A trader who is trying to make a living in the markets without a fully developed trading plan is in exactly the same position as the goldfish. Whereas one is merely a meal for an Arrowana, the other is routinely preyed upon by professional traders. At least with the goldfish the pain is over quickly. Traders without a plan can stretch out their torment for years.

My first trading plan was created in 1993, eight years after I started trading. It was a one-page document that has evolved over the years into the current fifteen-page plan that I use today. This evolved out of experience and from having other traders share their plans with me, most notably Mark Cook, who utilizes one of the most detailed plans I've ever studied. I update this plan annually. My plan expanded over the years as I realized the following truths:

- A superior per-trade tracking system had to be set in place.
- A specific day-to-day money management system had to be set in place.
- A methodology for holding specific trading setups accountable for performance had to be set in place.
- A reward and punishment system for myself had to be set in place.
- My plan had to evolve and take into account the setups and markets that best fit my personality.
- Not only did I have to incorporate trading into my plan, but I had to incorporate it into my whole life to really make the plan work. One reality of trading is that this is a profession that can take over a person and dominate their life. It is important to recognize this and bring a more holistic approach to your overall trading plan. This keeps a trader in the game for the longer term, helping to prevent burnout—a common occurrence in the trading world.

Every trader I've worked with has mentioned that the comprehensive business plan I make them write has been the deciding factor in their own performance. "It was when I turned the corner," is a common phrase I've heard used to describe the action of writing out such a detailed plan. What's in the plan? I'll show you the questions I make myself answer every year and take you through them step by step. After I'm done with this, I'll share a plan that was developed by one of the traders I've worked with. What follows are the questions and excerpts of the answers from my actual trading plan for 2005.

## WHY AM I TRADING AGAIN THIS YEAR?

The first question I ask myself each year is, why am I trading again this year? Although this might seem obvious, it is important to deliberately choose this occupation over everything else that's available out there. This is applicable to whether you are trading part time while you're holding down another job or are trading full time. Here is my answer:

The main reason I'm going to continue trading in 2005 is that I enjoy the financial independence and freedom that trading has to offer. I also love the fact that I can do this from anywhere, because I don't like to be tied down to any one location. I've never been good at taking orders, so I appreciate that I don't have a boss whom I have to placate. I enjoy meeting other traders because they are the most random, eclectic, crazy, and interesting people on the planet. I enjoy the mental challenge and stimulation that comes from trading, and I know if I stopped, I would miss it.

## HAPPY WIFE, HAPPY LIFE

This is where I take stock of everything else that is going on in my life and how it might affect my trading. By doing this, I figured out when I needed to hire my first assistant, when I needed to bring on another partner, and whatever else needed to be done to streamline my life for trading. Here's what I wrote down for 2005:

I have a lot of activities going on in my life besides trading. I'm actively involved in real estate investing, coin collecting, and traveling, and I have a lot of stuff going on with my Web site and other financial market-related programs. I also have a lovely wife who expects me to notice that she is a living and breathing human being, and I've realized how important it is to include her in my plans and keep her involved in the process, as well as being able to "leave trading at the door" and spend quality time with her. It's good for her, it's good for me, and it's good for us. Happy wife, happy life.

My wife and I are expecting our first child, and we are considering moving from Boston to Austin, Texas, where most of our family is located. I know that trading is my main occupation, and the only way I can continue with these other things is if I'm making profits from my trading. It is possible that I will drop some of these other activities if they become a distraction. I will compartmentalize and focus on trading during trading hours. To help with this, I have someone who runs the day-to-day operations of the Web site, have a cook and maid to handle all routine daily chores around the house and office, and someone else who helps manage my other investments. I will focus on writing newsletters that only pertain to my own trading, instead of writing about what I think other people want to know about. These newsletters are mostly for me to help force myself to clarify my own research and continue to find new trading ideas. Do not try to please all the people all the time.

I won't try to day trade if I am traveling or on vacation. It's okay to have swing trades on and manage existing positions, as long as I have a stop and target in place and I don't try to "out think" the position intraday. If I have distractions going on, I will not trade. Get rid of the distractions first. Examples include having uninvited guests over, morning phone calls, people instant messaging you in the morning asking about a trade, and so forth. Take care of the distractions. Ignore phone calls and instant messages until after 11:00 a.m. Eastern. Or better yet, turn them off. Don't be accommodating just to be nice. The path to hell is paved with good intentions.

## WHAT MARKETS AM I GOING TO TRADE?

This is where I lay out all the markets I'm going to trade. Beginning traders should be focusing on only a few markets. Once a trader decides, he or she should stick with those markets for a year instead of looking for the "next great thing."

For day trades, I'm going to trade the mini-sized Dow (YM), E-mini S&Ps (ES), E-mini Russell (ER), 30-year bonds (U.S.), and the major currency pairs in the forex markets. For swing trades, I will trade the E-mini Nasdaq (NQ), 10-year notes (TY), corn (C), wheat (W), soybeans (S), crude oil (CL), gold (GC), silver (SI), single stock futures, individual stocks, and stock options, in addition to swing trades in the major currency pairs in the forex markets I will allocate my total trading funds as follows:

- 25% intraday trades (ES, YM, ER, US, forex markets)
- 25% swing trades on futures (NQ, TY, C, W, S, CL, GC, SI, single stock futures, forex markets)
- 25% swing trades on stocks
- 25% swing trades on stock options

## WHY THESE MARKETS? WHAT SPECIFIC TRADING STRATEGIES AM I GOING TO USE?

This is a really important part of the plan. Traders should have a specific setup for each market they are trading. This way the setup can be tracked for performance. Each setup should be independent of itself. This means a trader could have a short on the YM for a gap play and a long on the ES for a pivot play simultaneously, and then track the performance of each setup separately.

For intraday trades, I will use the following plays:

- YM: gap plays, tick fades, and pivot plays
- ES: squeeze plays, scalper buys and sells, and brick plays
- ER: squeeze plays and pivot plays
- US: break of the high/low 15-minute bar, squeeze plays
- Forex Markets: box plays, squeeze plays, break of the high/low 15-minute bar

For swing trades, I will use the following plays:

- All futures and forex plays: daily squeeze plays, box plays, break of the high/low day, 8/21 EMA for swings (for single stock futures)
- All stock plays: daily squeeze plays, box plays, break of the high/low day, 8/21 EMA for swings
- All stock options plays: daily squeeze plays, break of the high/low day, 8/21 EMA for swings

The key with this is that if I don't have a specific setup in one of these markets, then I'm not taking a trade. I just wait until something sets up.

## HOW MUCH MONEY AM I GOING TO ALLOCATE TO EACH TRADING STRATEGY AND SETUP?

Determining how much money to allocate to each trading strategy and setup is, of course, critical. The key is to find an allocation that doesn't cause any stress, allows the chance for a trade to do its work, and won't violate any daily drawdown rules. One of the biggest problems I see with newer traders is that they are trading way too big in relation to their account size. Trading 10 lots on a $10,000 account is like introducing your mistress to your wife. Yes, you can do it, but that doesn't make it a good idea. (Luckily my wife has a great sense of humor.)

The following allocations are based on a per $100,000 basis. The number of contracts or the position size to be used are as follows:

| Trading Vehicle | Intraday Futures/Forex Each $100,000 | Swing Futures/Forex Each $100,000 | Stocks Each $100,000 | Stock Options Each $100,000 |
|---|---|---|---|---|
| YM, ES, US | 10 contracts | | | |
| ER | 5 contracts | | | |
| NQ, TY, C, W | | 5 contracts | | |
| S, GC, SI, QM | | 3 contracts | | |
| Forex | 8 contracts | 2 contracts | | |
| SSFs | | 10 contracts | | |
| Stocks | | | 15% of account toward each position | |
| Options | | | | 15% of account toward each position |

These numbers will seem conservative to some of you and aggressive to others. I've seen traders take a $100,000 account and start trading 60 ES contracts at a time. Pretty soon they are trading six contracts, because that's all the money they have left to trade. The goal with this plan is to make a living, not a killing.

## WHAT EXECUTION METHODS WILL I BE USING? WHAT PARAMETERS?

This is where I decide my primary execution method. Am I scaling in? Scaling out? Getting all in and all out? What is my risk-to-reward ratio? This is a lengthy part of the plan as I will write down sample plays for all my categories. I'm not going to do that with all my plays here, but I will spell out my parameters for gap plays.

For all of my intraday plays, I will get in all at once and scale out as the position goes my way. The target on the first half of my play will be small, the equivalent of 1 to 2 ES, or

10 to 20 YM points. Once I have this initial profit, I will give the second half more room to play out. For my swing plays, I will get in all at once and get out all at once, trailing my stop to protect any gains.

For 5-minute squeeze plays on YM, get in all at once, using 10 contracts per $100,000. Use a mechanical target of 10 points on the first half for choppy days, and 20 points on the first have for more volatile days, as determined by the volume on the ES on a five-minute chart (Chapter 5). If the target on the first half is hit, move your stop up to breakeven. Stay in the trade until one of four things happens:

- Your stop is hit.
- You get a reading of 800 ticks in the opposite direction of your trade.
- There is a reading of 1,000 ticks in the direction of your trade.
- The squeeze loses momentum.

I do this for each of my plays so there is no question as to how they should be executed. This is crucial because it ties in directly with the next portion of the plan.

## HOW AM I GOING TO TRACK AND RANK MY TRADES?

This is where I detail how I am going to track each of the setups I trade and how they are working. I track this information in Excel, which calculates a running average.

I will track all my trades and rate them as follows:

1. Target hit
2. Out at a different price from target, but profitable
3. Out at breakeven
4. Out at a different price from stop, but a losing trade
5. Stop hit

I will add up my daily score and divide by the number of trades to get an average. This provides a "grade point average" on the different setups and how they are doing. I separate the trades by the specific setup that is being used. At the end of the month, I will have an average by setup, and an overall cumulative average. This will help me to weed out the setups that aren't working. For example, I may have something at the end of the month that reads, "Gap plays: 4.24, squeeze plays: 3.57, pivot plays: 3.87." By looking at this I can see trends in these setups and potentially drop setups that aren't working, or allocate more funds toward setups that are working. It is imperative that traders do two things well in order to do this. First, they have to spend 10 minutes a day keying their trades into an Excel spreadsheet, or into a journal. Second, they have to follow their setups the same way each and every time. This brings me to an important rule regarding my trading plan:

*Any trade I take that does not fall into a specific setup or chart pattern I have outlined, I will label as an "impulse play."*

This includes plays in which I took a specific signal to get in, but got out of the trade too late or too early because I wasn't paying attention or because I was feeling hopeful or scared or whatever. This is a weakness, and if I succumb to this temptation, I must track it and see the impact it has on my trading. I know from past experience that the results of any of my "impulse plays" over time are poor, and this reminder keeps me from taking these trades. However, I do not want to get lax, and I will continue to write these down and track them if I take them. I will jot notes on these trades. Did I jump in too soon? Did I miss a fill? Did I chase? I have found that by tracking these things, I'm also holding myself accountable. The more I start tracking my trades, the fewer impulsive trades I take and the fewer overall amateur mistakes I make.

To this end, I also grade my trades on how well I followed the setup. I will give a trade a "5" if I followed the setup to the letter—whether or not it makes money. Any trade that is not a 5 is an impulse play. You have to be brutally honest with yourself here. If not, you're only hurting yourself and anyone who depends on your trading income.

I will also note any overall trends in my trading. How many days did I start off losing but ended up on the plus side? How many days did I start off strong only to give it all back? What was going on that day in terms of interruptions, phone calls, family stuff, and the like? I know from past experience that I get in trouble when I start off strong and start to go for "bigger trades with house money." I will keep track of any days in which I let greed get the best of me, then work on reducing the number of those days.

## WHAT ARE MY DRAWDOWN RULES?

If I am down by 15 percent for the month, I will cut my position size in half for the rest of the month. If I am down by 20 percent for the month, I will stop trading the rest of the month. If I hit a 30 percent total drawdown, it is time for a six-week break from trading. My daily drawdown max for intraday trading is $3,000 per $100,000. If at the end of the day I exceed this level, I am on probation the next day. If I exceed $3,000 per $100,000 again that week, I am done for the rest of the week. This is my punishment for breaking my trading rules.

I have to point out that many hedge funds and money managers are much more conservative when it comes to drawdowns and annual targets. A monthly drawdown of over 5 percent for a hedge fund can be devastating to its business, and an annual gain of 20 percent, year after year, opens the floodgates to billions and billions of dollars for any fund. I have a couple of comments on that.

First off, the day-trading strategies discussed in this book are not going to work on a $400 million fund. There is nowhere near enough liquidity to get in and out of the markets with that much money in that short a time frame. Many funds, however, will allocate a portion of their $400 million to take advantage of intraday trading opportunities I describe in this book. Out of $400 million, how much would they allocate? Maybe a million. That is ¼ of 1 percent of the entire fund.

I bring this up because people need to treat their trading account for what it is—a high-risk way to make a living. Most of a trader's funds should be kept in conservative vehicles—things like bonds or funds run by conservative money managers. Only a portion of total funds should be allocated to an aggressive trading account designed to generate monthly income.

## WHAT ARE MY PROFIT RULES?

My target daily average goal for intraday trading is $500 per day per $100,000. This is conservative and achievable, and it adds up quickly. I will focus on generating five $2,000 per $100,000 days per month. This means I don't have to trade every day. I know from past experience that my best trading days are Tuesday, Wednesday, and Thursday. Therefore, I will focus more on trading these days. If I am up over $2,000 per $100,000 before noon, I will continue to trade until I have a losing trade, at which point I will stop for the day. If I have a day in which I make $5,000 per $100,000, I will take the next day off to escape those feelings of euphoria that cause traders to do stupid things like double up on positions or trade without a stop. I will stop trading for the rest of the month at $20,000 per $100,000. I will track my daily equity curve through using an Excel spreadsheet.

I will withdraw 50 percent of my trading profits at the end of each quarter. I will never add money to an account that is down, and I will never meet a margin call. I will add money to an account that has proved itself with positive returns. The reason I will withdrawal profits is because this is the best way to protect them. It is with these profits that I get to invest in more real estate, buy more gold coins, pay for a family vacation, and fund my projects. It also is a reminder that the numbers on the screen are real and represent real cash.

## WHAT IS MY OFFICE SETUP GOING TO BE LIKE?

I have a separate condo that I have set up specifically for trading. The condo is sparse, one of the bedrooms is completely empty, and the other bedroom is set up as an office for my assistant. I have taken over the living room as my trading station. I have 5 computers and 12 monitors. I have cable Internet access with back-up dial up, plus two phone lines, a fax, and a cell phone if things go wrong. My goal this year is to get another assistant who helps only with order entry, and to program more of my trading setups to generate mechanical signals. I have had my trading office located at "regular" office space but found the solicitors and general banter too distracting for trading. Also, when other people in the office building found out I had quote screens all over the place, they would start stopping by to check out what the markets were doing. This was fine the first few times, but then it got real annoying, real quick. In contrast, in my private office, I have pictures on the wall that I enjoy and a large fish tank to watch when I want a break from watching the computer screens. And best of all, no unwanted interruptions.

## WHAT ARE MY REWARDS
## IF MY TRADING IS GOING WELL?

This is where I establish goals that motivate me to stick to my plan. I know that if I stick to my plan, my trading has a better chance of succeeding. And if I succeed, I get to reward myself.

If I hit 60 percent for the year, I will take the next four weeks off. If this occurs in the fourth quarter, I will take the rest of the year off. I could go for more money, but it's enough. For 2005, I want to spend two weeks in northern Italy and Switzerland. I want to take four long weekends and go to a beach and do nothing. I want to visit Australia, Hong Kong, Taipei, and Tokyo this year, whether on business or for pleasure. I like to watch movies, and I would like to upgrade my home theater system. I have a farm in southwest Nebraska, and I would like to buy another section of farmland in that area. I realize that I need to focus on the setups and not focus on the money needed for the rewards. If I focus on the money, I will lose. If I focus on the setups, I will win.

## ARE THERE ANY GROUPS, PEOPLE, OR ORGANIZATIONS I'D LIKE TO HELP OUT THIS YEAR?

I used to send money to the Salvation Army, but I don't really feel any impact when I donate money to big charities. I would rather help out individuals. Each year I find a struggling artist who has talent and support that person for a year, and I provide start-up funds to an inner city youth who wants to launch a business. My rule for this is that I never give the funds to people who find out that's what I like to do through an article and e-mail me. I look for people in my local area by asking teachers and other school personnel. I also like to spring for the occasional vacation that brings all the family members together.

## WHAT ARE MY SPECIFIC PLANS FOR STAYING "ON PLAN" THROUGHOUT THE YEAR?

This is where I add any notes I have gained from my own experiences to help me stay profitable in my trading.

After you have a $5,000 per $100,000 day, escape any feelings of euphoria by taking the next day off and doing something that humbles you like playing golf or flying a plane or sparring with a black belt in tai kwon do. Do not trade the S&Ps between 12:00 noon and 2:00 p.m. except if you are managing an existing position (do not initiate any new trades). Between 8:30 a.m. Eastern and 10:30 a.m. Eastern leave your instant messaging service off, do not check e-mail, and do not answer phones. In the trading room let people know you will not answer questions during this time. Minimize the trading room window so you do not read what is going on in the room. You can talk about what you are looking at and what you are doing over the microphone. If people have questions, they will have to wait. If they don't like that, they can leave. Do not trade anything during the overnight S&P session. Better yet, don't watch it either. If you quit early because you had a 20 percent month, physically get away so you cannot trade. Go to Cape Cod if it is summer or go skiing if it is winter. Do not trade after 12 noon on Fridays. Focus on trading lighter during the last three days of options expiration, or not trading at all. Review your performance during this time and consider this as your time off during the month. For the past year the market seems to do absolutely nothing during this time. Focus heavily on the first two trading weeks of the month. After the first two trading weeks are over, take the next two trading days off and get away from the markets. Give your brain a rest. Take off the entire week of Thanksgiving. Take off the last two weeks of the year. Plan your vacations in August so you won't be missing anything.

## WHAT AM I DOING ABOUT MY PHYSICAL HEALTH?

Your ability to trade effectively and consistently directly relates to your physical well being. You sharpen your mind through physical activity and plenty of exercise, as well as healthy eating. I'm going to share with you my recent health experiences. I debated about whether to include this or not, as this is a book on trading, not on health kicks. And, of course, I'm certainly not a doctor. However, I do feel strongly that optimum health is important for a trader, so I'll talk about my recent experiences and you can take it for what it's worth.

I've always been health conscious, though I certainly go through "less healthy" periods of time. I try to work out regularly, watch what I'm eating, not drink too much alcohol or caffeine, and take vitamins. Last year, when I was 34, I took a couple of physical fitness tests and detailed exams, and was surprised by the results. First off, my cardiovascular health and flexibility were rated as excellent. This means that my running and aerobic activity over the years were keeping me in good shape. That was where the good news ended. I then discovered my body fat percent was much higher than I thought, and I would need to lose 20 pounds of fat. This was a total surprise. Second, I discovered that I had an extremely low pH level, which means that my body was highly acidic. I then went on to find out the many pleasant things that are associated with having a continuous low pH/high acidic reading in the human body. Some of you will know what this means, while others of you won't. I'm going to condense this as much as possible and share it, so people who are interested can research this for themselves, form their own opinions, and make their own decisions regarding their health. I swear on my unborn child that this is not going to lead into a multilevel marketing pitch.

In a nutshell, a low pH level (high acidity) is the root cause of over 50 percent of all diseases leading to hospitalization, including all the killers like heart disease and cancer, as well as psychological diseases. More specifically, it causes plaque to form on artery walls, and it causes imbalances in the brain which lead to insomnia, anxiety, and impairment of memory. It also leads to calcium deficiencies as calcium is pulled from the bones to fight the high acidic levels in the body, which leads to weakened or collapsed vertebrae, poor posture, and back pain. A high acidic reading in the body leads to dysfunction of the digestive system causing indigestion, gaseousness, bloating, and abdominal cramping. Because of this, not enough nutrients get absorbed from the food we eat, and the entire body can experience malnutrition. This also causes undigested foods to ferment in the intestines, causing toxicity. High acidity also interferes with the basic functions of the colon, causing constipation as well as many other pleasant side effects. The list goes on and on with the immune system, respiratory system, urinary system, and glandular system all affected by a low pH level (high acidity) in the body.

I had no idea about any of this until I was told about it, and I was admittedly obstinate with the doctor when he was telling me about this. Did I have cancer? No. Were my bones weak? No. He assured me in time this would become a problem, but he did pinpoint an immediate problem, and that was with my digestive system. He asked me if I had to take antacids frequently because of heartburn. "Yep," I answered. He also asked, rather delicately I might add, if, upon emerging from the bathroom after "doing my business" I noticed a strong, almost embarrassing odor. This applied equally to any gas I might be passing into the atmosphere. "Uh, yeah, that happens sometimes," I said. He smiled and told me this was due to the high acidity in my system, which caused the digestive system to falter and not fully digest the food I was eating—which also was the cause of my extra 20 pounds of fat.

Before I embarrass myself further, let's jump into the next obvious question. What causes high acidity? Not surprisingly, it's the foods we eat—mostly the ones that are manufactured and come in cans or boxes. Even more so, it is based on what we drink. Sodas are the worst culprit, regular or diet. I used to suck down three or four Diet Cokes a day. I love sodas. Unfortunately, the more doctors I've talked to, the more convincing the argument that sodas are killers, just like cigarettes. Believe me, that is something I never thought would be coming out of my mouth. I stopped cold turkey and haven't had one since.

With respect to diet, I found it amusing that many of the things I thought were healthy were responsible for my current condition. In the mornings, I would pour soy milk on my cereal. Well, while soy is good for you, processed soy is like drinking soda, and most cereals are highly acidic because of the high proportion of refined flour in them. For lunch, I would have a sliced turkey sandwich, soup, and a diet soda. Well, the turkey is bad because packaged lunch meats carry nitrates that ruin a person's stomach. The bread was bad because of the refined flour, and of course the soda was bad. For dinner I would have something similar to what I had for lunch.

To top if off, I also found out that all of the vitamins I took were worthless because they were synthetic. This applies to every vitamin a person takes that lists ascorbic acid for Vitamin C, which is pretty much every vitamin. What about all the health benefits that you read about and hear in the media? It's called marketing.

Anyway, here is the list of foods by category, regarding overall health for the body. Foods that promote a healthy pH level are listed first, and the "killers" are listed at the bottom.

1. Eat all you want
   - Raw fruits
   - Raw vegetables (or lightly steamed)
   - Brown rice
   - Selected herbs
   - Unprocessed fruit and vegetable juices
   - Whole grains
   - Ezechiel bread (also referred to as flourless)
   - Drink one ounce of water for every two pounds of body weight each day.
2. Eat with some moderation—one part for every three parts from item 1
   - Clean meats, cooked rare
   - Roast fish
   - Eggs

- Raw dairy
- Unrefined molasses
- Raw nuts and seeds

3. Occasionally
- Processed cheese
- Commercial pizza
- Commercial butter
- Real ice cream (no gum)
- Canned foods
- Alcohol
- Coffee
- Pasteurized dairy

4. Not in this lifetime
- Soft drinks
- French fries
- Doughnuts
- Potato chips
- Refined protein powders
- Margarine
- Mayonnaise
- Hydrogenated oil snacks (salty snacks)
- Diet soft drinks
- NutraSweet/aspartame
- Processed soy (soy milk, soy cheese, soy protein isolate, soy lecithin)
- White bread

Admittedly, eating these foods from the first group on a regular basis took some getting used to. I love cereal, but now in the mornings I eat oatmeal with fruit. I love deli sandwiches and sodas, but now for lunch I eat a Greek salad with grilled chicken and water. For dinner I'll have vegetables, salad, and either chicken or fish. For snacks throughout the day, instead of grabbing something from the vending machine, I'll have an orange, a banana, or a handful of raw almonds that have been soaking in water. I still drink alcohol, but only on Fridays and Saturdays—and only a few drinks. The biggest challenge was cutting back on caffeine, but I went at it piecemeal, reducing consumption over the course of a couple of weeks. Once I adjusted, I noticed I had more energy because I was drinking so much water. The biggest change during the trading day is that instead of sucking on sodas and coffee and having my energy move up and down like a stochastic on a five-minute chart, I drink six bottles of water (16.9 ounces each) a day, and my energy level stays high and constant. The transition was difficult, but after four weeks of doing it, I couldn't imagine going back to my old habits.

I'm including this information because it was a real eye opener for me, and a big key to my improved health. One side benefit to all this, besides feeling better and sleeping better, is that I lost the extra 20 pounds I was carrying in five months, without increasing the amount of exercising I was doing. It was just a matter of eating foods that helped the functions in my body instead of harming them.

For anyone interested in more information, a good place to start is a book called *Alkalize or Die*, by Theodore A. Baroody. Also, you can go on Google and search for "acid and alkaline foods" or "high pH foods," and you will get all the information you need. If you are interested in the tests I took, feel free to contact me and I can give you more information. My own research has convinced me that by eliminating refined sugars and refined flours from our diet and significantly increasing our intake of clean water, we are preventing more health issues than just about anything else we could do. Good health and good trading go hand in hand.

## CONCLUDING THOUGHTS ON MY PLAN

This is the plan. The key here for me is complete and accurate daily records so that I can assess my trading, review my progress on a month-to-month basis, and make changes in my strategies based on my performance. I also want to incorporate other areas of my life into my trading plan, since trading is a very central and important part of my life.

I've shared my actual plan with a number of traders who have come up to the office to trade with me for a week. One of my goals in working with traders is to help them identify the markets and setups and timeframes that best suit their personality, and then from there help them to put together a game plan. Once they leave, they then e-mail their business plan to me, and I critique it for them and send it back. One of the traders who went through this process is Eric Grywalski. I've asked Eric if he would be willing to share the plan he created, because it is very specific to the beginning trader.

In spending time with him, I could see right away that he was highly intelligent and highly perceptive. Unfortunately, after the first few hours of trading, I could also see that he overanalyzed everything. Instead of jumping into a trade on a predetermined signal, Eric would continue to analyze the market to make sure the trade setup was really a winner. When he finally did get into a trade and was stopped out, his first statement was, "What am I doing wrong?" This tendency to overanalyze the markets is a problem for a specific group of traders, especially analytical and logical thinkers who are looking to make sense out of the "chaos and randomness" of the markets. To combat this, I had him focus on simple setups that required minimal analytics, and to formulate an exit plan with the same idea in mind—exits that were mechanical or that met a specific set of simple criteria. Eric had some trading experience on a swing basis before coming to visit, so he'd already had some experiences with the market under his belt. However, he was very new to intraday trading, and this is what he wanted to focus on. His plan follows, and I'll turn this over to him. Items in italics in his plan are my notes from the initial feedback I gave him on his first draft.

# A SAMPLE PLAN FROM A BEGINNING TRADER

My name is Erik Grywalski, and my trading plan was developed with the new trader in mind, using John's plan as a model. Defining a handful of solid setups, creating rules to govern my behavior in a limitless environment, and integrating proper trader psychology are key themes in my plan. As a beginning trader, I also wanted to focus on keeping my expectations realistic by not focusing on "making a killing in the market." Forming good habits early on and learning from my mistakes will be critical toward staying in the markets long term, which is every aspiring trader's ultimate objective.

Overall, my plan lays out three, high probability setups that I learned from John Carter and Hubert Senters during the week I spent trading with them. Gap, pivot, and squeeze plays allow traders to take advantage of market behavior that occurs on a fairly consistent basis throughout the trading day. Gap plays position a trader for the contra move that often follows morning gaps, while pivot plays anticipate potential turning points in the markets that are identified before the trading day. Squeeze plays allow traders to capitalize on the market's tendency to fluctuate between low- and high-volatility states.

Last, more important than the actual trade setup is trader psychology. Without establishing and maintaining a proper trader's mindset, consistent success in the markets will be unachievable. I strongly believe that this is an area that new traders often overlook because of their obsession with instant profits and is therefore briefly included in my plan. I would like to acknowledge Mark Douglas for his superb book, *Trading in the Zone*. All the core attitudes listed in my plan were taken from Mark's book, and all traders should put this book at the top of their reading list. Comments in italics are notes from John Carter that he inserted after reading the first draft of my plan.

## 2005 Trading Plan, Eric Grywalski

## Why Am I Trading?

I am trading because of my passion for the financial markets and long-lived aspiration of becoming a profitable, full-time trader. Trading will allow me to actively manage my money in all market situations, while having the freedom to work for myself in an area in which I have great interest. Being a student of the markets, I have gained an appreciation for some of the things that are critical for success as a trader. Proper mindset, strict money management, and trading with a predefined plan are just some of the more important areas to focus on when trading the markets.

With limited intraday trading experience, I realize the road ahead will be extremely challenging, and I have set expectations accordingly for my first year. The most important area often overlooked that will be critical for me will be to *establish and maintain* a trader's mindset. The ability to internalize and master the psychological aspects of trading is one of the most crucial skills that determine success. Indicators, charts, and the myriad other tools are helpful, but I must be careful not to overanalyze the market, and I must realize that trading is 90 percent mental. In general, proper attitude will produce better overall results than analysis or technique. With that said, my main goals during this first year are to learn how to execute trades well while achieving modest profitability. This means taking signals when they occur and managing my positions to maximize profitability.

## What Markets Will I Trade?

- Main contract: mini-sized Dow futures contract (YM)
- Hedging contract: E-mini S&P 500 futures contract (ES)

*Eric, the YM is a great contract to trade for newer traders. However, you need to have a backup plan. In situations where the eCBOT goes down or you have any computer problems, you will want to be able to hedge any "trapped" YM positions with the ES using one of the following options:*

1. *Take an opposite position in the ES market to offset YM position. As an example, if I am long two YM contracts, I will sell two ES contracts to hedge.*
2. *Use buy/sell stops in the ES market to hedge YM position. As an example, if I am long two YM contracts and the eCBOT goes down, I will place a sell stop for two ES contracts at a price level that is equivalent to my initial YM stop. This way, if the YM hits my stop and I can't get out of my position, I am hedged at my stop in the ES. However, if the market actually moves my way, I will still be able to participate in the move and liquidate my position once I am physically able to. —JC*

## Why This Market? Trading Strategies

The mini-sized Dow will be used for the following intraday trading setups:

- Gap fades
- Pivot plays
- Volatility expansion/five-minute squeeze plays

The mini-sized Dow has a better spread than the S&P and NASDAQ futures, which gives the beginning trader more room (levels) to allow trades to play out. Additionally, it is easier to track all 30 Dow stocks versus the 500 that exist in the S&P.

## Account Size and Number of Contracts to Trade?

An amount of $90,000 in start-up capital should be allocated in the following manner:

- $40,000 for trading capital
- $40,000 savings account
- $10,000 for first-year business expenses (home office, software, etc.)

## General Account Rules

- Withdraw 100 percent of any trading profits at the end of each month and place into savings account.
- Never add money to the trading account if the balance is below $40,000.

## Number of Contracts to Trade

- One YM contract per $20,000.
- Equal number of ES for hedging purposes.

## Trading Strategies

Three strategies will be used for intraday trading of the YM contract. I will follow only one setup at a time:

- Gap fades
- Pivot trades
- Squeeze trades

*Eric, if this is comfortable for you, simultaneous trades in the YM and ES markets may be considered. For example, if I am in a gap trade in the YM that hasn't filled and a five-minute squeeze play sets up in the ES, I will take the trade signal in ES using my standard squeeze execution procedure. This scenario is likely in a market that gaps up in the morning and consolidates all day before selling off into the close. In this instance it is okay to take both positions, just make sure you play them separately with their own, distinct parameters.—JC*

Each trading day will be broken down into two, 2-hour trading periods:

- 6:30–8:30 a.m. Pacific
- 11:00–1:00 p.m. Pacific

All trades must only be initiated during these two timeframes with the following exceptions:

- Management of existing trade that is still on from morning
- Five-minute squeeze

*A. Gap Fades*    The gap trade will be the first trade of the day that I will look for during the morning session. Gap trades are high probability trades that often fill on the same day. Intraday charts for this trade should be set with a 1:15 p.m. Pacific close and 6:30 a.m. Pacific opening to account for any overnight/morning gaps in price.

### Gap Trade Guidelines

1.  Using two-year raw gap data, take gap trades only from *Tuesday through Friday* and take only those gaps that occur *at or between R1 and S1 pivot levels*. Exceptions to this rule can be made if price opens near another significant level that has a high probability of providing support/resistance. As an example, the market gaps down below S1, but prices open right on the weekly pivot that also coincides with key daily chart support and/or a moving average (or fib level).

2.  YM gaps should be at least 20 points and not more than 60 points.

3.  Risk a maximum of 1.5 percent of total trading capital per trade.

4.  Around 6:20 a.m. Pacific time, evaluate premarket volume in key institutional stocks to gauge power of the gap. Specifically, review volume for MXIM, NVLS, KLAC, and AMAT along with other stocks tracked in One Chicago's

single-stock futures listing. Use underlying volume of cash market, not futures market.

## Volume Guidelines

- Light = < 30,000 shares
- Moderate = 30,000 to 80,000 shares
- Heavy = 80,000+ shares

Note: As a new trader, use a full position (two contracts) on only those gaps where there are less than 30,000 shares in premarket volume for the key stocks. These trades have the highest probability of filling the same day. With moderate volume openings, trade only one contract and use ½ gap fill as the target. Heavy volume openings are not to be faded.

1. Premarket volume takes precedence, but be alert during the gap trade if most of the sectors are moving in the direction of the gap. Ideally, look for at least five sectors moving in the opposite direction of the gap. Consider closing the position before stop is hit if the five sectors reverse and start to trade in the direction of the gap.

   *Eric, I would throw this idea about the sectors out—this will end up being an excuse to overanalyze the play, and you will end up getting out of the trades that you should have stayed in. Just focus on the premarket volume, set your parameters, and leave it alone.—JC*

2. If gap occurs with premarket volume over 80,000 shares and does not fill, look for the first buy/sell signal in the direction of the gap. This may be a pullback to a pivot or squeeze play after a consolidation of the morning's gap.

3. When the daily pivot precedes the prior day's close, look to lock in any gap trade profits at daily pivot.

4. Record unfilled gaps and keep price level handy as the market will often fill open gaps within 5–10 days.

Avoid gaps on the following days:

- Options expiration Friday.
- Rollover Thursday and day after.
- First trading day of new month.
- If after a narrow range day, the next day's gap is larger than previous day's range.
- Gaps where the opening price is outside the previous session's high/low.

## Gap Trade Execution Procedure:

1. When taking gaps, enter opposite the market using an "all-in" market order and place stop from fill price.

2. Stop price will be determined from the gap's size, as follows:

| Gap Size | Stop* | Potential Loss | % of Capital |
|----------|-------|----------------|--------------|
| 20 | 30 | $300 | 0.75 |
| 25 | 38 | $380 | 0.95 |
| 30 | 45 | $450 | 1.13 |
| 35 | 53 | $530 | 1.33 |
| 40 | 60 | $600 | 1.50 |
| 45 | 45 | $450 | 1.13 |
| 50 | 50 | $500 | 1.25 |
| 55 | 55 | $550 | 1.38 |
| 60 | 60 | $600 | 1.50 |

*Gaps 20–40 pts: use 1.5-to-1 risk/reward; gaps >40 pts: use 1-to-1 risk/reward.

3. After setting parameters, stay in trade until gap fills or stop is hit, but do not hold overnight and **do not trail stops**.

4. For two contracts and light volume gaps, the target is a complete gap fill. This price level should match the 1:15 p.m. Pacific closing price level from the previous day and should be set upon entry of trade. Use ½ gap fill as a target for moderate volume gaps.

*B. Pivot Level Trades*    Daily, weekly, and monthly floor trader pivots will be a second strategy used for intraday trading of the YM market. Pivots are leading price-based indicators that help anticipate market turns/points of consolidation and can be valuable entry points for both trending and choppy days. The basic strategy utilizes preplanned ("anti-impulsive") trades to either fade pivot levels on choppy days or buy/sell pullbacks to pivots on strong trend days. Daily pivots will be calculated using the 24-hour time period, while weekly and monthly pivots will use the high, low. and close from each of the previous week/month's trading range of the continuous contract (@YM).

## Pivot Level Calculations:

**R3:** R1 + (high-low)

**R2:** pivot + (high – low)

**R1:** 2× pivot – low

**Pivot:** (high + low + close) / 3

**S1:** 2× pivot – high

**S2:** pivot – (high – low)

**S3:** S1 – (high – low)

Daily, weekly, and monthly price levels will be drawn on the intraday chart each trading day.

## Pivot Trade Guidelines:

1. Use 144-tick chart for pivot strategy. Experimenting with other timeframes (89 or 233 tick) is okay to see what works best.

2. Add in 8 and 21 EMAs for confirmation (after entry) and seven-period RSI to spot bullish/bearish divergences. *This is fine, but make sure you are using this for confirmation after the entry, and don't use these to wait to get into the trade. — JC*

3. Consider using pivot strategy as the first trade of the day if an opening gap is a runaway gap where the gap does not fill because of strong buy/sell interest. On these days, look for price to pull back to a pivot level where an entry can take place before the market resumes in the direction of the opening gap.

4. Look to fade the first move to daily pivot and stay in trade until scalper buy/sell signal is generated.

5. If the market opens above the daily pivot, look for short entries for a move down to test the pivot and vice versa for openings below the pivot. If the pivot isn't tested during the morning session, look for a test in the afternoon.

6. For levels that have multiple pivots such as a daily and weekly, defer entry point to daily price level.

7. In general, for trend days, look to buy/sell pullbacks to pivot levels, and look to scale out at pivot levels above/below. *How are you determining whether a day is choppy or a potential trend day? This is another area where overanalysis can hurt a trader. For choppy days, it is okay to trade pivots, but remember you are fading the initial move to the pivot on these days. Remember to look at the ES volume and see if it is greater than 10,000 contracts per five-minute bar over the first six bars, which indicates a trend day, whereas volume of less than 10,000 contracts during the first six bars sets up a choppy day. —JC*

8. Utilize market internals to decide what action to take at pivots. For example, if the TRIN is falling and most sectors are green, focus on buying pullbacks to pivots and ignoring sell signals against pivots. In a choppy market, the internals are less critical, so look to fade rallies and declines to pivots.

9. Use midpoint pivots if the range between the seven daily pivots exceeds 40 points. Midpoints are not used with weekly and monthly price levels.

10. Moves to R3 or S3 are extreme, so keep emotions in check at these extended levels.

11. Daily R2/S2 will contain the market 90 percent of time, so be aware of a these levels when trading intraday.

12. Look for convergence of daily, weekly, and monthly pivots (and fib clusters). These levels are strong support/resistance areas to be aware of when trading.

13. If five-minute squeeze fires off in conjunction with pivot, stay in trade until momentum runs out.

14. After two losses in a row, quit using pivot strategy for that day.

## Pivot Trade Execution Procedure:

1. Use "all-in" limit orders to enter the market. Limit orders should be placed at the targeted pivot level +/– 3 pts. If buying at daily midpoints, just use nominal value for entry. *If trading more than 10 lots, use MIT orders (market if touched) to eliminate partial fills for both entries and targets.—JC*

2. Place an initial stop 20 points from the fill price. This represents a maximum draw down of $100/contract or .25 percent of total equity.

3. Sell/buy one contract after a 10-point profit and use the next pivot level as the target for the final contract.

4. After closing out the first contract, move the stop to breakeven +/– 6 points.

5. Consider using scalper buy/sell signals on 233-tick chart of ES to confirm the trade in YM at pivot levels. Confirmation should occur within 15–20 minutes. If confirmation doesn't happen, close out your position.

*C. Five-Minute Squeeze Trade*    Squeeze trades rely on the premise that stocks and indexes fluctuate between periods of high volatility followed by low volatility. The squeeze indicator captures the moment when the market goes from a low-volatility to a high-volatility state. The squeeze trade is the only trade acceptable to take during the 8:30–11:00 a.m. Pacific doldrums.

**Squeeze Trade Guidelines:**

- Use continuous contract (@YM) symbol when charting. Focus on signals in the five-minute timeframe for intraday trades.
- Red dots signify the contract is in a squeeze (Bollinger Bands are inside Keltner Channels).
- Blue dots signify that the Bollinger Bands have moved outside the Keltner Channels and volatility is increasing.
- Histogram measures move's momentum. Green bars on blue dots are long signals, and red bars on blue dots are short signals.

**Squeeze Trade Execution Procedure:**

1. Monitor a continuous five-minute YM chart for red dots. You should have at least two red dots before considering a potential squeeze.

2. Once a dot turns blue and closes blue for one, five-minute period, use an "all-in" market order to go long (two contracts) if the histogram is green and short if the histogram is red. Histogram appears above/below dots.

3. Set an initial stop of 20 points.

4. Scale out of one contract at a 10-point profit and move the stop to breakeven minus 10 for the second contract.

5. For the second contract, stay in the trade until momentum runs out on the histogram. This is indicated by the histogram's failure to make consecutive higher highs if long or consecutive lower lows if short. Wait for two consecutive higher/lower bars before exiting at the market on the second contract.

## Psychology

Psychology plays a very important role in trading, and the development of a proper trader's mindset should not be taken for granted. The unsuccessful trader has firm beliefs and expectations that are often not met by the market. When the outcome doesn't match the expectation, the trader feels pain and often views the market in a threatening way. Once this occurs, traders are doomed to fail unless they can recognize what is wrong and develop the proper winning attitude of a successful trader.

Adopt the following for trading success:

- **Every Moment Is Unique:** The trade either works or it doesn't.
- **Anything Can Happen:** Develop a resolute, unshakeable belief in uncertainty. The market has no responsibility to give us anything or do anything that would benefit us.
- **Markets Are Neutral:** The market does not generate happy or painful information, therefore, no threat exists. Our expectations formed from our original beliefs are the sole source of any happiness/pain.
- **Losses Are Okay:** Losing and being wrong are inevitable realities of trading since anything can happen. Taking small losses is part of a successful trader's job.
- **Accept Risk:** Fully acknowledge the risks inherent in trading and accept complete responsibility for each trade (not the market). When a loss occurs, do not suffer emotional discomfort or fear.
- **Monitor Emotions:** Learn how to monitor and control the negative effects of euphoria and the potential for self-sabotage.
- **Abandon Search for Holy Grail:** Attitude produces better overall results than analysis or technique.
- **Rigid Rules, Flexibile Expectations:** Adopt rigidity in your trading rules and flexibility in your expectations.

## Profit Goals

Income Goal = $20,000 full-time trading profits using two YM contracts (June–Dec).

$$\$20,000 \div 7 \text{ months} = \$2,857/\text{month}$$

$$\$2,857 \div 4 \text{ weeks} = \$715/\text{week}$$

$$\$715 \div 5 \text{ days} = \$143/\text{day}$$

$$\$143 \div \$5/\text{contract} = 29\text{–}30 \text{ points/day}$$

$$30 \text{ points} \div 2 \text{ contracts} = 15 \text{ points/contract}$$

## Profit Rules

- $143/day profit objective.
- Once my daily profit goal is obtained, stop trading for the day. *Eric, remember you will have losing days too. You will want $143 to be an average, not a stopping point on the day. If you make $300 one day, and lose $100 the next, then your average over the past two days is $100 per day.—JC*
- If I have a day in which I am up double my daily goal and the next trade is a loser, I will stop trading for the day.
- If I triple my daily profit goal before 9:00 a.m. Pacific, I will stop trading for the day and will take the next day off.

- If I meet or exceed my weekly profit goal ($780) before the end of the week, I will take the rest of the week off.
- Track daily P&L and convert to percent returns per day.

## Drawdown Rules

- *Daily drawdown maximum is 2 percent.* If I exceed this level by the end of the day, I cannot trade the next day. If I exceed 2 percent again that week, I will stop trading for the rest of the week.
- If I am down by 10 percent for the month, I cut my position size in half for the rest of the month.
- If I am down by 15 percent for the month, stop trading for the rest of the month.
- If I am down to a 20 percent total drawdown, it is time for at least a four-week break from trading until I can figure out and correct what I am doing wrong.

## Grade Card

Track and rate the performance of all trades as follows:

### Performance Scoring:

**5:** Target hit

**4:** Out at a different price from target, but profitable (time stop)

**3:** Out at even (scratch, time stop)

**2:** Out at a different price from stop, but a losing trade (time stop hit)

**1:** Stop hit

*Eric, this is good, but you will also want to grade how well you follow the setups you have chosen—in other words, how well you execute your plan. This is particularly important given your tendency to overanalyze what you are doing. You also tend to blame yourself when you lose money, i.e., "What am I doing wrong?" If you follow the setup the same way each time, then focus on what is "wrong" becomes the setup, not you personally. This way you focus on tweaking the setup, not blaming yourself. I would adopt the following scale to use to grade how well you actually executed the trade:*

### Execution Scoring

1. *Followed trade as dictated in your plan.*
2. *Followed trade entry, but closed out position before predetermined target was hit.*
3. *Followed trade entry, but removed stop and let position run past original target.*
4. *Entered setup late and didn't set target.*
5. *Impulse trade.—JC*

Add up daily scores and divide by the total number of trades to get an *average for both categories.* This will keep a grade point average of the number of trades you made that are profitable *and those that are executed as originally planned.* Track by trading method used (gaps, pivots, and squeeze) so you are able to rate each method and tweak as needed. Review the score at end of each month to see what needs to be modified.

Note: Any trade that does not fall into one of the three strategies outlined in this plan will be labeled an "impulse play." Impulse plays are a weakness because they violate your trading plan, so you must track them to see what impact they have on your trading. Write down notes on each trade and recognize if you jumped in too soon, missed a fill, or chased at an extended price.

I will also track various trends in my trading journal:

- How many days did I start off losing only to come back by the end of the day?
- How many days did I start off strong only to give it back?
- Were there interruptions during trading hours that may have affected my results?
- Did I decide not to trade because it was a narrow range day?
- Did I get too confident because of a good morning and trade outside my parameters?

## Office Setup

I will use one room in my house as my office, and it will be strictly for trading. The office will be set up with the following:

- Trading computer with three monitors using broadband Internet access.
- Day-to-day computer with separate broadband connection used for nightly research, e-mail, and as a back up to the primary trading computer.
- All computers will run with a battery backup and have Maxtor external hard drive.
- Antivirus and firewall protection.
- Spyware software.
- Printer.
- Separate phone line and cell phone.

*Eric, this is good. You and your wife also just had your first child (congratulations). How does this fit into your trading? Who is going to watch the baby during the day? Are you going to get a nanny, etc.? My wife and I are expecting our first child, and I'm in the process of hiring a live-in nanny to help with the daily tasks of raising children. This is so that daddy can sleep at night and be ready to trade the next day.—JC*

### General Trading Rules

- Do not hold any intraday positions overnight.
- As a day-trader, I am limited by time and range, so be keen to where the market is trading and avoid shorting/buying dead lows/highs of day.
- Parameters of trades are not to be changed once entered. I will define my profit target and stop *before* the trade is executed. After execution, I will let the trade play out to see what happens.
- Do not rush into a trade unless parameters are defined before the trade is placed. There will always be another opportunity down the road, and there is no reason to chase the market.

- Trade on the path of least resistance. For intraday trading use moving averages on 5-, 15-, and 60-minute charts to confirm market's short-term trend. If market dynamics are strong and moving averages are rising on all timeframes, do not take short signals. For mixed markets take long and short setups in line with buying/selling pressure of that particular day. Also, use a squeeze indicator to help with determining short-term market bias. If a daily squeeze exists on YM, focus on long setups and pass on shorts.
- Be aware of monthly and weekly pressures to be on the right side of the market.
- Focus on executing trades efficiently and not on P&L.
- Do not trade during lunchtime doldrums (8:30 a.m.–11:00 a.m. Pacific).
- Minimize trading on Fed days. Maybe look at the first ½ hour and last hour for any opportunities.
- During options expiration week, reduce your position size to one contract and consider trading only Monday to Wednesday of that week. Do not trade on Thursday and Friday.
- Trade light during the month of August, especially the last two weeks as volume dries up and the trade gets choppy. Focus on preparing for September trading when volume and players return to the markets.
- Consider taking time off during Thanksgiving week and during the last two weeks of December.

## What to Track
On a daily basis, keep track of the following:

- Market dynamics spreadsheet: tracks sector performance, advance/decline, breadth, etc., of the major markets. This should be done in both intraday and end-of-day formats. For intraday, data will be logged every ½ hour.
- Pending economic data and when it is being released, key earnings reports, and any upcoming Fed meetings.
- Review major markets and key sectors on 15-minute, 60-minute, and daily timeframes. Note position of moving averages to gauge supply/demand dynamics, oscillators, and key price levels on daily and 60-minute charts. Use monthly and weekly charts to help confirm support/resistance on shorter time frames. Look for confluence at price levels. From this information, a bias should be developed for the next day.
- Keep a trading journal that documents each trading day's action.

This is the end of Eric's trading plan.

## SUMMING UP THE TRADING PLAN

Eric put a lot of thought into his plan, and, as a result, he will not be staring at the markets each day wondering what he should be doing. This mental flailing around is what initiates most of the mistakes all amateurs tend to make. If you are a new trader without a plan, remember that you are going to be trading directly against Eric, and other people like him who have put a lot of thought into their trading plan. For every hundred traders who are out there, fewer than five have a plan as detailed as this. Who do you think stands a better chance of winning more consistently over the long run?

*The fun in trading comes from the thrill of the hunt, the anticipation of the kill. All the research, all the work culminates into a single moment in time when a trader makes a decision to pull the trigger and is shortly thereafter presented with the results. A trader who can string together enough consistent winners opens the door to a whole new life of independence. The lure of this challenge draws people of all ages and from all walks of life into the markets. Those who can face up to the challenge of drawing up a plan to pave the way will have the odds of success in their favor.*

# 20

## CHAPTER

# TIPS AND TRICKS FOR WHEN IT'S NOT WORKING FOR YOU, NO MATTER WHAT YOU DO

*Do not blame God for having created the tiger,*
*but thank him for not having given it wings.*

INDIAN PROVERB

## WILL CRY FOR FOOD—USING YOUR EMOTIONS TO MAKE MONEY

The biggest problem traders have is in controlling their emotions. I see it all the time. Traders know the setup they are supposed to follow, but they get swept up in their emotions and blow the trade. By stepping back and examining this process in more detail, traders can learn to use their own emotional reactions as indicators. Properly tuned, these emotional indicators, instead of leading to mistakes, can create great triggers to enter and exit a market. This is part of the transition from amateur to professional—instead of getting sucked into a trade because of emotions, use the emotional triggers to fight back and do exactly the opposite of what they are signaling you to do.

## THE FOUR SEASONS HOTEL TRADE

When I am in a trade that is going my way and I start to feel overly excited and the urge to add to my position, I instead use this as my trigger to set up a "double stop order." As an example, let's say I'm long 10 E-mini S&P contracts. The market is screaming higher. I find myself thinking of how many nights I could live at the Four Seasons on Maui with the day's profits. I recognize this feeling and immediately take the "Four Seasons Trigger" and place a trailing two-point stop for 20 contracts, double the size of my current position.

What happens is that I will stay in the trade as long as it is moving higher, but once the market turns, not only am I out of my position for a nice profit, but I also simultaneously get short 10 contracts. This process takes advantage of the market dynamics of human emotion in a very clean fashion. The selloff that occurs will be from other traders who succumbed to their emotions to buy at the top, because of fear of missing a move or the euphoria of having a current winning position. Once the market does reverse, it will be these traders who provide the fuel for the move down as they start dumping their positions once they can't take the pain of losing any longer. This is one example of how to get your emotions working for you instead of against you.

## THANK YOU, SIR, MAY I HAVE ANOTHER?

When I'm in a trade, I visualize what a newer trader would be doing—or what I would have been doing when I first started out. "If I entered here, where would my pain point be?" I've found that on the S&Ps a move of six points without any meaningful retracements is the maximum "uncle point" for most traders. When I see a six-point move without a retracement, I picture new traders and try to imagine the pain they are feeling. After about six points, I know they won't be able to take the pain any longer, and I step in and take the opposite side of this move, just as they are bailing out of their position and throwing cabbage at their screen.

As a professional trader, you will always be using a stop so you will no longer find yourself in this very real, very frequent, and very unfortunate position. Use your emotions to feel other traders' pain and figure out when they are going to throw in the towel.

## WHEN I TICK, YOU TICK, WE TICK

A more technical way to measure emotion is to watch the ticks. This is the same setup we talk about in Chapter 9. This time, however, if you are sitting there and the market is running away from you, instead of blindly jumping in, look at the ticks. Are they approaching +1000? They are probably getting close, as pools of amateur traders continue to buy at the market and tempt the goddess of good luck. The ticks are a great emotional balancing mechanism. A frequent surge of adrenaline that comes from watching a market move without you can be quickly tempered by a quick look at the ticks.

## DIVE, CAPTAIN, DIVE

My trading partners and I run an Internet-based trading room where people log in from around the world. One of the things we all like to do is watch how the newer traders react to the market action. There are "noises" that the people in the room can use. One of the classics is when the market is falling, falling, falling, and one of the free trials in the room posts that he or she is going short and initiates the "submarine dive, dive, dive" noise. Immediately upon hearing this, I know it is time to cover my shorts and go long. The experienced traders in the room also know this, and we all jump in and take the trade. The market usually reverses quickly, and once newbie traders say they are stopped out of the short trade, we cover our longs. It's emotion-based trading at its finest. Of course we then share this information with newbie traders. Once they catch on, we just have to wait for the next free trial to show up.

As a trader, if you find that you constantly short the lows and buy the highs, picture newbie traders getting so excited that they are about to literally "push the dive, dive, dive button." Do you want to be trading with or against these people?

## HIGH FIVE, BABY

Whenever traders I work with, or myself for that matter, start slapping one another on the back as the result of a good open trade that is racking up profits, I immediately snap alert and close out my position. This is the result of extreme emotion, and extreme emotion is not sustainable. I call this the "high five sell signal."

Any time you actually utter a noise or pound on something as the result of a trade that is going really well, it's a wake-up call for you to turn back into a professional trader.

## DISCOVER YOUR PERSONALITY TYPE AND FIND OUT IF IT'S HOLDING YOU BACK

One of the themes I've discussed in this book is the importance of finding the right markets and the right setups that best fit a trader's personality. People view the trades they are taking through one of the three dominant personality traits that all human beings share. Some of these personality types are naturally better suited to the world of trading than others. Unfortunately, there are also personality types that will not win at trading no matter what they do. However, there is a silver lining here. The reason these personality types lose is that they are unaware that their personality is the very thing responsible for their mounting losses and continued frustration. Once a trader learns about this, he or she can then use this information to turn their trading around.

The following 20-question quiz will help determine your dominant personality type. There is no right answer, and on some of these questions it may seem that there are two right answers. Just pick the one that makes the most sense in how it relates to you. Don't think about these too long. The faster you can move through this, the more accurate the readings will be, and the better information you will have to improve your trading. This is one of the personality profiles I have traders take when they come and work with me, so I can get a better idea of who they are and which markets and setups are best suited to their personality. Here we go:

1. When you think back to one of the best vacations you've had, what part of the vacation do you first remember?
   a. The sights and how the place looked.
   b. The different sounds you experienced.
   c. The way you felt while on vacation there.

2. When you think back to a person who captivated your interest, what is the first thing that really attracted you to them?
   a. Their appearance and looks.
   b. What they said to you.
   c. How you felt being around them.

3. When you are driving, how do you get around?
   a. I look for road signs or follow a map.
   b. I listen for familiar sounds that point me in the right direction.
   c. I follow my gut and get a sense of where I am.

4. When I play my favorite sport, I really enjoy:
   a. The way the sport looks, and the way I look playing it.
   b. The way it sounds, like the bang of the bat hitting the ball, or the cheering fans.
   c. The way the game feels, like holding onto a tennis racket or the feeling of running around the court.

5. Making a decision is easier when:
   a. I can see all the choices in my mind's eye.
   b. I can hear discussions from both sides in my head.
   c. I can sense how I would feel if either option came to fruition.

6. From the following list, I would say my favorite activities are:
   a. Photography, painting, reading, sketching, and films.
   b. Music, musical instruments, the sound of the sea, wind chimes, concerts.
   c. Ball games, woodworking, massage, introspection, touching.

7. When I am shopping for clothes, after seeing the item for the first time, the very next thing that I do is:
   a. Take another really good look at it or picture myself wearing it.
   b. Listen closely to the salesperson and/or have a dialogue with myself giving the pros and cons of buying it.
   c. Get a feeling about it and/or touch it to see if it's something I'd enjoy wearing.

8. During the times I find myself thinking of a former lover, the first thing that happens is I:
   a. Visualize the person clearly in my mind.
   b. Hear the sound of their voice in my mind.
   c. Start feeling a certain way about the person.

9. When I am at the gym, or working out, my feeling of contentment comes from:
   a. Seeing my reflection in the mirror improving.
   b. Hearing compliments from people around me about how good I look.
   c. Feeling my body get stronger and sensing it's more in shape.

10. When I'm doing math, I check my answer by:
    a. Viewing the answers to see if the numbers look correct.
    b. Counting the numbers in my mind.
    c. Using my hands and fingers to get a sense of whether or not I am right.

11. When I write out words, I verify the correct spelling by:
    a. Seeing the word in my mind's eye to see if it looks right.
    b. Pronouncing the words out loud or hearing it in my mind.
    c. Getting a gut feeling about the way the word is spelled.

12. When I love someone, I get an immediate experience of:
    a. The way we appear with each other through the eyes of love.
    b. Hearing or saying "I love you."
    c. The warm feeling toward that person.

13. When I do not like someone, I immediately experience dislike:
    a. When I see them coming toward me.
    b. When they start talking to me.
    c. When I know they are around.

14. When I am at the beach, the initial thing that makes me happy to be there is:
    a. The look of the golden sand and the beautiful sun and placid water.
    b. The sound of the thrashing waves, the howling winds, and whispers from afar.
    c. The touch of sand, the salty air at my lips, and the feeling of calmness.

15. In regards to my career, I know I'm on the right path when:
    a. I see myself clearly in one of the executive offices.
    b. I hear the president say, "You are one of the company's stars."
    c. I feel satisfaction in getting a promotion.

16. In order for me to get a good night's sleep, it is critical that:
    a. The room is dark with little or no light coming in from outside.
    b. The room is quiet without any distracting noises.
    c. The bed feels incredibly soft and comfortable.

17. When I get anxious, the first thing I notice is:
    a. The world seems slightly different to me.
    b. Various sounds and noises start to irritate me.
    c. I no longer feel a sense of ease and calm.

18. When I get focused and motivated, I immediately:
    a. View things from a brand new and positive perspective.
    b. Tell myself that this new state of being is going to open up new doors.
    c. Feel my body and mind getting excited.

19. When someone tells me, "I love you," my first reaction is:
    a. To form an image of us being together or that person loving me.
    b. To hear my soul saying something like, "This is amazing."
    c. A feeling of great satisfaction and contentment.

**20.** Dying, for me, is closest to:
    **a.** Seeing no more or seeing things in a brand new fashion.
    **b.** Hearing nothing ever again or hearing things in a brand new fashion.
    **c.** Feeling nothing ever again or feeling things in a brand new fashion.

Once you have completed this test, add up how many times you answered A, B, or C. For example, you might have A:6, B:4, C:10. These results will give you an idea about your dominant personality type. People generally react to and interpret the world around them through this filter. Get your scores together and we'll move on—you'll want to have taken the test before we proceed so your answers aren't influenced by what you read next. The goal here is to get an honest assessment of your personality traits and then learn how to best utilize those traits in your trading.

## PERSONALITY TYPES AND TRADING—WHAT YOU DON'T KNOW ABOUT YOURSELF CAN HURT YOUR TRADING

Nearly 60 percent of the population will have "A" as their highest scoring trait. This indicates that a person's dominant way in which they view the world is visual. It's not really known why this is so, but experts feel it has to do with sight being our strongest sense, and that, for the majority of us, we were taught from birth to depend on our eyes in order to make our way through life. Also, in today's world, our input is largely through television, movies, computer screens, and printed copy—all of which are heavily dependent on the eyes.

Visual people like daylight and are extremely mobile, and it's easy to find them in professions that allow them visual expression. Nowhere is this more observable than in the entertainment industry. Visual people are generally "movers and shakers" and like to move fast. Visuals are drawn to this industry and its related fields as a natural expression of who they are. These types of people naturally gravitate to professions such as painting, photography, and design. They also make great marksmen, firefighters, and pilots.

In terms of trading, visuals adapt quickest to this profession, as they depend largely on what is happening visually in front of them on the computer screen to make decisions. It doesn't mean they will make the right decisions, but they are most naturally adapted to the world of trading. If they are untrained in how the markets work, they will make the same mistakes as everyone else. Once they get some experience, however, they tend to be good at waiting for the charts to setup before taking their entries. Yet, only experience teaches them how to manage their exits. A visuals biggest weakness is watching the P&L fluctuate throughout the trading day. It would be better for them to cover that up (a business card taped to the corner of the computer screen works good) and just focus on the setups. Also, visuals tend to laser in on a price chart and ignore everything else, which can be a detriment to their trading. This is why it is helpful to have auditory alerts on things like high tick readings as well as listening to pit noise in the background so visuals don't get sucked into the extreme price action they are seeing on the charts.

If your highest score was "B," then your dominant personality trait is auditory. My accountant is highly auditory, and I've noticed that the sounds around the office occupy most of his attention. Auditory personality types relate to the world through the way things sound and in many respects are more sensitive to sounds than visual people are to sight. Auditory people can be easily distracted by the most inoffensive sound, which makes it seem like they are not paying attention to you during a conversation. In reality, though, they are strong verbal communicators—it's just they hear every sound coming their way and sometimes it distracts them. They enjoy talking with others as well as just talking out loud to themselves. Because of their innate ability internally to put thoughts into dialogue, experts believe most loners have this dominant personality type. Because of their heightened sensitivity to sound, auditories don't tolerate harsh or disharmonic noise as well as others do. Fire or ambulance sirens are major offenders, and you can spot an auditory easily by observing who on a street corner is holding his ears as an ambulance screams past. Also, they have an incredible ability to listen so thoroughly and with such intent that data is absorbed and processed in their minds very quickly, without needing to be translated into pictures. Because of this enhanced ability, auditories tend to gravitate to areas in life that permit the use of such superb listening and communicative talents.

In regards to trading, this personality type has one strong advantage—the ability to sit alone in front of a computer for days at a time without going crazy. That is an important part of trading, and this ability to be patient and wait and not feel isolated is a necessary trait to have. The downside of this personality type and trading is that a chart isn't really much use to them, and they frequently miss setups from simply not paying attention. Whereas a visual can stare at a chart for hours because the red and green lights are fascinating, an auditory personality needs additional input. Audio alerts and pit noise are important tools for auditories, and I know some of these personality types who don't even look at price charts. They just listen for audio alerts and then place their trades.

If your highest score was "C" then you relate to the world around you by how you feel. People with this dominate personality trait long to be understood and respected for being so in touch with their feelings. They tend to like a person because of how they feel when they are around them, or like a movie because of how it made them feel when watching it. When they laugh, they let themselves go and really feel the laughter, giving the person they are talking to a sense that they totally understand and agree with what was so funny. Type C personalities are able to translate visual images and acoustical data into feelings that are pertinent to them and those around them. Type Cs enjoy conversations but not for the same reason visuals or auditories do. They use dialogue to translate words, sounds, and images into feelings. While visuals and auditories are busy communicating with pictures and sounds, this type C personality is busily running through his vast storehouse of feelings and attaching sensory meaning to what the other person has just said.

Because of a heightened ability to feel, you would assume that type Cs are introverts. However, the opposite is true. Moreover, because of their superior sense of touch, type Cs make superior athletes. Any occupation that requires manual tasks is just plain easier for these types of personalities. Typical occupations that are tailor-made for them usually have hands-on or feeling parameters. Psychologists, woodworkers, potters, surgeons, actors, all types of mechanics, and other feeling- or sensory-based work are common callings.

For traders, this type of personality has the biggest struggle and usually doesn't make it until they figure out how their personality is working against them. A type C personality trader will wait until they sense when things are good or bad, or wait until they get a sense about whether what they are doing or are about to do is good or bad. They literally get into trades when it feels good to do so, and get out when they feel bad. This almost always puts them in just as a move is ending, and gets them out just as it is turning. For a type C personality, it feels bad to buy a market that is selling off into a pivot level. They would rather wait to see a bounce so that they can "feel good" that the trade is going to work out. Of course, by the time this happens, they should actually be closing out a position instead of initiating a new one. The solution to this is hard yet simple. If you are a type C, then just acknowledge that your feelings need to be faded. If you are excited and feel good about going long, then you should be looking at the short side and vice versa. If you are a type C don't despair. A type C who masters this will have a distinct advantage over other traders. A type C who is unaware of this will always face an uphill battle when it comes to trading.

In terms of personality, no one is going to be 100 percent anything. I am primarily visual, then "feeling" is not far behind, and finally auditory makes up a small portion of my overall "personality profile." I've learned to set up my charts to take the best advantage of my dominant visual personality, listen to my feelings to get an idea of what the amateur traders are doing and thus "fade my feelings," and set up audio alerts to make sure my eyes aren't the only thing that are responsible for my trading decisions. Learning this about myself made me a better trader.

## TRADING REALLY ISN'T FOR EVERYONE—ALTERNATIVES TO CONSIDER

The harsh truth is that trading isn't for everyone, but the problem is you won't know whether it's for you or not until you give it a shot. It takes guts, courage, and years to become good enough to do it for a living. My advice is to start out small. Whatever account you start with is your tuition money—you are going to lose it, and that is your educational fee for entrance into this world. Do yourself a favor and trade small until you start getting consistent with your setups. If after a few years it still isn't working out and you are getting ulcers or you figure out that you'd rather be playing golf, there are other options.

For me, I had to spend time and sit side by side with other traders before I turned the corner to consistency. In sitting beside these traders, it was helpful to hear them talk about what they were doing and why, but that was only about 40 percent of what I learned. The rest of it had to do with what they weren't saying or doing. They weren't getting upset if they missed a move. They weren't answering the phone when it rang. Also, there were many things and habits they did that they weren't even aware of until I pointed it out to them. It was these unconscious trading habits that I picked up that really helped me out as well—just observing and absorbing how a professional trader spent his day. To that end, if you really want to do this, I would encourage you to find an experienced trader and just spend a week sitting next to them. It was what turned the corner for me. If you can't find anyone, there are a few times a year when we will hold week-long "mentorships" at my trading office (see Figure 20.1).

**F I G U R E   20.1**

John Carter (outset) and Hubert Senters (closest in) showing Bill Shugg (center) how they trade.

Traders can sign up to come and spend time side by side with myself and some of the other traders I work with and just watch what we do. After a few days we will then have the visiting traders start making trades while we observe and make comments. If they do a good job following their own rules, we'll let them make some trades in one of our various funds that we run. Part of their homework while they are with us is to develop a full trading plan like the one I shared earlier. The goal is that when they leave, they will never have to wonder again what they should be doing when they are starting at the charts. They will have a plan to follow, and they will just wait for specific things to happen "according to plan."

There are also programs available in which specific setups can be auto-traded by a number of brokers. There are brokers who do this with my own setups and newsletter plays. However, the setups I use are shorter-term in nature, volatile, and not appropriate for everyone. (Our latest fund focuses just on currencies, and we continue to look for opportunities in this area as China looks to float its Yuan on the open market.)

There is no shame in throwing in the towel when it comes to trading. For many, quitting trading is the best trade they ever made. They are not stressed out, they let someone else manage their accounts, and best of all they understand what is going on because they have already been there themselves.

# 21
## C H A P T E R

# MASTERING THE TRADE

## AMATEURS HOPE, PROFESSIONALS STEAL

Professionals steal money from amateurs because amateurs hope, close their eyes, and unwittingly allow professionals to drain their accounts.

The sum of my trading experience is this: I've learned that being a professional is all about maintaining a specific state of mind while trading, and traders are never going to make consistent money until they achieve that frame of reference from which to operate. All the successful traders I know blew out their account at least once before becoming consistently profitable. Along these lines, I've composed a list of 40 "trading tips" for staying in this professional state of mind. These "tips" are not meant to make a trader conservative or hesitant. On the contrary, trading takes guts, and by following these tips traders will be given the key that will allow them to embrace risk and take the necessary chances required in the pursuit of capital gain. That is, traders will feel more compelled to take a chance because they know they are also going to fight to protect their capital. They won't freeze and lie helpless as it is whittled away.

This is a list I've developed specifically for myself. I'm using the term "you" as it refers to "me." Feel free to add to these or modify as best fits your own personality and trading style.

# 40 TRADING TIPS FOR MAINTAINING A PROFESSIONAL STATE OF MIND

1. Trading is simple, but it's not easy. If you want to stay in this business, leave hope at the door, focus on specific setups, and stick to your stops.

2. When you get into a day trade, watch for an 800-tick reading in the opposite direction of your trade for signs that you are wrong. This might allow you to get out of your trade before your stop is hit.

3. Trading should be boring, like factory work. If there is one guarantee in trading, it is that thrill seekers and impulse traders get their accounts ground into parking meter money.

4. Amateur traders turn into professional traders once they stop looking for the "next great technical indicator" and start controlling their risk on each trade.

5. You are trading other traders, not the actual stock or futures contract. Who is taking the other side of your trade? Is it an amateur who is chasing or a professional who has been patiently waiting for this entry all day? You have to be aware of the psychology and emotions on both sides of the trade.

6. Be very aware of your own emotions. Irrational behavior is every trader's downfall. If you are yelling at your computer screen, imploring your stocks to move in your direction, you have to ask yourself, "Is this rational?" Ease in. Ease out. Keep your stops. No yelling. The person who is screaming should be the one on the other side of your trade.

7. Watch yourself if you get too excited—excitement increases risk because it clouds judgment. If you are feeling peak excitement, it probably means the move is just about over. Tighten your stop and look to reverse.

8. Don't overtrade—be patient and wait for three to five good trades.

9. If you come into trading with the idea of making big money, you are doomed. This mindset is responsible for most accounts being blown out.

10. Don't focus on the money. Focus on executing trades well. If you are getting in and out of trades rationally, the money will take care of itself.

11. If you focus on the money, you will start to try to impose your will upon the market in order to meet your financial needs. There is only one outcome to this scenario: You will hand over all your money to traders who are focused on protecting their risk and letting their winners run.

12. The best way to minimize risk is to not trade. This is especially true during the doldrums, between 11:30 a.m. and 2:30 p.m. Eastern. If your stocks or other markets aren't acting right, then don't trade them. Just sit and watch them and try to learn something. By doing this, you are being proactive in reducing your risk and protecting your capital. The most common problem with losing traders is they always feel like they have to be in a trade.

13. There is no need to trade five days per week. Trade four days per week, and you will be sharper during the actual time you are trading.

14. Refuse to damage your capital. This means sticking to your stops and sometimes staying out of the market.

15. Stay relaxed. Place a trade and set a stop. If you get stopped out, that means you are doing your job. You are actively protecting your capital. Professional traders actively take small losses. Amateurs resort to hope and sometimes prayer to save their trade. In life, hope is a powerful and positive thing. In trading, resorting to hope is like placing acid on your skin. The longer you leave it there, the worse the situation will get.

16. Never let a day trade turn into an overnight trade. An overnight trade should be planned as an overnight trade before the trade is ever entered.

17. Keep winners as long as they are moving your way. Let the market take you out at your target or with a trailing stop. Don't use impulse exits. Every exit is taken for a specific reason based on parameters that have been clearly defined.

18. Don't overweight your trades. The more you overweight a trade, the more "hope" comes into play when it goes against you. Remember, hope to trading is like acid to skin.

19. There is no logical reason to hesitate in taking a stop. Reentry is only a commission away.

20. Professional traders take losses. Being wrong and not taking a loss damages your own belief in yourself and your abilities. If you can't trust yourself to stick to your stops, whom can you trust?

21. Once you take a loss, you naturally forget about the trade and move on. Do yourself a favor and take advantage of any opportunity to clear your head by taking a small loss.

22. In general, you should never let one position go against you by more than 2 percent of your account equity. Many setups work out better if you can use a larger stop. Instead of trading 20 E-mini contracts with a one-point stop, trade 10 contracts with a two-point stop, or 5 contracts with a four-point stop. The monetary loss is exactly the same, but one set of these parameters will work better on a particular setup than all the others. Find out what works best for your setup and adjust your parameters accordingly.

23. Get a feel for market direction by "drilling down." Look at the monthly charts, then the weekly, daily, 60-minute, 15-minute, and 5-minute to get the best idea of what the market is going to do in the short term. Always start with the larger timeframes and drill down to the smaller.

24. If you are hesitating to get into a position when you have a clear signal, that indicates that you don't trust yourself, and deep inside you feel that you may let this trade get away from you. Just get into the position and set your parameters. Traders lose money in positions every day. Keep them small. The confidence you need is not in whether or not you are right; the confidence you need is in knowing you execute your setups the same way each and every time and do not deviate from the plan. The more you stick to your parameters, the more confidence you will have as a trader.

25. Averaging down on a position is like a sinking ship deliberately taking on more water. This is ridiculous and stupid. Don't be ridiculous and stupid.

26. Try to enter in full size right away. If you pick up a half position first, don't add to it and create a full-sized position unless the trade is going your way.

27. Ring the register and scale out of your position. Have modest, mechanical targets for the first half of your position. Give the second half more room to run.

28. Adrenaline is a sign that your ego and your emotions have reached a point where they are clouding your judgment. If you are not in a trade, do not enter a new trade in this state of mind. If you are in a trade, stick to your parameters and walk away. If you are in a losing trade that has gone through your stop, exit your trade immediately and walk away from the markets.

29. You want to own the stock before it breaks out, then sell it to the momentum players after it breaks out. If you buy breakouts, realize that professional traders are handing off their positions to you in order to test the strength of the trend. They will typically buy them back below the breakout point—which is typically where you will set your stop when you buy a breakout. Use this information to make money off of amateur traders who buy breakouts.

30. Embracing your opinion leads to financial ruin. When you find yourself rationalizing or justifying a decline by saying things like, "They are just shaking out weak hands here," or, "The market makers are just dropping the bid here," then you are embracing your opinion. Don't hang onto a loser. You can always get back in.

31. Unfortunately, discipline is not learned until you have wiped out a trading account. Until you have wiped out an account, you typically think it cannot happen to you. It is precisely that attitude that makes you hold onto losers and rationalize them all the way into the ground. If you find yourself saying things like, "My stock in EXDS is still a good investment," then it is time to rethink your trading career.

32. Siphon off your trading profits each month and stick them into a money market account. This action helps you to focus your attitude and reminds you that this is a business and not a place to seek thrills. If you want thrills, go to Disneyland.

33. Professional traders risk a small amount of their equity on one trade. Amateurs typically risk a large amount of equity on one trade. This type of situation creates emotions that ruin amateurs' accounts.

34. Professional traders focus on limiting risk and protecting capital. Amateur traders focus on how much money they can make on each trade. Professionals always take money away from amateurs.

35. In the financial markets, heroes get crushed. Averaging down on a losing position is a "heroic move" that is akin to Superman taking a spoonful of Kryptonite to prove his manhood. The stock market is not about blind courage. Nobody hands out any awards to traders who picked the dead high or the dead low. Wait for a setup. This is about finesse. Don't be a hero.

**36.** Traders never believe that they will blow out their account. Always realize you will become a candidate for this if you don't stick to your trading rules.

**37.** The market reinforces bad habits. If early on you held onto a loser that went against you by 20 percent, and you were able to get out for breakeven, you are doomed. The market has reinforced a bad habit. The next time you let a stock go against you by 20 percent, you will hang on because you have been taught that you can get out for breakeven if you are patient and hang on long enough.

**38.** The true mark of an amateur trader who is never going to make it in this business is one who continually blames everything but himself or herself for the outcome of a bad trade. This includes, but is not limited to, saying things like:

- The analysts are crooks.
- The market makers were fishing for stops.
- I was on the phone, and it collapsed on me.
- My neighbor gave me a bad tip.
- The message boards caused this one to pump and dump.
- The specialists are playing games.

The mark of a professional, however, sounds like this:

- It is my fault. I traded this position too large for my account size.
- It is my fault. I didn't stick to my own risk parameters.
- It is my fault. I allowed my emotions to dictate my trades.
- It is my fault. I was not disciplined in my trades.
- It is my fault. I knew there was a risk in holding this trade into earnings, and I didn't fully comprehend them when I took this trade.

The obvious difference here is accountability. For amateurs, everything having to do with the market is "outside their control." That is not reasonable thinking and really just points to individuals who have, probably for the first time, had to confront their "real self" as opposed to the perfect self or idealized self they have constructed in their mind. This is also known as "living in a fog." People can drift around through life in their own private world, where they are pretty special and can do no wrong. Unfortunately, trading rips off this mask, because you cannot dispute what has happened to your account. This is also known as "confronting reality." For many people, when they start trading they are suddenly confronting reality for the first time in their lives. Just to see the world as it really is requires a lifetime of training, and for many people trading the stock market is their first real step on this journey. Some people say that traders are born, not made. Not so. If you choose to see the world as it is, then you can start trading successfully tomorrow.

**1.** Amateur traders always think, "How much money can I make on this trade?" Professional traders always think, "How much money can I lose on this trade?" Traders who control their risk take money from the traders who are thinking about the red BMW they are going to buy.

2. At some point traders realize that no one can tell them exactly what is going to happen next in the market, and that they can never know how much they are going to make on a trade. Thus the only thing left to do is to determine how much risk they are willing to take in order to find out if they are right or not. The key to trading success is to focus on how much money is at risk, not how much you can make.

## SURVIVING THE TRADER'S JOURNEY

Strategies fail because traders only have to have a couple of losing trades in a row before they throw out the whole system and go back to relying on their gut. Once traders are in this situation, they head into a downward spiral very quickly. Human emotions get people in at the dead highs and then human emotions get people out at the dead lows as they continually buy at the top out of greed and then sell the lows out of fear. Or, in the case of shorts, they sell at the lows out of greed and cover at the highs because of fear. And this is a cycle that happens over and over and over again. And it's never going to stop.

The financial markets naturally take advantage of and prey upon human nature, especially when it comes to greed, hope, and fear. The key is to remember that the biggest movements in the markets occur not when traders in general "feel like buying." They occur because groups of traders are all getting skewered at the same time and are forced out of a position. In reality, traders are not trading stocks, futures, or options. They are trading other traders. The profitable traders learn to be aware of the psychology and emotions behind the person who is taking the opposite side of their trade. Average traders understand only their side of the trade. Superior traders understand what's happening on both sides of a trade and know how to take advantage of situations that will hurt most traders. They know how to take advantage of human weakness, and, therefore, they are able to grind most traders into the ground like so much raw meat. In essence, winning traders steal money from losing traders.

My partners and I jokingly refer to the financial markets as the "Goddess of Temptation." The goal, of course, is for traders to develop a professional trading mindset that prevents them from succumbing to these temptations. Instead of being the *cause* of the ebbs and flows of the markets, traders need to jump the chasm that allows them to ride out these ebbs and flows on a course toward profitability.

Good skiers rarely worry about a route. They just go, confident that they'll react to changes in the trail as they come upon them. It's the same thing in trading: Traders have to have confidence in their technique. That is the beauty of mustering the right mindset before a trader starts the day—it enables the trader to feel like a good skier, nice and relaxed for the next unexpected turn.

## CONCLUSION AND FINAL THOUGHTS

Finishing a book must be similar to sending a child off to college, except in this case I'm not sad to see it go. It's a great process, and it even helped me to clarify some of my own trading ideas . . . but it's a lot of hard work. If it helps you to become a better trader, then the time was well spent. This book really discusses everything I know about trading up to this point in time. If you are interested in additional resources outside of this book, you can pay us a visit at our main Web site, www.tradethemarkets.com. We use this site to post our research on currencies, futures, stocks, and options, as well as post our mentoring and seminar schedules. We don't do these very often—just when the markets slow down as it gives us a break from our computer screens and allows us to interact with our clients. We usually do one in Chicago each year at the Sears Tower. This is a great location because we can visit the CME and CBOT and give people a real sense of how trading works. Beyond that, we look at places we would like to visit and schedule an additional seminar there. A lot of times these are based where we have clients that are interested in meeting with us. For example, due to meetings I've had with clients in China, I'm currently looking at scheduling a seminar in Hong Kong and Shanghai in 2006 and 2007. I'd like to bring in 15 people from the U.S. and 15 people from China and have everyone together for four days as a group. I think it would be a great experience for the people to interact with each other, make great overseas contacts, and learn about trading. For information you can view the websites, or call our offices toll free within the United States at 888-898-8118 (for international call +1 512-266-8659), or e-mail me at john@tradethemarkets.com. International callers can check the websites for the most up-to-date information on our direct office line numbers. Our main offices have recently moved from Boston, Massachusetts, to Austin, Texas.

When I kicked this off about 400 pages ago, I mentioned that intermediate traders generally fall into the following three categories:

- Those who know the setup like the back of their hand, but fail to make money because of a flawed trading methodology
- Those who know the setup better than their spouse's bad habits, but fail to make money because the setup is being used in the wrong market
- Those who know the setup better than the varied plot lines on *Alias*, but fail to make money because they can't stick to their rules.

The point of this, of course, is to emphasize the importance of establishing a trade setup from a multifaceted approach. Successful trading is a lot more than just, "What's my entry, and what's my stop?" In addition to the actual setup, there also needs to be a foundation from which to operate the setup. This foundation consists of the following: the right setup, in the right market, in the right timeframe, all of which tie into the trader's personality. How will you know when this all comes together for you? The first clue is that it will have nothing to do with how you feel about it. It has everything to do with the results. I've shared with you some of the setups that work for me. Find two setups out of this book that you can follow in a particular market in a particular timeframe, stick to your rules, and make them your own. Once you have two setups that work for you consistently, start looking at adding a third. There is no reason to rush into this. Take your time and master each step as you go.

As I state in the introduction, without rules, a trader is like a wounded antelope in the center of a lion pride. It is not a question of "if" the antelope is going to get whacked faster than a newly discovered FBI informant within the Mafia, but rather of "when." For traders without the discipline to follow their rules, the possibility of financial ruin is not a question of "if." It's only a matter of "when."

I work with traders all the time. The ones who turn the corner and eventually start making a living at this profession learn to stick to their rules. This is typically a painful process. There is only one guarantee I can give you in this business, and it is this: *If you can't stick to the rules you develop and, if you are always finding some excuse to enter or exit a trade earlier or later than your rules state, you will never, never make it as a trader.*

As a history major, I have to say that this is the most exciting time to be alive in the history of the world. Change used to occur over the course of centuries, and then decades, then years, and now change is taking place every day. One of my favorite fiction books of all time is James Clavell's *Taipan.* This book is based on historical facts and tells the tale of rival China traders Dirk Straun and Tyler Brock in the newly formed British colony of Hong Kong in the 1840s. They had to make their buying and selling decisions for vast quantities of spices, cotton, and tea using price quotes from London that were printed three months before. Can you imagine trading with quotes delayed three months? That is what people had to do less than 150 years ago. Today, when I'm in Hong Kong on business, I can type in real time and get responses in real time with a counterpart in London through instant messaging. Don't get caught up in any "wishing for the good old days" or any of that nonsense. Change is life, life is change. For traders, whether the markets go up, down, or sideways, whether the economy is growing or we are in the midst of a great depression, there will always be opportunities to trade.

After reading this book, it is my hope that you will have a better foundation for a plan to trade the markets successfully on a full-time basis: proven setups to play, markets that best fit that particular setup and a set of rules to apply to that setup. That is pretty much all a trader needs to survive and thrive in this greatest of professions. I wish you well on your trading journey.

> *Live your own life, for you will die your own death.*
>
> LATIN PROVERB

# INDEX

## ABOUT THE AUTHOR

**John Carter** is president of Trade the Markets, Inc. (www.tradethemarkets.com) and has more than 15 years of experience trading stocks, options, and futures. A CTA, Carter is principal of Razor Trading, a money management firm. He is a frequent speaker at industry events, including Trader's Expo, and is a regualr contributor to *SFO* magazine, tradingmarkets.com, and various Chicago Board of Trade publications.